D1116127

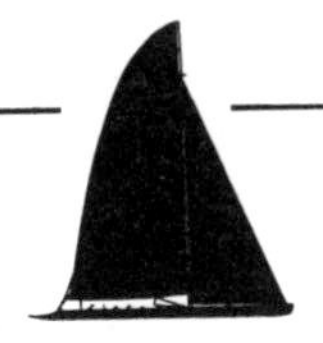

To The
Third Power

"The America's Cup is not just a sailboat race. It is a race of management, technology, teamwork, money, and — incidentally — sailing."

William Koch

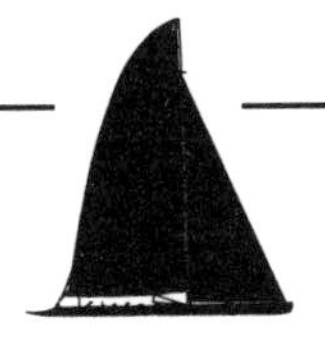

To The Third Power

The Inside Story
of
Bill Koch's Winning Strategies
for
The America's Cup

Paul C. Larsen

Tilbury House, Publishers
Gardiner, Maine

Tilbury House, Publishers
132 Water Street
Gardiner, Maine 04345

First printing: April, 1995

Library of Congress Cataloging-in-Publication Data

Larsen, Paul C., 1947–
To the third power : the inside story of Bill Koch's winning management of the America's Cup / by Paul C. Larsen.
p. cm
Originally published: West Palm Beach, Fla. : America³ Foundation, 1994. With new introd.
Includes bibliographical references and index.
ISBN 0-88448-147-6 (hardcover : alk. paper) : $24.95
1. America's Cup races. 2. Yacht racing — History. 3. Koch, Bill, 1940– . 4. Sailors — United State s— Biography. I. Title.
GV830.1992.L37 1995
797.1'4—dc20

94–46503
CIP

Text and cover designed by Edith Allard
Editing and Production: Mark Melnicove, Lisa Reece, Jennifer Elliott, and Chuck Prescott
Color Separations: Graphic Color, Fairfield, Maine
Printing (text and binding): Quebecor-Book Press, Brattleboro, Vermont
Printing (jackets): John P. Pow Company, South Boston, Massachusetts

10 9 8 7 6 5 4 3 2 1

Contents

Acknowledgments

Just as no one individual won the 1992 America's Cup for America^3, this book was the result of the hard work of a large team. The concept and majority of reporting was conducted by Choptank Word Bank, which also wrote and published *The Voice of America^3* newsletter throughout 1991 and 1992. Many factual and editing contributions were made by Bill Koch, Vincent Moeyersoms, Rick Wrightson, Will Robinson, Rick Burnham, Jerry Milgram, Peter Wilson, Sue Maffei-Plowden, David Rosow, Debra Cardillo, Gay Larsen, Ellen Bloom, Daniel Forster, Richard Callahan, Buddy Melges, Bill Shore, Win Fowler, and Roy Morrow Bell. Contributions to the text were made by many members of America^3 who are quoted throughout. A list of all America^3 members is found in the Appendix. *To the Third Power* is dedicated to all those who believed that the combination of teamwork, talent, and technology could move mountains — and proved just that in 1992.

Paul C. Larsen
March, 1995

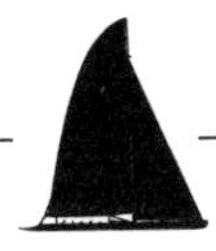

Prologue

It is perhaps the supreme irony, in an event whose history is filled with such, that the world's most famous sailboat race could be said to have been born on a farm. The year was 1848 and the place was a cow pasture in Sussex, England. Walking the fields were Prince Albert, husband of Queen Victoria, and a farmer friend, who confided he was on the verge of bankruptcy. After listening to the farmer's travails, Albert concluded his host's scientific knowledge of modern agricultural equipment and techniques was sorely lacking. When the Prince surveyed other area farmers, he discovered similar ignorance. The situation generated memories of his early years in Germany, where a succession of trade fairs displayed the newest machinery and innovations in an attempt to raise the consciousness of farmers and businessmen.

Albert decided to sponsor such a fair in England. At first he planned an international exhibition of the latest farm equipment, but as the idea took hold, it soon grew into a far more encompassing exposition. When "The Great Exhibition" opened in 1851, it was a celebration of international progress to date in the fields of science, industry, and art. For many Americans, it was an opportunity to show the world the results of their country's Industrial Revolution, now building to full force since its birth at the beginning of the century. The telegraph, steamboat, and locomotive were evidence of the nation's creativity and initiative, heralding an era of unprecedented growth and expansion.

By 1850, most of America had heard of the forthcoming International Exhibition. One of the sons of the Industrial Revolution, John Cox Stevens, was drawn to the challenge. From a family of scientists and industrialists that had invented the T-shaped railroad track, a bomb that was shot from a cannon, and the first propeller-driven boat, Stevens seemed eager to somehow be involved in a demonstration of his country's scientific achievements.

As a founding member of the New York Yacht Club as well as a wealthy industrialist with interests in steamships and a Hudson River ferry line,

Stevens had for years been a keen yachtsman who delighted in wagering on the swiftness of his sailboats. Prince Albert's world's fair provided Stevens the opportunity to indulge two of his favorite pastimes: fervent support of his country and yacht racing. Towards the end of 1850, Stevens and five friends formed a syndicate which commissioned one of the country's foremost yacht designers and one of the country's foremost shipwrights to produce, in the words of the builder, "a boat...faster than any vessel in the United States brought to compete with her."

Historians differ on Stevens's primary motive for building the new craft. One school of thought is that his heavily nationalistic beliefs led him to a desire to prove his country's boatbuilding proficiency. Others cite the more adventuresome side of his personality; he liked sporting contests and he enjoyed betting large amounts of money on them. Whatever his principal reason, on the day the International Exhibition opened in London, in New York a new schooner-yacht named *America* was declared finished and "ready to test her powers." She was soon on her way to England, where Stevens hoped to arrange some races with members of the Royal Yacht Squadron.

However, even before this "radical" schooner anchored off Cowes, word of her unusual appearance had spread along the waterfront. Considerably different from the British yachts, typically narrow and deep, *America* featured a sharp bow, wide beam, full stern, and low freeboard. Two steeply raked masts with no topsails and a single jib with no boom completed her look of an "out and outer," the term used then to define true racing craft. Despite the reaction of the 83-year-old Marqùis of Anglesey, who after a close inspection uttered the now-famous, "If she is right, then all of us are wrong," that opinion was not shared by English yachtsmen. When Stevens issued a challenge to any vessel of the R.Y.S. for a race in which he would wager the staggering amount of more than $50,000, there were no takers.

Instead, Stevens had to settle for a fleet race "open to yachts belonging to the clubs of all nations." The race offered a cash prize worth a little more than $500, accompanied by a rather ungainly silver trophy known as the "Royal Yacht Squadron Hundred Guinea Cup." It measured 27 inches high, 36 inches around, and weighed 134 ounces. Although called a cup, it was actually a bottomless ewer. The race drew seven schooners and eight cutters to the 53-mile course around the Isle of Wight on August 22. In front of thousands of spectators, *America* started last at 10 a.m., but by 5:50 p.m. she was twelve miles from the finish line and some seven-and-a-half miles in front of *Aurora,* the second-placed yacht. Almost three hours later, after the wind had died considerably, the race was over and *America* took the honors, the cash, and the "cup."

Through the ages, the story of Queen Victoria's query about the status of the race has become synonymous with yacht racing in general, and to some extent, with the fierce competitive nature of yacht racers. Although a number of historians dispute that it ever happened, the story goes that the Queen, aboard her royal yacht, asked who was winning the race. "*America,*" was the reply. When she asked who was next, the answer came back, "Your Majesty, there is no second." Myth or not, there are more than 20 skippers of America's Cup runners-up who would no doubt attest to the truth of the statement.

While this race is the most famous in America's history, and perhaps the most famous yacht race in world history, at the time neither Stevens nor his syndicate realized the significance of their victory. Stevens was still disappointed he could not arrange a high stakes match race, although he was somewhat placated by the growing reputation his vessel was earning, both for her swiftness and her scientific achievement. Queen Victoria and Prince Albert paid a much publicized visit to the yacht the day after the race around the Isle of Wight, a visit that went a long way toward establishing friendlier relations between the two countries and demonstrating the potential of the developing nation on the world's stage.

America was to race only once more under the management of Stevens and his syndicate, which sold the schooner to an Englishman. When the Americans traveled home, it was with the expressed promise to return to England with another yacht, but that never happened. What did endure was the Royal Yacht Squadron's idea of "a race for the clubs of all nations."

The cup *America* won was passed among the sailors for awhile, but no one was quite sure what to do with it. There were suggestions of melting it down and making medallions out of the silver for distribution to the families of the men on board. For some time the trophy was largely forgotten and was stored in an attic. In 1853, Stevens, who held the position of commodore at the New York Yacht Club, posted "a race for all nations" with a prize of $500. Not enough interest was shown, but the challenge was renewed in 1857. For this race, George Schuyler (an ancestor of Bill Koch's) recovered the cup and presented it to the New York Yacht Club, calling it the "America's Cup." The first challenge for the silver urn, now the oldest trophy in sports, was raced in 1870.

In the 143 years since *America's* accomplishment, only 23 men have won the America's Cup. More people have led expeditions to climb Mount Everest; more men have been president of the United States.

The challenge offered by the America's Cup is both ambiguous and darkly formidable. Like war, the Cup is a comprehensive test of resources, technology, tactics, and ingenuity. It demands as much business acumen as athleticism. While mandated in the Cup's Deed of Gift as a "friendly competition between nations," the regatta has always been characterized by hostility. No quarter is given. Campaigns have historically included espionage, dirty tricks, open accusations of cheating, and at times, actual litigation. In this race, the ends often justify the means. It is more a contest of design technology and organizational skills than sailing.

Sailboats are the slowest vehicles that race. Marathoners can run 20 miles faster than today's Cup yachts can sail around the 20-mile course. In a fleet race, there can be satisfaction even at the back of the pack. But the Cup is a best-of-seven series of two-boat match races. One either wins or finishes last. And one does so in painfully slow motion, in the most public of forums, complete (since 1987) with live, on-board cameras and microphones that record every grin and grimace. The winner is heaped with glory. The loser — previous accomplishments aside — leaves beaten and empty-handed, humiliated by the failure of his best innovations, stunned by an enormous expenditure of money that was for naught. And since it is an international contest, the winner's flag always seems to fly a little brighter, while the colors of the loser's fade. Those who fail on Everest have considerably more satisfaction. There is no disgrace in being bested simply by the elements of nature.

It is not surprising that syndicate heads who choose to enter the America's Cup fray have certain things in common. Success and wealth have stoked their egos and built their self-confidence. Even greater challenges, the search for some new Herculean accomplishment and perhaps increased exposure on the world stage are motivating factors. History proves that what may be sports' most unique contest has for almost a century and a half attracted many of the world's most unique individuals.

England's Sir Thomas Lipton, who founded the tea company, tried for 31 years to win the Cup, and failed. Another challenger, T.O.M. Sopwith, the British aviation pioneer, found that his best effort was not sufficient to win. It wasn't until 1983 that the United States of America finally lost a Cup match. That year, a team fielded by Australian beer baron, Alan Bond, won in its fourth attempt.

In the 1930s, famed American heir and sportsman Harold Vanderbilt picked up the challenge to defend the Cup, and succeeded twice before World War II put a temporary hold on Cup competition. In the 1970s, outspoken American media and sports magnate, Ted Turner, steered to victory on his second try.

In 1980, after 130 years of routine, one-sided American victories, San Diego businessman Dennis Conner transformed Cup competition into a full-time professional occupation. Conner won the Cup, lost it to the Australians three years later, and won it back in 1987 in the turbulent waters off Fremantle, Australia in what may have been the most exciting America's Cup ever. In 1988 New Zealand's Michael Fay registered a surprise challenge with a 130-foot monohull. In what became the most litigious Cup in history, Conner answered with a catamaran that sailed over the ocean's surface to easy victory. When asked about the sporting nature of his defense, Conner said, "There has never been any sportsmanship in the America's Cup. Anyone who thinks so is kidding himself."

In 1992, newcomer Bill Koch entered America's Cup XXVIII. Businessman, heir, scientist, and yachtsman, Koch, like Vanderbilt, played a dual role in the America^3 syndicate. He managed the entire effort and skippered the yacht. While Vanderbilt had his ace, Sherman Hoyt, beside him in the cockpit, Koch shared the helm with Olympian Buddy Melges.

Koch's team entered the game two years late. The challengers had never looked stronger or better prepared. Money was in place, new technology had already been developed, the world's best sailors were scattered among eight challengers from seven nations. For many months America^3's goal looked unattainable. Las Vegas bookmakers considered the fledgling group a 100 to 1 shot to win the Cup. The team's supporters among the international yachting press could be counted on one hand. To many observers, Koch was thought to be too inexperienced and his insistence on the scientific method in all phases of crew training and boat preparation was considered too didactic.

But to the more historically oriented observer, Koch's approach was reminiscent of John Cox Stevens and the original *America* syndicate. Both syndicates were built on a high regard for the truth of science and the art of the boatbuilder. Both placed a huge importance on boat speed. And like Stevens, Koch is a businessman/scientist/heir who wanted to prove to the world the superiority of American technology.

Another commonality between the original and the most recent winner of the "Hundred Guinea Cup" is the emphasis put on management. Decisions made by key individuals of both syndicates eventually spelled the difference between success and failure. In Koch's case, his determination to hold steadfast to his original tenants of teamwork, talent, and technology, even in the face of internal dissension and public skepticism, proved all-powerful.

The story of the America³ victory has more to do with science and management than with sports and athletic heroics. Koch set the agenda from the beginning, and his brilliance is better demonstrated by his selection of team-oriented individuals to manage his plan than it is indicated by when he tacked or how he drove.

Managing the intricate dynamics of an America's Cup syndicate has become an art in itself. In Stevens's day, the *America* syndicate was run by five men, the yacht was raced with 21 sailors on board, and the entire endeavor is estimated to have cost less than $25,000. The America³ syndicate grew to more than 200 people and cost approximately $68 million. Stevens's main concerns were the building of the boat, the cut of the sails, organizing the voyage to Europe, and arranging races in which he might recoup some of his expenses. Koch worried about tank testing, composite material developments, computer assisted design programs, personality clashes, ego battles, rule changes and disputes, physical conditioning programs, dietary management, boatbuilders' timetables, dealings with the press, industrial and technological espionage, compound and boat security, accurate weather reporting, a possible crew mutiny, match racing strategies and tactics, and on and on.

In the beginning, there was little success. Schedules went awry, budgets were prematurely spent, the concept of team was undermined by the ego of individuals. Yet slowly and persistently, America³ improved. The sailors finally overcame Team Dennis Conner in the defense finals, and squared off against the Italians in the Cup match. On Saturday, May 16, 1992, Koch's yacht *America³* won its fourth race against Italy's *Il Moro di Venezia,* and successfully defended the America's Cup. With the victory, Bill Koch joined the very exclusive club of those who have won this elusive trophy. *To the Third Power* is the story of how he and his team managed to win.

"Boatspeed is a science,
sailing is an art."

William Koch

Magic (D) 1870

Cambria (C) 1870

Columbia (D) 1871

Sappho (D) 1871

Livonia (C) 1871

Madeleine (D) 1876

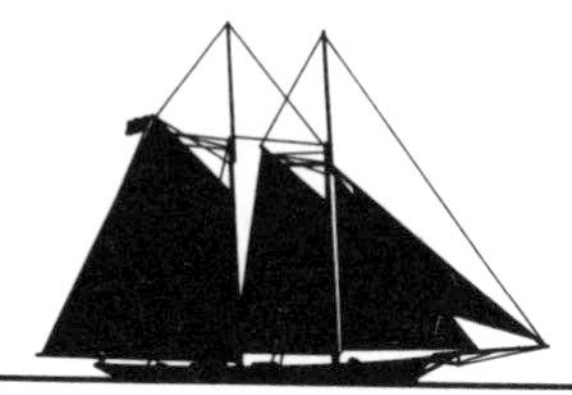

Countess of Dufferin (C) 1876

Mischief (D) 1881

Atalanta (C) 1881

Puritan (D) 1885

Genesta (C) 1885

Mayflower (D) 1886

On page viii: a profile of the schooner-yacht *America,* the racing vessel that started it all. She was modeled after New York pilot boats. Above: silhouettes of America's Cup contenders ("D" for defenders and "C" for challengers) from 1870 to 1992. When *America* won the Hundred Guinea Cup in 1851, the rules of the race called for the winner to be determined only on elapsed time and did not handicap the boats by size. By 1870, for the first challenge, a rating rule was was established that resulted in elapsed time being corrected depending on waterline length. The rating rules were change

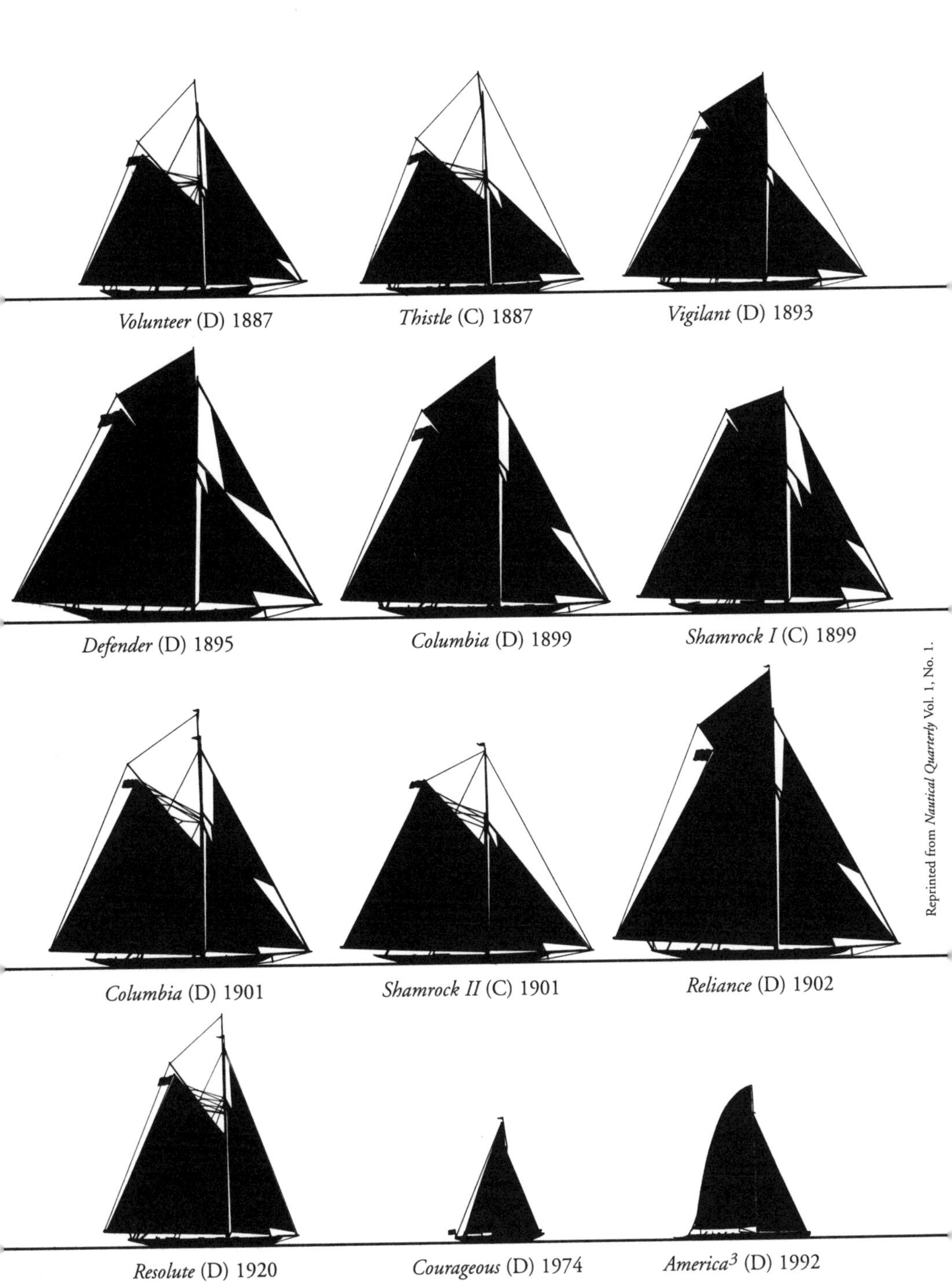

again over the years, in 1871, 1876, 1882, 1920, 1930, 1958, 1988, and 1990. Among the changes considered were length, weight, displacement, sail area, overhangs, and the shape of the hull. Schooners and cutters were the dominant designs from 1870 to 1887. Races from 1893 to 1920 were conducted in "the great sloops," measuring from 106 feet to 144 feet. J-Class boats ruled the Cup waves from 1930 to 1937, and the 12-Meter era ran from 1958 to 1987. Following the catamaran mismatch in 1988, the IACC formula was adopted.

"I did not win the America's Cup, the entire team did."

William Koch

Out of the Fog

1

Fog covered the North Atlantic, obscuring the brilliant spinnaker colors of the 22 sailboats racing across Narragansett Sound. The weather was not particularly unusual for the waters surrounding Newport, Rhode Island, and on this mid-June day in 1990, few people walking the streets gave it much notice. Nor did they realize that just offshore a watershed event in the history of yacht racing was taking place.

Attempting to make its way through the fog, the fleet was competing in a regatta organized by the New York Yacht Club. Five classes of yachts, measuring from 30 to 85 feet, had met the starting gun. As visibility became increasingly difficult, nine skippers decided in favor of safety over a possible trophy and turned their craft towards shore. For the more experienced long-distance racers, any thought of quitting was anathema.

Not only were these fiercely competitive yachtsmen willing to risk the dangers of ocean sailing in hopes of victory, but they also rode the waves with some sense of expectation. For several weeks preceding the regatta, word had swept the waterfront that a new "maxi" was about to be launched. To most sailors, the news was met with the same excitement exhibited by movie fans at a Hollywood premier. The maxis — so named because they are the largest boats racing under the IOR (International Offshore Rule), a rating system that attempts to classify non-equal boats into equal categories by using time handicaps — are today's thoroughbreds of the sea. They are among the largest, fastest, most expensive sailboats built to race. Their owners are among the most successful, most competitive, and richest men in the world.

Because there are only a handful of maxis in existence, the launching of a new one is a rare and special event in the world of yachting. Anticipation grows steadily and breeds a hundred inevitable rumors. And because this particular boat, and its particular owner, were the subject of some of the wildest speculations ever uttered along the docks, the attention of sailors around the globe was drawn to the fabled New England city on this pea soup of a day. Only a few knew how this new boat had come to be.

Since its official birth in 1979, the maxi class had been in flux. Once dominated by Europeans like Baron Edmund de Rothschild (*Gitana*), Enrico Recchi (*Benbow*), and William Whitehouse-Vaux (*Mistress Quickly*), the early 1980s saw a shift in power and performance to American owners like Jim Kilroy (*Kialoa*), Huey Long (*Ondine*) and George Coumantaros (*Boomerang*). In the late '80s, the Italians, led by industrialist Raul Gardini, took command. Honorary members of the class like King Juan Carlos of Spain and the Aga Khan gave it the high profile of a very exclusive international club for the rich and powerful.

With such celebrity, it is not surprising that when, in 1984, William Ingraham Koch joined the maxi club after purchasing the German Frers-designed *Huaso,* not much notice was given or taken. What was surprising was that Bill Koch, born in Kansas and infinitely more familiar with the prairie than the sea, more comfortable on a horse than a boat, should decide at age 45 that he wanted to go sailing. And not just sailing around buoys at the local yacht club. He wanted to go to sea on an 80-foot sailboat with a crew of 30 and race in places like St. Tropez, Sardinia, Hawaii, St. Thomas, Majorca, and Antibes.

There have been grand entries into yachting before, people who have entered the sport with boats as large as their dreams. But it is safe to say that no other debut has come close to making the impact that has been made on sailboat racing by newcomer Bill Koch.

Koch may not have had any experience in designing, building, outfitting, and racing maxi yachts, but he did begin the game with a very clear plan in mind. *Huaso* a cruising boat, would be revamped into a racing boat and serve as a platform on which Koch could learn the sport, develop a crew, and use as a benchmark against which other designers he intended to retain could measure their ideas.

Scientist and Businessman

With twelve years of study and three degrees from M.I.T. (the Massachusetts Institute of Technology) behind him, Dr. Koch, the scientist, saw the maxi class and the world's oceans as a huge laboratory in which he could test a whole range of theories dealing with such subjects as physics, mechanics, hydrodynamics, experimental materials, meteorology, and velocity predictions. And after thirteen years as an employee of his family's company and now chairman of his own corporation, Bill Koch, the businessman, had certain ideas about management he was eager to apply to his new sport.

If Bill Koch's entry into the world of racing big sailboats was accompanied by a wait-and-see silence, his approach to yachting was soon the talk of the circuit. He wasted no time in asking the rhetorical question: How can I figure out in advance how fast a boat is going to be? The difference between Bill Koch and others who had been struggling with that riddle for years was that Koch had the resources and the scientific background to begin formulating a Grand Plan that would possibly yield some new answers.

In his methodical manner, Koch interviewed a number of the world's leading yacht designers. To each he posed his question: "What makes a boat go fast?" He was not pleased with the answers.

"I thought I was asking them a straightforward question that seemed to me to be at the very heart of their profession. What I got in response were mystical answers. To me, boat speed is a science, sailing is an art. The problem, I discovered, is that most yacht designers are artists who fall in love with their work." And once in love, it was difficult for the creator to alter the creation.

This inflexibility bothered Koch, a man whose entire higher education was based on experimenting; test it, make a change, test it again, repeat the process, try an alternative, test it again and again, and when you're finished with all of that, test it again. Schooled in the scientific method, he wanted to use it in real-world situations. Thus, he postulated that the way to balance art and science was to use the creative ideas of designers, but final decisions would be made according to science, a more objective discipline.

Then a friend introduced him to Dr. Jerry Milgram, naval architect and professor of Ocean Engineering. At M.I.T., Milgram's academic specialties are studying satellite images of ship wakes and oil spills. But in yachting circles he is known as a heady innovator, and something of a mad scientist.

Jerry Milgram was among the first to apply high-end scientific technology to yacht design with success. He created a stir in the 1960s when he used photographic measurements to create models of 12-Meter sails that he tested in the wind tunnel. In the '70s, he did research on the redesign of *Intrepid*, the boat that won the America's Cup in 1967 and 1970. Along the way Milgram had theories that resulted in some strange-looking boats (a cat-rigged Concordia, for instance), but they were always examples of scientific logic being applied to reveal a weakness in a rating rule. While Milgram's boats weren't always fast, or appreciated by the yachting community, his points were well-taken, if grudgingly so.

Koch and Milgram are a good match. Koch, with a degree in chemical engineering, is familiar with fluid- and hydrodynamics and is intrigued by technology. One of his guiding principles is that science makes the decisions while intuition comes up with ideas. "I have a technical bias," Koch says. "There is no magic involved. Fundamental scientific principles are the way to go. The guy who wins a boat race is the most objective."

From Milgram, Koch received a different perspective and answers radically different from those he heard other designers utter. So he developed a project in which science would be the final arbiter in all decisions and those decisions would be the basis for all developing technology. That project, ongoing for years, came to be known as "the Matador Program."

Like any good scientific approach, Koch's plan called for basic research in a variety of sectors. Instead of rushing off to the store for a new boat, he picked up *Huaso*. He changed the name to *Matador*, after the Matador Land and Cattle Company in Texas, his father's favorite ranch. Koch gutted *Matador*'s interior to make it more race worthy, purchased (for $500) non-commercial rights to a bull's-head drawing from the Picasso estate for use as the boat's logo, and went racing.

The boat did poorly at first, and Koch soon figured out why. "I made a basic management mistake," he admits. "I thought that inviting the top-notch sailors, the so-called 'rock stars' of sailing, to race *Matador* with me, would be the quickest way to success. I soon learned otherwise. They argued among themselves, they were rude, they never worked as a team."

It was a lesson well learned and one that would have an enormous impact on Koch's sailing philosophy. His hope from the beginning was that he could develop a crew that held team goals higher than personal glory. The rock-star route had proved a dead end, so he began to dismantle and rebuild at the same time. He reasoned that if he could gather a solid core of team players who would enjoy the experience in general and working together in particular, he could mold the entire crew after them.

Attitude, Teamwork, Ability

"I decided I should pick the crew myself," said Koch and he came up with a formula. Each crewman would be rated on a one-to-ten scale in three categories: attitude, teamwork, and ability. "They had to score nine or ten on the first two," Koch says, "and at least five on ability." The de-emphasis on ability speaks volumes about Koch's priorities.

It began to work. *Matador* started doing better, often finishing second and third. In the first world championship *Matador* entered, the boat's mast broke and still finished second. Today that mast, now repaired, stands as a flag pole at Koch's Nauticus (Latin for sailor) Marina in Osterville, Massachusetts. It serves as a constant reminder of what a mistake can cost. In the four World Championships *Matador* entered, she finished second in three of them. An impressive record for most yachtsmen, but Koch wasn't interested in second. He wanted the fastest boat in the world, sailed by a well-coordinated team interested more in sailing perfectly than in furthering their own careers.

Sailing in the afterguard (the so-called "brain trust" made up of the helmsman, tactician, and navigator) on grand prix race boats is always tricky business. The boats are so demanding, and the desire to win is so strong among owners, that full-time professional racers have taken over the key jobs: helmsman, tactician, navigator, sail trimmers. Owners racing these boats are comparable in their involvement to owners of Indianapolis race cars. Industrial developer Jim Kilroy successfully skippered *Kialoa*, the maxi. John Thompson, who owns a bearing company in Long Island, successfully skippered *Infinity*, a well-known 50-footer. But the rest tend to assign themselves a less crucial job and let the pros run the show.

Racing sailboats today is a complicated, high-tech, water-borne chess game of finesse and strength, timing and good tactical calls. The infusion of electronic aids over the past ten years has helped, moving the data from the seats of revered skipper's pants to digital screens. But to do well in a hot fleet, a skipper has to anticipate the data and respond by second nature. That takes time, experience. No two situations are ever quite the same. Today's best sailors have been racing continuously since grammar school.

Bill Koch started at age 45. He is a studious man who soaks up information like a sponge and retains it like an elephant, and he applied himself to the process with vigor. But he had a lot of ground to cover.

"Bill's goal was to go racing with friends, or people who would become friends," Vincent Moeyersoms says. Moeyersoms is a congenial, ambitious fellow who turned his love of sailing into a successful management career. He was born in Belgium, where he studied physics. Then he went to sea, racing the Whitbread Round the World Challenge in 1981. He is a veteran of two Admiral's Cups, five SORC's, three Kenwood Cups, and five Maxi World Championships. He worked on *Condor* (a hot maxi) for two years, eventually becoming skipper. He moved to *Matador* when he heard Bill Koch needed crew.

"It was a learning program for everyone, and he wanted it to be enjoyable," says Moeyersoms. "It was tough because of the various sailing abilities of the people. They represented different levels of technical expertise, and different ways of life. The *Matador* crew was the most diverse of any boat out there. But Bill stuck with it. It was two or three years before the afterguard, the permanent crew, the weekend sailors, and Milgram's scientific team gained mutual respect and really began talking to each other."

Koch pursued his attitude/teamwork theory, and worked on crew motivation. Each member was required to read Robert Axelrod's book *Evolution of Cooperation,* a Koch favorite. He has probably spent more money on uniforms than any owner in the history of the sport. "We're a team," he says. "Teams wear uniforms. We tuck our shirts in while racing — no shirts off. We're shipshape."

This was part of Koch's management/leadership philosophy. He was adamant about making everyone part of the team, and the fact that everyone wore the same uniform, whether he be an accountant, security man, or sailor, served to reinforce that idea. It also strengthened the "no stars" dictum. Koch's view is that everyone on the team is of equal importance. "Everyone wins, or no one wins," he says.

Koch's views on teamwork were in large part shaped by his experiences on the basketball court at M.I.T. When he tells the story, he reminds listeners that the esteemed institution of higher learning has never exactly been known as a jock factory. But because the university did offer athletics, and because Bill's height made him a natural candidate for basketball, he tried out for and made the freshman team. Bill's twin, David, possessed of more athletic ability than Bill, and for that matter, perhaps any other student at M.I.T., was destined for stardom and selection to several Small College All-American teams.

During that first year, the freshmen team did about as expected, losing more than winning. A lot more. But the youngsters did no worse than the varsity, which won a grand total of one game the entire season.

In Bill's sophomore year, he graduated to the varsity, where his skills weren't enough to change the fortunes of the team: another season with but a solitary win. If discouraged, neither Bill nor the team showed it, but clearly the athletic department had seen enough. Out with the old coach, in with a former high school coach named Jack Berry.

"Jack was a tough, no-nonsense character," says Bill. "He was determined to make a success out of us M.I.T. nerds, and he was going to do so with one player who could make most teams, my brother, and the rest of us, who would have been sent to the showers within five minutes of the first try out on any serious college team. He organized the team around everyone's individual strengths and weaknesses, teaching us only one play because he said we weren't smart enough to remember any more. He drilled us over and over on that one play so we wouldn't make any mistakes and he instilled in us the thought that if we played as a team, we could win."

Berry made them believe in themselves and he told them they were winners and that he did not care what the rest of the world thought. He made them practice hard and he preached the gospel of teamwork. In Bill's junior year, the team won half of its games. The seniors had the longest winning streak and the least points scored against it of any college team in the entire nation.

The answer was plainly attitude and teamwork. "What my basketball career showed me," says Bill, "was that you can take inferior talent and mold a better team around them than far superior players just by stressing, and executing, teamwork. We had no stars. We just fought it out together."

He divided the *Matador* crew into team sections: foredeck, mast, grinders, trimmers, afterguard. He held team meetings before and after the race. The crew boss made sure everyone had a job — even occasional guests — so everyone would feel part of the *Matador* family, acquire the *Matador* spirit. He established a prize for the guy who best exemplified attitude and teamwork. The previous winners got to select the next recipient. At lavish *Matador* crew dinners, in addition to Steuben and Swarovski crystal awards, he issued *Matador* underwear.

"I've sailed on other boats," Koch says, "where there is nothing but anger and hostility. On *Matador*, things were harmonious, pleasant. We had fun. We were a real brotherhood."

Matador did well, but she wasn't a winner. She came close, but couldn't make that last hurdle that distinguishes champions. The word on the circuit was that no matter how many changes they made to *Matador*, and there were hundreds made to keels, appendages, sails, deck layouts, hardware, etc., the boat just couldn't beat the newer maxis or the more experienced crews. It began to look as though the timetable of using *Matador* as a training vessel, while Koch put plans in motion for designing and building a "breakthrough" boat, would have to be modified. Koch originally thought the program would take two years. It lasted more than five.

Two Research Programs

At the same time he bought *Huaso*, Koch began two research programs at M.I.T., both under Jerry Milgram's direction. One was theoretical, aimed at advancing the theory of why sailboats move through the water. Under reexamination would be the Velocity Prediction Program (VPP), a relatively new, evolving formula meant to predict a particular boat's speed under given conditions with certain sails hoisted. As part of this M.I.T. study, Koch built a scaled-down maxi: a 30-foot, sailing version of *Matador* that contained a space frame hitched to the hull in six places with strain gauges. Everything that attached the sails to the boat — mast, traveler, winches, jib cars, and shrouds — was fixed to the space frame. Every change in tension on any of the above would be recorded by the strain gauges. This boat, in effect, measured the forces the wind exerted on the boat. The data was collected by an on-board computer and compared to boat-speed fluctuations.

The second program was aimed at designing the fastest maxi in the world. It was the most comprehensive research and development program ever undertaken to build a boat by anyone, anywhere, with the possible exception of the U.S. Navy. Given Koch's belief that in theory yacht design is a science, but in practice it is an intuitive art, he wanted to test the full spectrum of possibilities. He wanted to test as many ideas as possible.

In order to generate those ideas, Koch approached more than 20 yacht designers, some famous, some unknown, and requested entries to a design contest. The requests generated more than 50 entries received by Milgram and his staff. Separate studies were done on rudder and keel shapes. At the time, this approach to sailboat racing on any level, was highly unusual.

Forty-five of the designs were built as 1/3-scale models that were tank tested. A dozen of the best models were made into small sailboats and then raced against each other. Among them were 1/3-scale models of existing maxis Koch built as control boats. Twice he invited the other maxi owners to Cape Cod to compete in regattas using the scaled-down versions of their yachts that were accurate right down to paint jobs and logos.

The sailing models were tested for handling, tacking ability, acceleration, and wave resistance. Real polar diagrams (accumulated VPPs for all points of sail) were written for each model and compared to tank test data. The data was analyzed. Discrepancies were noted. The models were retested in the tank. Some of the shapes developed for keels and rudders were tested full-size on *Matador*.

So it was with the basic research and the design contest, both of which developed more offshoots than ivy growing up a brick wall. One of these projects involved the development of both hardware and software for predicting wind patterns over a given section of water. "Going up a weather leg the second time around," Koch says, "chances are the major shifts will occur in the same place. Of course then you have to fight the cultural problem of convincing the less science-minded sailors to believe this and take advantage of it."

The *Matador* research and design program for Koch's maxi was managed under the same precepts used to develop his crew. Team players were sought. Ideas were encouraged and discussed. Flexibility was cherished, especially as the program headed into unknown territory.

"There were basically ten people on the team," says Vincent Moeyersoms, who coordinated the process. "It was a new way of working. The computer gives you the lines very quickly. The designers only optimize the lines and appendages. Structure and construction are not things they have to worry about. The tank and wind-tunnel tests give us a sense of whether what the computer is telling us will work. We always sent our own guys to the tank to get a hands-on feel for the control variables: temperature and pressure changes, wear and tear on the equipment. Because you rarely see more than a two percent difference in a test. Sometimes that two percent is noise. You have to learn to tell the difference."

Two designs appeared to fit the boat speed requirements. One was developed by Bill Cook and the other was drawn by Buddy Duncan and Penn Edmonds. Koch liked what he saw, but he told the designers to put the two boats together and work on producing an even faster boat. Back to the drawing boards. The effort paid off. The final boat design by the team of three was for a very large, heavy yacht. From the start, the choice drew criticism from yachting's cognoscenti. First, it was said, Koch had passed up the services of the leading maxi designers in favor of relative unknowns with maverick ideas and a university professor with ethereal theories and an experimental approach. Next, he approved plans for a boat that was tc weigh almost 100,000 pounds and measure 85 feet when everyone knew the smartest maxi designers favored shorter and lighter, recommending 70,000 pounds and less than 80 feet. This would be a whale in a school of barracudas.

If Koch's choice of designers and design confused the docksiders, they were totally perplexed when word leaked out that the new boat would carry a trim tab, a maneuverable device on a boat's keel used to correct side slipping so the boat could sail in a straight line. This was a signal, so it was said, that the boat's keel was too narrow and wouldn't afford enough lift, causing the boat to head for third base when the skipper was steering to first.

Koch was undaunted by the sniping. This was not the first time in his life he'd had someone tell him "You can't do that." In fact, it might be said that much of Bill Koch's personal and professional life is the result of him listening to such suggestions and replying "Yes I can, and I'll show you how." Being told no seems to be an impetus for Koch to get things done.

Construction was begun at Eric Goetz Custom Sailboats, Bristol, Rhode Island, in the summer of 1989. Goetz had started by building in wood, completing more than 50 wood-epoxy hulls before he switched to synthetic materials. Now he is the foremost builder of composite sailboats in the country.

And now, in the North Atlantic fog, the results of all the time, effort, and expense of this five-year experiment were finally about to be displayed for all to see. The new boat had been launched a month earlier and even before the champagne bottle was smashed on her bow, and long before her first race, she generated a stir of excitement and curiosity throughout the sailing world.

So much about the boat was unusual if not unique. Design, engineering, material, even her name: all different. She was the first maxi built entirely of composite materials, predominantly carbon-fiber. As rumored, she was long and heavy. And her name, *Matador²*, that's "*Matador* Squared" as in to the second power, seemed to define the scientific approach to yacht racing.

During the sea trials, that approach was under close scrutiny and when gear broke and other problems arose, murmurs of doubt could be heard on the waterfront. But Koch was so convinced that his methodology was correct that he walked the deck confident and calm.

Through the years *Matador²* was being designed and tested, Koch concentrated on *Matador*, trying to absorb as much about big league sailboat racing as he could. After his initial experiment with "big name" sailors, he continued to make his own crew selections, using the attitude/teamwork/ability formula he had devised. Over the years a core group had formed, including a number of old friends and trusted loyalists. Several knew Bill Koch from Osterville, others from business. Names that were frequently found on the crew's list were Vincent Moeyersoms, Rick Wrightson, John Osmond, Fred Curran, Peter Grubb, Lou Varney, Bob Leach, and Carl Lessard.

Hundreds of top sailors and "wanna-be's" passed through the *Matador* Program over the years, but this small group served as the nucleus and would find themselves on board the majority of races *Matador²* sailed after her launching. They exemplified the Koch approach to teamwork. They worked well with each other and their focus was on the team's goals. And now that they were aboard the new boat, an electric sense of excitement passed among them.

Matador² vs. Boomerang

Matador² had only one opponent this day. The former maxi-class world champion and long-time nemesis of the first *Matador*, George Coumantaros's *Boomerang* circled the new boat in pre-race maneuvers. Koch had come to like and respect Coumantaros a great deal. The shipping magnate had become Bill's mentor in the ICAYA (International Class 'A' Yacht Association) and had passed on much advice to the novice. Coumantaros is a real gentleman of the old school whose approach to the sport is without the claws and bared teeth sometimes exhibited by other maxi owners. Just as he and Koch found much in common, so too did the crews of the two boats. They helped each other out when necessity dictated, and they were often found at the same post-race watering holes.

Now, as the two maxis dodged and ran at each other, crews aboard the boats in other classes watched them and instant evaluations were whispered across the water. If *Matador*^{2} was indeed a "breakthrough" boat, she would be well-tested by *Boomerang*. The legendary maxi, with a seasoned crew, was always a step ahead of the first *Matador*. If this new one was to get anywhere in the class, she'd have to get by, or at least be close to *Boomerang*.

As the countdown to the starting gun began, Koch was at the wheel and Gary Jobson, the former three-time All-American sailor, veteran of three America's Cup campaigns, and television sailing analyst was calling tactics. Perhaps the second (to Dennis Conner) best known American sailor, Jobson seemed in many ways the epitome of the rock-star persona Koch found unacceptable. But he'd raced with the *Matador* team many times over the years, a good indication of his outstanding sailing skills as well as his political savvy. Also, Koch considered him a friend.

Matador^{2} took the start and headed upwind on the left side of the course. *Boomerang* worked the right side and before long the two boats lost sight of each other in the deepening fog. With visibility so impaired, the afterguard turned to the boat's electronic nerve center to get their bearings. Rows of blinking screens displayed digital numbers conveying wind and boat speed, position on the course, range and distance to the next buoy, and other information used by the afterguard to make critical decisions. But even with all the data flowing, the loss of visual contact with left those aboard the new maxi wondering exactly how fast they were going and how that compared to their opponent.

The course was spread across 22.8 nautical miles of water. Koch, at the wheel, implored his crew to drive themselves as hard as they could; to give *Matador*^{2} a true test of just what she could do. The 30 men aboard pushed the boat hard, sailing in a vacuum, scanning the horizon for any sign of *Boomerang*.

During the three-hour race, the fog thickened and the wind dropped from eight knots to four, shifting from an easterly flow to directly out of the south. While the varying conditions may not have been ideal for the maiden race of *Matador*^{2}, they did present a fair challenge.

As the two maxi boats headed towards the finish line, the yacht racing world held its collective breath, anxious and curious about the results. Not only would this race answer many of the questions competitors and arm-chair sailors had about Koch's radical design and testing theories, but it might also have an impact on the sport's quintessential regatta — the America's Cup.

Word had spread among Cup syndicates and organizers of Koch's five-year design and testing program, of his comprehensive use of "space age" materials, and his almost total reliance on science to arbitrate tough problems. If *Matador*^{2} showed well against her proven rival, much could be learned from Koch's methods. But if she didn't do well, as so many suspected, the more traditional approaches to yacht design, testing, and organizational management would continue to be favored.

And so, a simple race between two boats off the New England coast was taking on immense proportions. And out there, in the fog, during the race, no one really knew what was happening. The afterguards in both boats stood before the instrument and computer screens, mesmerized by the data that continuously changed before their eyes.

And now, almost three hours after the start, the crew aboard *Matador*^{2} could make out the committee boat and the finish line. They continued to scan the waters around them for any sign of *Boomerang*. None was found, even as the new boat crossed the line. The jubilation aboard *Matador*^{2} was somewhat tempered by the fact that no one knew where was or what had happened to her.

After five minutes passed, then ten, and still no sign of , speculation that the former world champion had dropped out of the race began to spread. *Matador*^{2} might be fast, and she certainly seemed to be an improvement over the first *Matador*, but there was just no way she was a ten-minute improvement. Stop watches continued...12 minutes...14...16. Something was wrong, something serious had happened to *Boomerang*. Seventeen minutes, 18, and wait, there she is, there's *Boomerang*, and she's sailing perfectly well. When she crossed the line and her crew nodded congratulations to the victor, there was a stunned silence aboard *Matador*^{2}, *Boomerang*, the committee boat, and the few other vessels circling the finish line.

Matador^2 had just beat *Boomerang* by 18 minutes and 58 seconds. Koch's new boat had gained almost a minute per mile over her rival. Such a quantum leap in speed had never been seen in the history of yacht racing. This was more than the "breakthrough" boat the *Matador* team had hoped for. This was a rocket ship!

Don't Give Up the Ship

2

While one race does not the fastest boat in the world make, the crew aboard *Matador*² knew they had just experienced something quite remarkable. The word "unbelievable" was perhaps the most overused exclamation uttered by the still-stunned team as their boat headed back toward the Newport docks. Even Bill Koch, who had planned for this moment during more than five years of testing and hundreds of hours of pushing, cajoling, inspiring, encouraging, and provoking his designers, scientists, and technicians, had a difficult time fully realizing what had just happened. New boats are expected to beat older boats if the designers and builders do their job correctly, but no one could have predicted a 19-minute margin over a former maxi world champion. The victory was roughly equivalent in sport to Secretariat's incredible win of 31 lengths in the 1973 Belmont Stakes. Nothing like it had ever happened before, and few believe its equal will be seen again.

If Koch and his crew were nonplused over what they and *Matador*² had just achieved, they were not exactly prepared for what was about to occur. Sailing is not a sport in the United States that draws a lot of media attention, but there is perhaps no greater word-of-mouth network than sailors with a story to tell. It took no time at all before the tale of *Matador*² was told. And when it was heard by America's Cup movers and shakers, its impact went far beyond a friendly sailboat race on a foggy summer's day.

Ever since man affixed a sail to a boat and caught the wind for the first time, he has sought ways to make sailboats go faster. Today there are thousands of competitions held throughout the world in which men and women seek to prove the superiority of their craft and their own skills. Most of these contests are administered by local yacht clubs or sailing organizations and their results are of little interest to anyone except the competitors themselves. With the exception of the professional match racing circuit, several long-distance races, a couple of around-the-world endurance marathons, and perhaps a rare big-money challenge designed to attract press, very few sailboat racing events garner much general attention.

The singular event recognized internationally as the pinnacle of yacht racing competition offers the world's oldest, regularly contested sporting trophy — the America's Cup. Since 1851, its rich and colorful history, fraught with controversy and heartbreak, yet replete with wondrous characters and outrageous incidents, has excited and intrigued countless sailors the world over.

At the time of *Matador²*'s improbable victory over *Boomerang,* the status of the America's Cup was at one of its lowest points ever. It was not until 1983, when *Australia II* beat Dennis Conner's *Liberty* to take the Cup out of the United States for the first time in the event's then 132-year history, that the regatta began to attract much widespread attention among the general public; most followers concede Conner's loss was the best thing that ever happened to the Cup. That viewpoint seemed to be supported when in 1986-87 fifteen challengers from six nations competed in the waters off Fremantle, Australia.

By now television had entered the game and the live pictures of sleek boats being pushed by strong winds and courageous sailors through turbulent seas mesmerized millions throughout the world. Conner's comeback victory continued the drama of his 4-3 defeat in Newport and now the public seemed to have a wholly new perception of the sport. The old adage that yacht racing is as exciting as watching grass grow, if not retired forever, was at least silenced for years to come.

As the scene shifted to San Diego, the event had reached its peak, but in less than a year its glistening image began to tarnish. The downfall began when New Zealander Michael Fay walked into the San Diego Yacht Club in July, 1987, and presented a written challenge to the club's commodore. According to Fay's interpretation, a single yacht club can challenge the defending yacht club in any size boat that complies with the formula set forth in the Deed of Gift, the oft-amended 1857 document that serves as the rules of the game. What resulted was an end to all plans for a multination challenge in 12-Meter yachts (used for Cup matches since 1958) and the beginning of the court-forced mismatch between a 130-foot monohull and a catamaran.

While the Cup was held hostage in dry-docked litigation, it became apparent that a whole new formula was needed both to resurrect the event's public image and to avoid similar incidents in the future. Committees were formed, proposals were made, rules were changed. Even as the New York

Supreme Court was still considering the legal ramifications of the monohull/catamaran race, the powers that be within Cup circles forwarded a plan that included the suggestion for a new class of boat. To be called the International America's Cup Class (IACC), the new boats would be designed and built to a complex formula in which sail area, waterline length, displacement, and weight were considerably adjusted compared to the 12-Meter formula. The idea was to present marine architects and boatbuilders with a vast challenge to explore the speed frontier. The obvious result was a new look to the fading image of the America's Cup and the hope for closer and more exciting competition.

Although 12-Meter yachts were, for all intents and purposes, the face of the modern America's Cup, replacing the majestic but anachronistic J-Boats used from 1930 to 1937, by 1988 they were considered dinosaurs. Criticized for being too heavy and short on sail area, the twelves performed admirably in Australia's heavy weather, but it was feared they would give a slow motion perspective to the San Diego event, where the average wind speed is not even 10 knots (in Perth it is over 24 knots). By contrast, the IACC boats, at 75 feet with 70 percent more sail area and 30 percent less weight, were promoted as speed machines compared to the lethargic twelves.

When the move was made from the 65-foot 12-Meters to the 75-foot IACC boats, the new class was often said to be "pretty much like the maxis." While designers and technicians might argue, a quick analysis of the formula and the description of the new materials now allowed in hull, deck and sails, indicated there were more similarities to the maxi class than there were differences. And the comparison was seen as positive for the Cup because the maxis had a reputation as the most exciting and sexy class of racing sailboats. Thus, those mounting America's Cup campaigns cast a curious eye toward the waters in which the maxis were racing.

What filled their line of sight in June of 1990 was the phenomenal success of *Matador²*. It didn't take long before the realization hit that if such a quantum leap in performance could be achieved in the maxi class, then use of the mountains of test data and technologies developed to produce *Matador²* might produce the fastest IACC boat in the world. And wasn't that just what every America's Cup syndicate from San Diego to Tokyo was seeking?

The living room of Bill Koch's house in Osterville, Massachusetts, looks like a maritime museum. A large room, it has been reduced by the size and heft of its furnishings. A thick, round sheet of glass lies upon a large ship's wheel to form a central coffee table. Huge binnacles and an engine room telegraph flank the fireplace and hearth. Beautifully restored, hand-carved figureheads are on display. Smaller nautical antiques (sextants, brass telescopes) and seafaring paintings complete the decor.

One wall is taken up by a canvas that measures nine by seven feet. It is a romantic, dramatic, close-in rendering of a naval battle that took place on June 1, 1813; *Shannon* (British), defeating *Chesapeake* (U.S.). In the painting, the two ships are side by side. The hand-to-hand combat between the crews is at full pitch. Men are portrayed fighting with cutlasses, daggers, and fists. One dazed sailor grips a harpoon as he searches for a victim. Another climbs aloft seeking advantage, or perhaps escape. The carnage depicted is considerable.

The central focus of the painting is an officer, sword in hand, who has apparently paused in his exertions, taken center stage, and drawn himself into a proud command posture for the artist's benefit. This is the captain of the *Shannon,* relishing, if prematurely, his victory over the U.S. vessel. James T. Lawrence, captain of the *Chesapeake,* an ancestor of William I. Koch, is not pictured. He is lying below, mortally wounded, about to issue his famous last words which would be adopted as the U.S. Navy's major credo: "Don't give up the ship."

Explaining how it came to be that at the age of 45 he suddenly took up grand prix yacht racing with such a passion, Bill Koch often refers to the similarity of the Kansas prairie to the sea and to Captain Lawrence. "It was in my blood," he says, regarding the painting with a trace of amusement born of fortuity.

When he bought his first big boat in 1984 he could as easily have purchased a professional sports franchise, or perhaps gotten into thoroughbred horses, or Formula One race cars. Besides the absence of those activities in his blood — although Koch was a fair basketball player at M.I.T. — each sport presented a practical problem for this man, then in his mid-40s: as owner, Bill Koch would have to be an observer. That role was not acceptable. From the outset, Bill Koch wanted to play. If he was to put a team together, he wanted to be part of that team. Although he'd spent 13 years in the family business, he'd never felt, nor seen exhibited by other employees, his perception of team spirit.

Fred Koch, Oilman

Koch Industries, according to *The Wall Street Journal,* is the second largest "closely held" corporation in America (its revenues rank it with Amoco and Shell Oil). The company began when Fred Koch, Bill's father and the son of a Dutch immigrant who started a small town newspaper in Quanah, Texas, invented a thermal cracking process that extracted more gasoline out of crude oil than existing methods. The major oil companies sought to dismiss the innovative Koch by immobilizing him with lawsuits.

So in the 1920s and '30s, Fred Koch went to Russia and built 15 refineries as part of Stalin's first five-year plan. He became a multi-millionaire before he was 25 and fought a battle against the U.S. oil companies in court for 20 years. His tenacity was ultimately rewarded by a string of legal victories and his fortune increased exponentially. Upon his return to the U.S. in the early 1930s, he continued to build the Wood River Oil and Refining Company (which later became Koch Industries) into one of the industry's major companies. His death in 1967 ended the fabulous career of one of America's most interesting and maverick oilmen.

Bill is one of four brothers. The boys were raised to be tough by their gruff, self-made father who was determined that his sons would not become society bums. From childhood on, all the boys labored summers on the family's west Kansas ranch, mending fences, digging ditches, and herding cattle. They were also treated to the kind of excursions most boys can only read about: hunting safaris in Africa and the Arctic.

Until high school, Bill attended public schools in Wichita, Kansas. He then applied to Culver Military Academy in Culver, Indiana. The school told him he wasn't a good enough student to be accepted into the winter school, but if he attended the summer school he would be reevaluated. It was not the first or last time Bill Koch was told he couldn't do something.

Bill enrolled in the Culver Summer Naval Academy, where he first saw a sailboat. In 1958 he graduated from the winter school in the top one percent of his class. Now he was told that although his good grades were a result of his hard work and determination, he wasn't smart enough to attend M.I.T., his first choice for college. But he was accepted anyway and he flew east to attend college. Years later, Bill speaks proudly of his three degrees from the highly respected Massachusetts institution, his graduation in the top 10 percent of his class, membership in two honorary societies, and receiving the coveted Hunneman Prize for outstanding originality in chemical engineering.

While preparing that thesis, he also began working for the family business by forming Koch Venture Capital at an office in Cambridge. After graduation, he assumed full-time duties as president of Koch Venture Capital and set about finding new businesses whose technology might be combined with a division of Koch, or even with the mainstream of the oil business. In practice, it was very much an entrepreneurial job and it gave Bill a sense of running an independent, free-wheeling business. It was an experience he could borrow heavily upon years after when he began to manage his sailing enterprises.

In late 1974, Bill joined a company that Koch Venture Capital had financed, the Koch International Trading Company. He worked his way up through a variety of responsibilities in Koch Industries until he became president of Koch Carbon, a division he started for the company. At the time, the division was the world's largest dealer in petroleum coke. Bill also held the position of vice president of corporate cevelopment for Koch Industries.

In 1980 Bill brought his concerns about how the company was being run to the attention of his brother. He felt the treatment of the minority shareholders was unfair, that the dividends were too low, and there was not enough liquidity, among other issues. Particularly bothersome to him was a criminal conviction concerning the Federal Oil Lottery that the company had received. A dispute between the brothers erupted and developed into a bitter lawsuit and protracted negotiations. Finally in 1983 it was settled when Bill, his brother Fred, and his father's cousins sold almost half interest in the company back to Koch Industries. Bill left the company a multimillionaire many times over.

Bill Koch then started his own company he called Oxbow: "a bend where a river changes course." He has built it into a diversified business with more than 400 employees and revenues close to $500 million. Oxbow operates four companies. Oxbow Power develops new electrical generating plants as well as owns and operates five power plants fueled by geothermal steam and natural gas capable of supplying a city of 370,000 year round. Oxbow Carbon and Minerals, which mines coal and sells over four million tons a year of petroleum coke, coal, ash, gypsum, and other materials, is now the world's largest trader in petroleum coke. Oxbow Realty owns and develops residential and commercial properties in Massachusetts and Colorado, and Fibercast Corporation is one of the world's largest manufacturers of high-tech composite pipe.

A semi formal atmosphere prevails at Oxbow. Koch usually wears his suit jacket in the office. Once, as he sank into a comfortable chair to talk, the jacket of his pinstripe suit fell open to reveal a flash of hot pink lining. He explained that the late Emilio Pucci was a friend of his, that all his business suits are lined with silk Pucci fabrics. "That's me," he said with a grin. "Conservative on the outside, wild on the inside."

Bill Koch moved to Cape Cod when he began pursuing his interest in the sea. In Osterville, he built the mini marina/yacht club Nauticus to hold the sizable fleet of small boats he began to accumulate. The handsome facility won architectural awards. In his home, he hung his stunning, museum-quality collection of marine art.

Bill Koch began sailing with a vengeance the same year he started

Oxbow. His first offshore experience was a Caribbean cruise in 1982 with his wife, Joan, and another couple, Franklin and Brenda McCann. The vessel was *Vanda*, a classic wooden schooner. "Bill brought all these books with him that would have put me to sleep," Franklin McCann says. "But he studied them. Scientific stuff like vector analysis, lift coefficients, laminar flow...it was like he was doing his doctorate all over again. He taught himself all this stuff. He used to ask the captain if he could not push the boat a little faster. But *Vanda* was old, the captain's pride and joy, his livelihood, built in 1905. Forget it. Bill got bored. We left the charter early. It wasn't satisfying his competitive juices."

Koch's entry-level boat was an 85-foot Little Harbor ketch ordered from the famed New England sailor, sailmaker, and boatbuilder Ted Hood. Since delivery wasn't scheduled until spring, 1984, Koch purchased an old Hood 40-footer in 1983 and entered the Southern Circuit. Hood skippered, Koch crewed. Halfway through a race from St. Petersburg to Fort Lauderdale, Koch observed the largest boats in the fleet, going in the opposite direction with their sails down.

Koch turned to Hood and asked: "What are those boats?"

"Maxis," replied Hood.

"Where are they going," wondered Bill.

"Home," said Ted. "They've finished the race."

Koch, who by then was cold, wet, cramped, and wondering if this was really the way sailboat racing was meant to be, said, "Next time, I'm going to race one of those." Hood smiled his acknowledgment.

"I've been trying to get you in one of those for the last two years," said the man whose familiar blue oval logo adorns sails from Boston to Bali on everything from dories to maga-yachts.

Later, Koch commented, "I noticed the maxis did it a lot faster. They looked like fun. I like big boats. I'm a big person. I need the space."

He took delivery of the 85-footer, which he named *Jayhawk*, after the mythical Kansas state bird, and went cruising with the McCanns and another couple, Al and Robyn Surprenant. "He sailed like a man possessed," Al Surprenant recalls today. "There wasn't a pinch of nauticalness among the three women. And Bill's idea of cruising was to sail for two weeks...without ever stopping or getting off the boat. It was a running joke. We'd pull into a cove and the women would plead for a five-minute walk on the beach."

The group was sailing off St. Barts one morning during Christmas week. It was howling, 40 knots with 20-foot seas. When Joan was emerging from the head, the boat smashed into a big wave. The jolt threw her to the floor and up against the john. She suffered bruises and immediately determined she had had enough. Once she was on her feet again, she walked up on deck, pointed at her husband, who was behind the wheel, and shouted, "Billy, stand this ____ing boat up straight right now!" The captain entered her request in his log as "the quote of the day" and Bill turned around and headed back to St. Barts.

Koch didn't care for cruising. "I ended up eating too much and drinking too much," he says. "I had a captain and crew...there was nothing else to do, no objective. I decided racing was the way to go, only on a big boat."

It was at that point Koch bought *Huaso* and began the testing and design programs that produced *Matador*^{2} and now had the six declared American defense syndicates scrambling for his assets.

From the outset of his sailing career, Koch had gone on record as having no America's Cup interest. Louis Cabot, a summer neighbor in Osterville, says Bill virtually ignored the subject when it would arise. Cabot is a crusty Bostonian, a man in his 70s with a shock of white hair over a weather-beaten countenance, and the quiet, challenging manner of a gunfighter. He is descended from the powerful family whose prominence is perhaps best defined in the famous New England saying: "The Lodges speak only to the Cabots, and the Cabots speak only to God." He was with the Cabot Corporation from 1948 until 1986 — most of those years as president or chairman — and has been a director of a dozen different companies along the way. He was chairman of the Brookings Institute and served on federal commissions on defense management and higher education.

No America's Cup Involement

Louis Cabot introduced Bill to his old sailing friends, one of whom, Jack Fallon, acted as his mentor in the early days of Koch's sailing career. Cabot sailed on *Matador* when he could and when conversations about the Cup would come up, the Bostonian would ask: "Why not get involved?" And Bill would say, "No, no, not the Cup. You can't be your own boss...too political." Cabot would shrug, let the subject die for awhile, but he was always convinced that Koch could be a major player.

In conversations about the Cup, Koch would tell Cabot: "I don't want to have anything to do with the America's Cup for three reasons. It costs too damn much money, there is too much publicity and I'm a private person, and it turns too many of the competitors into enemies. In the maxi class, all my competitors are my friends, and we stay that way, win or lose."

Koch's first brush with the Cup didn't go well. "In 1987 after Michael Fay's challenge," Koch says, "Gary Jobson urged me to offer to build San Diego a 90-foot waterline boat. We were deep into the *Matador*^{2} program, and I probably had more technical information on big boats than anyone.

I asked Jerry Milgram if we had the time to design and build a 90-footer, and he said we did. So I made the offer. Malin Burnham's response was a rebuff: 'Okay, but if you beat Conner, Conner will sail your boat.'"

Burnham was both president of the newly formed America's Cup Organizing Committee (ACOC), and Stars & Stripes syndicate chairman at the time. A well-known West Coast sailor in his own right, he'd been through several America's Cup campaigns and was privy to the controversies, chicaneries, and political infighting that seem to stalk the event. He had known Conner since, as a boy, Dennis used to patrol the docks of the San Diego Yacht Club, always looking to be crew on a racing sailboat. When Conner, representing the New York Yacht Club, lost the Cup in 1983, Burnham was horrified at the club's treatment of his friend. Not one member on the Defense Committee attended the final press conference with the helmsman nor gave Dennis any gesture of support. This abandonment may go a long way to explain Burnham's mistrust of the East Coast racing establishment of which he believed Koch to be a part.

When asked about the rumor that Koch had offered to build San Diego a boat, ACOC Executive Director Tom Ehman told the press, "Talk is cheap." Ehman, who had been at the center of a number of unsuccessful America's Cup campaigns, is well known for many unfortunate public statements. While no one paid much attention to Ehman's bluff and blunder, Koch was stung by the attitude presented by both Ehman and Burnham. His offer was made in good faith and he was treated with ridicule. The whole experience further soured him on the Cup, reinforcing all the negative feelings he had about it.

"After the IACC rule was formulated in 1988," Koch says, "Gary again proposed that I sponsor a campaign. I asked him how he saw it. He said he'd skipper, I'd be 17th crewman. I said no way."

The "17th man" was the position on board left for owners or corporate honchos or celebrities or contest winners whose seat was basically a payback for their monetary contributions or personal involvement. When on board, the 17th man was encouraged to "watch, but please don't touch." He was usually seated in the very stern and any real involvement was frowned upon.

That was the end of any Cup speculation until that fateful day in June, 1990, when *Matador^2* put *Boomerang* on the horizon behind her. Osterville neighbor Rick Wrightson, a close friend and trusted business associate of Koch's, had often discussed different scenarios for some type of Cup involvement with the Kansan. Wrightson is a native Californian who received a degree in management from Northeastern University and then attended the Boston College Graduate School of Arts and Sciences. A longtime entrepreneur, he had started and developed a business involved with computer peripherals, which he eventually sold to a large manufacturer. He was living in London with his family when Koch asked him to return to the U.S. to run a business Koch was thinking of buying.

Wrightson, who sails his Wianno Senior and J-30 out of the Wianno Yacht Club in Osterville, had sailed aboard both *Matador* and *Matador²* for eight years, including six maxi world championships. Wrightson's head for business and interest in sailing appealed to Koch. As a detail man, Wrightson had become one of the few close confidants of Koch.

Wrightson recalls that after the *Boomerang* race, he got a phone call from a friend who had been approached by Lee Smith, a veteran Cup player, and Buddy Melges from the now-defunct *Yankee* syndicate. They wanted to meet with Koch. "I said that Bill's attitude about the Cup could be put in one word: 'Never.' But I was sailing on *Matador²* that weekend and it couldn't hurt to ask. I was surprised when Bill said he'd meet with them." Koch divulged to Wrightson that he had given the Cup very serious consideration once again and he was thinking of making a run for it. He asked Rick to come on board and utilize his business start-up experience to help get the new endeavor underway.

"Initially, I had no interest in getting involved in any sailing program outside of the maxis," says Bill. "But when I continued to receive so much interest from other sailors and syndicates, I began to take a little bit of interest in the America's Cup myself. When Dennis came and offered to buy my technology, I really knew I had something."

As Koch's interest increased, he did what he does with every project he undertakes. He began to study it from every angle possible. "I read everything I could get my hands on about the America's Cup," says the perpetual student. "In particular, I read every word Dennis had published. Great generals say know your enemy. Dennis isn't an enemy, but I sure as hell knew I'd have to battle him to get to the Cup. I wanted to know how he thought, what his values were, how his mind works."

Koch knew before he'd made up his mind to enter the Cup that Dennis would be a formidable opponent. Dennis's oft-repeated slogan of "you have to make a commitment to the commitment" and his credo of "attitude, attitude, attitude" is not far from Koch's trilogy of "attitude, teamwork, and technology."

"In reading the history of the America's Cup," says Koch, "I boiled it down to two very simple principles. First, a slow boat has never won the America's Cup, only fast boats have won. Second, the team that has won is the one which made the least mistakes, not the one that was the most brilliant. Our management philosophy developed from these two historical principles. Boat speed is a science, not an art. Sailing is an art. We have to combine the two in the right mix. Use science to develop boat speed and use training and crewwork to develop a team that makes no mistakes." On the latter point, Koch liked to use the quote attributed to the Foreign Legion: "Train so hard that war is easy."

When word got out that Bill Koch was listening to what would-be Cuppers had to say, members of every fledgling defense syndicate came after him to beg, borrow, steal, or purchase his technology. Among the first to visit were Bill Shore and Buddy Melges. Shore, who is president of Shore Sails, had been Melges' navigator for the America's Cup matches in Fremantle, 1987, on *Heart of America*. Shore, Melges, and Ohio businessman/sailor Chuck Inglefield had begun assembling a syndicate for 1992 called Yankee.

Low on funds and with prospects dwindling, Shore felt the organization still had a lot to offer. There was Melges, of course. Buddy is a natural leader with the enthusiasm and drive of a competitor half his age, with twice the maturity, and three times the experience. One of the most charismatic personalities in the sport, his down-home euphemisms and back porch stories have served to teach and extract laughter from several generations of younger sailors. "Beloved" is an accurate description, although a word his own modesty would never condone. Buddy's list of yachting accomplishments — including two Star World Championships; an Olympic Gold medal (Soling); a Pan Am Games Gold Medal (Flying Dutchman); five E-Scow and seven Skeeter ice boat National Championships; three-time Rolex Yachtsman of the Year — is staggering.

Yankee also had some potentially interesting technology in place with NASA, and Shore had experience running an America's Cup sail development program. Despite Koch's previous reluctance to be associated with the Cup, the idea now began to intrigue him. The meetings he was having with syndicates like Yankee sent a clear message of the vast potential waiting to be tapped. He had a very good idea of what big-league sailing was all about from the time he'd spent on the maxi circuit, and the sport excited both his intellectual and competitive nature. While in his own mind the success of *Matador²* proved the validity of his reliance on the scientific method and his personal management principles, he fully realized the difference between the maxi circuit and the America's Cup. Only a handful of owners raced maxis; the Cup attracted the best talent and deepest resources from the world's most developed nations. It might be the same game, but this was a different league. This was the ultimate challenge in the sport and it presented the ultimate challenge to Bill Koch the scientist, the businessman, and the sailor. It was beginning to prove just too much to resist.

By the end of June, 1990, nine American defense syndicates had formed and representatives from each were scouring the land and corporate boardrooms seeking support in the form of talent, technology and cash. Few were getting very far. Everyone but president George Bush acknowledged the country was in the grips of a recession and most companies were announcing vast lay-offs, not sponsorships of a boat race.

The ACOC Defense Subcommittee had been, since March, increasingly concerned about the lack of progress the syndicates were making in raising funds. As the marketers continued to bump into each other outside the doors of the few corporate directors who granted them audiences, it became apparent the overall defense effort was becoming diluted at best and self-destructive at worst. ACOC thus decided to establish a June 28, 1990 deadline by which time each syndicate would be required to substantiate that they had $6 million in resources.

Sharks in the Pond

From the beginning, Dennis Conner was perceived by most Cup observers as the defender-apparent. Now the most experienced America's Cup sailor in the world, he had brought the Cup back from Australia and placed it on a shelf of honor at the San Diego Yacht Club; the same club where years before he had been inducted as the youngest member, the same club that bordered the waters on which he had sailed all his life. Members of ACOC realized Conner would most likely emerge as the defender, but they were determined to create a defense plan that would foster competition which would sharpen Dennis' skills. The approach they took has been described by Tom Ehman, executive vice-president, general manager and chief operating officer of ACOC, as a "sharks in the pond" plan. Simply defined, it meant that ACOC would license only what they considered the strongest syndicates and let them compete against each other for the necessary assets needed to mount a successful effort. As the sharks circled their prey, the blood of Cup campaigns (top sailors, technology, money), it was thought the battles would only strengthen the eventual survivor as that syndicate gobbled up the most useful remains of the competitors' soon-to-be carcasses.

Out of the nine syndicates vying for licenses from ACOC, only four received them: Team Dennis Conner, Beach Boys America, Isler Sailing International, and Triumph America Foundation. While these four seemed to demonstrate the most strength, Ehman later conceded ACOC granted the licenses with the understanding all the defenders were shaky but it was hoped they all would become viable in time.

After the licenses were granted, increased energy was focused on recruiting Koch by each of the remaining syndicates, several of the syndicates that didn't make the cut, and by ACOC itself. Ehman was increasingly worried the "sharks in the pond" strategy might not work out as planned because the sharks were little more than guppies at this point. He decided to launch a full court press on the still-reluctant man who had just days before demonstrated to the world he had the stuff that makes yacht racing champions. But whereas the other syndicates were looking East to form either a coalition or an outright absorption of their embryonic organizations, Ehman had a different agenda. He was hoping to entice Koch into the game because he felt Bill could best be used to tune-up Conner and in the end, the maxi man would turn over his considerable sailing assets to the San Diego helmsman. That, according to Ehman and the rest of ACOC, was perceived as a winning combination.

From early 1989 and throughout 1990, Ehman dealt with Gary Jobson, who he knew was relentlessly attempting to convince Koch to mount a Cup campaign. The two served each other's purposes well. Jobson had the ear and the confidence of Koch, and Ehman could provide the ticket to sail. And although the man from ACOC may have originally been motivated by the idea that Koch and company would provide the perfect trial horse for Dennis, he was charged with building the strongest possible defense effort and Koch's involvement would certainly provide just that.

Another press on Koch was launched by Larry Klein and Brodie Cobb, who had formed Triumph America in April of 1990. Klein is a San Diego sailor who had been named Yachtsman of the Year two months previously and was slated to head up the sailing side of the syndicate. Cobb is from Dallas and saw himself as the director of the business operations and marketing program. Neither had any prior Cup experience and Cobb's fundraising experience was limited to what he represented to be a $200,000 Olympic campaign. Both visited Koch a number of times, sailed on *Matador²*, and consistently tried to secure his backing for their fledgling syndicate.

When Dennis Conner came calling, Koch paid particular attention. Seemingly an unlikely pair, this former draper from California and the multimillionaire from Kansas, both had great respect for each other. Conner was the one man in the world most identified with the America's Cup. A veteran of five finals, the only man to lose it and win it back, he had almost singlehandedly brought sailing in general and the America's Cup in particular to the attention of the public throughout the world. After his comeback victory in Fremantle, he and his team were invited to the White House, paraded down New York's Fifth Avenue, and feted and lionized throughout the country. Dennis is the only sailor whose image has appeared on the cover of *Time* magazine.

Sitting across from Koch, the vaunted helmsman had a plan, actually several, and he had a strategy. It was a strategy that had served him so well in America's corporate boardrooms when he mounted his assault on *Australia:* appeal to their patriotism. America needs your support to prove to the world we're still first in technology, that we can get the job done. It worked then and Dennis believed it could work now because, after all, Bill Koch understood the concept better than most. He was indeed a patriot, and his life had been centered around business and science. But what Bill Koch was, Dennis reasoned, that his boardroom brothers weren't, was a sailor. Dennis greatly admired Bill's maxi program and his courage to stand behind the wheel. Bill believed Dennis to be the best sailor in the world.

Dennis proposed a number of scenarios involving Bill, everything from advisor to co-helmsman. He also offered to buy Koch's technology. But while Bill was deciding, he heard back from several members of his technical team that Conner was trying to hire them. Recalling Capt. Lawrence's famous plea, that may have been the final incentive Koch needed.

While Conner's actions were perceived by Koch as neither illegal nor unethical, simply an example of the helmsman's well-known penchant for leaving no stone unturned in his never-ending quest to seek every advantage possible, the situation made the Kansan realize the time had come for a decision. He had what America's Cup syndicates most covet and he had to decide whether to use it himself, sell it, give it away, or ignore the whole thing. Actually, his only real choices were to use his resources or let another defense syndicate do so. Koch's loyalty to his country and his belief in the superiority of American technology precluded him from working with a challenger or sitting on the sidelines.

Koch told Jobson, Wrightson, Moeyersoms, Cabot, and one or two other trusted advisors he had decided to keep an open mind about the Cup and asked each to make suggestions about the best way to proceed. During one meeting at Cabot's house in Osterville, Koch began to outline what kind of an organization he had in mind, should he decide to enter the game. He turned to Cabot and asked the man who had advised presidents, generals, and corporate giants what he thought.

Somewhat stunned by the enormity of the contemplated endeavor, Cabot said "Let me make sure I have this straight. You're thinking of entering the America's Cup, where you have had no experience. You're thinking of starting from scratch, finding designers and builders to put together this new boat that no one has ever sailed, and hiring maybe a couple of hundred people to run dozens of different departments in what will amount to a small corporation. You're thinking of moving the whole show to San Diego and building what will amount to a small waterfront village. You're thinking of being on the boat yourself, steering some of the time. You're thinking of going up against Dennis Conner, who by now, does all of these things in his sleep. You're thinking of raising a king's ransom to pay for this. And you're thinking of doing all this in just seventeen months. Is that what you're thinking?"

A grin spread across Koch's face as he heard, for perhaps the first time, just how outlandish this idea might sound to outsiders. "Yes, Louie, I guess that's just what I'm thinking."

"Then know this, Bill. If I were the chairman of a Fortune 500 company and you came to me with hat in hand and outside in the lobby was Dennis Conner with an even larger hat, I'd be looking to fill his hat with my sponsorship dollars."

"But you might be wrong," said the Kansan.

"So I might, but you better get used to hearing that."

Cabot fixed his eyes on his neighbor and said "Bill, I think I know you pretty well and if that's true, then I believe almost everything about an America's Cup campaign that you would run would be different from what all the others will do. Parts of that I like. Very much. Parts of that I don't like. Just be prepared to hear a thousand times that your different way is the wrong way. You'll hear it on the docks, in the boardrooms, from the press, from your competitors, maybe even from people on your own team. But if you do it, do it your way. Do it differently. And stick to your guns."

"Louie was, and is, a great advisor," says Koch. "He foresaw things, told me how to handle certain situations that might occur. And they almost always did occur. When I called him up to ask if he would participate in starting an America's Cup campaign, he first said he'd think about it and get back to me. I told him I had a lot of people approaching me with a lot of different scenarios. Louie said, 'if you are going to do it, you ought to distinguish yourself from all the others. There are a lot of people who think the Cup is becoming too commercial, so if you are going to do it, why don't you do it in a Corinthian way with no advertising.'

"The suggestion struck me as a great idea. I told him how much stock I put in the ideals of teamwork and attitude and that Corinthianism fit in perfectly with the overall concept."

Koch's first concern was whether he'd truly receive equal treatment from ACOC. He knew as well as anyone that Dennis was San Diego's favorite son and he was well aware of the trial horse strategy. Even while he was meeting and being courted by syndicates alive and dead, Koch needed absolute assurance that if he did make a run for the Cup, that run would be made on "a level playing field." Jobson, who had discussed the potential ground rules with Ehman on several occasions, assured Koch that ACOC would go out of their way to accommodate him. At a July meeting in Chicago attended by Koch, Ehman, several members of the ACOC Defense Subcommittee, and Buddy Melges, Bill was told that no conflicts of interest between ACOC's members existed in their friendship with Dennis Conner. It was also clearly communicated to Koch that they would gladly issue him a license whenever he requested it.

One evening while still in the throes of deciding, Bill was at dinner with the author Patrick Robinson, another Osterville summer resident, and close friend of Koch's for a number of years. Robinson, an Englishman who has parlayed a Fleet Street journalism career into six international best-selling nonfiction books, has been close to the America's Cup scene for more than a decade. His *Born to Win*, which he wrote for John Bertrand about the Australian's historic 1983 Cup victory, is generally considered the best description of actual Cup racing ever written. Koch solicited Robinson's views on a variety of Cup issues.

After the two discussed pros and cons and Koch heard Robinson's unequivocal support, Bill raised his glass of wine and as he touched Patrick's glass, said, "Well, then, I guess I'll do it. I think I have to 'cause it's sort of in my family. I can't just give up the ship, can I?"

Bill Koch had made up his mind, and with those few words he changed the course of the 1992 America's Cup, and quite possibly every Cup competition to follow.

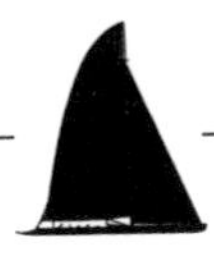

Not Just a Boat Race

3

When he later explained his decision to enter the Cup fray, Bill Koch was characteristically analytical. "I thought about it rationally," he said. "It was evident that I had something valuable. *Matador²* was very fast. I had an organization in place. I had the technology in place — or I thought I did. I had the funds, and my business is organized in such a way that I could take the time. There are so many factors. It's rare in a lifetime to have them all in line. If the Cup was still being sailed in 12-Meters, my technology would have been irrelevant. But with a new boat it made sense. Here was the chance to go for the gold. Why not? It was an opportunity to show that my management style, my Corinthian ethic, my ideas about teamwork, could compete on a world-class scale."

Given his experience in building boats and sailing teams, Koch believed he had a handle on scheduling and costs. His estimate on time was too optimistic and his prediction that he'd have to spend perhaps $25 million of his own money was woefully short. But what Bill Koch may have lacked in prescience, he made up for in tenacity. Fred Koch's 20-year battle for justice hadn't gone unnoticed by his son. As determined as his father had been in his ambitions, once Bill set his sights on the Cup, there was nothing to deter him.

As the word spread that Bill Koch might make a run for the Cup, those who know him best expressed surprise. It seemed out of character for a member of one of America's wealthiest families, who had heretofore always gone to great lengths to protect his privacy, to suddenly enter a situation that demanded he subject himself to public scrutiny.

"I didn't like the publicity aspect," Koch says, "but I thought Gary could manage that. I would involve good friends, avoid the back-stabbing." However naive that statement might have been, it does indicate a cornerstone of Bill Koch's America's Cup philosophy. Just as in the *Matador* program, Bill believed that the formula to Cup success was found in testing and teamwork. At that point, what the press thought or wrote was of little concern. Besides, Jobson had a knack for handling the press; indeed, as ESPN's sailing correspondent, he was one of them.

August of 1990 was a busy month for all concerned with this Cup syndicate that was forming around Bill Koch. Jobson went to the Cape on August 6 for a meeting with Koch, Louis Cabot, and Vincent Moeyersoms. The syndicate unofficially began that day. Koch gave the go-ahead for the design process to start, and the organization began to take shape.

Although the core group of his *Matador* team was in place, Koch knew a vast expansion was necessary. He would build his America's Cup organization using the same procedure he'd used successfully in building organizations at Koch Industries and the Oxbow Corporation.

"I learned long ago I can't do everything; no one can. I also know there are plenty of people who are smarter than I am or have more expertise in particular fields. My management approach is simple. I give people who work for me all the responsibility and authority they need to do the job. Then they have to define that job. If I have to tell them what to do and how to do it, I have the wrong person. They need to tell me what they're going to do. My job is to make sure the priorities are straight and the focus is sharp. Then it's just a matter of going out and doing it."

As the small group discussed their individual responsibilities, the first clouds began to form; clouds that later would erupt into an unpleasant storm that threatened to drown the syndicate.

"I had been holding out for skipper," says Jobson, who had twice served as a Cup tactician and felt ready to move up. "But Bill said he and I should be co-skippers. We debated that issue, but that was the deal. I swallowed hard, but went along."

"I told Gary he could be co-skipper," Koch says. "But I was skipper."

It was evident from the beginning that who would steer the boat was going to be a pivotal issue with Jobson, although Koch made it clear from day one he wasn't about to be merely a land-based owner or the 17th man. All who had sailed with him since he began with *Matador* in 1984 agreed that Bill Koch had come a long way in a short time. He'd been an adept student. On *Matador* Koch had the helm the lion's share of the time, and had done very well. But the America's Cup is match racing against the best hired guns in the world, and the challengers would pull out all the tricks.

San Francisco ace Paul Cayard had become an Italian resident and was skipper for the Italians. Kiwi Chris Dickson, who came close to winning the Challenge trials in 1987, had been hired by the Japanese. The New Zealanders had San Diego-raised Rod Davis, and David Barnes. Marc

Pajot, for years one of the highest paid athletes in Europe, was sailing for the French. And down the road was Dennis Conner, still one of the toughest competitors on any race course. If sailing had a hall of fame, these guys would be among its most recent nominees. All of these proven match racers have been sailing since childhood. They are tough, resolute, crafty, and at the top of their game.

But Jobson was philosophical. It appeared he would be starting the boat, then calling tactics — not a bad situation. And Jobson had grown to respect Koch. He once spoke of a disqualification *Matador²* had suffered for tacking too close to a competitor. "Bill was cool when it happened," Gary said, "no problem. Three days later he said to me, 'The mistake was lack of confidence in the boat. We should have dipped him and passed him on our next crossing. We shouldn't have taken an unnecessary chance to win.' He's thoughtful, analytical, and he never forgets anything."

An important factor in Jobson's decision to play was the central authority Koch would bring to an America's Cup syndicate. Syndicate power has always been vested in a board of directors. Win or lose, all syndicate operations have been adversely affected by the internal struggles and compromise decisions that have characterized syndicate boards. As a hot skipper with a tough, street-smart businessman's persona, Dennis Conner developed the clout to take charge of his own syndicate from 1980 on. But Conner didn't have it all in hand. His biggest loose end was money.

"This time the guy with the money will be in charge," said Jobson, who had suffered through two Cup campaigns under syndicate boards. "And he'll be sailing on the boat, and he's a technocrat. He's one authority who will settle all arguments. Now that's an advantage." Jobson's rationale would come back to haunt him.

As for Koch's intention to drive the America's Cup boat, "The value of the helmsman is overrated," Jobson said in August. "There are so many great ones. The difference between them is really the boat, and the support they get — sails, crew, logistics, tactician. Today's perfect helmsman isn't a Ted Turner, or a Tom Blackaller, or even a Dennis Conner. It's someone who keeps his mouth shut and does what he's told. Bill will eventually recognize that the real fun isn't steering, but pulling it all together." What Koch did come to see was that the real fun was both steering and pulling it all together.

The part about the boat making a difference was at the core of Koch's rationale for skippering. He had seen what a difference the boat had made in the maxi class. He was confident the same difference could be realized in the IACC class. Dennis Conner's oft-quoted remark that his grandmother could win sailing *Matador²* was music to Koch's ears.

Such discussions were academic, because Bill Koch made it clear from the beginning that he believed management control was as important to success as any other factor, perhaps the most important. And since there was never any debate about who would head the syndicate, there needn't be any argument about his decisions. Those who knew Koch best weren't worried about the steering issue. They agreed that when the time came, he would do the right thing.

In late August (1990) there was a large meeting at Koch's house on the Cape. Among the issues discussed was what to name the syndicate. A public relations firm had been asked to supply a list of names, none of which struck the right bell. Other names were discussed, some votes were taken, and the name "Alliance America" seemed to capture the most interest. And then Bill Koch suggested "America^3," but there wasn't much support voiced for it. For the following weeks leading up to the official announcement, the working title of the syndicate was "Alliance America." But Koch was unhappy with the name from the beginning and continued to push "America^3."

There was logic in Koch's suggestion of "America^3," a scientific image he liked. If *Matador^2* had been a quantum leap over *Matador,* the hope was that his eventual IACC boat would be another leap in design evolution. Hence, the cubed idea: to the third power. And there was Koch's three-part motivational philosophy: attitude, teamwork, and talent. He also pointed out the symbolic reference to three great sailing areas of the United States, all represented by sailors in the room: the West Coast, the East Coast, and the Great Lakes. Another alliterative trio — talent, teamwork, technology — was in the offing.

The name "America^3," what it meant, and Koch's support of it, fit into his overall management style. Having learned to live by the scientific method — trial, error, more refined trial, more useful error — and trust its value, Koch's way is organized chaos. Stir the pot, see what boils to the top. Take the best ideas and improve them. The only problem would be time. There had been no particular deadline for the *Matador* program, but the first set of Cup trials was on January 14, 1992, just 17 months after Koch made his commitment, and more than two years after some of the challengers entered!

Koch also asked key members of his embryonic syndicate to write a game plan for how they should proceed. What he received was not exactly what he had in mind, so in September he composed the "America^3 Manifesto" himself. The document was distributed with a request for comments. Some drifted back and it was Jobson's critique that Koch found most encouraging. "If you do even half of what is in this manifesto," commented one of

America's most experienced sailors, "you will win the Cup." But for the most part reactions were swept along with the current of events. With the millions of details that needed to be attended to, the manifesto was soon forgotten, but the plan and philosophy never were. Towards the end of the campaign, Rick Wrightson retrieved a copy from a file and read it again for the first time in more than a year-and-a-half. He was astounded by how closely what had actually occurred paralleled what Koch had written should be done. Today, the manifesto stands as a testament to Koch's vision.

Typewritten over some ten pages, the document's first words were: "GOAL: To win the 1992 America's Cup." These were followed by a simple statement that serves as the ultimate definition of the America³ syndicate. "OBJECTIVE: To win the Cup in good taste and without commercialism; using high standards of sportsmanship, honor, and integrity, and by combining teamwork with advanced high technology and entrepreneurial management. The effort will not be built around any one individual but around the team as a whole."

The manifesto went on to cover areas such as management, technology and operations, the sailing program, fundraising and marketing, and finance and accounting. Subjects as disparate as security, the non-profit status of the syndicate, wind-tunnel testing of keels, computer simulation, number of boats to be built, meteorological data, electronic measurement systems, the crew rating system, and physical fitness were all covered. But perhaps most telling of Koch's perspective on his new challenge is how he saw the priorities: "The America's Cup…is not just a boat race. It is first a fundraising race. Second, it is a race of technology. Third, it is a race of managerial skills. Fourth, it is a race of teamwork. And finally, it is a sailboat race."

After the manifesto was written and circulated, the action moved to Newport in September, for the beginning of the World Maxi Championship that Koch wanted very badly to win for several reasons. First, although he was convinced *Matador²* was the fastest sailboat in the world, he knew his one race against *Boomerang* was not enough proof for the yachting world. Second, now that the word in Cup circles was out that he was in, the World Maxi Championship would go a long way in establishing his credentials for fundraising, attracting talent, and convincing any skeptics he belonged in the defender ranks. And the line-up in Newport listed names that were also found on America's Cup syndicates around the world.

Passage Di Venezia was owned by the late Italian Raul Gardini and helmed by Paul Cayard, two major figures for the challengers. French America's Cup helmsman Marc Pajot would be at the wheel of *Emeraude.*

Longobarda, current maxi champion, would be sailed by two prominent members of Team Dennis Conner, longtime Cup tactician Tom Whidden and Californian John Bertrand. John Kolius, helmsman for the New York Yacht Club's campaign in Fremantle, would steer *Vanitas.* Heady company for Koch and *Matador²*; beating these guys would speak volumes about his boat and his ability behind the wheel.

There was also a personal reason why Koch wanted the Championship. Aboard the first *Matador* he had raced Raul Gardini's *Il Moro Di Venezia* 38 times, winning just 11 races. The two men, both fabulously rich and powerful, had never become close friends. A fierce rivalry had developed both on and off the water. Gardini, who lived the life of the European nobility, had more than once made caustic comments about the Kansan. Koch had held his tongue, but victory in the Championship over the Italian would certainly give him great personal pleasure.

In the seven races in Newport, *Matador²* showed the entire fleet its stern in five races to win the series. Gardini and Cayard, winners of two races, came in second. Two more series remained to determine the annual champion: Miami and St. Thomas. Koch's maxi won in Florida and came in second in the Virgin Islands. And so in the first four regattas *Matador²* raced, her record was three firsts and one second, enough to be crowned the 1990 Maxi World Champion.

Believing he had accomplished his goal with *Matador²*, Bill Koch now turned his full attention to the America's Cup. Even while concentrating on the Championship and having already set his own Cup wheels in motion, Koch was still engaged in negotiations with ACOC. The talks centered on the key issue: could ACOC assure Koch of the "level playing field" on which he insisted. Koch is a tough negotiator, and his experience in this area, gained from so many years in the rough and tumble energy business, served him well with ACOC. He had reason to suspect that august group of pressing for home court advantage. But in the weeks following the July meeting in Chicago, the financial prospects for the four licensed syndicates had not improved at all.

Koch knew the ACOC Defense Subcommittee wanted him in in the worst way and he pressed his advantage. He was after a contract that eliminated surprises down the road. He wanted a fair set of trials with the winner designated by points accumulated, not by selection committee, as the New York Yacht Club has done for more than a century. And he didn't want ACOC empowered by some subtle, small-print clause to take over his boat, his team, his technology — or to select the defending helmsman. Koch's perception of these potential road blocks was unusual for a freshman player. But his game plan was well-researched. His goal was to eliminate problems with a dogged persistence as he encountered them. In the end, an 11-page Defense Plan was drafted. This legal document was a revision of the original Defense Plan that had been adopted on December 18, 1989. It covered America's Cup and IACC World's management; budgets; equal rights clauses for all potential defenders; establishment of a Conflicts Committee; marketing; promotion; licensing; fundraising; availability of the Cup itself; promotional obligations of ACOC and syndicates; trials scoring and selection process (by accumulated points only); measuring and certification of yachts; and syndicate financial obligations to the Partnership for America's Cup Technology. The amended document is dated October 1, 1990.

On October 2, Vincent Moeyersoms, Rick Wrightson, and assistant Ellen Bloom had opened a syndicate office in Weston, Massachusetts, and had begun work. Three days later, Koch held a press conference in New York to officially announce that he was seeking to defend the America's Cup. "The day of the press conference, a number of us met beforehand," Louis Cabot says. "We were still discussing names. Bill arrived late and announced he didn't like the name 'Alliance America.' He said he couldn't stand it and he still liked 'America^3.' We talked for ten minutes, took a vote. Only three people liked it, but Bill said he was going into the press conference and announce we were called 'America^3'." Later, Gary Jobson would say: "The vote was 7 to 3 against using 'America^3.' Bill Koch cast the deciding vote."

Koch also told the small group he wanted to announce that the distinguished New Englander, Louis Cabot would serve as chairman of the new syndicate. Koch asked if there were any objections and when none arose, he marshaled his troops together and marched into the packed conference. Until then, Cabot had been somewhat reluctant to take on the task.

If there was some confusion and discord among syndicate members over the name and management structure, there was none from the group of reporters who had gathered inside a large meeting room in the Waldorf-Astoria. Intentionally or not, Koch's cubed idea gave them a number of angles for fresh stories about the oldest competition in sport.

Jobson served as moderator and spokesman, and between him, Vincent Moeyersoms, Bill Koch, and Louis Cabot, the main themes of the campaign were articulated. In the following day or two, the country's most respected yachting journalists filed their reports on what they had heard and those themes were now set in print across the nation.

"America^3," wrote Carolyn White of *USA Today*, "intends to be first in 'teamwork, talent and technology,' industrialist Bill Koch said Wednesday in New York." Barbara Lloyd of *The New York Times* pointed out the difference between America^3 and all the other announced Cup syndicates, defenders and challengers, "Koch plans a noncommercial effort. His boat and sails will be devoid of advertising slogans and emblems." *The Washington Post*'s Angus Phillips added, "Jobson and Koch envision an old-style, Corinthian campaign in sharp contrast to the highly commercial efforts planned by other Cup aspirants. 'I like doing things contrarily,' Bill Koch said. 'We can do a program without turning it into the Indianapolis 500.'" Bill Center wrote in *The San Diego Union*, "The foundation of the America^3 Team is design. Koch, Heiner Meldner and Jerry Milgram — all holders of doctoral degrees — worked together on a $3 million project that compiled technical data for the construction of *Matador*^{2}." And Dave Philips took up the same subject in *The Providence Journal*, "Technology, technology, and technology are what Bill Koch and his associates in this country's newest America's Cup syndicate are counting on to help them win the 28th America's Cup match."

The public launching of America^3 couldn't have gone better. It was a major story in the major papers and the goal of getting the word out was accomplished. Yet there was one unsettling moment that occurred during the question and answer period. Jobson had introduced just minutes before the key members of the syndicate and all the individuals who sat in the front of the room. One of the journalists, obviously a veteran of America's Cup controversies and politics of the past, rose and said, "Gary, you've just introduced four world-class helmsmen in you, Buddy Melges, Larry Klein, and Bill Koch. You can only race one boat in the Cup itself. Who's going to steer it?" A murmur spread through the room as Jobson deflected the question. There was no follow-up, but it was a question that would trail the campaign even until the final race.

A partial answer to the question began to develop shortly after the news conference. Both Jobson and Klein headed for Baltimore to participate in the Columbus Cup, a major match racing event founded the year before by local civic leaders and businessmen, including Jobson. Gary had used his influence to arrange for Klein to skipper one of the boats. The idea was for him to gain match racing experience which would benefit the Cup campaign.

The boats used in the regatta were J-44s and eight teams were competing. The format, as in most match racing events, called for each skipper to draw a new boat for each day's racing. The skippers were allowed to bring three crew members who would serve as the permanent crew, to be augmented by four individuals selected from a pool of local sailors. And because the boats were being donated for the event by local owners, each owner and one owner's representative would sail aboard the owner's boat.

Columbus Cup Controversy

Problems with Larry Klein began as soon as he appeared for the regatta. When he drew the names of his four local crew members, one of them was Linda Stearns. Despite the fact that Stearns is one of the most accomplished offshore sailors in the country, a sailmaker by profession, an experienced fleet and match racer, and a sailor who had more experience on J-44s than Klein, the Californian was outraged that he would be forced to sail with a woman.

He called Jobson and complained, beseeching him to "fix it for me." Jobson told him the idea here was to get match racing experience and that was what counted, not necessarily winning. But Klein was determined to win the Columbus Cup in order to better his chances of grabbing the wheel for the Cup campaign.

Klein refused to even speak to Stearns, continuously complained to the Columbus Cup Committee, and generally made life miserable for everyone aboard his boat and on land. Eventually, Stearns decided it wasn't worth the fight and resigned her position, despite the Committee's support of her. Ironically, the boat assigned to Klein the day Stearns stepped aside came with a woman as the owner's representative. Klein made a beeline to the Committee chairman to complain again, but the chairman was fed up and told him so.

Klein's behavior continued to come into question when he exhibited extremely poor sportsmanship by verbally abusing jury members when a call went against him and he was disqualified from a race. At press conferences, Klein generally appeared sullen and disgusted, refused to apologize for his behavior, and implied women sailors weren't strong enough to compete on bigger boats.

The press had a field day with the entire affair as headlines screamed: "Klein Makes Waves With Anti-Women Arrogance," "Yachtsman of Year Flunks On Attitude," and "Sexism Controversy Leaves Klein Vulnerable." Jobson, caught in the middle between his positions as adviser to the Columbus Cup and member of America^3 and his previous friendship with Klein, was quoted in the papers as saying "I thought it [Klein's behavior] was a disgrace. He won't be invited back. You don't get everyone mad at you — the jury, the race committee, the Columbus Cup and your crew — and then walk away leaving a favorable impression."

The impression made by Larry Klein on the managers of the America^3 syndicate was disastrous. Only days before the sailor had been introduced as a potential helmsman of the new America's Cup effort. He had been present in many meetings when Koch pronounced the importance of attitude.

Now, in his first public appearance as a representative of the syndicate, Klein had, in Jobson's word, "disgraced" the new campaign.

Jobson, well aware of Koch's insistence on attitude and that the syndicate portray a unified, "clean" image, met with Klein and requested that he make a formal apology to Linda Stearns and the Columbus Cup organizers. Klein said he would, but later told Gary he had thought it over and he didn't believe he had anything to apologize for to anyone.

After reading reports in the press and receiving a summary from Jobson, Koch agreed with Gary that an apology was needed. He said that if Klein came clean the syndicate would stand behind him. When Klein refused to do so, it was apparent that the incident would have a negative impact on the syndicate and adversely affect fundraising. All this before the new campaign had really gotten underway.

Klein's reaction to the request by Jobson and Koch was that Jobson was blowing the whole thing out of proportion for his own self-serving reasons. This despite Gary's using his influence to get Klein into the regatta and counseling him during the furor. And, of course, Gary hadn't written the damning newspaper reports.

Klein went to Louis Cabot and repeated his accusations about Jobson. He insisted he had been framed by the Annapolis sailor. Cabot decided to conduct his own investigation, which included speaking with many individuals who were involved in the incidents in question. His conclusion was that Klein's activities were actually worse than what had been reported to America^3. He found not a scintilla of evidence to support Klein's defamation of Jobson. By November, the decision to terminate Klein was made.

Klein's reaction to the sacking was predictable. He told Koch he was outraged and extremely angry. Koch explained that Klein had been fired because he had embarrassed the syndicate and that he was a liability in terms of fundraising, public image, and sense of teamwork. Klein then claimed that because he was a "professional athlete," he should receive a severance package commensurate with that status, which meant he should be paid for the rest "of the season," meaning throughout the entire campaign. Koch said that was ridiculous, that Klein had only been officially on board for a month, and that there was never any guarantee that he would have made the team anyway. He offered to pay him for three months. The termination and severance issues were taken to the board of America^3 where they were unanimously supported.

In a separate but concurrent affair, Brodie Cobb was also let go from the America^3 syndicate. The decision was based primarily on his ineffectiveness as a fund raiser and the difficulties he was having working with other members of the rapidly expanding syndicate staff. There were also a number of incidents that had occurred in which Cobb's integrity was suspect.

Both Klein and Cobb were incensed by their dismissals and soon filed a $50 million lawsuit alleging fraud, wrongful termination, loss of prospective business advantages, and theft of trade secrets, among other things. On the day of the America's Cup Ball, Koch received a letter which read, in part:

"I am Brian Dennis Sean Monaghan. I and my firm have been retained to bring you to justice or, in the alternative, to strip you of a few million bucks to partially compensate my clients, Larry Klein, Brodie Cobb, and Triumph America.... Can I deliver? Ask around.

"There is a less expensive and less painful way — settlement. If you have any interest in genuinely pursuing that alternative, please have your counsel contact me. If a settlement is finalized by May 2, 1991, I will refrain from alerting the media that the Complaint has been filed."

The letter was so unprofessional and so transparent that this was an amateur attempt to shake down Koch for "a few million bucks" with the veiled threat of running to the press with the non-story. The Koch camp had a hard time believing the letter was legitimate.

Koch, no stranger to litigation or would-be intimidating tactics by lawyers, asked San Diego attorney Roy Morrow Bell to look into the situation. Koch's instructions were to make it clear that neither he nor the America³ Foundation were subject to blackmail or extortion. Bell, who knew Monaghan, was saddened by the ambulance-chasing approach of a colleague, but was determined to raise the proceedings to a higher plane. His partial response, written with tongue implanted in cheek, was as follows:

"Dear Brian Dennis Sean (a/k/a/ Patrick) Monaghan:

"We represent William Koch and have been provided with a copy of what purports to be a letter from you, threatening to strip our client of some 'bucks.' From my life's experience and professional relationship with you, I am convinced to a moral certainty that someone off-balance has stolen your letterhead and is sending letters out, supposedly from you. I just thought I would let you know that, so that you could do something about it...."

What followed was some two years of the discovery process in which Monaghan for the plaintiffs and Bell for the defendants deposed witness after witness, the list of which reads like a *Who's Who* in sailing.

Finally a trial date was set for early May, 1994, but when a series of pretrial motions set before the court by Monaghan failed, he and his clients realized that what they thought was their case was rapidly dissolving. As Monaghan's visions of pocketing Koch's millions began to blur, he and his clients offered to settle out of court for what attorneys call "nuisance value" the week the trial was to begin. Koch, who believed from the beginning there was no merit to what he saw as a frivolous lawsuit, wanted his day in court, but chose, in the end, not to inconvenience his friends who were prepared to travel from around the world to testify. While the terms of the settlement are confidential, what the America^3 Foundation will say is that the affair was resolved at far less than what the trial would have cost, at far less than Koch's original severance offer, and at no cost to Bill himself. Thus ended one of the uglier incidents of the 1992 America's Cup.

And so, within days of announcing his syndicate, Bill Koch was already embroiled in the politics and nastiness he so wanted to avoid. The early favorable press notices had been replaced by stories of intemperate behavior by one of his team members. Ugly firings and lawsuits took his time and concentration away from the tasks at hand. Welcome to the America's Cup, Mr. Koch. How do you like it so far?

The syndicate now had little more than a year to organize a team, build a boat, choose a crew, and tend to the millions of details included in each of those actions. Enter David Lowry, a fast-gun industrial real estate developer from Temecula, California, via London, Cape Cod, Maine, and Minnesota. Lowry is a wiry man in his 40s with a perpetual head of steam up. He always looks a bit distracted, as if he's forgotten — or just remembered — something important. He's got the rapid, deadpan delivery of a stand-up comedian.

In the early days of America's Cup XXVIII, Lowry had approached his friend Elliott Lott, the president of the Beach Boys singing group, with the idea of involving the famous band in the famous sailing race. Initially the idea took hold, and while sailing wags were producing lines about "the sloop *John B*," Lowry was forging ahead as he attempted to assemble an America's Cup team.

The San Diego Yacht Club accepted the Beach Boys as a legitimate syndicate on July 31, and two days later Lowry was on his way to Europe to offer the French a deal for their IACC boat. He convinced the French that selling the boat would give them the opportunity to build a new one. The French agreed.

America^3 approached the French about their boat the same week. The French wanted to deal with America^3, but they felt they had an obligation to Lowry. Lowry ended up with the boat, but within a month money pressures rose to the danger level. He met with Koch and offered to sell America^3 half interest in the French boat. But Koch had a different idea. What if America^3 took over the assets Beach Boys had developed?

"I figured I couldn't beat Koch," says Lowry, "so I better join him. He struck me as a trustworthy, honorable man. And by the first of the year, the

Gulf War was building. The economy was in the toilet. Corporate America was sitting on its hands. I had to sell the boat."

Designer Doug Peterson saw Koch's buyout as a generous gesture. "He didn't have to do it," Peterson said. "He could have said no thanks, waited until we defaulted on payment of the French boat, and simply bought it. I found him sympathetic towards our effort, a man with good intentions." In addition to the French boat, Koch also got Peterson, two other top designers in John Reichel and Jim Pugh, and a bag of test data. But he could have negotiated separately for all that as well.

In less than four months, Bill Koch had completely shaken up the 1992 America's Cup defense scene. Gary Jobson had moved from ESPN broadcaster to co-skipper and vice president of America^3. Peter Isler had terminated his defense effort and had joined ESPN as a broadcaster. Triumph America, Yankee, and Beach Boys syndicates had all been acquired at least in part by America^3. John Bertrand joined Dennis Conner. Buddy Melges and Bill Shore found a home at America^3.

There were now only two syndicates competing for the right to defend the Cup: Team Dennis Conner and America^3. The defense trials would be a showdown from day one.

A Tern for the Worse

4

During the second week of January, 1991, the 40 sailors who had been invited to try out for the crew of America³ descended upon San Diego. At dinner the evening before this initial training camp began, a 7 a.m. meeting the next morning was announced. One sailor got up extra early to do his habitual stretching exercises. Was he ever surprised to find out that the 7 a.m. "meeting" entailed 90 minutes of stretching and jogging supervised by Dick Dent, former trainer for the San Diego Padres baseball team. Many were the groans and gasps of pain as 40 men, bridging a variety of ages, weights, and physical conditions, struggled to perform the routine Dent presented.

Koch, always serious about his own physical conditioning, asked Dr. Robert Leach, the Chief of Orthopedic Surgery at the University Hospital in Boston, former orthopedic surgeon to the Boston Celtics and a member of the U. S. Olympic Committee to become the official America³ training advisor. Known to the team as "Dr. Bob," Leach was consulted by Larry Mialik, who established the program. Dent administered it.

A few days into camp, the morning exercises were augmented by an after-sail visit to the San Diego Chargers' weight room, thanks to Mialik's intercession. Mialik had played tight end for the Atlanta Falcons and Chargers during his NFL career. He and Charger coach Dan Henning were old pals.

If their physiques were an indication, a third of the squad was familiar with weight rooms. The rest wore apprehensive looks as they eyed the kinetic challenge of the sparkling white and chromium machines reflected tenfold in the mirrored walls. Scattered above the mirrors were signs: "Physical domination"; "Expect nothing but the best"; "Don't take anything for granted"; "Kick ass." Dent and the Charger trainer quickly had everyone doing what they could do, and soon a sense of quiet pride began to radiate along with the sweat. For many, that would change to chagrin the next morning, when brushing the teeth revealed a puzzling new stiffness across the shoulders. It was only the beginning of a long season.

Those who knew Bill Koch were not surprised that he would start his America's Cup program with an emphasis on physical conditioning. Koch carries only 190 pounds on his angular, 6-foot 4-inch frame. At 52, his boyish face displays a pale, sun-sensitive complexion topped with an unruly thatch of golden blond curly hair. His blue eyes are steady, equally capable of warming with sudden friendliness, or chilling with icy dismissal.

Koch works religiously on his lean physique. Weight rooms are as integral a part of his life as are helicopters and exotic wine cellars. At the first evening meeting, Koch spoke about the physical side. "There's an average weight limit on these boats of 198 pounds per man. There's a lot of extra weight in this room that's got to go. Dick Dent is going to be measuring everyone's fat content. We're aiming at 10-12 percent. We're not going to be fat, dumpy American heroes. We're going to have the best bodies out there."

Complimenting the physical side was diet. Buddy Melges kept looking for the bacon and eggs, but he never found them at the training table. The emphasis in the dining room was on high carbohydrates — plenty of pasta — fresh vegetables, delectable California greens, and lots of fruit. Fish and chicken were staples. No one saw beef for two weeks. Koch made a dietary alteration after a few days when he determined that the meal at night was too heavy. So pasta dishes were served at breakfast for the heartier souls. Lunches on the boats were cold pasta, vegetable, and salad sandwiches in whole wheat pita bread, washed down with Gatorade, juice, or mineral water. The "real people" beef eaters were grumbling, but only mildly. Training table fare was delicious.

Sarah Lessard ran the kitchen. She had joined her husband Carl in San Diego when he flew west looking for a compound site. After learning to cook at home, she polished her skills working on yachts. Feeding 80 people at a clip was a new experience for her, though one would never know it by the high standards she struck and maintained throughout the program.

Physical fitness was another area that began on track and stayed there. The rest of the program would have its ups and downs during a six month shake-down period, but Dick Dent and company were as reliable as sunrise. Having food and fitness the two factors everyone could count on was a blessing. One might not know where the boats were or who was on first on any given day, but good meals, good workouts, and thoughtful physical care were always a sure thing. That was an important stabilizer.

What was not so stable were several other parts of the overall organization. Although Bill Koch had established that the management of America³ was among the most critical elements to potential success, there was no way to foresee many of the obstacles that suddenly appeared after he set up the syndicate. Not even he, a proven manager in several successful multimillion dollar corporations, could anticipate that a group of birds would come close to completely scuttling his developing America's Cup campaign.

Earlier in the Fall, Koch had asked Carl Lessard to make a reconnaissance trip to San Diego to scout for possible properties the syndicate could either acquire or lease. Lessard returned to Osterville, where he was managing Koch's Nauticus Marina, with the unhappy news that most of the prime sites had been snapped up by challengers and those that hadn't carried outrageous price tags.

After that, he became a habitually red-eyed weekend commuter. Then in early December, 1990, Carl and Sarah moved to San Diego.

Rick Wrightson had overall responsibility for finding a compound site. Lessard was his long-distance collaborator in the hunt.

"He was my guardian angel at the beginning, my partner at the end," Lessard says.

"I'd get to the office at 7:45 a.m.," Rick says. "Carl would call a few minutes later — 4:45 a.m. his time."

"I'd call again at 5 p.m. — 8 p.m. Rick's time, he'd still be there," Carl says.

Wrightson, trying to hold together a million projects from Boston, frequently found himself on a cross-country flight to attend meetings Lessard had set up. He also sat in on a number of zoning board meetings. David Dick, a San Diego attorney, became an indispensable ally as he advised Wrightson and America³ on the subtleties of city and state laws. Dick, who spent hours working for the sailing team, never sent in a bill. "He was one of our most important contributors," says Wrightson. "I'm not sure we could have accomplished what we did without his help."

From the outset, Lessard was a marked man. "The property owners and contractors were like a pack of salivating dogs," Lessard says. "Gardini had come in and bought Gerry Driscoll's yard. They thought everyone would go that big. They envisioned five or six American syndicates, and 15-20 challengers. They had dollar signs in their eyes. Their first question was, 'What's your budget?'"

From Junkyard to Compound

Lessard scoured the waterfront, dickered with a number of greedy property owners, walked away from several extravagant proposals, and then set his sights on the dilapidated Bay City Marina at 4960 North Harbor Drive. He'd originally passed on this site because of its junk yard condition, the confusion of ownership after several bankruptcies, and a plethora of complications associated with the property. It was an on-again, off-again negotiation that took weeks and contained more twists and strange characters than a novel by Elmore Leonard.

Carl realized that *USA-2* would arrive from France before he'd have a place to put her. Not to be deterred by such momentary delays, he figured if he couldn't bring the boat to a dock, he'd bring a dock to the boat. While the haggling continued on the Bay City Marina, he leased a 178-foot barge from R.E. Staite Engineering, Inc. and put a crane on it. He appealed to the Port Authority to tie it up at the Tenth Street Terminal. The request became a political football when the Port Authority was pressured by waterfront property owners who felt they might lose America^3 as a client if the syndicate had someplace to go. But the press was watching the situation with interest, and Lessard used that. "The Port Authority reluctantly let us tie up," Lessard says. On New Years Day, 1991, Carl and Stu Argo — a big-boat sailor from Michigan who would become the starboard sail trimmer — painted the deck of the barge.

Now the Phillipe Briand-designed IACC sloop, formerly designated F-1, had temporary quarters and it effectively made America^3 the first U.S. Cup syndicate to have a boat in the San Diego waters.

Lessard, with one headache cured, returned to his attempt to secure a land facility. In the end, on March 9, a few phone calls dragged the principals to a 6 a.m. meeting. Rick Wrightson, Carl Lessard, attorney David Dick, and Vincent Moeyersoms met with representatives from the land owners. The meeting fell apart and the A^3 team adjourned to the San Diego Yacht Club. There Vincent Moeyersoms stretched himself out on a table trying to curtail back spasms. Amid this odd scene, a proposal was suggested which later received approval from both sides.

Carl was one proud negotiator when he reported to Koch that the syndicate now had a San Diego home. All that was left to do was clear out the junk and replace it with the state-of-the-art equipment needed to efficiently operate an America's Cup boatyard. Koch congratulated Carl and reminded him he needed to acquire the proper permits from the different city agencies that watch over such construction. "No problem," said Carl, who believed the really hard part was behind him.

That was until he heard about the birds. Nesting terns to be exact. "They are protected, Mr. Lessard. We have very strict ordinances here. You can't be putting in pilings, using jackhammers and bulldozers, making a lot of noise during their mating season."

"When are they due here?" asked an increasingly chagrined Lessard.

"In little over a month," was the chilling answer. Lessard was told he simply didn't have enough time to do what he planned, so he should wait until next year. Lessard knew any delay would be disaster. After months of searching and debating and squeezing and walking away from deal after deal, he finally had a site and he wasn't about to let a bunch of birds get in the way of his planned progress.

Once again Lessard was not to be dissuaded. He knew that Gerry Driscoll, a longtime San Diego boatyard owner and former America's Cup sailor, had great influence with the San Diego power structure. Lessard asked Driscoll for help. Driscoll responded by walking the permit application through official channels, a process that normally takes two to three months. He accomplished the task in four hours.

Now America^3 had its permit, but it came with a limited time warranty. It would expire on the first day the nesting terns arrived.

"In 38 days, we put the compound together," says Lessard, who coordinated compound construction and worked closely with Ray Carpenter of R.E. Staite Engineering. Carpenter helped Lessard pull off the impossible. "We started removing the old pilings within an hour of signing the agreement," says Lessard. "There were a lot of balls in the air. We worked sunrise to sunset."

In 38 days, all the old docks were removed and new concrete pilings and docks (1,000 feet plus) and a Travelift ramp were installed. Two old buildings were razed and two 5,000-square-foot metal buildings were erected. A 150-ton Travelift arrived on three semi-trailers and had to be assembled. During the demolition phase, all electrical, water, and compressed air lines were run underground. All the concrete work — pilings and Travelift ramp — cured just in time to begin launching boats, and for the arrival of the nesting terns.

As more sailors and support staff arrived in San Diego, the problem of where to house them arose. This was not a weekend regatta. Personnel from all parts of the country were leaving homes and jobs to join what, at that point, could only be described as something of a pipe dream. No first-time effort had ever won the modern America's Cup. No syndicate had ever quite approached the event the way America^3 planned. Those who signed on did so with a great deal of faith and no doubt some trepidation. So to add housing dilemmas to what may have been a growing anxiety would have retarded any progress made on the water.

Koch asked his old friend from Osterville and *Matador* days, Fred Curan, to see what he could do to solve the problem. Koch wanted the team concept to apply to living quarters as well. Curan was to try to keep as many of the crew in near proximity to each other as possible. It was not as easy as renting a house, a dorm, or an apartment. Individual needs had to be taken care of — single, married, married with children, allergies, smoker/non-smoker, would/wouldn't double up, etc. Curan scoured the city and outlying parts, as well as worked with each person to try to discover what best suited him or her. In the end, most of the crew was housed at the Oakwood Apartments, a stone's throw from the compound. The complex became a central meeting place for off-duty social activities and helped to instill the sense of team Koch had hoped for.

While workouts, nutrition, housing, and securing a compound were all important elements of the America^3 campaign, there was no doubt in anyone's mind that the sailors needed to start sailing. Many of the challenging nations had built their first boats and were training at sea. Some already had two boats. The U.S. defender hopefuls had yet to build a boat and thus were handicapped from the beginning.

Given the early lead enjoyed by many of the challenging nations, having *USA-2* was a godsend. It meant America^3 sailors were on the water at last. America^3 had a boat under construction, but delivery was four months away. *USA-2* made New Zealand's two IACC boats perched on the apron of its handsome new Coronado Island compound seem a little less daunting. There was only so much to be done with one boat, but starting basic orientation would be progress.

America^3 purchased the French boat for two reasons: to make tension measurements and to use it for crew training. The syndicate's managers realized that no matter how much experience the team's individual sailors had had, no one had ever sailed an IACC boat.

The IACC boats are big, impressive, slightly intimidating when one first steps aboard. The deck is broad, sweeping. The mast towers 104 feet above the deck. The mainsail, with its full battens and extreme upper roach, looms overhead like the side of a tall building. Everything about the boat is different from, and much bigger than, a 12-Meter. It is light for its size, and carries enormous sail area. That means it will accelerate and decelerate quickly. Sailing one is a new game, from the mechanics of tacking, to trimming the relatively small jib, to steering. Crew mistakes are quickly apparent and costly.

And there is that enormous, pesky, asymmetrical spinnaker to deal with, 5,000-square-feet of cloth anchored to the end of a 35-foot pole that extends 10 feet beyond the forestay. Jibing takes a powerful crewman at the mast who can horse the inboard end of the pole high on its track, and then down again after the outboard end swings inside the forestay. This maneuver has to coincide with an assist from Mother Nature to blow the clew of the sail around in front of the boat so it can be sheeted in on the other side. Race-quality jibes would take a lot of work and experimentation.

John Bertrand, the Beach Boys skipper, had sailed *F-1* in France for several weeks before it was sold. He said when his squad first tried to jibe the boat with the asymmetrical chute up, it took twelve attempts.

Legs four, five, and six of the new, made-for-television America's Cup course would be a series of spinnaker reaches forming the letter "Z." They would involve an initial set, two jibe-peels, and a final takedown. Sail selection, handling, and crew work would be critical on the Big Z.

Gary Jobson, vice-president of sailing and co-skipper, divided the crew into two groups. Every day, one group began unraveling the mysteries of *USA-2*. They found the IACC boat very physical. For the first couple weeks, everyone was coming in beaten up. The grinders especially had a workout. Their day began with hoisting the mainsail — a sustained, two-minute effort. Sheeting in the small jibs wasn't bad, but on asymmetrical spinnaker jibes the grinders amidships were cranking in nearly 200 feet of line as the new sheet blew around the front of the boat. The mains'l grinders were also dealing with a long workout on jibes. Tacking, they would earn their keep as the main was eased a foot, then cranked in as speed built. In low gear, one foot equaled twenty cranks.

The backstays were critical. On jibes, the trimmer hauled as hard and fast as possible to secure the new backstay as the main passed the centerline, then scrambled to get the handle in and winch it home. On tacks, it took more than a minute, working hard, to get those final clicks on the winch as the readout climbed to as much as 20,000 psi. Adjusting the traveler on the wind was a mountainous task that required both hands and determination. It was apparent that the IACC boats required a lot of muscle, even in the afterguard.

Learning to manhandle the big pole was a project for the foredeck crew. The sewer man was working in quarters more cramped than a 12-Meter, horsing around sails that are bigger and heavier. The point man was constantly shinnying like a monkey up the foreguy to the pole end for jibes and takedowns, suspended over the water. And the pit crew was up to its knees in line trying to coordinate its heavy, precision work with the foredeck's needs.

The second group of America^3 sailors went off to polish tactical match racing skills on two chartered Catalina 37s. Koch, Jobson, Melges, and Bill Campbell were doing most of the driving on the boats. Campbell is an E-Scow champion and Naval Academy graduate with several years' experience navigating missile submarines.

The syndicate asked several experienced umpires to call the match racing so the skippers and crew would become used to the on-the-water judging system employed for the first time in America's Cup racing. In one series Koch was paired against Jobson and beat him in all six races. For Koch it was proof he could hold his own against those who thought he had no business behind the wheel. He felt his credentials confirmed when one of the judges drew along side the Catalina and, laughing, said "Bill, I think you better find a little better skipper for the other boat. You need some competition out here!"

It was bump and grind with the Catalinas. More than once raised voices were heard across San Diego Harbor. Both Catalinas sported scuffs of red and green paint from harbor buoys after only a few races. Koch smiled one evening as he commented on the Catalina action. "I hope we'll get the kinks out before we start sailing two big boats. It's a lot cheaper to wreck the Catalinas."

At that, Melges shook his head. "There you go, getting frugal again."

The Syndicates Structure

Evening meetings rounded out each day of training camp. It was a dawn-to-bedtime schedule that Jobson had organized, but then America^3 was definitely in catch-up mode. The French boat had been launched in March, 1990. The French and Italians had match-raced in July, 1990. In September, 1990, the Italians launched a second boat. The Spanish launched a boat in November, 1990, and New Zealand and Japan had been gearing up since 1988. Bill Koch didn't announce his intention to defend until October, 1990, and if America^3 had a boat launched in time for the IACC World Championships in May, 1991, it would be remarkable. There was a lot of ground to cover.

After everyone had signed a multi-page confidentiality agreement, Koch broadened the view for the crew. He opened the door and invited the players in to hear the game plan. Koch may not have been as seasoned a sailor as many in this group, but as an experienced manager he had a plan. He realized that input from world-class sailors would be important and he wanted everyone to feel a part of the team.

At the first evening meeting, Koch went over syndicate structure in his soft-spoken way. He recalled a seminar he had conducted on finding and starting small technology companies as a grad student at M.I.T., where he earned a Ph.D. in chemical engineering. The seminar was attended by Ken Olsen of the Digital Equipment Corporation. "Olsen said Digital's success was not based on doing one thing outstandingly, but on doing everything reasonably well," Koch said. "That's what we must do. We can't rely on any one factor."

The crew work, Koch said, is like a ballet dance. "If anyone tries to stand out, it will destroy the whole movement. The winning boat makes the fewest mistakes. We will go to great lengths to insure teamwork." He reminded the assembled crew — still aspirants at this point — of the formula that had proved so successful on *Matador²*: "Attitude, teamwork, and ability — in that order."

He repeated that everyone on the team was of equal importance. Sailors, scientists, maintenance people, sailmakers, everyone would meet and exchange ideas on a variety of issues that would arise. When a problem occurred, there would be a team approach to its solution.

He told them he had initially been repelled by the America's Cup. "I've seen the Cup breed enemies. I don't want that to happen here. I want lifelong friends out of this. We're all here because we love to sail and we want to win. But we want to win with pride and dignity, honor and friendship." Koch's lofty goals were admirable. Whether or not they could be realized in the caldron of animosity historically generated by America's Cup competition was the question.

In some ways, the evening meetings were the highlight of each day. The America³ Foundation's Chairman of the Board Louis Cabot warned against complacency, urging the crew to think "meaner, tougher, and faster." Gary Jobson talked about the course and the tactics involved. Buddy Melges discussed boat speed. Bill Shore spoke about the sail development program he was managing.

Vincent covered a large blackboard with more than 50 names of people working on the design and technical side. Moeyersoms was now America³'s executive vice-president of technical operations (coordinator of design, technical research, construction, sail development, instrumentation, shore operations, coaching, tenders, and scheduling), and chief operating officer of the syndicate. Halfway through his presentation, Vincent's beeper went off. Throughout the campaign, he was pulled in many directions at the same time.

There were visiting professors to this elite master class on sailboat racing. San Diegan Peter Isler, the old Conner hand who had tried in vain to start his own defense syndicate, came to talk about the competitors. Sailmaker, senior U.S. Sailing Association juror, match racer, and Lightning and Thistle champion Dave Dellenbaugh lectured about the racing rules and the brand-new on-the-water judging.

The America's Cup Organizing Committee's Gene Trepte (director and defense chairman) and Tom Ehman (executive director) went over race committee management and the new race course. Ehman seemed more curt and aggressive than ever. He said he was proud of the race course, "having had a lot to do with its design." Ehman was asked about the logic of the "button-hole" at the bottom mark of the "Z," where the lead boat had to round to port, make a 270-degree turn (or a 360-degree turn if that boat decides to tack right away), and potentially have a close encounter with the trailing boat. "I hope no one gets hurt," Ehman said, "at least not badly. If a boat sinks, they better get it on tape."

A few evenings later, San Diego Charger coach Dan Henning lectured on team play. Larry Mialik introduced Henning. "The two of us," Mialik said, throwing an arm around Henning's shoulders, "have something in common that no one else in this room shares — we were both cut by the Chargers."

Mialik is one of the new breed of crewmen found currently on the bigger race boats. His initial qualifications were his strength, his athletic ability, and his commitment to teamwork. Those were prerequisites enough for being able to grind a winch through 40 or 50 tacks on a weather leg without losing the rhythm, or collapsing from exhaustion. Sufficient sailing skills could be acquired along the way.

By the time America³ began, Mialik had undergone plenty of training. A Midwesterner, Mialik was logically "discovered" by Buddy Melges's scouts while he was working at a University of Wisconsin sports clinic. He ended up on Buddy's *Heart of America* crew. Gary Jobson got to know Mialik in Australia, and later recruited him for the successful *Matador* campaign in 1987. When it was time for America³ crew selection, Mialik was a proven Koch regular, a winch grinder who had learned all the moves and emerged as a team leader.

At this early stage of the campaign, finding a way to make the team gel was uppermost in everyone's mind. It was a big team — 40-strong — and it included a lot of talent. The average age was 32. Among the titles the sailors held collectively were five Olympic medals, 34 national championships, and 21 world championships. They had sailed in 29 America's Cup campaigns. The potential crew also included one experienced woman (Whitbread 'Round-The-World Race veteran Dawn Riley) and several men who had never sailed before and others who had taken up the sport only in the past six years, including the president of the syndicate and skipper himself.

Jobson had done most of the crew selection, with suggestions from Koch, Melges, and Moeyersoms. Jobson had parlayed a stellar collegiate sailing career — followed by an America's Cup win (as tactician with Ted Turner on *Courageous* in 1977) — into a successful sailing consultation business. Over the past ten years, his emergence as a broadcaster (the America's Cup in Fremantle, 1987, for ESPN; the 1988 Olympics for

NBC, among others) and public speaker has made him one of a very few well-known personalities in yachting. And he has continued racing and kept current with others who do the same. His on-board experience, coupled with a five-year stint of coaching at the Merchant Marine Academy, give him the background to make personnel evaluations. His knowledge of world class sailing talent is comprehensive and his opinion of who was right for which job was expressed to Koch often. Koch continuously stressed the value of attitude, a concept Jobson shared and incorporated into his crew recommendations. But this game was going to be tricky. Only sixteen crew (and alternates) would end up on the boat — if, in fact, they won the right to defend the Cup. With a multi-boat program, there would have to be a two-team split at some point. That is always a sensitive, potentially divisive moment.

"The emphasis has got to be to play down the individual," Coach Henning said. "In a team sport, all-stars mean nothing. The joy is winning. Everything else is last."

High Tech

5

While the focus of the America³ syndicate may have been on San Diego in the first months of 1991 as the sailors trained and the compound was constructed, there was intense activity in several other American cities as well. If the emphasis in Southern California was on physical labor, matters more cerebral found prominence elsewhere.

After Koch's August directive to begin the design process, Vincent Moeyersoms rounded up the team that produced *Matador²*, made a couple of substitutions, and charged them with planning an IACC program. At the time they numbered about ten. Before the Cup was over, the number of people involved in design, construction, sails, and instrumentation would grow to more than 125.

"This was the core group," says Moeyersoms. "During the early days we were principally concerned with establishing an overview of the entire design program; trying to foresee what problems might lie ahead and then devise ways to avoid them. Work began on a whole array of parallel projects. We looked at hull shapes, different keels and spars, appendages, construction methods and all types of materials, sails, rigging set-ups, deck lay-out, instrumentation, everything we could think of that would affect boat speed in any way. We met regularly and discussed our ideas. Many we threw out, the better ones we kept."

The drill was for the designers to come up with as many wild ideas as they could by using their intuitions and then by using the scientific process they would select the best of them. This process was fundamental to Koch's management philosophy. He believes in letting creative people create. But even more so, he believes anything new must be tempered and tested by science.

Although the team had the testing data developed during the five years of the *Matador* program to use as a benchmark, they generally considered the America's Cup fertile ground for all sorts of new ideas and experiments. As Jerry Milgram, the M.I.T. wizard who played a key part in the *Matador* project, liked to say: "The Phoenicians invented sailing several thousand years ago and there has been little advancement since then."

That may be somewhat of an overstatement, but there is a ring of truth to Dr. Milgram's analysis. With the advent of steam-powered engines in the 19th century, followed by the invention of the internal combustion engine, the use of sail-powered vessels was no longer economically viable. As a result, there have been relatively few technical innovations in the last hundred years. Those that have been made, such as the use of fiberglass in constructing boats, originated in other industries.

Although the America's Cup was established as a challenge to designers, scientists, and technicians to look beyond the status quo, it is ironic that its modern day administrators have been so slow to embrace technical breakthroughs. The introductions of bendy spars, wing keels, Mylar and Kevlar sails, composite building materials, and speed-enhancing riblets were all met with suspicion of rule-breaking and generated initial controversy rather than rightful acclaim.

With a keen eye on recent history and a genuine sense of fair play, the design committee searching for a new boat to be used in 1992 set out to found a class of racing yachts that could both utilize the innovations of the past and allow room for those of the future. While some believe they actually went too far in sacrificing safety for speed as masts broke and gear exploded, most designers and technicians involved in the '92 Cup were grateful for the extended parameters they enjoyed.

To make the breakthroughs that all Cup syndicates seek, today's yacht designers have a number of tools at their disposal which until recently were nonexistent. Chief among these is the personal computer, which accomplishes a variety of tasks essential to design. As the computer has become more powerful and more versatile, it seems it is being used for everything from drawing hull lines to analyzing competitors' shapes to acquiring real-time data while sailing. What used to be done by hand over a period of months in the days of such America's Cup boats as *Ranger* (1937), *Columbia* (1958), *Constellation* (1964), *Intrepid* (1967), and even *Courageous* in 1974, now has been reduced to a matter of hours as CAD-CAM (Computer Assisted Design, Computer Assisted Manufacturing) programs attack a myriad of problems.

Yet even with the advancement of computerized design programs and the use of the personal computer, Koch's technical team found the scientific

Drawings supplied by Dirk Kramers.

From the drawing boards of the America³ design group, a sketch of the sail plan and deck layout of USA-23. The sail plan provided initial sizes for mains, jibs, and spinnakers. Items that needed seminal development were asymmetrical spinnakers and reachers for the 135-degree, 100-degree, and running legs of the course; and strong, light, full-length battens for the big mains (270 square meters).

tools being used in yacht design and boat speed prediction inadequate for their needs. The *Matador* program, the most extensive attack on boat speed in modern yacht racing history, had proved the worth of creating new scientific and technological tools. For the America's Cup, Koch charged his team with concentrating on developing the fundamentals of yacht design and the basic science of boat speed. Koch was convinced that if his technical team fully understood what tools could do and what the data they produced meant, they could design the fastest boats in the world.

The problem of inadequate tools was also recognized by the defense committee. Defense design programs, to say nothing about defense programs in general, had been in limbo ever since the status of the next America's Cup was to be determined in court as a result of Michael Fay's surprise challenge. Potential U.S. Cup entrants didn't know if the outcome of courtroom deliberations would result in their being challengers or defenders; if they would race in Auckland or San Diego. Fundraising, organizing, training, and design plans all came to a standstill in America, while other Cup nations raced ahead with their programs.

By May, 1990, the legal system had finally ground out its verdict and the official word was the 1992 America's Cup would be held in California. Defenders now had to play catch-up and the area in which they had fallen behind the furthest was design. The defense committee had recognized the problem and had sanctioned an organization called "Partnership for America's Cup Technology" (PACT) to jump start the defense technology efforts. The idea was that PACT would serve as a reservoir of scientific and technological knowledge and resources from which the defending syndicates could draw. PACT's mission, under the leadership of longtime Conner crony John Marshall (who had recently split from Team Dennis Conner), was to develop the scientific and technological tools needed to design fast boats. In other words, PACT was supposed to be doing a major part of what America^3 was taking on itself.

America^3 objected to PACT's existence from day one and continued to do so throughout the campaign. The syndicate managers had chosen from the very beginning to pursue a design course based on science and technology. They would commit millions of dollars, untold hours, and immense human effort to that pursuit and they believed their discoveries should be proprietary. But now they were being told that their $100,000 entry fee which gave them official status as a defender, was going to support PACT. That money, plus small contributions from corporate and private sources, was to provide the needed funding for the development of design tools. But compared to the America^3 budget, PACT's resources presented little more than a bare cupboard.

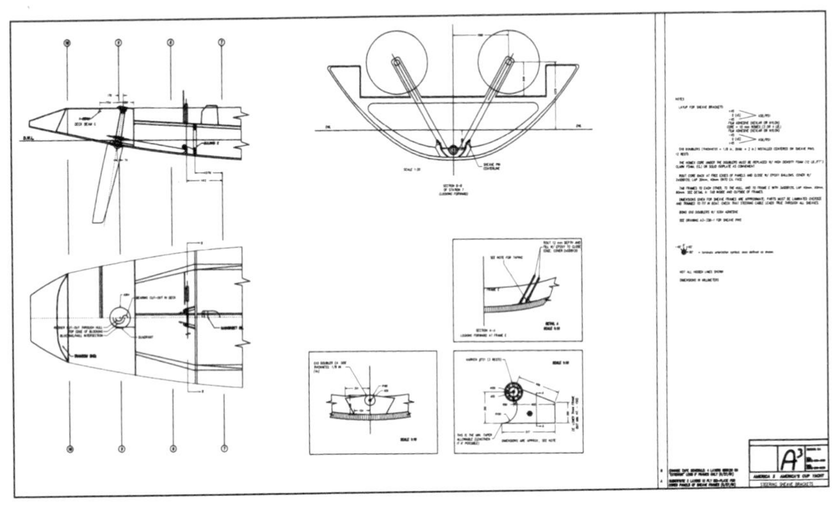

Detailed section drawings of steering system. These CAD (computer-aided design) drawings were used principally by the engineering department to determine exact placement of equipment, dimensions of gear, thickness of core, etc. Seen here are rudder, wheels, steering cable, steering sheave brackets, doublers, and steering quadrants, all drawn with quick tacks and jibes in mind.

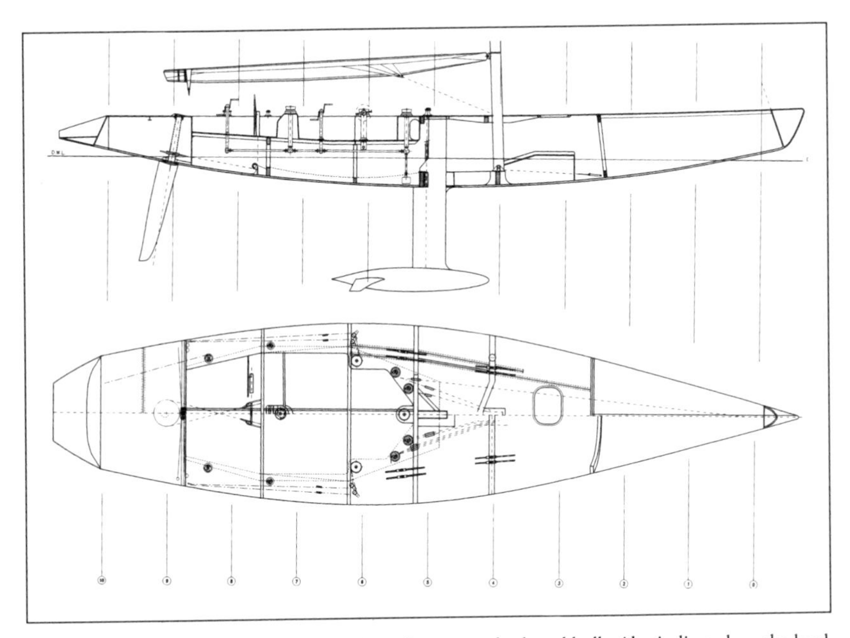

Internal structure layout showing positioning of maststep, keel, and bulb. Also indicated are the level and depth of the cockpit as well as the platform under the forward hatch. Hundreds of similar drawings were prepared throughout the design and building processes as changes were made to certain sections or an overall design was radically altered. Imagine making the changes by hand.

REVISION	DATE	DESCRIPTION	RELATED DRAWINGS	COMMENTS
A		CHANGE RUNNER WINCHES TO BARIENT #839a MOVE PORT JIB HALYARD FORESPAR CLUTCH ADD KEEL HOLE MOVE AFT TWO HALYARD BLOCKS SLIGHTLY FWD CHANGED PEDESTAL X LOCATIONS MOVE BUTT LIFT DEFLECTOR SHEAVE AFT 850mm AND CHANGE TO SWIVEL BLOCK ON EYESTAP ADD SM. PADEYE FWD OF FOREDECK HATCH MOVE AFT PEDESTAL AFT 247mm CHANGE STAYS'L PEDEYES TO MED. SIZE MOVE FWD JIB TRACKS FWD CHANGE OUTBD #3 TRACK END STOPS MOVE MAINSHEET ROLLER CLOSER TO WINCH	A3-746 A3-724	LOCATIONS LISTED WERE INCORRECT AS PER P.WILSON FAX 4 FEB 92 AS PER P.WILSON FAX 4 FEB 92 AS PER P.WILSON FAX 4 FEB 92
		MOVE AND LOCATE SIDE DECK SUPPORTS CHANGE FAC VALVES BY PRIMARIES TO SINGLES MOVE RUNNER WINCHES INBD 40mm ADD BOOM CRUTCH SOCKET MOVE TOPMAST BLOCKS INBD OF RUNNERS	A3-704	TO AVOID INTERFERENCE WITH RUNNER LEAD

Detailed plans for the deck layout of *America*³. This particular plan carries a number of instructions to the boat's builders, such as "move topmast blocks inbd. of runners." Such instructions resulted

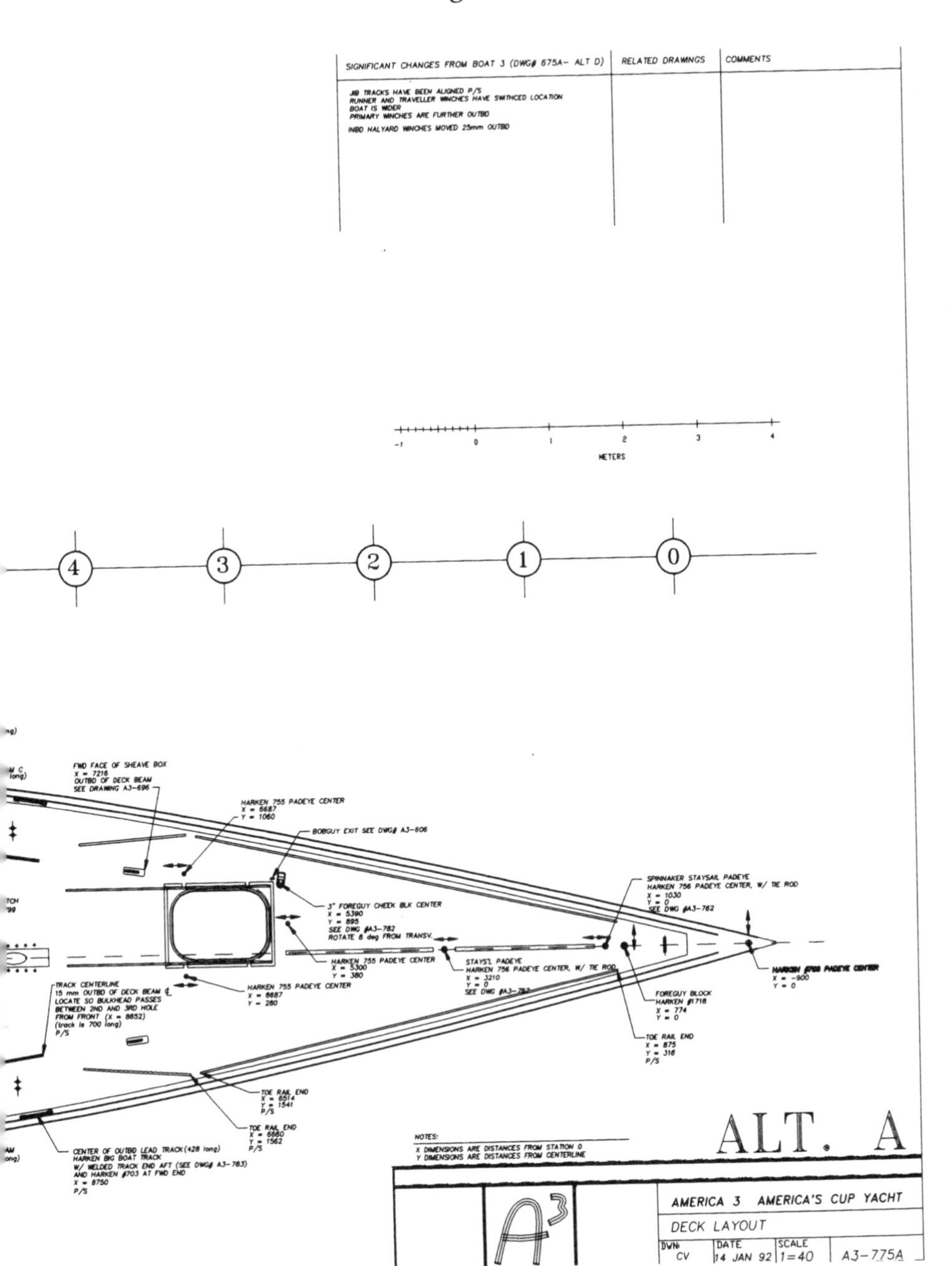

from load and engineering studies of previous plans. The 0-11 circled numbers designate different "stations" of the boat from bow to stern. Detailed drawings of each station were also made.

Comparison of IACC Yacht with 12-Meter Yacht

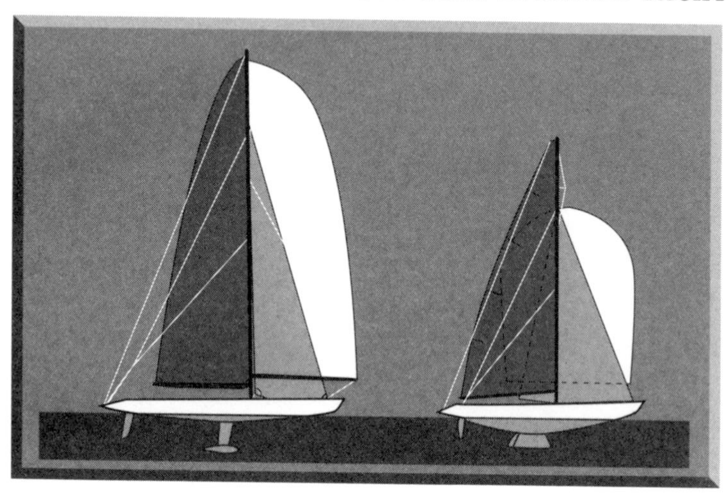

As the 12-Meter era came to an end, the International America's Cup Class (IACC) yacht was developed. Twenty percent longer than a Twelve, it weighs 30 percent less, has 40 percent more draft, and its total sail area exceeds that of its predecessor by 70 percent. The IACC boats are big, impressive, and slightly intimidating; the deck is broad, sweeping. The mast towers 104 feet above the deck, the mainsail, with its full battens and extreme upper roach, looms overhead like the side of a skyscraper. Everything about the boat is different from, and much bigger than, a 12-Meter. It is light for its size, and carries enormous sail area. That means it accelerates and decelerates quickly.

Dimensions of IACC Yacht

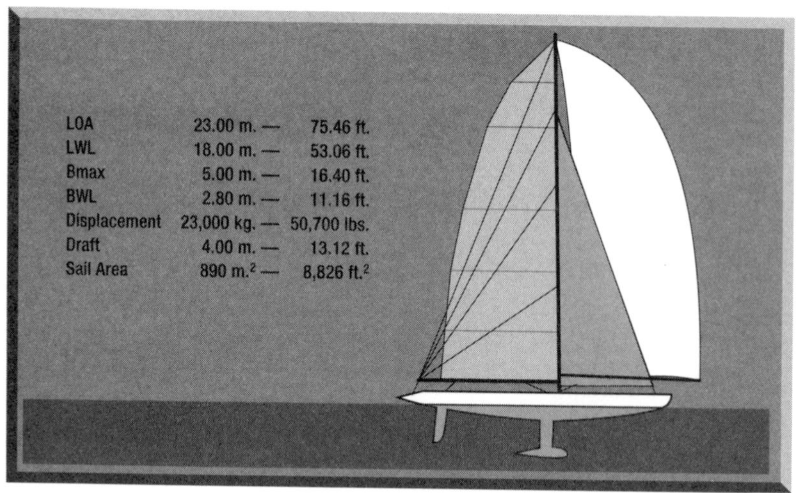

LOA 23.00 m. — 75.46 ft.
LWL 18.00 m. — 53.06 ft.
Bmax 5.00 m. — 16.40 ft.
BWL 2.80 m. — 11.16 ft.
Displacement 23,000 kg. — 50,700 lbs.
Draft 4.00 m. — 13.12 ft.
Sail Area 890 m.² — 8,826 ft.²

All diagrams © Mike Samuel

America's Cup Course

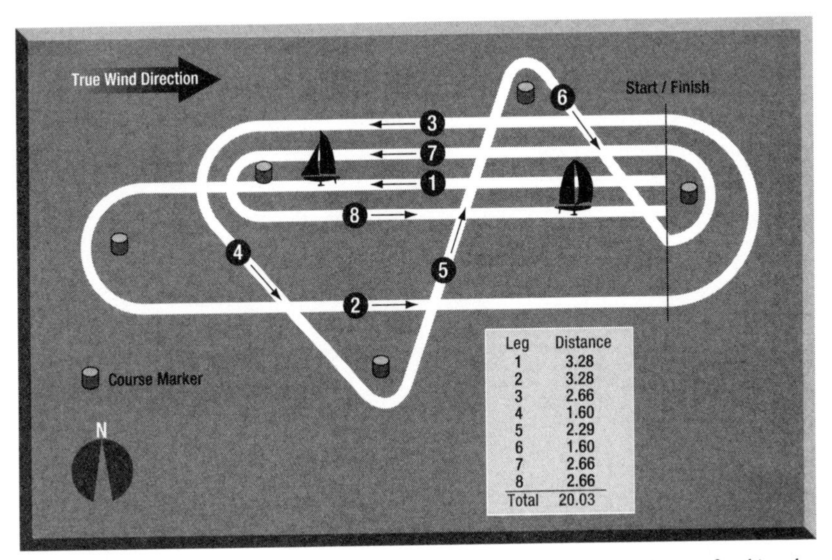

The class of boats was not the only innovation in the 1992 America's Cup. In hopes of making the event more exciting for the television audience, race managers included three new reaching legs during which the huge, brightly colored asymmetrical spinnakers were flown, sometimes propelling the boats to as much as 16 knots of speed. The "buttonhole" at the botton mark of the "Z" was subject to controversy as the lead boat had to round to port, make a 270-degree turn (or a 360-degree turn if that boat decided to tack right away), and potentially have a close encounter with the trailing boat. Critics felt safety gave way to television ratings. Thus, no reaching legs in 1995.

America³'s objections to PACT's existence focused on three points. First, because America³ was starting with its own reservoir of scientific and technological knowledge (from the *Matador* program), they believed that anything PACT might come up would fall short of what they already had and would help the underfunded Team Dennis Conner more than it would help them. Second, PACT proposed that it have access to America³'s confidential data, clearly a proposition of no benefit to America³. And third, PACT was competing for sponsorship in the same marketplace where America³ and Team Dennis Conner were seeking funding. Even though TDC was receiving some benefit from PACT, they joined America³ in objecting to PACT, saying that if they had their share of the PACT budget, they could spend it more wisely.

The man who ran the technology program for Koch's team saw PACT as a bit of a loose cannon. "Each defense syndicate was supposed to have a direct say on what PACT should or shouldn't do," says Vincent Moeyersoms. "We would have these long meetings that resulted in little more than a waste of time. America³ and Team Dennis Conner agreed on

Polar Diagram

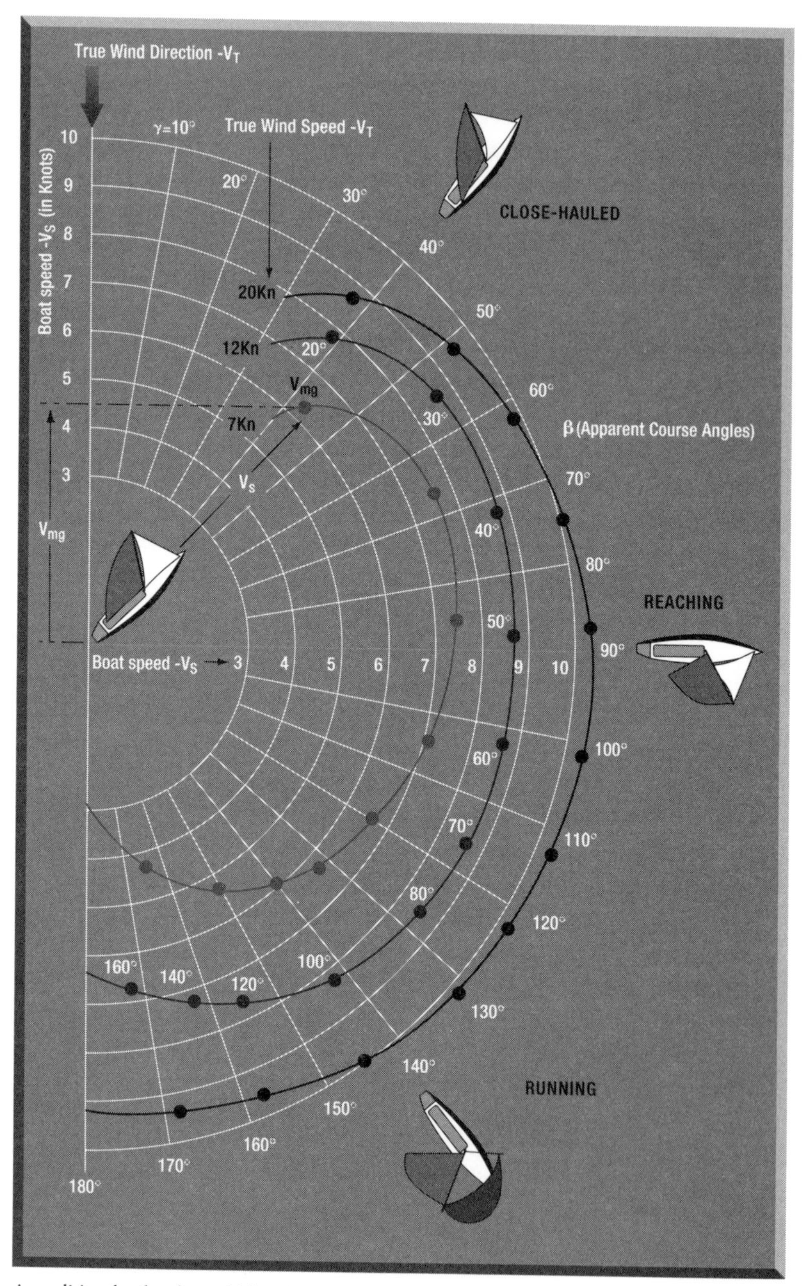

A traditional polar chart which estimates a 12-Meter yacht's performance on different points of sail in smooth water at three different wind strengths.

what PACT should do, and then PACT would go off and do whatever they wanted. Their actions rarely coincided with what the defenders asked."

How successful was PACT? "We received no meaningful information from them," says Moeyersoms. "About the only thing we ever got was a computer program that never worked. Their projects were much more long-term. They were of no help for 1992."

Velocity Prediction Program

Among the most important tools designers use today are velocity prediction programs (VPPs). They allow the designer to answer the question Bill Koch asked when he first began to sail: "How can you predict a boat's potential speed before she is built?" The ability to estimate the maximum potential speed of a sailboat in a given wind condition allows the naval architect to compare two or more sailboat designs. It is enormously valuable and time saving.

Predicting a sailboat's speed based on her design began in the 1930s and was initially carried out by hand. The development of VPPs made such calculations much easier. The perfect boat design is really a balancing act of the forces generated on the hull and the sails by water and wind. As these forces vary, when the wind increases or decreases and its angle changes or waves build or flatten out, the sailboat's speed is always affected. VPPs measure these forces, compare and contrast them, and ultimately predict their overall effect on boatspeed.

The balancing act continues when different sail shapes are used, wind speed and angle vary, the length of the boat is modified, the angle of heel changes, and so on. It is a game of variables that before VPPs would try the patience of even Job.

Professor Milgram had several advantages over many of the other designers working across the world. VPPs were actually first developed by Justin E. Kerwin, M.I.T. professor of Ocean Engineering, the same department in which Milgram teaches. He had been working with this data from the beginning and probably had more experience than any other academician or technician. He also had the experience of *Matador²* behind him.

Milgram knew that the Achilles Heel of VPPs is found in the scale-model approach. Usually, a generic model based on comparing predicted and actual performance is used. However, inaccuracies occur when the boat's rig to be evaluated has different proportions than the one used to generate the model.

To avoid these inaccuracies which render the VPPs basically worthless, Koch funded a program in which Milgram and his students and staff developed and built the "M.I.T. Sailing Dynamometer" which measures sail forces directly on a 35-foot sailboat. The Dynamometer is a test boat that differs from an ordinary sailboat in that all rig components, mast, chainplates, winches, lead blocks, traveler, etc., are attached to a rigid frame that is structurally separate from the hull. This frame is surrounded by the hull and deck and is connected to them only through six load cells. Signals from the cells are interfaced through a signal conditioner to an on-board computer, which also records outputs from sailing instruments which provide wind speed and direction, boat speed, heel angle, heading, etc. The computer also records signals from additional precision inclinometers, which measure heel and pitch angles. When all this data is mixed together in a type of high tech soup, it becomes the first course in a feast of scientific calculations that result in the most accurate VPPs modern technology can achieve.

The overall length of 35 feet was chosen because it would be large enough to obtain good sail force data yet small enough to be handled by one or two persons. In order to develop an IACC mathematical scale model, the Sailing Dynamometer was fitted with a scale model of an IACC rig.

The most difficult technical task of the Sailing Dynamometer project was obtaining real-time windspeed and direction measurements with consistent accuracy. The major problem here was that wind instruments affixed to the mast were affected by mast twist. This problem was solved by installing a video camera at the masthead and focusing it on marks drawn on the deck. The location of the marks in the video frame determined the amount of twist in the mast.

Video images were also used to measure sail shape. A computer-interface video system with specialized software was developed. High resolution video images of the sails were taken from a motorboat and then fed into the computer. The images appeared on the computer screen and the operator could scan the tape, pause on any frame, and be able to perform any necessary measurements and calculations on screen.

When these measured sail shapes, along with wind and heel angles, were entered into a computational fluid dynamics computer program developed by the Atlantic Applied Research Corporation in Burlington, Massachusetts, a sufficiently accurate sail model was achieved. By using this sail model, maximum speed prediction error was reduced by a factor of ten.

Reasonably certain that the computer modeling was producing as accurate data as possible, America^3 staff members began using the M.I.T. Sailing Dynamometer daily in San Diego. In addition to all the other instrumentation, a cellular phone was always aboard which was used to contact M.I.T.

to solve problems as they occurred. As Milgram later said, "For the first time in history, there exists a measure of how well a sailboat can actually work!"

Armed with the data from five years of the *Matador* program and the knowledge of how VPPs work and can be worked, Jerry Milgram found himself in front of the wind tunnel at Hydronautics Research in College Park, Maryland in January, 1991. Beside him were several members of the America^3 design team: Buddy Duncan, Rob Scala, and Dr. Heiner Meldner.

In the tunnel's test chamber was the M.I.T. Sailing Dynamometer. Between runs (approximately ten minutes at 200 mph), yaw, rudder and trim tab angles were changed. During each run, data on drag, lift, yaw angle, side force, and a half-dozen other effects were being constantly fed into computers. For the small group gathered to run tests on some early keel and rudder shapes, science was what yacht design is all about and science depends upon data. In Maryland, data collection had been underway for the America^3 program for four months.

At one point the group paused long enough to watch one of General Schwartzkopf's press briefings from the Persian Gulf, complete with extraordinary video of bombing runs. It was a sobering moment. As the war unfolded, people wondered if there would be a 1992 Cup match. Afterwards, Jerry Milgram jumped in his car to drive to the water test tank, which was conveniently located 40 minutes from the wind tunnel. Milgram was overseeing the early testing for the design program in addition to maintaining a full schedule at M.I.T.. He was short-tempered this day, talking about giving the whole thing up. Co-workers were ignoring this behavior. "Jerry's overwhelmed because he is a critical piece of the program," said one who knows him well. "He's overworked, overloaded, but he loves it. He's a hyper guy, happier when he has too much to do."

Milgram was also slightly preoccupied about the tactical oil spill Sadam Hussein had loosed upon the Gulf. Several students Milgram had taught at M.I.T. about the technology of oil spill cleanup were on their way to the Middle East. Milgram had reason to be anxious.

The test rig at Hydronautics Research looks like a recreational vehicle from a road warrior movie. It bridges a water canal measuring 25 feet wide, 13 feet deep, and 410 feet long. A scale model about 20 feet LOA attached to the rig was moved through the water at different speeds. One hundred five runs were needed to complete one test.

Bill Koch has great faith in the wind tunnel and water tank. He considers them the great arbitrators. Exhaustive tunnel and tank testing made *Matador*^{2} the speedster she was. "In the five years of the *Matador* program,"

Schematic Diagram of Sailing Dynamometer

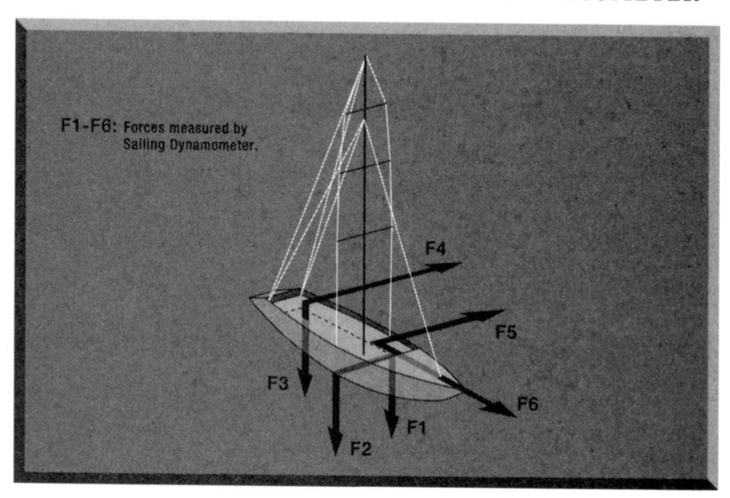

A schematic diagram of the sailing dynamometer's internal frame shows the forces measured by six load cells positioned throughout the boat. The load cells are interfaced to a computer through signal conditioners and a multiplexed analog-to-digital converter.

Inboard Diagram of Sailing Dynamometer

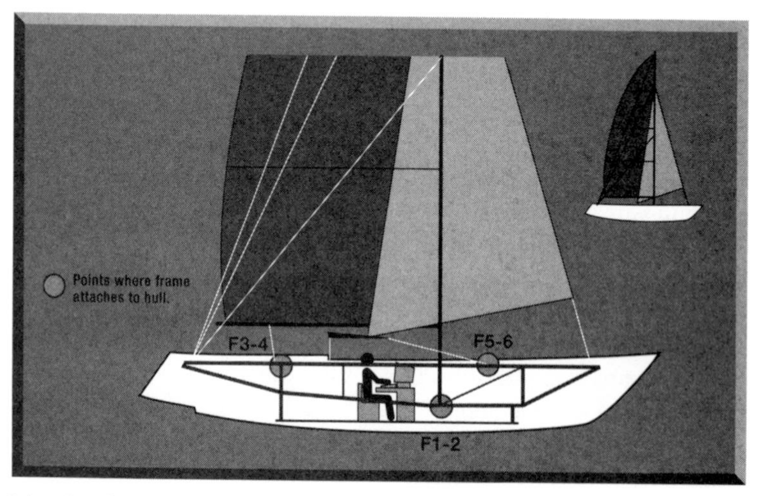

Inboard profile of the load boat in which the external keel and rudder are not shown. By setting up all channels, the user, seated inside, allows the aerodynamic forces and moments on the entire rig to be measured while the vessel is under sail in real wind and while undergoing the unsteady motions due to sea waves.

Koch says, "we had developed the tools to accurately analyze test results." Koch was demanding. When a second test bettered the first, and a third bettered the second, Koch ordered more. "Nature is not linear. There will be maximum points in the data," Koch says.

Milgram and his people proceeded with confidence. They knew most of the peculiarities of these potentially misleading facilities. At one point, Milgram considered heating the water in the test tank to match water temperatures in San Diego.

The Hydronautics facility is dreary as a cave: dark, damp, and dank. Being there looked like tough duty, but Milgram, Daniel Lemere, and John Mass were continually buoyed by the secrets it revealed. There was also the tank testers' own brand of humor that lightened up the long days. One of the favorite quips shared with visitors was, "Yeah, I understand the Italians did twenty runs before they filled the tank."

Eighteen Months in the Tank

Testing would continue for a year and a half. In the end, more than 1,000 hours of tank time was spent testing 34 different hull models with various appendages to determine displacement trim. At 105 runs per test well over 1,500 miles were run in the tank — 400 ponderous feet at a time.

America^3's first boat, *Jayhawk* (USA-9), was under construction without the benefit of any test data. "We had to get a boat started," Milgram said with a shrug, obviously unhappy about the pressure. "So we took our best shot at it. It will be interesting to see how we did." *Jayhawk* was designed about the same time Bill Koch was announcing his campaign. *Defiant* (USA-18), was also designed and built without the benefit of tank test results.

Having been research director of the program that produced *Matador*^{2}, Milgram wasn't exactly working in the dark on USA-9. But in today's world of computer precision, an IACC boat is significantly different from a maxi. Milgram and the team applied proven concepts from the maxi research program, and photo intelligence from the French and Italian boats. The latter was a bust. The measurements taken off the photographs proved to be inaccurate.

Milgram, at the suggestion of Bill Koch, began a maxi tank testing program right after Koch bought *Huaso* in 1984. It produced ten different major modifications to old *Matador* before *Matador*^{2} evolved. Along the way, a solid design and technical team was formed. It was this group that provided the nucleus for America^3.

HULL RESISTANCE MODEL

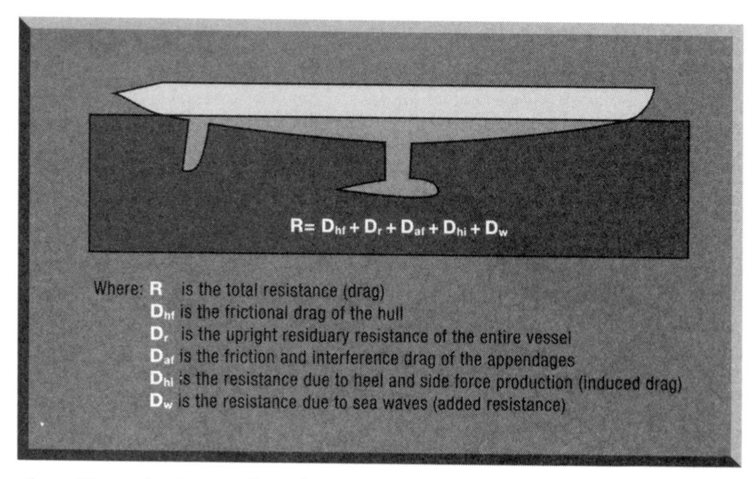

$R = D_{hf} + D_r + D_{af} + D_{hi} + D_w$
Where: R is the total resistance (drag)
D_{hf} is the frictional drag of the hull
D_r is the upright residuary resistance of the entire vessel
D_{af} is the friction and interference drag of the appendages
D_{hi} is the resistance due to heel and side force production (induced drag)
D_w is the resistance due to sea waves (added resistance)

Above: The total resistance of a yacht moving through the water is shown in formula. Opposite: In their constant quest for speed, yacht designers and scientists are continually trying innovative ideas, in recent years, one focus of their attention has been different appendage configurations. The ruder and keel systems shown here were used by different syndicates during the 1992 Cup to varying degrees of success.

Heiner Meldner, a theoretical physicist who had taught at Stanford University, did the wind-tunnel testing for *Matador²'s* keel. Then he supervised construction, figuring out how to cut a foil shape out of a single piece of stainless that measured 16 feet by 6 feet by 1foot. He designed in the trim tab, figured out how to hinge and control it, then solved the problem of how to attach the heavy, exotic rig to the boat.

A native of what was West Germany, Meldner was the youngest full professor in Berlin in 1972. That same year he wrote a paper on neutron sources so revealing that both the work and the author were essentially "seized" by the U.S. government. Meldner became a U.S. citizen and went to work at the Lawrence Livermore Laboratory, in San Francisco, developing nuclear weapons. His work was so classified he had to proceed alone, picking up engineering, fluid dynamics, and a few other disciplines along the way. Meldner holds five major U.S. patents that are forever classified. He has more than 5,000 hours on Cray computers, among the fastest number-crunchers made.

Meldner met sailmaker Lowell North in the 1970s when he went shopping for sails for his Soling. He questioned North's design methods. "I was being a typical German-professor type," Meldner says with a grin.

Different Rudder & Keel Systems

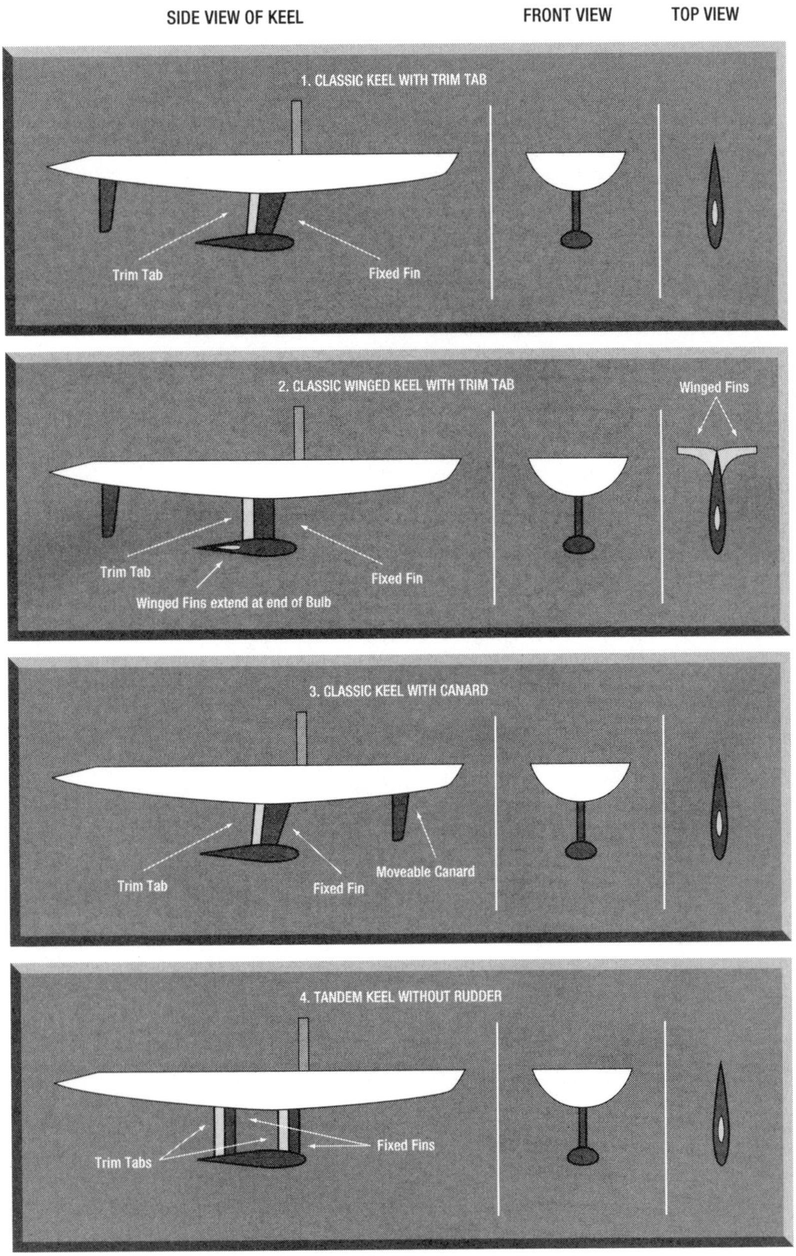

SIDE VIEW OF KEEL

FRONT VIEW

TOP VIEW

1. CLASSIC KEEL WITH TRIM TAB

Trim Tab

Fixed Fin

2. CLASSIC WINGED KEEL WITH TRIM TAB

Winged Fins

Trim Tab

Fixed Fin

Winged Fins extend at end of Bulb

3. CLASSIC KEEL WITH CANARD

Trim Tab

Fixed Fin

Moveable Canard

4. TANDEM KEEL WITHOUT RUDDER

Trim Tabs

Fixed Fins

A
D
F
I
J
10
K
4
9
8
16
14
G
12
7
6
13
15
17
J
11
K

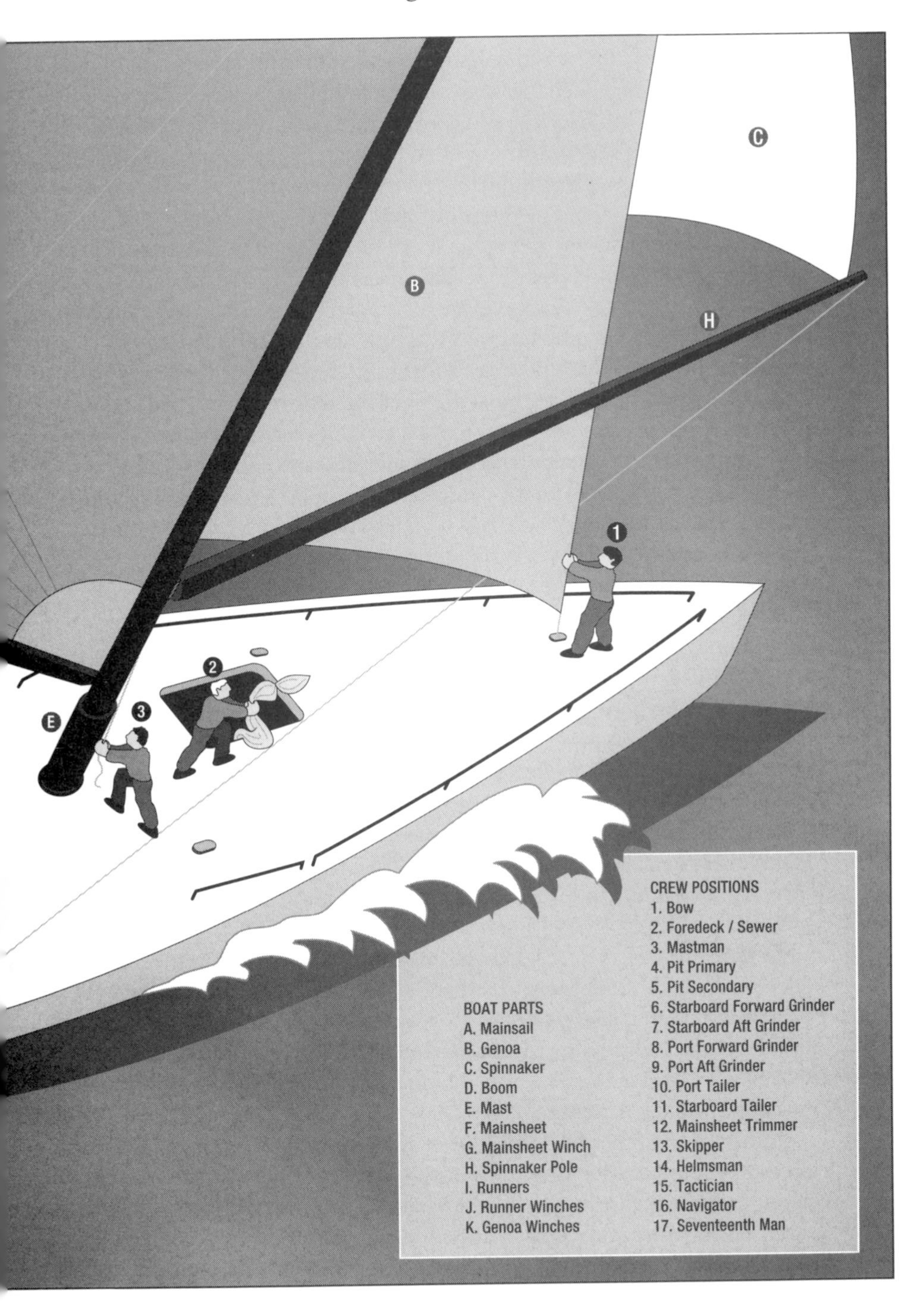
C
B
H
1
2
3
E
CREW POSITIONS
1. Bow
2. Foredeck / Sewer
3. Mastman
4. Pit Primary
5. Pit Secondary
6. Starboard Forward Grinder
7. Starboard Aft Grinder
8. Port Forward Grinder
9. Port Aft Grinder
10. Port Tailer
11. Starboard Tailer
12. Mainsheet Trimmer
13. Skipper
14. Helmsman
15. Tactician
16. Navigator
17. Seventeenth Man
BOAT PARTS
A. Mainsail
B. Genoa
C. Spinnaker
D. Boom
E. Mast
F. Mainsheet
G. Mainsheet Winch
H. Spinnaker Pole
I. Runners
J. Runner Winches
K. Genoa Winches

"I didn't know what he was doing, but I wanted to make sure he was doing it right." North suggested Meldner write a computer program that would rank four sails North had already tested on the water. Meldner did, scoring 100 percent. Intrigued, North suggested he try to design a faster sail. When Meldner did that too, North quickly gave him a contract.

By his count, Meldner has been involved with eleven different Cup syndicates since working on *Enterprise* in 1975-77. As part of the four-man design team that produced Tom Blackaller's radical *USA* for the 1987 America's Cup in Australia, he earned a reputation as something of a free thinker. *USA* was the only boat in Fremantle that did not have a real keel; instead, attached to the hull, was a torpedo-shaped mass of lead at the end of a thin aerofoil-shaped stem that provided righting moment. Two rudders provided lift to prevent the yacht from slipping sideways: a traditional steering rudder in the aft section and a bow foil measuring about six feet deep and two feet wide. This canard system showed moments of great potential, but Blackaller's late entry and lack of adequate funding prevented a true test. However, the theory was again put into practice in the 1992 Cup when several yachts used modified canard systems.

As America^3's technical director, Meldner's main mission was to come up with fast appendages, and to develop the best possible composite laminates and structures. He worked well with the people involved at the laboratory level, many of whom he knew from the weapons business. Hercules, Inc., is one example.

Hercules is a multibillion-dollar international company that makes rocket fuel, missile casings, advanced composite structures for satellites and aircraft, and is the largest supplier of carbon-fiber in the U.S. Meldner suggested that Hercules could build a hull that was lighter, stiffer, and stronger than any available. On his recommendation, *USA*-9 was built at Hercules, in Clearfield, Utah.

At the time, this was a closely-guarded secret. Many syndicate employees knew only the code word "Herbert" for the mystery location where the boat was under construction. Eric Goetz Custom Sailboats in Bristol, Rhode Island, built the molds for *USA*-9. Outsiders logically assumed that Goetz, who built *Matador^2*, was building the boat. That misinformation was reinforced by America^3.

Although the other boats were built at Goetz because Hercules was not accustomed to boat building methods, Koch felt the project was very successful because the Utah company did build all the masts, booms, and spinnaker poles, which proved to be the strongest spars in San Diego. Hercules was also instrumental in developing the technology for the materials used in fabricating the hull. Koch was after a breakthrough, and he understood the risks involved. America[3] got its lighter, stronger, stiffer boat, but not without headaches. Peter Wilson, manager of construction and engineering for America[3] yachts, said Hercules expected a foot-thick stack of drawings two months in advance for every element of the boat. The reality was a single sheet three days early if they were lucky. On some days, it was a pencil sketch on a wood scrap. It was the price of playing catch-up. Wilson found himself between two worlds on a collision course.

To an observer, the design and technical program seemed unwieldy. There were so many people and parts scattered across the country. As Milgram said, it was "design by committee, with no dissenters," meaning that ideally, agreement on all aspects should be sought. "It's like a cottage industry," Milgram said. "Sometimes it's difficult, sometimes it's not. You have to keep visiting the cottages. The best thing is that everyone is free to have input into everything. Toughest of all is communication."

Design team member Jim Taylor spoke of the diverse characters involved, and the egos. "Meetings were unusual. The team worked well. To me it was a testament to the guys who selected the people.

"Despite all the technical input, decisions were still made by two or three people. The technical side didn't try to force what the boat had to be. The whole idea was to try what might work, not what you know will work. This concept was a lot easier for Milgram than me. There aren't too many owners who are willing to risk their nickel. But Koch is a scientist in tune with the experimental method. He is a good communicator. He related to us, and that was critical.

"At our first design meeting I expected a Donald Trump character. Instead, Bill turned out to be an insightful, low-key guy. His penetrating questions had people scratching their heads. The guy at the top has a lot to do with the project all the way down the line. Bill had a group of individuals there, self-starters, and he was set up for that."

Don't Sink the Boat

As Koch said many times, "The whole idea behind experimenting is to leave as little to chance as possible. I expected mistakes, ideas that didn't work, differences of opinion, competition between our designers and scientists. To me, that's the environment most suitable to the creative process. I believe mistakes are good as long as you learn from them and don't sink the boat. But to learn from a mistake, you first have to admit you made it. If we didn't make mistakes, we weren't trying to improve."

And throughout the entire process, Koch would arrive periodically and push his team to come up with the swiftest boat. "A slow boat has never won the America's Cup," he would remind them.

Integrating the East/West factions of the design team presented what was sometimes a challenge given the differences in distances and personalities. San Diego designers Doug Peterson, John Reichel, and Jim Pugh often had different approaches to their work than the East Coast contingent. The hearty Pugh is the Rod Stephens (a legendary designer) of the group, the sailor who helps conceive boats, then brings them to potential once they are launched. Reichel is quiet, thoughtful, a talented naval architect. Peterson first drew boats in his grammar school text book margins. His innovative One-Tonners hit it big in the 1970s, and he has been a force in yacht design ever since. Until they went on their own in 1988, Reichel and Pugh worked for Peterson helping produce many successful boats.

By January, 1991, Eric Goetz had long since completed the molds for *USA*-9 and had begun those for *USA*-18. In a separate shed, Goetz's crew was building another large boat: *USA*-11 for Dennis Conner. It was a tribute to Goetz's capability that both American syndicates had gone to him for boats.

"With the IACC boats, we were pushing the envelope, learning amazing stuff," Goetz said. "It's chemistry. Put the wrong resins together and nothing will stick." The IACC boats are made with "pre-preg" carbon-fiber, meaning cloth already impregnated with resins. The cloth is applied to the structure, then baked in a huge oven. A temperature of 200 degrees (F) must be held for four hours. What to build was much more of an issue than how to build it. An ambitious, four-boat program had to be completed for America³ in one year. There were hard launch dates for each boat. Construction and engineering manager Peter Wilson used a software program to establish equally hard deadlines for ordering materials, and for completing stages of construction. With raw materials and products coming into Bristol and San Diego from all over the world — all of them custom-manufactured and produced, and with the Goetz operation going to a six-and-a-half day, two-shift work week for the first time ever, it was a frantic undertaking. The details were staggering. The pre-preg carbon-fiber came across country in refrigerator trucks and was stored in a freezer until used.

There were days when the tension was palpable. As Dr. Bill Unkel put it, "It fills life and goes beyond. No matter what else is going on, this project always wins. The deadlines are fierce. But it's a good group, everyone working his tail off. You have to rise to the challenge. Everyone else does." Unkel, a lecturer at M.I.T., is a software specialist who devised and wrote many of the programs for the *Matador* project. Now he was working full blast creating programs that could be used to collect data while sailing, then figuring out how to harness them into a complex, real-time telemetry network. If Koch needed an example to personify his "attitude" requirement, it was Unkel. A nonsailor, Unkel worked all night and caught naps during races. He soon became the head of the electronics, instrumentation, software and meteorology department.

Down the street from Goetz, at Hall Spars, Dirk Kramers, chief engineer of America³, was doing the engineering for the boats. Kramers' career includes stints at Huisman's yard in Holland, Minnefords on Long Island, and Hood Yacht Systems, where he worked with designers Buddy Duncan and Jim Taylor.

"So many people, so little time," Kramers said with a smile. He was collaborating with Steve Tsai, a leading composites expert from Stanford University, who was analyzing hull laminates. "But I'm spending a lot of time explaining the peculiarities of boats and where the loads are. The loads move around, of course. Two mediums [air, water] are involved, and waves. Burt Rutan says sailing is harder than flying. He says it's amazing that man learned how to sail first."

Moeyersoms had instructed Kramers to build a boat that "cracks, but doesn't break. We need to find the structural limits." Koch wanted to take chances on the first boat. "Koch says if we overbuild we won't learn anything," said Kramers. "But it's scary. We're looking for cracks, not catastrophes. The task is to run like hell toward the cliff and stop just before you go over — wearing a blindfold."

A peek at the tip of the design-and-technical-team iceberg made one wonder how Moeyersoms was coordinating this diverse, sometimes cantankerous group, numbering, in January, 1991, more than 50 people. "We have meetings every three weeks," Moeyersoms said. "The meetings clarify things. It's a global approach, totally open. We encourage people to stretch out and not worry about being wrong.

"There's no jealousy. Bill's approach is that we pay well, and in return America³ retains ownership of all the work, all designs. It costs more, but you can make more objective decisions. We still have people pressing for their ideas, and there's a little friction that occurs early on. But it doesn't last. It just takes awhile for people to feel their input means something.

"Bill is demanding, he expects the best, but he doesn't hold anything back that you need. And when you hit a road block, Bill is the one who will make the decision.

"Everyone is overworked. There isn't much time to communicate. I tell them, pick up the phone, no one is going to call you. Sometimes they don't do it. That's why the meetings help. But mainly we have to rely on people's initiative. Like that line of coach Bill Parcells: 'Expect nothing, do something, blame nobody.' There is no place here for guys who do nothing. It seems to be working. People quickly slip into a niche."

Leader of the overworked was Moeyersoms. It was rare to see him eat lunch sitting down. "He's key," Louis Cabot said of Moeyersoms. "He was at the heart of the *Matador²* program. He's very self-confident. He doesn't express a lot of strong opinions. Sometimes he's almost passive. But he has the presence and ability to clarify issues, direct discussions. He's creative. What he's doing is a remarkable feat."

"He's a great people person," Rick Wrightson said. "He understands what the designers and technical people are doing. You can't bullshit Vincent. I leapt into this project just to be able to work with him."

"There were lots of loose ends at first," Louis Cabot said. "Vincent stuck in there, put out the fires, got it organized so everyone played a role. He's definitely one of the heroes of this thing."

The overall list of design and technical programs carried out by America³ was staggering. Following is a list of these programs:

Design Tools
VPP improvements
CFD modification
Data analysis: Tank Testing — Wind Tunnel
Sailing Dynamometer:Sail Forces — Sail Shapes and Sizes
RMP design

Design
Hull: 75 designs
Appendages: 135 configurations
CFD modeling of appendages
Rating procedures
Optimization and modification of 4 boats
Modeling performance of competition

Technology
Composite Research: Materials — Laminates — Bonding
Scale Structural Testing: Keel fin — Mast Tube
"Cuben Fiber" — Sail material development

Engineering
Hull and Internal Structure — Low weight and high stiffness
Mast and Rigging design
Keel fin: Composite — Steel
Booms and Poles
FEA modeling:
Hull and Internal Structure — Keel fin
Mechanical systems: Steering — Tab — Kelp Cutter
Quality Control Program
Weight Monitoring Control Program

Full Scale Testing
256 days on the water — 1 & 2 boat testing of hulls, booms, masts, rudders, keel fins, bulbs, wings, trim tabs, and sails

Scale Testing
102 Tow Tank Tests
343 Wind Tunnel Tests

Sail Program
Design, engineer, build, test, and improve 250 sails: Mainsail, Genoas
Spinnakers — asymmetrical — symmetrical
Cuben Fiber sail cloth development
CFD modeling of shapes and parameters
Scale testing on sailing dynamometer — 10 upwind, 10 downwind sail configurations
Shape digitizing systems — Masthead Cameras: Real Time Offboat video
Optimum Sail Configuration Chart: Wind speed and angle dependent
Carbon fiber batten development

Construction
4 America's Cup boats (1 built at Hercules Aerospace, 3 built at Goetz Custom Sailboats)
8 115-ft Carbon IACC masts
9 Booms
12 Spinnaker poles
8 Rudders
9 Keel blades
15 Keel bulbs
8 Reaching struts
10 Trim tabs
1 Hull tooling for Hercules Aerospace
3 Mast mandrels
37 Tank models
132 Tunnel configurations
Real time temperature monitoring system
for boat cure cycle

Instrumentation
Electronics — Basic instrumentation on all boats
Software — Racing yachts performance and tactics: 2 boat testing
— Evaluation of competition
Telemetry of Data/Encryption
Meteorology:
— Daily forecasts
— Long term forecasts and climatology
— Correlations and projections
— Current measurements
Guzzini
"Gust Buster" — Electronic visualization of wind pattern
Keel video — Looking for kelp
Pre-race data collection at 4 corners of course
Communications — secure networks (wireless) for voice and data

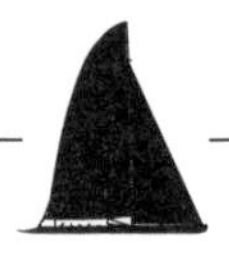

Corinthian Conversations

6

Money. For some 140 years, it has been as critical to success in the America's Cup as a fast boat or a clever skipper. The history of the event is as tied to finances as it is to weather conditions. In its earliest days, it relied upon the super wealthy of the world to build boats and mount crews. In fact, the boat for which the Cup is named, the famous schooner *America*, was built with money in mind — its owners hoped to make and win large wagers on her speed. The Cup's very first challenger was Englishman James Ashbury, whose father had made an enormous fortune in the railroad industry. Ashbury, a member of twelve different yacht clubs, amassed his own war chest to battle for the Cup and bankrolled the *Cambria* and *Livonia,* unsuccessful efforts of 1870 and 1871.

Since then the annals of Cup matches have been filled with names like J. Malcolm Forbes, the Earl of Dunraven, J.P. Morgan, Sir Thomas Lipton, Harold Vanderbilt, T.O.M. Sopwith, and Alan Bond, some of the world's wealthiest individuals. And while those same annals are filled with the legends of great seamanship and advanced technology, there is no argument that without these gentlemen's checkbooks their America's Cup syndicates could not have afforded the technology, crews, facilities, and support services needed to sustain a campaign. The simple fact is that the America's Cup is one of the costliest sports in the world and always has been. It takes money, big money, to play.

Over the decade leading to the 1992 match, both defender and challenger budgets had grown exponentially. For the 1983 Cup, it has been reported that the seven challengers and three defenders spent less than $18 million as compared to the more than $150 million budgeted for the 15 challengers and four defenders in 1986-87. In 1992, one syndicate alone, Il Moro di Venezia, is said to have spent more than $200 million.

Even with men of great wealth like Italy's Gardini and America's Koch, the 1992 America's Cup syndicates had to rely on several other sources for funds. For many past campaigns, syndicates relied on "gifts-in-kind" to supply them with everything from winches and sandpaper to shorts and shoes. While this helped defray expenses, it hardly took care of the mountain of bills that always accumulate in any Cup effort, even the ones that don't make it past the first few months of organizing.

What is needed and cherished most is cash, and until 1983 that was largely found in the form of large donations from individuals seeking tax deductions. During 1983's defense of the Cup, 18 U.S. companies paid $30,000 each for the right to use the America's Cup emblem in their advertising and promotion programs. By 1986, the focus was on corporate *giving*, with the emphasis on giving. "The America's Cup is a sport in transition. We are not a professional sport, but we're no longer amateur in the traditional sense because it has become so expensive. We need grassroots support, contributions of $5 and $10 in big numbers. But this isn't enough. We need the support of corporate America, and this sport has never had that before," said a project coordinator for one of the American syndicates.

At that time corporate America was having difficulty understanding how to leverage its investment. Sports marketing was not something new to either Madison Avenue or Wall Street, but what corporations were being offered by Cup marketers was.

Well aware of the astronomical costs of mounting what was now as much as a two-year sailing campaign complete with multiple boats, the event's organizers relaxed Rule 26, the international rule that somewhat prevented the display of logos on hulls and sails, for Fremantle. This infuriated the old guard, the Corinthians, who preferred their sport not go the way of the Indianapolis 500. But absent a Lipton or Vanderbilt in every camp, there simply was no other way to accommodate all those who wanted to win the America's Cup. So an experiment of sorts was suggested. As in everything political, a compromise was reached: no logos on boats in the actual races, but they could be used and photographed during practice.

It was one thing for a company to write a check to a tennis tournament and be able to see its logo beamed out across the world as John McEnroe cranked up a serve, but it was quite another thing to be told by sailors-in-suits that banners and billboards weren't allowed in this sport. Trying to explain to a CEO that his company's logo could fly on a spinnaker in practice and might catch a frame or two of a local television news spot, but it couldn't fly in the actual races seen by millions the world over just wasn't getting it done. More energy was spent inside boardrooms attempting to define Rule 26, than on what a particular syndicate had to offer.

However, enough corporate money flowed into Cup coffers in 1986-87 to convince the powers that be that allowing "tasteful" display of sponsor logos on boats, sails, appendages, booms, and clothing would make for closer competition in the fundraising wars. The 1988 Cup, known as the great mismatch between Conner's catamaran and Fay's monohull, was the first to see sponsor advertising on the actual racing yachts.

As Bill Koch wrote in his manifesto: "Before the America's Cup is a sailboat race, it is first a fundraising race." Syndicates around the world preparing for the 1992 Cup in San Diego learned that lesson quickly. Corporate headquarters from Madrid to Manhattan, Perth to Paris, were besieged with proposals and pin-striped promoters.

Koch's manifesto also stated that America^3 would be a Corinthian campaign. With a single stroke of his pen, he returned his syndicate to the days when the Cup was "clean." That didn't mean America^3 would not seek corporate contributions; far from it. What it did mean was that his fundraisers would have to come up with more enticing programs and offer more innovative results than the competition.

Koch was looking for approximately one third of the overall budget to come from sources outside his own pocket. To achieve this goal, the America^3 fundraising team concentrated on five specific programs: 1) Broad-based direct mail soliciting relatively small donations; 2) Corporate donations; 3) Individual, large donations solicited personally; 4) Retail sales with profits funneled to operations; and 5) Use of a syndicate newsletter to solicit donations of any type.

Shortly after the syndicate was formed, a development office was opened in Newport, Rhode Island. The initial projects completed from there were several sophisticated direct mail tests and the publication of the first issue of the *Voice of America^3*, the four-color newsletter that would serve as the syndicate's primary disseminator of information. As personnel changed and new staff was added, the office moved first to Herndon, Virginia and later to Fairfield, Connecticut. While the address may have changed, the major responsibilities of the office did not. Raising money and making sure all contributors were kept abreast of progress were priorities one and two.

David Rosow joined America^3 in late March, 1991. An aggressive businessman who took over the development of Stratton Mountain in Vermont, and who is currently in the golf business (course construction, equipment manufacture, senior tours), Rosow came on board as vice president of development, and as a director of the America^3 Foundation. In time, he was promoted to executive vice president and his responsibilities increased to the point where he effectively managed all of the non-sailing and technical operations. Rosow, Koch, and Moeyersoms became the senior management team of America[3]. David proved himself particularly valuable in negotiating with Team Dennis Conner and ACOC on a variety of issues. A Connecticut native, he is owner of *Springbok,* a race boat he campaigned in the 50-Foot Association. His wife, Jeanne, also joined the effort.

A $15 Million Goal

The goal of Rosow and his staff was to raise $15 million for the syndicate. His job description soon grew to include a variety of responsibilities including the handling of media relations, a sore point throughout the campaign. In the modern America's Cup game, the role of public relations is pivotal for a variety of reasons, chief of which is money. Presenting the right image is a key to fundraising. Corporate sponsors and individual donors want to be sure "their team" is well represented in the press and that they represent themselves well. Almost from the beginning, Koch and his different way of doing things — his emphasis on scientists, his "no rock stars" system, his Corinthian concept — all this flew in the face of the prevailing wisdom on how to run a successful America's Cup program.

From day one, Gary Jobson had been in charge of the media. This may have been Koch's greatest management mistake. On the face of it, no two philosophies could have been more different. Jobson is the embodiment of the sailing rock star — many think he invented the term, others think it was invented about him, and another faction thinks he invented it about himself. There is no one in the United States who has done more to bring the sport of sailing to the attention of the general public than Gary Jobson. But his detractors claim it was all done more to promote Gary than to promote sailing. This is the knock he received at America[3]. Here was Koch preaching "team" while his chief disciple was spreading, at least in the eyes of many within the syndicate, the Gary Gospel.

Jobson also represented the traditional approach to winning the Cup. Hire the best designers, they'll draw a fast boat. Hire the best sailors, they'll make it even faster. Boat owners stay on land or sit in the back and watch the real sailors work. One can only wonder what he thought of Koch's "no ego but the ego of the boat" dictum. One wonders what he thought when Koch poured so much money, time, and effort into the scientific method. If Koch wanted someone to sell his plan to the press and public, one wonders how he could have selected the sport's quintessential self-promoter.

By the time Rosow took over the PR program, a bunker mentality had set in. The demands of the press were interfering with both sailing practice and the operation of the syndicate. The media was distracting the team from their focus on winning. They had clobbered Koch, his ideas, his program, and his admittedly poor performance in the Worlds to the point that whenever someone showed up with a pen, microphone or camera, America³ members dove for cover. Rosow surveyed the situation and saw that the press was not exactly helping the cause, so he favored the implementation of a closed-ranks strategy. Simply put, since the press isn't cooperating with us, why cooperate with them. The compound became off-limits to almost everyone with a press card, which only served to infuriate members of the fifth estate to the point of generating even more bad press.

As Rosow's responsibilities grew in other areas of the campaign, he eventually passed the PR job on to Will Robinson in April, 1992. Robinson had been a television news director in Los Angeles and is generally considered to have salvaged something of a better image for Koch and the "technology nerds" the press loved to jump on. He figured that since the closed-camp strategy didn't work, maybe an open-the-doors-and-windows one would.

When Rosow came aboard, Wrightson was in the middle of establishing the syndicate's elaborate security system program — no small task. As with all the syndicates, security was a high priority for many reasons, chief of which was to make sure the boats were kept safe throughout the campaign. Wrightson had fulfilled many administrative duties for Koch in the past and today continues to help run the America³ Foundation.

Aiding Rosow, Wrightson, and Koch on the finance side was Brad Robinson. Robinson had a similar position within Koch's Oxbow Corporation and he expressed interest in working with the America's Cup team. Koch's offer included responsibilities similar to his job at Oxbow, but Koch told him when the Cup was over, he couldn't guarantee him his corporate position would still be available. Robinson decided to take the chance because he liked what he saw at America³, and it is a measure of his competence that when the campaign was over, Koch asked him to return to Oxbow.

With the move west of more and more of the America³ team, the offices on the compound filled quickly. Wrightson and Lessard, the duo that oversaw the acquisition of the old Bay City Marina site, now were charged with finding more space. Activity at the compound itself was frenetic, 18-hour days were the norm, and in those early days it seemed that every airplane that landed in the Southern Californian city brought more bodies eager to help the effort.

By now Wrightson and Lessard knew their way around San Diego real estate and regulations, and obtaining a floor in a nearby office building seemed like child's play compared to their earlier compound controversies. The new offices housed staff working on development, public relations, administration, and accounting.

When the offices were acquired there was less than a month until the

IACC World Championship. This event, held in the waters off San Diego in May, 1991 was primarily designed to showcase the new class of racing yachts and to give some indication of the progress made by the different Cup contenders. It was also a prime reason to fly in potential sponsors for some subtle arm twisting.

At America³, arriving guests meant housing and food and spectator boats. The development team worked on invitations and catering and chartering boats in those weeks leading to the Worlds. The direct mail solicitations continued and the marketing program for corporate donations was almost in place, but the emphasis now was on the upcoming competition. If America³ could draw the right corporate and private individuals to San Diego and then put on a good enough show, chances of building the bankroll would be greatly increased.

It was perhaps the first sign of potential success for the syndicate that on the first day of the Worlds the America³ docks were filled with spectators and lined with enough boats to accommodate all of them. The first big challenge to the shoreside team was met without a hitch. On the water, the racing yachts didn't fare as well.

While Bill Koch's Corinthian approach may have kept a number of the more aggressive sports-minded companies from coming aboard, certain aspects of the campaign, stressed by the marketing team, clearly appealed to others. America³ positioned itself as a rookie effort, an underdog, while aligning itself with the spectacle of the oldest continuous sports competition on Earth. Companies looking to associate themselves with the event in a more low-key manner than other syndicates were offering became America³ targets. And always, always, the advanced technology the syndicate was built around and identified with in the press was stressed.

One of the first forays into corporate boardrooms was made in the Maynard, Massachusetts, headquarters of the Digital Equipment Corporation, the second largest computer manufacturer in the country next to IBM. Rick Wrightson headed a team of Dr. Jerry Milgram and Dr. Bill Unkel that executed a well-conceived plan that highlighted the many similarities between the two high-tech organizations. There was much at Digital that promised success for the young syndicate. Koch admired the company's founder, Ken Olsen, and often quoted the scientist and businessman to his America³ team. Also, Koch and Olsen both graduated from M.I.T., where Milgram was currently one of the better known professors. The M.I.T./America's Cup connection was further strengthened by the fact that Nathanael Herreshoff, designer of more Cup victors (six, from 1893 to 1920) than any other designer, was also a M.I.T. graduate.

The obvious appeal, beyond old school ties, was technology. Milgram, who had used computers to his design advantage for a number of years, and Unkel, who headed the syndicate's instrumentation team, presented a convincing plan of how DEC's equipment and resources would, yes, interface with America³. Digital's Ralph Dormitzer was intrigued by what he heard and he secured approval from Olsen and two vice-presidents, Jack Smith and Dom LaCava. Dormitzer worked closely with the design and technical teams at America³ and became the chief liaison between the syndicate and DEC as the company provided nine DEC 3000 and 5000 workstations that were used on site by the designers for VPPs, race modeling, computational fluid dynamics, and finite element analysis.

DEC also donated a number of 386 and 486 personal computers, laptops, and printers (laser and color) which were used by syndicate staff members in all phases of the campaign. Priority access to Digital's VAX9000 supercomputer at M.I.T. also proved to be enormously beneficial. This system enabled the designers and engineers to log in from wherever they were working and run fast, advanced calculations and modeling. Digital also lent technical support for several new technologies such as voice recognition used in certain security applications. The company also provided one of the most indispensable elements of the campaign — cash.

Technicians and Technology

In return, DEC made good use of the America³ Foundation's available talent, enlisting Milgram, Unkel, Meldner, Moeyersoms and members of the sailing team to speak at corporate functions. America³ was the centerpiece of the company's "DEC World" trade show, where *Jayhawk* was displayed. The idea was to show employees, dealers, distributors, and retailers how the company's products and resources were being used in real world situations. These were exciting applications of DEC technology and the sailors and scientists were impressive in front of large groups. But perhaps nothing matched the excitement a group of twenty DEC guests experienced the day they sailed aboard one of the America³ boats and witnessed a dismasting. The group proved as stalwart as the sailors when they all gathered the next morning for another day on the water.

America³ next approached Chevrolet. The huge car and truck manufacturer had already expressed interest in the Cup and had assembled a task force to investigate potential opportunities. What appealed to Digital Equipment Corporation also appealed to Chevrolet — the shared interest in advanced technology. There was also the possible scenario of a United States versus Japan final, a battle quite familiar to the American car maker and one which had the marketing and promotion people scurrying to their thesauruses searching for superlatives.

Chevrolet General Manager Jim Perkins, Manager of Sales Promotions Mike Valerio, and Assistant Manager of Passenger Car Advertising Lew Eades worked with the America^3 team for more than a year. During that time, the company shipped 22 cars and trucks, including Corvettes, Suburbans, and Blazers to San Diego enabling the sailors to transport themselves and their mountains of gear around the city. Despite elaborate security precautions, the syndicate soon discovered the Suburban was a favorite item in Mexico and several were stolen.

A "Corvette Cup" Regatta was organized and Corvette management used it as a dealer motivation program in which the top 100 Chevrolet dealers were sent to San Diego in November where they sailed on board America^3 boats with the Cup sailors. Both groups considered the promotion a huge success. Corvette sold a lot of cars. America^3 received sponsorship dollars and high-profile exposure along side "America's sportscar."

With the Worlds completed, the fundraising emphasis turned to special events held in cities like Fort Lauderdale, Dallas, Chicago, Osterville, Boston, Long Beach, New York, and San Diego. The usual program was a cocktail party and dinner, then an address from Bill Koch or one of the America^3 Foundation's board members bringing guests up-to-date on the progress of the team. This was usually followed by footage from a film well-known sailing photographer and videographer Phil Uhl was shooting on the syndicate. These events were key to the overall fundraising drive and were quite successful in securing support.

As Rosow and Wrightson continued knocking on corporate doors, the direct mail and Voice of America^3 programs were generating individual donations ranging from \$10 to \$100,000. More than 35,000 people contributed. A matching gifts program, called the "Corinthian Fund," was established to equal all individual donations of \$25 to \$100. Founding contributor Mrs. Frances Morss had been an avid sailor since the age of three and a devoted supporter of the America's Cup since 1930.

The gifts-in-kind program was also growing quickly. Almost every issue of the Foundation's newsletter announced new companies joining the campaign. Before the final race was over in May, 1992, dozens of companies had provided a myriad of supplies and services.

What the America's Cup represented to the Adolph Coors Corporation was sun and fun — young, athletic people pursuing a goal on the water. The image tied in with their general marketing plan and they aligned their Coors Light product with America^3. In addition to cash, the company supplied bottles and cans and kegs for use at many of the social functions sponsored by the syndicate. They also set up an 800 number soliciting contributions for America^3.

Coors leveraged their sponsorship by using America^3 boats and sailors in a 30-second television commercial. Members of the sailing, coaching, and maintenance teams were selected by the commercial's director. Used to long days on the water or in the compound, the "actors" spent hours in front of the cameras as take after take was made. The work was grueling, but when televised, the ad was beneficial to both Coors and America^3.

By August, 1991, having considered proposals from both America^3 and Team Dennis Conner, Polo/Ralph Lauren decided to become a sponsor of America^3. Soon the entire team was outfitted with blazers, pants, shirts, sweaters, sweatshirts, shorts, hats and jackets. Like Coors, Polo decided to use the sailing theme in their advertising and the company sent fashion photographer Bruce Weber, known for his Calvin Klein ads, to San Diego. The America^3 ad was seen in dozens of publications and ran for almost a year.

The Hercules Corporation in Clearfield, Utah, is a leader in the manufacturing of carbon-fiber and composite structures. The technical team at America^3 suggested the use of their facilities and expertise early in the campaign, and negotiations between the two groups centered around the building of *Jayhawk* (US-9). Hercules donated much of their time and materials, and were considered among the most important corporate donors.

During a year of continuous corporate solicitation, many marketing, advertising, financial, and chief operating officers from companies as disparate as banks and ice cream manufacturers considered proposals from the America^3 Foundation. Some gave immediate rejections, a few gave immediate acceptances, some came back with counter proposals, and some negotiated ad infinitum. In the end, AT&T, Motorola, *Newsweek* magazine, Chase Manhattan Bank, *Yachting* magazine, and Mount Gay Rum joined the other corporations that had made substantial cash and product gifts.

"We set a goal of raising $15 million in the very beginning," says Bill Koch. "I knew our Corinthian approach was different from everyone else, but I thought we could turn that to our advantage. Some companies liked the idea of seeing their name all over spinnakers and hulls. Others, the ones who came on board America^3, appreciated what we had to offer. Other syndicates, defenders and challengers, spent a lot of time telling companies what they could and would do for them. We told potential donors who we were, what we believed in, what we were doing, and how we were going to do it. If that fit in with their idea of the America's Cup or their own philosophies and marketing approaches, all the better. In the end, the companies that agreed to support us all walked away very happy they had done so. I don't think that has ever happened before — that all sponsors were pleased with what they got out of their involvement with the America's Cup."

The $15 million goal was almost met. By the time the books closed on America's Cup 1992, the America³ Foundation had received checks from more than 35,000 individuals. Corporate sponsors made up the difference.

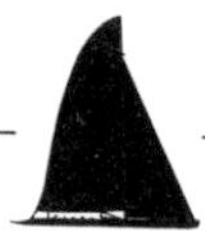

Everything But the Bullets

7

Activity at 4960 North Harbor Drive became frantic as the May 4 date for the IACC World Championships approached. The compound was by no means finished, but on April 20, when *Jayhawk* arrived by truck from Utah, it was functioning. The security system, including 16 television cameras that covered the perimeter of the compound, was in place, complete with a staff of 13 security officers who were on duty 24 hours. Passes bore photographs. They were color coded for access to various areas, and required. No pass, no entry, no matter who you were.

America³ won "best supporting celebrity couple" with the arrival of Ted Turner and his fiancee Jane Fonda. Ted sailed as America³'s first 17th man on *Jayhawk* in the practice race. Jane spent the day on *Firewater*, the syndicate's command vessel. After the race, coach Fuzz Spanhake, a New Zealander, picked up Ms. Fonda in the rubber boat to escort her to *Jayhawk* for the sail in. Having been told Fonda was a film actress of some note, Spanhake dutifully asked if he might have seen one of her films. Fonda began naming them, from *Klute* and *On Golden Pond* all the way back to *Barbarella*. Fuzz kept shaking his head. In desperation, Fonda finally told Fuzz she had also done a workout video. Fuzz brightened. That he'd seen.

For many business enterprises, the start-up phase can easily take three years. America³'s planned life expectancy was only 20 months, so it made sense that Phase Two began just nine months after start-up. It might have begun even earlier, but the all-consuming pressure to be ready for the IACC World Championship had suppressed a number of issues that needed attention. Chief among them was the role of Gary Jobson.

As co-skipper, Jobson was head of the sailing team program, medical/fitness program, public relations, publications and video production, and was listed as one of five vice-presidents of the syndicate. He was the syndicate's major spokesman, and he was an integral part of fundraising and sponsorship. But from January, 1991, when the team assembled in San Diego, Jobson and Koch developed a few fundamental disagreements about policy that began to fester. Perhaps the problems related back to when Jobson imagined he would be skipper and Koch would be 17th man.

Jobson's disagreement was three-fold. It had to do with naming a first-string crew; selecting a permanent afterguard; and determining a helmsman. The latter specifically meant how much Koch would steer the boat. This was an issue that became a regular media story that continued throughout the campaign and threatened to disrupt the America^3 sailing team on a number of occasions.

While the media played up the steering issue and the date of defender Trials loomed ever closer, Jobson became more insistent on obtaining a clear statement on his three issues. By contrast, Koch had a hard time understanding Gary's problems. His view was that he'd made as clear a statement as could be made on all three questions in his manifesto, written before the campaign even began. He'd repeated his stance a number of times in crew meetings, and once again during the Worlds, said "I will remove all politics from the crew selection. I'll select the crew myself, based on two criteria: attitude and teamwork." And Jobson, who had sailed with him for seven years, knew the Kansan's stubborn adherence to his philosophy.

As tension built between the two dynamic personalities, crew members were almost forced to take sides. The entire situation came to a head when Koch received a call from one of the syndicate's directors, who said several of the crew had called him to say Jobson was lobbying for support among several key sailors to get them to commit to leaving America^3 if he, Gary, quit.

With all this swirling around them, Koch, Jobson, and the crew attempted to prepare for the Worlds. Koch faced a personal dilemma that tested his strength as the syndicate's leader. On the one hand he had been preaching, since writing his manifesto in September 1990, the importance of teamwork, that America^3 would not be built around any one individual. On the other hand, he had enormous respect for Jobson and considered him a close friend. Also weighing on his mind was what a Jobson resignation or dismissal might do to the whole program. He sensed that resolving the "Gary issue" might be one of the most critical acts of the entire campaign. And it proved to be just that.

If the Worlds had been more successful for America^3, the situation might have cured itself. But success was not in the cards. *Jayhawk*, built at Hercules in Utah and shipped to San Diego in kit form, arrived on April 20, just 12 days before the first practice race of the Worlds. By the time the boat was assembled, fitted with keel and spars, and measured, the crew had one sailing day prior to the practice races.

The day of Race 1 was atypical for San Diego — 15 to 18 knots of wind over sloppy seas. Breakage across the fleet was estimated at considerably more than $1 million, including the dismasting of Japan's *Nippon-6*. *Jayhawk* retired with hydraulic and genoa track problems.

The carnage on the course led to one of Koch's most-quoted remarks. When asked for his reaction to the IACC boats, Koch said he thought the people who came up with the rule to which the boats' design had to comply, were "idiots." What bothered him was the fragility of the boat (many Cup observers speculated the boats could never have been used in the conditions off Fremantle, Australia) and the extreme costs involved in design, testing, building, and replacing equipment.

Other opinions were voiced at the press conference, several in support of the new boats. Chris Dickson, the New Zealander who was sailing for the Japanese and collecting a pot full of yen, pointed out, "Only the best sailors should be out there. These boats are like Formula One race cars. An amateur should not drive one."

Koch, obviously the target of the remark, bristled at the intended slight. In response to a reporter's query for a reply, Bill said, "I am an anachronism out here. I'm not a hired gun." Koch's term stuck, and throughout the competition the phrase "hired gun" would be leveled against both Dickson and the American turned Italian, Paul Cayard. The idea of selling out your country for money incensed Koch.

The highlight of the regatta for America³ was *Jayhawk*'s victory in Race 3. Jobson was the starting helmsman and he hit the line in good position just as the gun went off. Koch was steering on the seventh (weather) leg when he ground down *Nippon-6* during an impressive display of pure boat speed. On the final leg, the America³ team passed New Zealand for the win.

Other than that race, there was little to cheer about. The victory was not enough for *Jayhawk* to emerge from the fleet-racing part of the Worlds to enter the match racing phase in which only the top four boats participated. *Jayhawk* ended up sixth out of nine boats and *USA-2*, the former French yacht, was next to last.

As expected, two of the best-prepared foreign teams — New Zealand and Italy — finished one-two-four (Italy's second boat was fourth). Japan's three-boat program finished out of the money. The surprise was *Stars & Stripes* (*S&S*), Team Dennis Conner's recently launched new boat. Conner looked good on the starting line, and fast upwind. *S&S* was first four times at the weather mark. But the Team Dennis Conner (TDC) boat suffered from a shopworn sail inventory, and a tight budget. For that reason, although *S&S* finished third in the series, TDC dropped out of the finals to save wear and tear on what might be its only boat.

TDC's withdrawal elevated *Nippon* into the finals. *Nippon* finished fourth after *Il Moro di Venezia* (15); *New Zealand* (12); and *Il Moro di Venezia* (1).

A World of Trouble

Koch's reaction was subdued, but determined: "The Worlds were a really bad experience for us. The boat broke a lot, and there was no time to fix it. People were discouraged. The direction of the design program was in question. And the enormity of the budget hit me for the first time. It was going to cost three, maybe four times more than we projected. The low point for us came right after the Worlds. The publicity we suffered as a result of crew and boat problems made it look like a disaster. In the end, being such a severe underdog was very beneficial to our effort. But at the time it was very difficult."

The poor performance had another repercussion as well. Even before Koch officially announced he was entering the America's Cup, members of ACOC and the Defense Committee began to talk privately about a future merger between Dennis Conner and Bill Koch. From the beginning, no one really believed a first time Cup effort, mounted by a guy who only began sailing eight years ago, had any kind of chance. Especially against Dennis. But what Koch discovered later was that Malin Burnham, president of ACOC and Dennis booster number one, believed that the only way to keep the Cup in San Diego was to have Bill join the fray, get his nose bloodied in battle by Dennis a few times, and then when he was softened up enough, he'd be ready for a merger with the Californian.

It seemed to be a winning scenario. The world's greatest helmsman teamed with one of the world's wealthiest men. Who could beat that? And when things looked so grim at the end of the Worlds, Burnham and ACOC increased the pressure on Koch, both privately and in the press, to merge with Conner. "It's the only way to keep the Cup...do it for your country...it would be an unbeatable team...."

Koch saw such a plan as more disruptive than productive. "We would have spent more time and effort on merging the two philosophies and the two cultures than on actually training to win the Cup," he would say later. But as the pressure increased, Koch and his team felt they were being forced to answer the growing pressure. Privately, Koch let Burnham know he had no interest in a merger. Right or wrong, he would continue his own campaign. The refusal caused a small rift between the two and later, when ACOC continued to press for a merger and disparaged Bill's sailing abilities in the press, Koch counter-attacked by accusing the organizers of mismanagement, a charge that was already being argued in the press and one that was substantiated by a river of red ink across the financial books even before the event was concluded.

Koch respected Burnham and wished no ill will to grow from his decision, but a merger would go against everything he had told his team from day one. While the public and private sniping from both sides never escalated into much more than a mild battle of words, Koch moved to end the friction by sending Burnham the book *Evolution of Cooperation*, and offering a truce, which was accepted.

Another incident during the Worlds helped define Koch's approach to personnel questions. The French boat, which was the first one in camp and by far the slowest, quickly earned the nickname "The Scud" because of its inherent resemblance to Sadam Hussein's wildly inaccurate, impetuous, and erratic guided missile. Clearly outclassed, the boat really had no business in the Worlds, but Koch thought his team should get race experience, and he saw an opportunity for attitude evaluation as well.

With a few exceptions, the Scud crew raced with high spirits and a vengeance. Their starts were excellent, their crew work was superb. The boat took on amazing quantities of water, and there was no pump on board, which slowed them even more. Their motto was based on what they called Scud technology: "If there's a lighter, better, faster way, we're not interested." The culmination of their efforts was a fourth in one race.

"A fourth!" exclaimed Scud crewmen Bob Billingham. "Can you believe that? Scud getting a fourth? What a crew, what a team, what incredible spirit!"

Koch placed Buddy Melges and John Kostecki on the yacht, later admitting this was solely "an attitude test." Kostecki is one of the top sailors in the country, the winner of six world championships in J-24s, Solings, 6-Meters, and Sunfish, as well as the Silver Medal in Solings in the 1988 Olympics.

"Buddy performed exceptionally well," says Koch. "Didn't whine, didn't complain, just did the best he could. Kostecki was just the opposite. He wanted off the Scud and on *Jayhawk*. He said he should be allowed to steer more. It was an attitude test and Buddy won. During my talks to the team, I told them that no one was indispensable, including me."

Following the Worlds, the "Gary issue" came to the fore. For several weeks in June, Koch and Jobson discussed their disagreements at length. Koch continued to be baffled by Jobson's reluctance to accept his philosophy, a philosophy that had been written before the campaign began and was reiterated almost daily. He sensed a crisis was near, one that would bring his entire management approach into question and potentially destroy everything that had been accomplished to date. His handling of the situation may have been the most crucial reaction of the entire campaign.

Koch and Jobson took several long walks together during which they attempted to work things out. Koch believed Gary was becoming increasingly depressed and he attempted to bolster him up. "I'd been through so many situations with him that I knew one of his greatest weaknesses is mental toughness. He is a great sailor, yet in tough situations, Gary tends to give up. It was one of my jobs on *Matador* to boost him up whenever he got down. I mistakenly thought he was just going through one of his regular downs. I had no idea he was plotting a crew revolt."

As the two men began to drift further apart, several incidents occurred that forced Bill to come to a final decision about Gary. During a conversation with John Kostecki about the steering issue, Koch was told Kostecki understood his reasoning, but "I just wish I had talked to you first. Gary didn't tell me the full story." Koch noted the comment to himself, but it would resurface within the next several days.

Koch then found out that during the Worlds, Jobson had leaked inside information to the press which was meant to discredit Bill's sailing abilities and put pressure on him to get off the boat.

Next, Gary had arranged for Ted Turner to bring several state governors to visit the America^3 compound, where they were feted at a reception, all without Bill's knowledge. This was followed by Gary's giving ESPN permission to fly a logo-emblazoned spinnaker on the boat, free of charge — this in the face of the syndicate's strict "no advertising" dictum. Bill claims that he was never consulted about this action, although Gary disputes that claim. Later, it came out that at the same time Gary was negotiating a contract to be an on-air commentator for ESPN.

"I went ballistic," admits Koch. "It was clear Gary had his own agenda."

Koch left immediately to keep a long-planned reunion with his son Wyatt in Boston, but as he flew across the country, he agonized over the situation. When he landed, he received a phone call from Bob Chilton, the syndicate's vice-chairman, during which he was told that several members of the crew had told Chilton that if Gary quit, all the best sailors would quit with him. Koch asked him who would leave, but Chilton refused to say. "Thanks for your loyalty," Koch replied sardonically.

The next day chairman Louis Cabot called to say he'd also heard from Chilton and following that call, he'd done a little investigating on his own. "It seems," said Cabot, "that when Gary was recruiting these guys, he told them, 'don't worry about Bill Koch. He'll be off the boat before the trials start.'"

The news stunned Koch. He felt betrayed. If anyone should understand how he ran a team, how he managed people, it was Gary Jobson. He thought of Gary as a close friend. The two had sailed thousands of miles together, shared many a laugh, toasted each other a hundred times. If there was one man more responsible than any other for getting Bill Koch into the 1992 America's Cup, it was Gary Jobson.

Koch needed to talk to someone who might make some sense of all this. He met for a drink with his friend Bob Leach, the sports doctor, and told him his story. Leach replied that he saw the situation as an obvious attempt by Gary to increase his responsibilities within the syndicate. He told Bill he thought the timing was particularly bad, that if he was to try a power play, he would have done it just before the Finals, when Bill wouldn't have had much recourse.

Meaner Than a Junk-Yard Dog

On Saturday, June 24, Koch called Gary from Boston and asked him who had authorized the ESPN spinnaker and the CNN governors' visit. Jobson remained silent. Koch said, "Gary, I'm sorry, but I'm going to be meaner than a junk-yard dog when it comes to winning the America's Cup." He told him there is no I in the spelling of team and he said he'd meet with him first thing Monday in San Diego.

Seeing the handwriting on the wall, Jobson decided to jump before he was pushed. On Sunday, he spent the day calling people in the media and explaining he was "quitting" the campaign because he and Koch no longer saw eye to eye on the important issues.

Finally, on June 26, Koch, not knowing Jobson had already resigned to the press, asked Jobson to resign graciously. Their final interview was tinged with sadness. While Koch felt betrayed and he still did not fully understand Jobson's actions, it was important to him the two not part enemies, but as friends.

"I'm here because I love the sport and because I believe we can win the America's Cup if we follow the principles set out in our manifesto. I also believe you love the sport, but I think you could serve it best by leaving and returning to ESPN. It seems to me you don't like the way I'm running our program, but I'm not going to change it for you or anyone else. You want to be skipper and steer the boat. I've made it clear that isn't going to happen, so I think it best we split now. We'll agree to say nothing bad about you; you agree to say nothing bad about us. You didn't resign, you weren't fired. You simply found a better opportunity."

Jobson raised no argument. He stood, offered his hand, and said, "Good-bye, Bill."

Koch had offered him a six-figure severance check, and asked that he agree that neither party would publicly say anything negative about the other. Initially Gary agreed, but when he was asked to sign a written agreement to that effect, he refused.

As expected, the press buzzed with this news following Gary's call the night before. "Bill wants to do things his way," Jobson told *The New York Times*'s Barbara Lloyd. "He wants to decide the makeup of the team and the afterguard. I felt it better that I step aside if I can't do that."

Koch told *USA Today*, "I regret Gary leaving very much, he's a talented guy. (But) he wanted to select the afterguard, and I'm going to select the afterguard. That's what it boils down to."

Privately, Koch was disappointed and puzzled. "I was shocked Gary thought he could take over. He had sailed on *Matador²* long enough to know my style, to know how stubborn I am, to know that I have the deciding vote in this syndicate."

To further complicate matters, helmsman Buddy Melges was hospitalized for back surgery shortly after the Worlds. The prognosis was that Melges would be out of the lineup for 6 to 12 weeks. On June 27, *USA Today* headlined, "America³ owner nearly alone as team dwindles."

The embattled Koch was gamely philosophical in remarks to his crew. He was sticking to his guns, and there was comfort in that. "Gary put a great deal of emphasis on PR. We no longer will. A good article in a magazine does not win the race; only good performance does. We make no apologies. We have learned a tremendous amount to this point about design, the other boats, what crew performance has to be, how to handle and race the boats, and how late I can stay up and still be effective the next day. The time to break gear and make mistakes is right now. We'll learn from the mistakes and not make 'em again. Hey guys, this is good news. We now know what we have to do to win the Cup."

Privately he was grim. "The Cup is three times bigger than I thought, and three times nastier. This isn't a sailboat race or even a sporting event. It's more like a war, with everything but the bullets." After a pause he added: "But in war, it's winning the last battle that counts."

There was speculation fueled by Louis Cabot and David Rosow about the effect Jobson's departure would have on the sailing team. After the Worlds the team had a two-week break. Would everyone return? Would anyone return?

On the day that Jobson left, the crew still in San Diego met to discuss the situation. In less than 10 minutes they decided to support Bill Koch. Crew who were on vacation were called and informed of the decision.

"There was no mass defection. In fact there wasn't one defection," Bill

Campbell said. Campbell is close to Jobson. The two grew up together in Toms River, New Jersey, competing in a variety of boats. Campbell is a cool helmsman with a good tactical sense. He's also a dedicated team player with solid self-possession. As he said at one point, "My role is being reliable, dependable, and ready to be wherever I'm needed." That wasn't just talk. The day after Jobson left he had gone to Koch and offered to manage the sailing team. Koch accepted the offer.

Campbell was recruited by Jobson for the 1983 *Defender/Courageous* campaign. The two have sailed a lot of miles together. Now the backup guy was standing in for the star, and in this case the effect was calming. "Gary knew how to do the job. Now we're learning it," Campbell said, implying a bit more delegation in the scenario. "The new boat is coming, the designers are here...I would say the crew is very upbeat. Continuity is being maintained. We are not going to fold up because we lost a key guy. Everyone seems to feel, 'I can do this.'"

Koch spoke with each member of the crew the morning after Jobson left. "He asked me if I had a problem," main trimmer assistant Bob Billingham said. "He was concerned. He was straightforward, up front about the whole situation. I was touched by his directness and confidence. It was a confidence I hadn't seen. He wasn't the least bit nervous or insecure. I thought, he's not worried about Jobson leaving at all. He looked me in the face and asked if I was still on. I said I was."

There was definitely more delegation, more leadership surfacing. Some of those picking up the pieces were mast man Mike Hein, a former *Matador* crewman, who had spent many weeks at Goetz on the construction end; bow man Jerry Kirby, whose positive outlook never faltered, and whose carpentry skills had made him valuable during compound outfitting; mast man Peter Craig, who had taken on the crew scheduling task and, of course, Buddy Melges, who came out of the hospital with new direction.

"The stint in the hospital gave me an opportunity to assess the situation," Melges said. "My lay-up was good timing, because after the Worlds I was out of the loop. If pressed, I would have had to support Gary. We only had a year left. I didn't think that was sufficient time to build to the level we needed to reach. Bill came to visit me in the hospital. He asked if I would stick with him. I said yes. I was surprised I said that. My recuperation gave me time to look things over before I started sailing again."

During his relatively short, somewhat miraculous recuperation from surgery to correct a very bad spinal problem, Melges went on a one-man coaching and pump-up spree among the crew. Every day Buddy was seen talking with various groups about problems and situations; teaching, telling jokes, and being cheerful. Speaking after dinner, Melges can be very entertaining. On the America[3] docks, he was inspirational.

"Buddy was an angry guy early on," Louis Cabot said. "He liked to bitch. There was a lot we all had to be patient about."

Now Melges was thinking positively, especially on the matter of steering, an area where he had a vested interest. "I think we need to give Bill as much time as possible on the helm," Melges said, "make him the best sailor possible, so when he gets in a shit fight he'll know when to get help.

"Gary tried it one way," Buddy said, "letting Bill go it on his own. Now we'll try it another." It was the beginning of an afterguard marriage between Buddy and Bill Koch that would go the distance. Like many marriages, it would have moments when the crockery flew. But the growth curve that makes successful marriages work would sustain.

Melges has just the right mix of sailing skill, maturity, patience, country humor, charisma, foxy political acumen, and toughness for his role. He could lay criticism on Koch and Koch would listen. "Some of your tacks really sucked yesterday," Melges said at one morning meeting. "I thought you were going to tear the gudgeons off the damn boat." Buddy admitted that the timing of such a fusillade was important. But criticism was part of the job, if only to give credence to praise.

Credit Koch for learning to take it. It had to be tough stuff for a man used to doing whatever he wants, whenever he wants. Koch said once that people deferring to him was a terrible problem; that deference was such a negative, self-destructive way to proceed. A measure of Koch's continuing maturity throughout the campaign was that he recognized the diversity of opinions from the ever-growing number of people joining the team and he encouraged all individuals to speak their minds.

One individual who did speak his mind, unfortunately did so during a night of partying at the Worlds Ball, where the liquor flowed freely. Bob Chilton revealed to Richard Callahan, an America[3] board member, that he believed Bill Koch had no business sailing on the boat. Callahan, an attorney for Koch's Oxbow Corporation and a personal friend of the skipper's for more than a decade, said simply: "You must not know Bill very well."

Chilton's comment was indicative of his growing dissatisfaction with the way the syndicate was being administered, and with his alliance to the Jobson train of thought. Earlier, Chilton had suggested he manage the syndicate. Koch heard the same suggestion from Geoff Mason, David Lowry, David Rosow, and Brodie Cobb. All used the same argument: Bill needs help managing so he can spend time sailing. Koch believed just the opposite: he needed to be on board so he could more effectively manage.

Boardroom battles, corporate restructurings, grabs for power were nothing new to Koch and such situations within America^3 actually confirmed his belief that managing an America's Cup syndicate wasn't much different from managing a business.

Although no sailors left when Jobson did, Chilton resigned shortly thereafter. There was, and is, no animosity between him and Koch. Just two ways of looking at things.

Kelp Cutters Blues

The overall situation would get worse before it got better. Two months after the Worlds ended, America^3 agreed to race the French in a best-of-five series dubbed the Lafayette Cup. Melges was still recuperating. It was just a tune-up regatta raced in the bay, but it was well-attended. It turned into a media field day for hammering America^3. In the first two races, *Jayhawk* became entangled with kelp. In race two the kelp had such a grip on the boat that *Jayhawk* retired after falling behind by 10 minutes.

While the Lafayette races produced little to be encouraged about, two positive developments did grow out of the thrashing. It became apparent that the San Diego kelp beds might become as important a factor in boatspeed as all the other elements the America^3 technical team was studying. Immediately after the Lafayette Cup, Koch instructed the technical men to design a "kelp cutter" which would slice the stuff off the keel quickly and efficiently, preventing the slowdown they were experiencing. The technicians replied that it couldn't be done. Kelp had long been a problem in the San Diego waters and many attempts at inventing some way to keep it off or get it off the bottoms of sailboats had failed.

It was not what the skipper of *Jayhawk* wanted to hear. Hadn't he heard the "it can't be done" litany throughout the *Matador* program and in the early stages of the Cup campaign? It was beginning to be a familiar refrain, and yet he'd had a string of successes to disprove the notion.

As Koch's patience was sorely tested, he replied with a one-word epithet comparing their answer to a walk in a cow pasture. "We have to solve it. We are going to solve it. Because if we do not solve it, we can't win the America's Cup. The team that best solves the problem may find itself with a big edge over the opposition. Make this a priority. I want a team of designers doing nothing except finding a way to get that crap off our keel. Study it, research it, and test it. But get it right. And get it done." It took some time, but the technicians figured it out and an innovative kelp cutter was added to America^3's ever-growing list of equipment.

After the third race in which *Jayhawk* fouled *Ville de Paris* at the start and never recovered, crew morale was low. Several helmsmen had taken their place behind the wheel with no apparent difference in results. Before race four, Koch called his afterguard together and announced he would steer. He stayed at the wheel from start to finish and it was the only race *Jayhawk* won.

If Koch's helming abilities were still an issue among the crew, as they certainly were in the media, that race went a long way towards putting an end to any dissent on board. However, the press generally chose to ignore the point, preferring to emphasize how far the French had come from their seventh place finish in the Worlds, one place behind *Jayhawk*, to their 4-1 rout some sixty days later. An exception to the press bashing was Peter Isler's commentary on ESPN in which he pointed out how ironic it was that the only race won by America^3 was the one in which Bill Koch drove throughout.

With dogged determination, America^3 took its testing programs into the hot, windless San Diego summer. After the Worlds, the team had gone on a seven-days-a-week practice schedule. Day after day *Jayhawk* and *USA-2* logged many hours of base and sail testing. Base testing provided critical, full-size, on-the-water data for the design team about boat speed and the effectiveness of various appendages. Sail testing fed information into Bill Shore's sail development program.

Shore started Shore Sails in Newport, Rhode Island, in 1973. A chance sail on *Heart of America* in 1987 landed him the navigator's job with skipper Buddy Melges. He also helped manage *Heart's* sail program. He started with America^3 in the fall of 1990, hiring Win Fowler, who managed a Shore loft in Maine, as his assistant. "Our goal," Shore said, "is to have the fastest, lightest, and fewest sails."

Shore first contacted sailmakers who had maxi experience, signing up Halsey, North, and Sobstad as builders. That scheme added talent to the program. Per Andersson and Larry Leonard (Sobstad) were working on mains'ls, jibs, and spinnakers. Andy Halsey and Peter Wheeler (Halsey) were concentrating on asymmetrical spinnakers; and Dave Hirsh (North) was designing genoas and reaching asymmetrical sails. The result was good competition and politics that were, as Vincent Moeyersoms said, unbelievable. "We only had North people on the final sailing team," Vincent said. "Their view of sail selection was tainted by their loyalty." Moeyersoms said if he didn't see the progress he expected, he would wake up a loft with a visit from competing sailmakers. He said that worked well.

The basic maxi sail plan provided initial shapes for mains, jibs and symmetrical chutes. But three items needed seminal development: asymmetrical chutes (A sails) and reachers (R sails) for the 135-degree, 100-degree, and running legs of the course; and strong, light, full-length battens for the big mains (270 square meters). As for the A and R sails, "The shape/size/fabric combinations were virtually infinite," Shore said. "It was a very complex issue."

The use of asymmetrical spinnakers dates back to the 1800s. But the cumbersome sails fell out of popularity fifty years ago. They made sense once again for the lighter, faster IACC boats. The IACC VMGs improved by sailing higher jibe angles off the wind. Even on the 180-degree legs, A-sails would prove faster in under 12 knots of wind. Modern materials and jibing techniques made these sails essentially brand new items. It would be many months before satisfactory A- and R-designs would be achieved.

Shore had talent and good tools at his disposal. Engineer Peter McCarthy was collecting and running computer analysis of sail shape data provided by mast cameras. Jack Kleene applied computational fluid dynamics to assess the lift and drag of sail shapes. "Jack had a substantial influence on shapes," Shore said. "He opened up the tops of the genoas, made them more open-leached for a better slot effect."

Shore also had access to the sail force boat, the 30-foot "floating dynamometer" that was originally built for the *Matador²* program. The Force Boat, run by Bruce Sutphen and Eric Steadman, proved to be a useful tool for analyzing changes in sail sizes and shapes. In tank and wind-tunnel testing, sail force coefficients are usually empirical data. With a scaled-down IACC rig in the Force Boat, actual sail force numbers were obtained.

It was handy for testing roach profiles, and A-sail development especially. Instead of building a full-sized sail, a 1/4-sized sail could be tested on the Force Boat with reliable results. "Mainly it told us if we were going in the right direction," Shore said. Full-scale testing was done with two boats sailing a straight line to compare sails.

With all the gear and information at his fingertips, Shore said the problem of fastest, lightest, fewest remains a human one. He could be speaking for the design team as well. "The Computer Formulated Design (CFD) work was absolutely pure. But it assumes flat water, and it doesn't measure how fast a certain shape will tack. Most think two-boat testing is the best, but maybe not. It relies on accurate positioning information (GPS), and the concentration and technique of the two helmsmen; whether or not the boats are encountering the same waves at the same rate; the precision of trim.... The variables are endless.

"Our group had to decide what to test and what not to test. And when the tests didn't agree, which one was on track."

Shore says the heart of the program was the link between the technical and practical sides. Fifteen members of the sailing team — many of them from the "Who's Who" of sailmakers — participated in sail development through six "task" teams: Care; Performance Tracking; Testing; Shape Restoration (recutting); Shape Tracking; and Batten and Spar Development. They met with Shore's technical team weekly to plan and evaluate tests.

Perhaps the greatest innovation in sailmaking was announced in February 1992, just ten days after the Italians had announced their breakthrough in carbon-fiber sail technology. Inside the America³ camp the timing was significant. The word among insiders was that they had reduced their development deficit from two years to just ten days. When one of the Italian designers saw the new American sails, he said they made those of his syndicate look "prehistoric."

As was the case through the R&D department, a number of very secret programs were underway. One was labeled the "B" (black sails) research program and it was investigating the possibility of using carbon-fibers in new sail fabrics. In the summer of 1991, Koch suggested to Heiner Meldner, who was in charge of the "B" program, that the effort should be expanded by considering the use of ordered polymers such as liquid crystal fibers.

By October 1991, various hybrid carbon, polymer, and liquid crystal filament concepts had been manufactured at the Composite Structures Laboratory at Stanford University. The liquid crystals align themselves in the direction of the force exerted on the sails. Hundreds of tests were performed there and several of the more promising material panels were added as patches to an actual racing genoa sail. Tests performed in secret in the early mornings on *Jayhawk* and *Defiant* proved successful and several weeks later sufficient material was produced to build a full-scale racing mainsail.

The sailors liked what they saw and quickly Halsey, North, and Sobstad were given enough material to go into production. By the time America³ had made it to the Final matches against Italy, their yacht carried a full inventory of the new sails with the exception of downwind, symmetrical spinnakers. Actually, two different types of sailcloth were manufactured: one for the mains'ls and genoas, and the other for asymmetrical spinnakers. The new material was about 50 percent lighter and 50 percent more stretch resistant than any other material available, as well as being considerably stronger. It also was much more resistant to sunlight and all tests indicated that the racing life would exceed that of competing materials by at least a factor of three. Koch and his scientists consider the development of the new fiber one of their most significant technological achievements, all the more impressive considering it was developed in just six months.

There was another innovation resulting from the *Jayhawk*/*Defiant* testing that later proved to add to boat speed. Peter Grubb had mentioned to

Bill that trimming the runners (traditionally a job of the afterguard that supports the rig and adjusts mast bend and headstay tension) would help trim the sails through the bad waves of San Diego. In one test, Koch was aboard *Jayhawk* and Melges was steering the significantly faster *Defiant*. Koch asked tailer Per Anderson to trim the runners in conjunction with another tailer trimming the sails. In five straight tests, as the runners were being trimmed in this manner, *Jayhawk* outperformed *Defiant*. Koch saw this as a key to speed and he suggested the runner winches be moved forward of the keel. This would allow the lazy tailer (stationed on the windward side of the yacht and without trimming responsibility on a tack) to trim the runners. The suggestion was met mostly with jokes and ridicule. The trimmers said the runners were always handled by the afterguard, keep the winches back there. Finally Koch told Moeyersoms to move the winches on *Defiant* and *America*^{3}. He did and the performance of both the boats was increased.

"That was another reason for me being on the boat," Koch said later. "I wasn't fettered by tradition."

Darth Vader at the Helm

8

In August (1991), to break the monotony and improve testing with more wind, the boats, tenders, and crews were moved to Long Beach for ten days. Testing was the priority. The September deadline for finalizing the design of boat #3 was fast approaching. But the three coaches were allowed crew training days on occasion.

Fuzz Spanhake sailed the last two Whitbread-Round-the-World Races on *Lion New Zealand* and *Fisher & Pykel.* Before that he'd been on the 1987 New Zealand America's Cup squad. Fuzz, a sailmaker by trade, had been with America³ from the outset. Other coaches were Eric Johnson, a collegiate sailor, grand prix racer (fleet and match), and professional coach; and Graham Hall, who joined the team in May, 1991. Hall won the Mallory Cup in 1969. An active match racer in the 1970s, Hall coached the U.S. Naval Academy sailing team to five national championships in the 1970s and 1980s.

The training schedule the coaches wrote was like a computer game. It consisted of levels that went from basic to impossible. It covered every eventuality the three could think of, including starting drills; dip practice; low-speed tacking; flying the spinnaker without a pole; stalls; and emergencies: broken sheets, winch failure, blown chutes, and men overboard. The latter turned out to be important. The America³ Swim Team was a popular organization. Twenty-three sailors took a total of 32 unintentional dunkings.

As one sailor said, "These boats are big, scary mothas." In waves, they bucked like Brahma bulls. At best, a mistake would cost time; at worst, breakage or injury. The crew had to be able to handle the boats blindfolded if they wanted to be in the game. Next to a maxi crew of 30, an IACC team of 16 is the biggest team in sports. And 16 is a minimal number for such a demanding boat. The smooth, orderly coordination of 16 men in every situation was like running a no-huddle offense in football. It would take a lot of practice. And crew practice wasn't being allotted much time.

Another aspect of the coaching program that was consistent throughout the campaign was the complete indifference of the coaches to individual egos. No one was spared, not even the boss. When Koch made a mistake, he was called on it. For some of the sailors with many years of experience, corrections to their technique or style was not always easy to swallow. But in the end, as each crew member found that he was treated no differently from the sailor beside him, the coaching tactics tended to reinforce the team concept.

In August, Bill Campbell arrived on the scene. Campbell has been sailing and skippering maxis since he was a teenager. He'd also had the shore jobof handling the*Matador* racing program. He was with Dennis Conner's *Freedom* campaign in 1980, the year Conner startled competitors and altered the sport by turning professional and making the America's Cup a business. Campbell was hired by America³ as coach and reconnaissance specialist. He was immediately dispatched to Australia to have a look at the competition.

When he returned to San Diego, Campbell turned his attention to the foreign syndicates practicing daily off Point Loma. He began accumulating an extensive photographic file on each boat. Some photographs were digitized to provide accurate measurements. Pictures of sails were carefully duplicated on computer programs. "I had never seen an IACC boat," Campbell says. "I had to get oriented by looking at our boats, then begin comparing. There were a lot of factors — A sails, R sails, the power of the boats, their stability. It was a new game. The object was to build a mental inventory of each boat. Of course the boats were changing all the time.

"With a new boat, we all had to learn that a bad feel on the helm might be fast. It turned out the boats are stable, and they like power, especially on the reaching legs. The main may be luffing, and there's lots of helm pressure, but it's fast."

Campbell would eventually accumulate over 2,000 rolls of film on the challengers and *Stars & Stripes*. It was an invaluable, well-indexed collection that provided a picture history of the competition's sail inventory, mast movement, changes in boom length and displacement, deck layout, and underwater alterations.

"The greatest luxury," Campbell says, "is that we were able to work in close to all those teams for several months, because no one took America³ seriously. They would wave at us, kid around. They thought we were a joke, totally screwed up. We learned a lot. We'd cruise around in *Guzzini* and take all the shots we wanted.

"After we beat Team Dennis Conner in that first race in January, 1992, the door slammed. The challengers began to complain about our 'spying.'

When we showed up they harassed us with chase boats. When they saw a helicopter, they would bring their rubber boats alongside to churn up the water so we couldn't photograph their keels. But by then it was too late."

Guzzini was an innocuous, 30-foot Bayliner that became the most notorious boat in San Diego. It was used originally with casual observation in mind. At first, the idea was to install an underwater periscope which would be able to view and film competitors' keels. A couple of America³ scouts would pose as beer-drinking fishermen while they got in close to challenger practice sessions. But word leaked out about the device and it was never used. When that idea fizzled, *Guzzini* was used for a variety of jobs. At one point the boat was fitted with a scaled-down IACC keel for testing a top-secret kelp-cutting device that was being developed. Bill Unkel then commandeered the boat as a floating weather instrument platform.

When challengers continued to complain about America³'s alleged "spy program," Bill Koch couldn't resist turning up the heat. The boat was fitted with an array of high-tech antennas, including a flat-black construction on the foredeck made of metal pie-plates and swirls of wire. While paranoid observers may have judged this configuration to have the ability to bounce electrons off the most distant galaxies, the pranksters at America³ knew that bakers could make more sense out of the set-up than even the most seasoned code breakers.

How much real "spying" was conducted by America³ will probably never be accurately determined, but it is fair to say the information received in no way compared to the psychological edge the team gained over most of their competitors. Nor did it come close to equaling the sheer fun the team derived from the controversy.

One particular incident was often referred to as proof of the elaborate electronic surveillance equipment being used by America³.

"Discard the Jack"

One day a deck hand on *Guzzini* spotted, through long-range binoculars, Dennis Conners'operations chief playing computer poker. He zoomed in on the lay-out of the cards, then called up Conner's tender on the radio to advise Bill Trenkle: "Keep the King. Discard the Jack."

Within hours the diversion had escalated into a major international incident. Word spread to the managements of all syndicates that Koch had tapped into the electronic systems of all his competitors. Phone lines between the compounds were engaged. Calls for espionage oversight committees were made. A consensus that something had to be done to stop Koch was taken. Bill's reaction, expressed between spasms of laughter on

North Harbor Drive, was that Trenkle had lost the game anyway. So much for our advice, he muttered.

Not everyone saw the issue with the same degree of humor. *Guzzini* took a lot of heat, especially from Italian skipper Paul Cayard. He began a short-lived campaign to bring these nefarious acts of America³ to the attention of the public, through the media, and especially to Cup organizers and rules watchers. The more Cayard talked, the more incensed he became. Working himself into a rage, he thundered he would protest the Americans under Rule 75 (the fair sailing rule) and bring criminal charges against Bill Koch. In an effort to diffuse the situation, the chief of America³ called Cayard and attempted to point out the possibility of overreaction among the Italian-led remonstrations. Cayard slammed the phone down in wrath. On another occasion, Cayard was asked who he thought would win the America's Cup. "*Guzzini*," he snapped.

Undeterred, Koch stated publicly: "It is my business to find out everything that I can about my opposition. We have never done one thing that could possibly be judged to be illegal. And I shall continue to instruct my people to do anything, repeat anything, that will increase our overall knowledge of the boats against which we may have to race."

The day *The New York Times*' Barbara Lloyd suggested that Darth Vader was at the helm of *Guzzini*, Bill Unkel made a quick visit to the costume shop. The following day Vader and several of the more ghastly apparitions from the bar scene in "Star Wars" were seen aboard *Guzzini*.

"*Guzzini* is named after the Great Guzzini," the whimsical Unkel explained, "an Italian clairvoyant who could look into the eyes of the enemy and know his intentions. Of course the enemy had to be thinking in Italian. The Great Guzzini's English wasn't so good. His French was terrible. A Kiwi accent would have blown his mind."

Before August was over, Bill Koch would follow Melges into the hospital. For several years Koch's shoulder had been bothering him. Orthoscopic surgery removed the bone spurs that had been aggravating muscle tissue by the motion of steering and he was back in action in time to make the 1991 World Maxi Championships in Sardinia and St. Tropez.

The logic of taking time away from Cup preparation to race the maxi series was questioned. But, Koch organized his America³ team into two maxi crews and added a few *Matador²* regulars. While many of the challenger crews took holidays, America³ sailors and shore team workers happily left the San Diego grind to go racing. Again, Koch stressed teamwork and pointed out that those he took to Sardinia included team members who weren't sailors. Everyone needed to work together to get the job done, whether it was in Italy or California, whether they were helmsman or maintenance man. They needed to rely on each other, respect each other. Win or lose, there would be no blaming each other.

In retrospect, Koch's decision to race *Matador*^{2} was a turning point for the entire America^3 program. One benefit that arose was that the crew gained confidence in Koch's technology program. Following the not-so-inspiring performance of *Jayhawk*, a number of the sailors weren't convinced that the great emphasis on science was paying off. But once they stood aboard *Matador*^{2} and felt her speed as she left the other maxis in her wake, they became believers.

Again, Koch took a page from his continually evolving management book and put theory into practice. "I felt we all needed a change of scenery," says Bill. "I wanted to see more unity between our maintenance guys and the sailors. More teamwork was needed and I thought if we got away from the daily routine and everyone changed jobs and positions, we'd come back with a better appreciation of each other."

It worked. *Matador*^{2} didn't just win the World Championship. The sleek white boat ran off with it. In Sardinia, *Matador*^{2} won six out of seven races. In St. Tropez, she finished 1, 2, 1, 4,1, 2, 3. The shared European experience, the successful racing, the good times, all served to weld the America^3 crew into a much tighter unit. In both glittering international ports the competition was good, the nights balmy, the social scene brisk.

For Bill Koch the experience was very satisfying. It had been the sweet taste of his new maxi that had persuaded Koch to undertake a Cup campaign. The repeat maxi Worlds win reinforced the value of his technological approach. That, and being removed however briefly from the San Diego sniper wars, renewed his resolve for going after the America's Cup.

The performance Andreas Josenhans turned in as *Matador*^{2}'s tactician was an added bonus for Koch. Loft manager for North Sails East, Josenhans has registered a hefty string of world championships (Stars, Solings, Etchells, Sonars, One-Tons) as crew. He's a methodical, quiet man with a habitual twinkle in his eye. He trusts logic. Built like a nose guard, he loves an athletic challenge. A highly ranked water skier in Canada where he grew up, Josenhans once set a water-ski speed record towing behind a float plane at more than 100 mph.

Koch says he discovered Josenhans's tactical ability in an Etchells fleet race in San Diego. "In one race we came from last to first, all on shifts and positioning," Koch said. "He has a good level of maturity. A bad start doesn't wipe him out."

Josenhans was obviously pleased about the Sardinia regatta. "It's rare when one gets to register six bullets," he said. But he wasn't too keen on his new job, which he correctly figured would follow him back to San Diego. "I'm a mainsheet trimmer," he said. "Win or lose you can say you did that right. Tactician is not a rewarding job. All day you see opportunities you missed. The only perfect move is one so easy that no one needs a tactician to call it. And it's the one job everybody second-guesses. You win, it was easy. You lose, you blew it."

Perhaps the most satisfying maxi Worlds win for Koch was the race in Sardinia against the Whitbread maxis, ketches that fly on the reach. *Matador*^{2} rounded the final mark dead last, and passed the entire fleet on the last beat. "Bill started and drove the whole race," Josenhans said. "It was raining, chilly, terrible weather. Bill wanted to hand off to Buddy on the last leg. Buddy told him, 'No chance. You got us into this, now get us out.'"

While Bill and Buddy were in Sardinia, Billy Campbell had made a major personnel move back in San Diego. Becoming increasingly irritated with one of the crewmen who had shown potential as the best mast man in camp, Campbell determined the sailor's perpetual lateness and absence from the morning work-outs and sail training sessions were detrimental to the team. The sailor was fired. The decision was questioned by a number of America^3 members who felt losing the sailor's skills might backfire down the road. But Koch backed Campbell. Once again, talent took a backseat to attitude.

When Koch returned from Sardinia, he stopped in Boston to see Wyatt, but ended up spending ten days in bed with pneumonia. The physical grind of the long campaign was evidenced by this incident and by two other hospitalizations during which Koch underwent surgery for other ailments.

The Big Rig Caper

Back in San Diego, the design team had been climbing the walls. With two months left before the final design for boat #4 had to be in the hands of Peter Wilson and Eric Goetz, Moeyersoms, Milgram, Meldner, and company had their attention diverted by an anomaly in the IACC rule. Jerry Milgram called it the Big Rig Caper.

"It appeared," Milgram said, "that the rule allowed the use of sails measured as spinnakers on upwind legs. This was a phenomenal distraction for us. We heard that New Zealand was testing in this area, and we observed the Italians going upwind with masthead sails they took down when we got close. The sails worked because there were systems for rolling up the extra material when on the wind to create a straight luff. The result was enormous additional sail area that was 'free.' If this concept proved legal, we could have smaller mains. This made the optimum boat longer and wider because of reduced measured sail area. There would have been sail handling problems because of the extra cloth, but the boats would have been trains upwind."

For a month, the design and technical teams worked overtime evaluating big (one foot longer) boats. Four boats were actually designed. Several foggy mornings, an America³ crew left before dawn to secretly test the big rig. The correspondence with the measurement committee regarding interpretation of the rule was voluminous. "It was very expensive in terms of time, money, and meetings," Milgram says. America³ worked with the measurers to have the Big Rig ruled illegal and finally, it was.

At the same time the Big Rig Caper was being played out, the design team was struggling to come up with a significant improvement over *Defiant* (USA-18). If the third boat was only marginally different from *Defiant*, then why bother to build it? Koch sat down with the design team and told them he didn't accept their theory that they had reached a plateau. He told them they had to come up with new ideas, do more tank testing if they had to. "You will always find something better if you look hard enough."

Koch often said that since the science of testing, designing, and building sailboats was still very much in its developmental stages, many of the good ideas came out of intuitions and hunches. This is why he set up his testing, design, and building programs to include as many technical people as possible, all of them encouraged to deliver as many "wild ideas" as they could. Tests were then performed in an effort to determine the best ideas and those were then used as a cornerstone for improvement. "We wanted to use the designers as the creative force and the scientists to marshal that force," said Koch.

New data (that is still classified) came from the test tank. "This design insight led to a new batch of models that tested much better," Milgram said. Using the models, the team collected data on these specific design features, and how to relate them to the rule. Young naval architects Daniel LeMere and John Mass were still putting in long hours at the test tank, refining the numbers on the new models. Inaccuracy in some of the models disrupted testing. Perhaps it had to do with time allowances for model construction, which had been reduced from six weeks to ten days as construction deadlines approached and passed.

Koch pushed for more testing. He didn't mind delaying construction if there was a chance the tests would lead to a faster boat. He believed they would.

Both the Big Rig and the new design tangent raised hell with the construction schedule. At Goetz, the building of the third boat (USA-23) had begun before the Big Rig Caper had been put to rest by the measurement committee. "We thought the new design ideas were good," said Milgram, "but we kept the original boat #3 going at Goetz as an insurance policy that cost $20,000 a week. From August 1, 14 complete designs were done for boat #3. At least 20 more were put through computer modeling programs."

At Goetz, USA-23 was started three times. The first stop-work order came at the initial stage of the mold. The builders began again with a new set of plans. The second stop-work order came after six manic weeks of double-shift effort. This time, a finished mold was on the floor, gleaming and beautiful. "I was on the phone to Vincent the night before," Wilson said. "I told him the carbon-fiber was out of the freezer, thawing. This was it. He had to decide whether or not to continue with this mold. He said, 'Cut it up.'

"The next morning I gathered the guys. I told them first that America³ had come up with a really fast design. Then I pointed to the mold and said, 'This isn't it.'" Wilson said disbelief quickly shifted to fury. One worker picked up a sledge hammer, walked over and punched a hole in the mold. Soon the whole crew was reducing its creation into junk.

"About two hours later," Wilson recalls, "Milgram called, said he had an idea how to use some of the mold for the new design. I said 'Jerry, you don't understand....'"

In October, the sailing team got another infusion of talent. David Dellenbaugh was added to the ranks. A hot small-boat sailor (Lightning World Champion, 1991), a proven match racing tactician (two Congressional Cup firsts as main trimmer for Dave Perry — 1983 and 1984), Buddy Melges' tactician on *Heart of America*, and a United States Sailing Association senior judge, Dellenbaugh joined the team as tactician and starting helmsman.

America³ decided another tactician was needed so that the team would have two tacticians and two navigators for two boats. Suggestions were taken from many sources and a list of possible tacticians was drawn up. Then an ad hoc committee of six sailors ranked each name on the list. This collaborative effort produced Dellenbaugh as the number one selection.

"Dave has always been the best at what he does," said Dave Perry, who grew up playing Little League Baseball and sailing with Dellenbaugh in Connecticut. "He's a student of the sport. After each Congressional Cup race, we'd go back and work on starting line solutions using beer bottles on a pool table. Dellenbaugh watches, learns, fills up notebooks."

Dellenbaugh is a thoughtful person not satisfied with easy answers. Not long after graduating from Cornell University, he took a six-year break from competition when he was concerned about the long-term effects it might have on him. During that time he drove a school bus in Boston, becoming involved with inner-city and environmental problems.

Well-known big-boat navigator By Baldridge also arrived in camp. Before navigating *Matador*[2] to the 1991 World Maxi Championship, he did the same for *Kialoa* in 1984. "He was outstanding, talented, and tactically smart," *Kialoa* owner Jim Kilroy recalled. "Calm, with a great sense of humor. He thought things through in three dimensions."

Kimo Worthington joined the team as a helmsman and mains'l trimmer. A veteran of two Cup campaigns (*Clipper* 1979, and *Eagle* 1987), Worthington has done well in boats from Finn dinghies to 50-footers to 70-foot ULDB sleds. He was in the midst of a Star Olympic campaign when he was asked to join America[3]. Hard-working, humorous, talented, and a natural leader, Worthington was another example of what Koch meant by attitude.

Another October arrival was Irish sailor Harold Cudmore. Cudmore was helmsman on the United Kingdom's *Victory 83* for Peter deSavary until the two fell out, and skippered *White Crusader* (UK) in the 1987 Cup Campaign. Cudmore is a skilled match racer, a fierce competitor with a reputation for taking no prisoners, and an acerbic wit. "The ultimate match race is an aerial dog fight," Cudmore has said. "The loser dies. The winner has the satisfaction of killing him."

Cudmore gazed at the breadth of America[3] — all the talent, teamwork and technology — and shook his head. "It's incredible," he said with delight, his black eyes twinkling. "The American way, high-end. There's everything here but match racing skills need to be improved."

The infusion of talent was originally planned as a tactic to build a sparring team. Koch wanted his troops to become battle hardened.

When asked what he did during his two weeks in camp, Cudmore said, "I told them just give me a boat and a wheel and let me test the system, go at 'em. The names of the three trimmers were all I needed. I adapt quickly. Proceed with gay abandon. They told me just don't wreck the boats."

Cudmore had never sailed an IACC boat before. He was admittedly out of match racing practice, and not used to San Diego's bigger-waves-than-wind conditions. Even so, he quickly got the upper hand. "He showed us his tactical mind," Josenhans said. "We worked on standard match racing moves — timed runs, quick luffs. The gloves came off, and we got in close. That's how Harold is. We luffed him once and our rigs hit. Could have trashed the mast. And once the bow on 18 rode up on 9's transom. It was good. We got used to maneuvering in close. We improved our discipline on starting drills. The bowmen got better at calling the line. We were better for having him here. A lot of what he said and did stuck."

"We had some close ones, burned out some chutes," Cudmore said. "Their boat handling is great, but the back of the boat is rusty. I gave them an agenda. What they pick out is their business."

Cudmore brought two umpires with him so the crew would experience on-the-water judging, which would be used in the Cup for the first time. Melges, Koch, and others took turns in the judges' boat, and several queries developed that were passed on to the ACOC.

Cudmore also recognized immediately that the team's time-on-distance work was sorely lacking. Practice starts were a real weakness. Cudmore knew that Conner was a master at time-on-distance starts and he warned that unless they improved, Dennis would win every start and probably go on to win every race. From that point on, the team went through daily drills for almost a month until Buddy was able to put the bow on the line when the gun went off.

Koch liked what he saw. He had been after someone who would test — beat up on — his troops. "He was a big help to us," Koch said of Cudmore. "He improved our starting techniques, and his debriefings were good. He'll be invited back in January."

Koch gave his team a week off for Thanksgiving. Then it would be back to work. They took Christmas day off, and New Year's Day. The rest of the time they worked. There was no choice. Round 1 of the defense trials was slated to begin January 14 with a race against Team Dennis Conner.

Plate 1: An aerial view of America's Cup champion *America*^{3} carrying sails made of the syndicate's proprietary fabric, "Cuben Fiber."

Plate 2: Matador^2 was the result of an extensive five-year research and development program that produced one of the fastest yachts ever built. That program served as a springboard into the America's Cup when the design formula was changed to

create the current International America's Cup Class (IACC), not dissimilar from the maxi class. The data and scientific tools used to build *Matador*^{2} were found to be transferable to the new class.

Plate 3: The design team, made up of marine architects, scientists, and technicians. Back row (L to R): Daniel La Mere, Doug Peterson, Jerry Milgram, Bill Koch, Vincent Moeyersoms, Fernando Frimm, and John Reichel. Front row (L to R): Phil Kaiko, Jim Taylor, Heiner Meldner, Jim Pugh. Missing are Penn Edmonds and Buddy Duncan.

Plate 4: The America³ Foundation Team. For a full listing, see the Appendix.

Plate 5: Jayhawk rounds the final leeward mark in the last race of the 1991 IAAC World Championship. (Because the mainsheet trimming system failed during the prestart, trimmer Andreas Josenhans was forced to trim from the halyard pit.)

Plate 6: Buddy Melges, at the helm of *Defiant*, approaches the weather mark and begins to bear off the wind as the spinnaker is hoisted behind the genoa. Trimmer Mike Toppa eases the sheets.

Plate 7: On a sun-soaked afternoon, *Stars & Stripes* squares off against *Defiant* in the early rounds of the defender trials. Note the different downwind sail selections:*S&S* chose a traditional symmetrical chute while *Defiant* flies an asymmetrical kite.

Plate 8: In Race 7 of Round 3, *Stars & Stripes* suffered a spectacular dismasting as a result of a fitting failure in the running backstay system. $500,000 worth of sails, spar, and rigging began to sink.

Plate 9: The wind catches a Cuben Fiber asymmetrical spinnaker as the crew works to fill it.

Plate 10: Members of the Kanza indian tribe from the State of Kansas were present when tribal head Wanda Stone christened *Kanza*. The boat's name reflects Bill Koch's upbringing in Wichita.

Plate 11: Bill Koch and Paul Cayard pose beside the America's Cup as it was displayed at the San Diego Yacht Club.

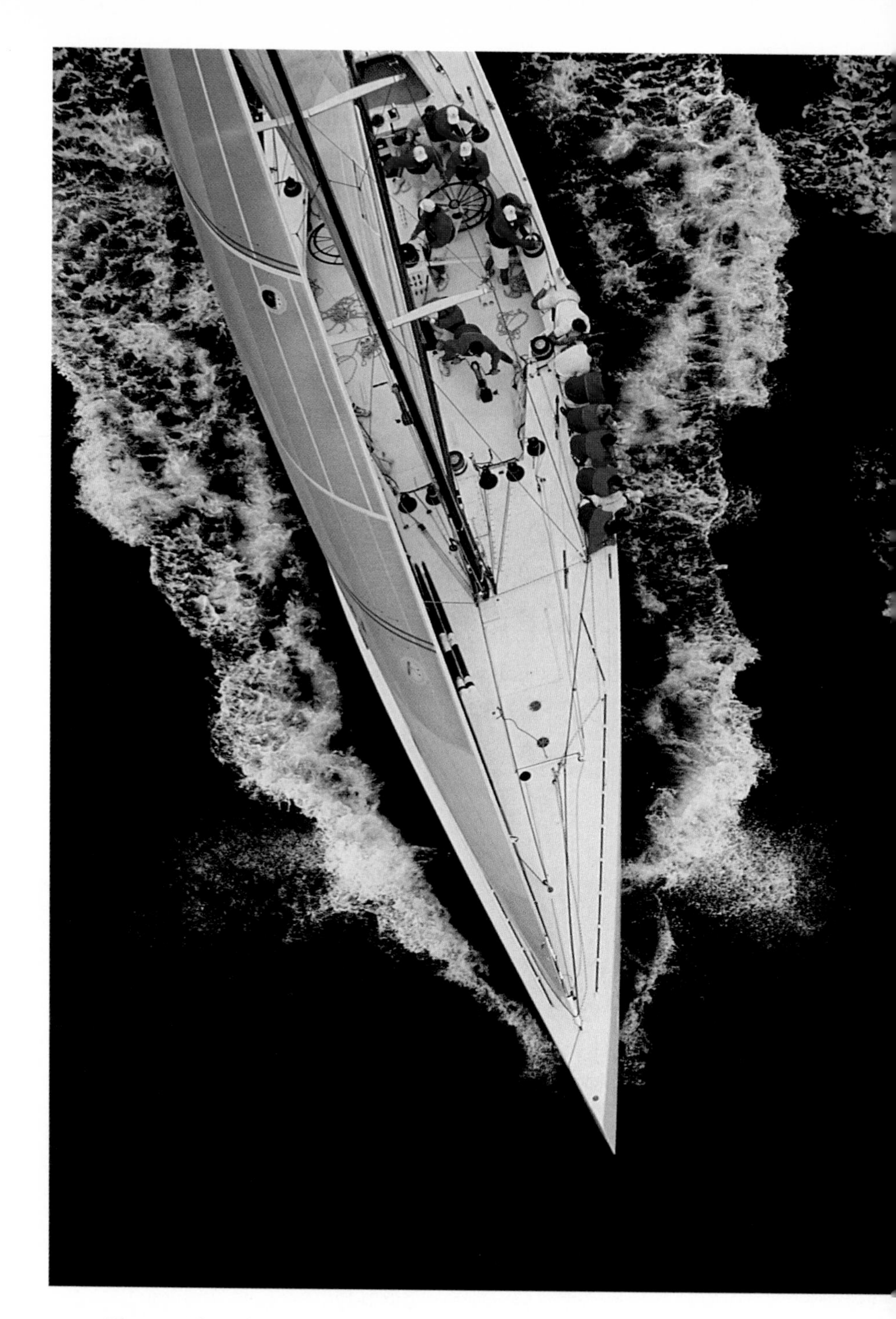

Plate 12: After a leg one "slam dunk" by *Il Moro* in Race 2, *A*^{3} tries to get bow-out enough to pinch Cayard off and force him to tack.

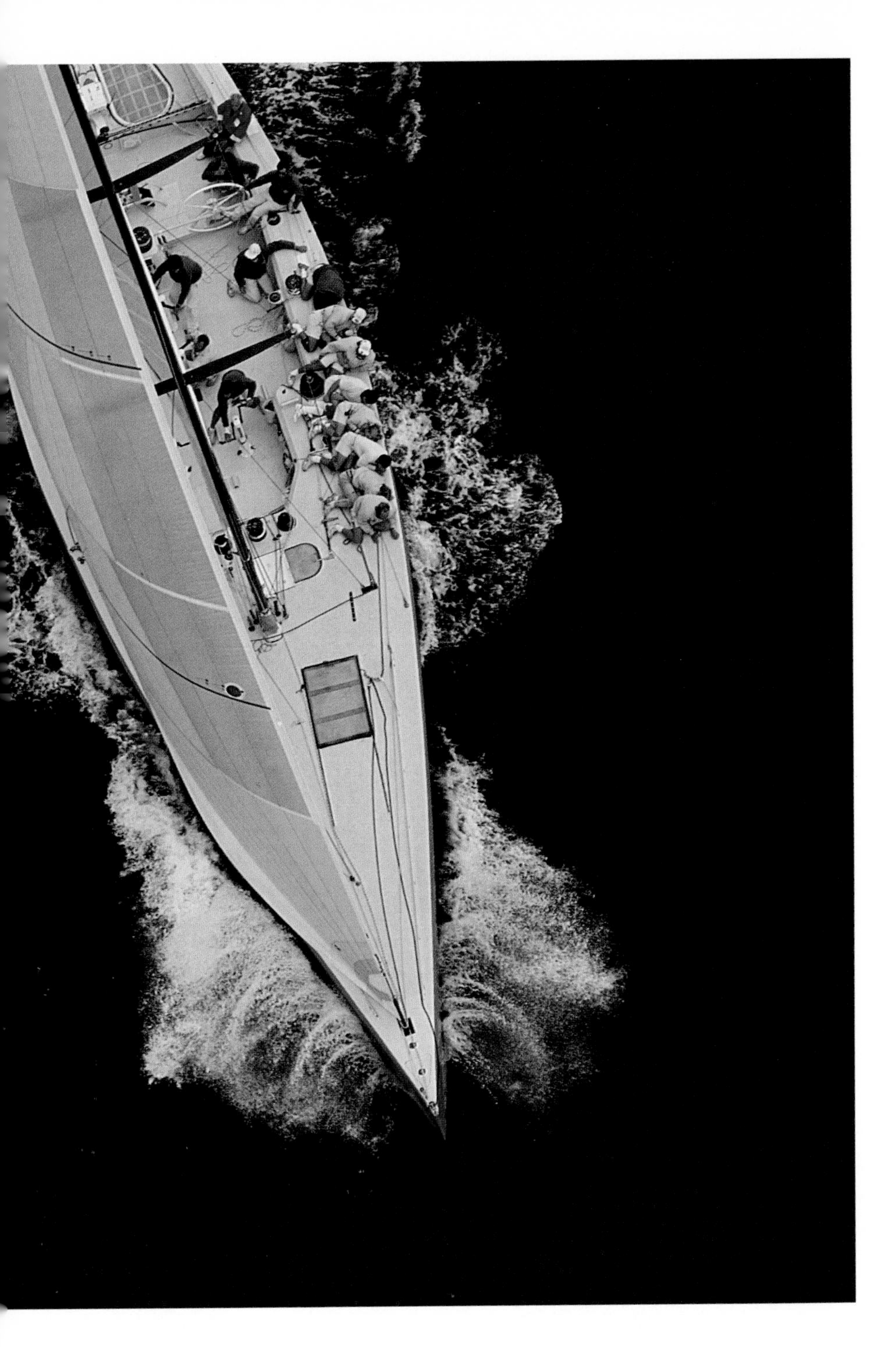

Plate 13: Vincent Moeyersoms shares in the jubilation aboard *America*^{3} after the "rookie" team crosses the finish line in the final race of the 28th America's Cup.

Plate 14: The America^3 team continues the celebration ashore.

Plate 15: "I did not win the America's Cup, the entire team did." — Bill Koch

Plate 16: During the 1992 victory parade, *America*^{3} flew an all-white chute with a sunflower emblem, a tribute to Koch's boyhood home in Kansas. Here, Merritt Carey of the new Women's Team checks the rig during a practice sail.

Plate 17: The America^3 Women's Team is made up of sailors, weight lifters, Olympic rowers, body builders, and other athletes. It's the first time in history an all-women team has competed.

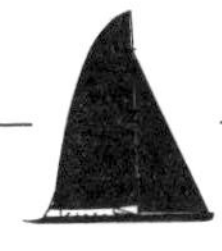

Happy New Year

9

America³ welcomed the new year. Out with the old, in with the new. The year 1991 had been one of turmoil, anxiety, pressure, stress, change, disagreements, false starts, law suits, controversies, and disappointments. This — 1992 — was the year of the America's Cup. In just two weeks, the defender Round Robin Series #1 would begin. All slates were wiped clean. What happened the year before no longer mattered. Past transgressions were forgotten as the focus on racing intensified. All that mattered now was what would happen on the water. Gentlemen, hoist your sails!

For the trials, three separate "slots" had been established and agreed upon; two for America³ (slots A and B), and one for Team Dennis Conner (slot C). This system would prevail through Round 1 (one point per win); Round 2 (two points per win); and Round 3 (four points per win). The points leader would enter Round 4, the semi-finals, with a two-win bonus. The second boat would receive a one-win bonus. The third boat would receive no bonus. The highest-scoring boats in Round 4 would race in the defense finals, a best-of-thirteen series. The system was slightly less complicated than cricket.

While it was true America³ would have 32 sailors on the water and Team Dennis Conner would sail with 16, and it was equally true sailing at this level is as much a team sport as any played today, most docksiders referred to the coming battles simply as "Koch versus Conner." There was a certain sense of history and headline that came with reducing these multi-million-dollar and multiple-person efforts to just two men. After all, how many spectators could identify the starboard winch grinder aboard *Australia II* when that yacht turned the America's Cup world upside down? Or for that matter, how many Cup watchers could name the entire crew aboard *Stars & Stripes* as she headed toward the starting line for her first 1992 race?

And what a contrast, this Koch vs. Conner match-up. The unproven rookie vs. Mr. America's Cup. Kansas vs. California. The businessman/sailor vs. the sailor/businessman. The mad chemist vs. the seasoned professional. A man whose entire approach to the game was in question vs. the man who wrote the book on Cup preparation.

Koch had come to sailing late in life, taking some 45 years to discover "it was in my blood." When Conner was 44, he'd been on the water for tens of thousands of hours, won countless races, had an Olympic medal, and had won and lost and won the America's Cup.

Koch, the scientist, filled his design team with scientists. Conner, the sailor, filled his design team with sailors.

Koch is a man of many interests: business, science, art, fine wines, several sports. His life has been shaped by boardroom battles, chemical equations, and Monet acquisitions. Conner once wrote: "For the better part of my life I've been a sailor. It's my hobby, my passion, the way I've chosen to live my life. It's what I've spent more time at than anything else, and it's certainly the one thing I do best. Most of the values and philosophies I live by are the result of lessons I've learned while racing sailboats. When I'm on the water, I'm at peace and almost always happy, especially when I'm winning."

Yet for all their dissimilarities, the two men who so fervently desired to be the Cup defender, had at least one thing in common: respect for the opponent. As Conner said in an ESPN interview on the eve of the trials: "I'm a Bill Koch fan. I think frankly that the San Diego Yacht Club, the America's Cup defense, and America are very fortunate to have Bill Koch involved here. This man is doing it his way and he has a very good chance of being successful. I think the man is a winner." For his part, Koch said simply: "I think Dennis Conner is the best sailor in the world."

While the mutual admiration society might have been a show for the cameras and all part of the great psych-out game athletes love to play, there was much truth to the fact that both men knew they were up against as strong an adversary as they had ever been. Conner knew Koch's financial resources and technology program were elements far beyond his reach. How ironic for the man who had invented the America's Cup multiple-boat campaign to be entering battle, because of the lack of cash, with just one boat. Koch knew Conner had a boatload of world-class sailors whose practice time far exceeded that of his team, and that those sailors would drag every fraction of a knot out of the boat. He also knew there was no team anywhere more loyal and devoted to their skipper than the *Stars & Stripes* team was to Dennis. And both men knew that the other was a fierce competitor who hated to lose and rarely did so.

There was little doubt that Dennis Conner was the hometown and sentimental favorite. There was also no question that Bill Koch and his program were still little understood by the media, by the average fan, and from the discord exhibited in previous months, by some of his own team. But despite the naysayers and the 100-1 odds posted in Las Vegas, Koch doggedly stuck to his philosophies. Still, with only days to go before the racing began, he refused to name an A and B team.

"There were several reasons I kept rotating the crew," said Koch later. "Overall, we were constantly seeking improvement at every position. I wanted everyone familiar with working with everyone else. Racing from January to, hopefully, May is a long grind, both physically and mentally. I wanted a team whose members were interchangeable. I needed to be totally confident that if someone got sick or hurt, his substitute could do the job without missing a beat. Not designating A and B teams kept everyone on their toes. Certain individuals may have thought they were first-string material, but they had to go out and prove it every day. They also had to look at every other crew member as an equal. I believe this method built morale and intensified everyone's competitive spirit.

"I also believed we had a very good chance of placing two boats in the Finals. If that happened, I would need two first-rate crews, not a first-string and a second-string."

What was known about the ensuing showdown with Conner and company was that America^3 would race *Jayhawk* and *Defiant*. USA-23, to be known as *America^3*, was still in Rhode Island undergoing the final phase of the building process. But until only hours before the first race, the names of the starting boats were all that was known. Koch hadn't even said who would drive them. Most people, inside and outside the compound, assumed Bill Koch, after all the furor over his driving, would helm *Defiant*, the faster boat.

But when opening day dawned, Bill Koch stood in front of his several dozen sailors and told them Buddy would steer *Defiant* and Dave Dellenbaugh would call tactics. He would skipper *Jayhawk* with Bill Campbell as starting helmsman and navigator, and Andreas Josenhans as tactician. After posting the full crew lists, he walked to *Firewater*, from which he would watch the race he'd spent seventeen months preparing for.

A Stunned Silence

The sailors sat in stunned silence. No one had expected this. Koch was making a statement, but no one was quite sure what it was. Could it be that he wanted to show his confidence in Buddy? Was it that he truly believed it didn't matter who was on which boat, that everyone really was equal in his eyes? Did he have such faith in the design team and the improvements to *Jayhawk* that he had no doubt the boat would win? Or was it that he believed *Jayhawk* and *Stars & Stripes* were equal in speed and he wanted to see how he and his crew would perform under the pressure of going head-to-head with the world's greatest sailor? Whatever, no one asked and Koch didn't answer.

With one minute left before the start of the first race of the defender trials, *Defiant* (USA-18) and *Stars & Stripes* (USA-11) were on the wind, sailing toward the left side of the line after a mild skirmish. *Defiant*, with Dave Dellenbaugh at the helm, was ahead and to leeward in the light air, just where she wanted to be. *Stars & Stripes* was forced to tack away to the right. A few minutes after the start, the two boats came together. *Defiant* tacked in front of *Stars & Stripes*, again forcing the blue boat off to the right. Among America^3 partisans, joy and hope were the emotions of the moment.

After a frantic year of running behind, a year of putting a multimillion dollar business on line; of tank and wind-tunnel testing; compound building; sail testing; crew training; fundraising; designing and building boats; and the personal upheaval that goes with total commitment to an America's Cup campaign, the first cross was a moment of hard-won satisfaction. At the first weather mark, the joy was unrestrained: it was *Defiant* by :36. Over the next seven legs, *Defiant* added almost a minute and won by 1:34, in what the San Diego Union called a "flawless" performance.

The trials had actually begun with verbal sparring between Bill Koch and Dennis Conner at the opening press conference. Koch stood his ground when the subject of the IACC boats arose. Yes, the boats were fast, and fun to sail, he conceded with a smile, "But not so much fun when you are paying the bills." Koch maintained that the boats were fragile, expensive, dangerous, and bad for the Cup. He predicted they would go the way of the prohibitively expensive J Class.

Even with a one-boat program that was hamstrung by lack of funds, Conner disagreed. "I think the IACC boats will be around for a long time," he said.

Resolution of that discussion would be years away. The more pressing interest had to do with the long-awaited confrontation on the water.

While America^3 had a two-boats-to-one edge, Conner's boat had displayed excellent speed at the Worlds in May. That made *Defiant*'s competitive edge in the opening race particularly satisfying to America^3's brain trust. And while *Stars & Stripes* still sported a thin inventory of work-in-progress sails, and looked generally rusty on the race course, the sails, crew work, tactics, and sail calls on *Defiant* got high marks.

The America³ pre-race routine on the water was established as the trials began. On race day, the weather and current boats departed before 9 a.m. to take readings. Two race boats left the dock at 9:30 a.m., each towed by its rubber chase boat (capable of 40 to 50 knots). But before leaving the dock, counter-espionage measures were taken. Part of the America's Cup game has become trying to find out as much as possible about the other guy's boat. When *Australia II* arrived in Newport for the 1983 match, her hull was draped in a "skirt" to keep her revolutionary wing keel a secret. It worked to some extent, but it also drew attention to the yacht's underside and prompted more than one scuba diver to attempt furtive reconnaissance expeditions.

America³ boats were dressed not only with skirts that covered the entire bottom to prevent measuring, but also with "panties" to obscure the keel. It was calculated that if both the panties and skirt were dropped at the dock, a skin diver had about 60 seconds to swim in, take photos or obtain a measurement of the keel, and swim away. A scheme was devised by which the skirt was dropped at the dock, but the panties were retained until the boat reached mid-harbor and then were dropped at random locations.

Once clear of the channel, *Firewater* took both boats on a stern tow. *Firewater* was not only the mother ship for the race boats and small support vessels, complete with spare parts locker (everything but a mast) and tool room, but she was Command Central. With all telemetered data coming to *Firewater*, she was a floating war room. With his electronics team, Bill Unkel kept the data flowing. Coach Fuzz Spanhake ran the pre-race, two-boat testing from the bridge. Sail shapes were videotaped on the bridge, digitized, and ferried to the race boat. Meteorologist Chris Crabtree collected his data and made final weather calls from *Firewater*. Bill Shore coordinated sail calls from a chase boat, using *Firewater* as a floating sail bin.

On *Firewater*'s flying bridge, the brain trust collected about an hour before the start. The core of this group included Harold Cudmore, Spanhake, Bob Campbell, sailing team afterguard members not racing, design team members, and Vincent Moeyersoms, who came aboard from a chase boat in time for the start. The flying bridge had readouts of all data from the race boat, and a television picture of the race course (after ESPN began live coverage). It was here where all pre-race decisions were coordinated: sail combinations, preferred end of the starting line, preferred side of the course, and other tactical considerations.

Round Robin #1 quickly developed its own pattern. *Defiant*, with Buddy Melges at the helm, went undefeated throughout the series. It wasn't a walk, by any means. In Race 1, *S&S* made it exciting at mark 5 when she cut *Defiant*'s lead to :20. In a dying breeze, *S&S* came on when *Defiant* sailed into a hole and slowed to a crawl. With both boats on the wind on starboard, *S&S* slipped up under *Defiant*'s lee, established an overlap, then slowly stuck her nose ahead for the first time in the race. A jubilant Conner raised both arms as he sensed a kill. But *Defiant*'s afterguard had quietly spotted a new breeze filling in ahead. Moments after Conner's gesture, Melges and Company tacked away and found themselves on the layline and moving. Conner had to sail three boat lengths to clear his air before he could tack. By then it was over.

When *Defiant* reached the dock and Melges was buffeted by a thousand congratulations, he smiled and waved and nodded his thanks. And as he walked toward land, he was heard to say, "That ain't coaching, that's racing. A whole damn lifetime of racing." One person who knew what he meant perhaps better than anyone was Dennis Conner.

The older *Jayhawk* looked strong on the starting line, but couldn't stay with either *Defiant* or *Stars & Stripes* once the races began. Skipper Bill Koch and crew showed they were in the fight. In Race 5, *Jayhawk* threw 42 tacks at *Stars & Stripes* on the first weather leg. While this was on the extreme side, most of the races included a flurry of tacking, putting to rest the apprehension that no tacking duels would occur between IACC boats because of their big wind shadows.

Trailing by :45 at Mark 1 in the same race, *Jayhawk* gained on the reaches, then initiated 27 more tacks on the second beat. By Mark 4, *Jayhawk* had cut *S&S*'s lead to :11, but even with her superior sail inventory, that's as close as she got. In Round Robin #2 (starting February 8), *Jayhawk* was replaced by America^3's third boat, USA-23 — *America^3*.

In Race 6, *Jayhawk* beat *Defiant* off the line in 6 knots of breeze after a good skirmish, and held on for a dozen tacks as Melges attacked. Then Campbell, who steered the start and the beginning of the leg, tacked on *Defiant*'s weather bow (going for a slam dunk) as *Defiant* crossed just below *Jayhawk*. Campbell was late. Melges put the nose down and coolly inched his way through *Jayhawk*'s lee. It was an important, and misleading moment. The timing of a successful slam dunk is always critical. This would be one of only two instances on the 1992 America's Cup course that the slammed boat would successfully sail out from under the coverage. But America^3 afterguards, perhaps with this incident in memory, would continue to try.

Race 7 was perhaps the highlight of the series. After starting even with *Defiant*, *Stars & Stripes* picked up a favorable, 15-degree shift on the right and led by: 35 at the weather mark. *S&S* seemed quicker in more breeze, a fact Jerry Milgram confirmed. "Dennis's boat is faster," Milgram said with professorial logic, "when it is going faster." *S&S* held *Defiant* off until leg 5, when the America[3] entry quickly closed the gap with a burst of speed credited to a handsome new reacher that had been put on board that day. *S&S* changed sails in desperation, but the maneuver only slowed them more. A thousand yards from the mark, *Defiant* rolled over the top of *S&S*. It would be the only pass on a reach during the entire America's Cup regatta. *Defiant* avoided a sharp, last-second luff from Conner followed by a protest flag. *Defiant* answered with a flag of her own.

The first on-the-water judgment in Cup history disallowed both protests. *Defiant*'s sail change and rounding was smooth as silk, while *S&S* struggled to pick up the pieces. *Defiant*'s winning margin was :50.

For America[3], Buddy Melges and Dave Dellenbaugh were the MVPs of the first series. Melges got a kick out of the IACC boat. "It felt like the scows and the Star boats I grew up with," he said. "It's got big horsepower in the sail plan. It responds well and accelerates quickly. The sound of the bow wave and the noise of the water along the hull tell me a lot about what the boat is doing, just like in a scow."

One should not underestimate the value of Melges' scow experience. The first year he moved into Star boats, he won the World Championship in a tough fleet of 104 boats. To prove it was no fluke, he won the Star Worlds the following year as well. As a helmsman, he has great sensitivity. "He has jets," Andreas Josenhans says of him. "I can only say that about a couple other guys I've sailed with."

The question about how Buddy would fit into big-team bureaucracy was still on the table. On small boats he is used to calling everything. And his only significant match racing experience had been in Fremantle, where seamanship often counted over tactics.

Dellenbaugh's crafty work on the starting line was a pleasure to watch. Most of the time when the gun went off, Dellenbaugh had won the side of the course he wanted. Tactically, Dellenbaugh and navigator By Baldridge — an impressive reader of wind patterns — combined to make excellent calls.

Crew Confidence

Bill Koch was happy with his team's auspicious beginning. "I'm pleased with our crew work," he said. "This first set of trials gave everyone confidence that we can do battle and win. It showed that our design predictions are on track. We learned a lot about which sails work and don't work under racing conditions. And we learned how good *Stars & Stripes* is. We now have a benchmark for comparing our new boats."

Stars & Stripes improved dramatically during the series. At the post-race press conferences, *S&S* crew members frankly admitted using the series to profit from America³'s research and development in all visible sectors: from sailing techniques to sail shapes, and especially sail trim. *S&S* trimmer Bill Trenkle said Round Robin #1 was "pre-season…a training vehicle for playing our way into shape." And Dennis Conner, who can be as crafty behind a microphone as he is behind a wheel, congratulated Bill Koch for developing a program "with no apparent weaknesses." Koch took that with a grain of salt.

The early trials are "spring training" for everyone from race managers and judges to the teams themselves. The races don't count for much in terms of points, and the hope was that sailing in May would be quite different from the light, incredibly unstable winds offered in January. During one January race, the wind shifted 270 degrees. Another day was so fluky the boats finished after sunset. The photographers loved it — "Conner Bites the Dusk," the *L. A. Times* headlined over a rare sunset shot of USA-11 — but it made for poor racing.

The early competition was valuable in this new America's Cup boat-valuable for fine-tuning a syndicate's overall package. Even with all the time and energy put in over the past year, Koch said he wished he had another year. So did Milgram, and Moeyersoms, and Heiner Meldner, and Bill Shore.

"Any research program reaches a stalemate," Koch said. "Then a new idea flows in and it takes off in a new direction. If we had more time we could test more variables, more keels…we'd know which boat was better under which conditions." But he admitted another year of such intense sailing might raise havoc with the crew.

In an effort to keep the crew cohesive, Koch reshuffled the teams labeled "red" and "blue" for the January series. His move was consistent. "We are all the same team," Koch maintained. "I don't want to create a division. We don't want any mushrooms here," he says, a reference to the nickname selected by Dennis Conner's trial horse team in Fremantle in 1988: those kept in the dark and fed bullshit. Conner's subs even flew their own mushroom burgee.

Observers, including a number of crewmembers, who thought they had spotted a stellar combination on board *Defiant,* were perplexed by Koch's intention to reshuffle the lineups yet again. After *Defiant*'s sparkling performance, it was a difficult decision. Koch put it off for a week while he held dinners at his house for small groups of crewmembers. Of thirty-eight responding to Koch's question, only two specified who they wanted to sail with. The rest put the ball back in his lap. On the afterguard question, all abstained. Koch stuck with his philosophy.

"Buddy was an A and B team guy when he first arrived," Koch said, "but by the start of the trials he believed in the system. We have two equally good teams out there. Any combination could make a first team. Each sailor knows the others' idiosyncrasies. We have a strong bench. If anyone gets sick, or hurt, substitution would be smooth.

"I spent a lot of my athletic career on B teams. It feels terrible. It's demoralizing. There's always resentment coming from the B guys, and superiority from the A guys. The result is that the B players never develop their skills. If we'd split into A and B off the bat, some of our best guys would have been put on B or even cut. In such a long campaign, some guys start high and wear out. Others rise to the occasion. It's a long, drawn-out process that requires stamina and inner drive. It's not apparent right away who's got it and who doesn't."

Making an A/B distinction was going to be tough with so much talent. The red/blue plan put everyone on an equal basis, and kept enthusiasm up. But sooner or later 16 people would have to be named as a first team. How that was done (and when) would be as delicate as disarming a bomb; or as disruptive as exploding one.

Most of the crew wasn't eager for an early decision, especially those who had been involved with Cup campaigns in the past. All of them wanted a chance to show their stuff in a real match race situation. They went along with Koch's red/blue crew philosophy, but most of them wanted to know when a decision would be made. Consensus was that the first team should be picked by the semifinals.

The afterguard was a separate issue. Racing advisor Harold Cudmore was back for the duration, and was close to Koch on team matters. In Cudmore, Koch saw someone with no ax to grind, no hidden agendas. He also liked Cudmore's clear, incisive viewpoints. But on the question of choosing an afterguard, even Cudmore hit the wall. Harold suggested Bill select the afterguard he wanted for the finals and let them practice together. "That is a logical way to proceed," Koch admitted, but in the end he decided to shuffle the afterguard as well.

"I wanted to sail some with Buddy, one of the world's best helmsmen," Koch said, "find out how we worked together. I needed to know when he was steering what I would do on the boat. And Buddy hadn't sailed with Bill Campbell. He wanted to do that. He wanted some days off the boat as well."

Koch said the job he really coveted was starting helmsman/tactician. "I love the intellectual, judgmental process that's involved," he said. "But good starters and tacticians are like chess players. They have good pattern recognition. I don't have the experience for that. And the Cup isn't the place to go to school. If we want to win the Cup, I'll have to take a position where I can help, and still be intellectually involved."

A Scalded Dog

10

Not many San Diegans shared the joy of the America³ team over its performance in defenders Round Robin #1. The hometown boy, the champion of the world, Mr. America's Cup, their man Dennis Conner had been made to look mortal. This wasn't the script the Californians had written and rewritten since the better-left-forgotten monohull versus catamaran debacle had changed the rules and once again thrust San Diego's skipper into the limelight, the shadow of which would bring credit and dollars to their city. Their script called for Dennis to take on the world's best and demolish them as he had done so many times in the past. And this time, it would happen in his, and their, own backyard.

The press, both local and international, didn't take kindly to this upstart group either. Dennis was the story here, not Bill Koch. "Cubens" (as in "America Cubed") was the description someone hung on those inside the America³ camp, a somewhat derisive term meant to symbolize the "nerd factor" characteristic of these scientific types. But when the press picked up the term, those inside the North Harbor Drive compound wore it with pride. After all, Round 1 seemed to validate the Koch approach. The emphasis on scientific testing, the refusal to name a starting team, the absence of stars and reliance on teamwork, all this was beginning to pay off. It doesn't matter what you call us, they seemed to say, as long as you call us over the finish line first.

Koch himself was too busy to pay much attention to what anyone was saying, but there was a situation that was beginning to rankle him. Several of his crew reported the San Diego Yacht Club had refused them service because they were wearing A³ clothing. This, combined with the middle-finger greetings of more than a few spectators on shore, hit the Kansan hard. Had the yacht club forgotten his team was racing under their own auspices? Was sportsmanship an ideal entirely lost on this city?

But Koch, like his team, determined to make his statement on the water. And even though the first round wasn't that significant and there was still a great deal of racing to be done, Koch was already quite confident his boats would prove faster than *Stars & Stripes*. *Defiant* had shown this, and if all the testing done on the new boat proved accurate, *America*^{3} would be another leap forward. For here was the boat that was the real beneficiary of all the testing that had produced *Matador*^{2}, as well as all that had been learned since the maxi's birth. *Defiant* and *Jayhawk*, built under severe time pressures, were really only modified *Matadors*. And while these two IACC yachts were used in San Diego as platforms to study everything from rigging placement to crew selection, a test tank in Maryland held the secrets to who would win the 1992 America's Cup.

If there is one story that typifies Bill Koch's reliance on scientific data as well as his personal management style, it is the story of the creation of USA-23, later christened *America*^{3}. Thirteen times Koch's design team had come to him with "final" plans and thirteen times they'd been sent back to the drawing boards. Each time they told the boss it's the best they could do, and each time Koch said he didn't think so. Those drawings were interrupted twenty times to build new models and retest again. "The more we experiment," Koch said over and over, "the more mistakes we make, but the more we learn and improve. If you are not trying new things, you are not improving. We will keep trying, keep doing new things until we find the best way. Don't be afraid of mistakes. Any mistake is a good one, as long as you learn from it and don't sink the boat!"

Already, the Goetz Boatyard had built three new hulls, only to be told a new design was coming. Once the boatbuilders were six weeks into the job, with the entire staff on double-shifts, when Moeyersoms called to say "scrap it." Frustration built to intolerable levels.

Koch had been through this before. How many times had he been told during the *Matador* project that "this plan is the ultimate; we can't do any better?" But in the end the team produced the design breakthrough they were all after. Koch was looking for the same thing here, the design that would give him the fastest IACC boat in the world.

Towards the end of the process, with almost no time left on the clock, Koch ordered another round of tests. He'd studied all the data over and over and he believed he had discovered an anomaly. He wasn't exactly sure what it was, but something didn't ring quite true.

Build and test two new models, the boss told the technicians and designers. Don't have time, came the answer. Find the time, insisted the boss. Eric Goetz tells us he absolutely needs the final plans now if you're going to get the boat in the water for Round Robin #2. I'll handle Goetz, said the man who doesn't hear the word no.

"The Cup Is In Your Hands"

Koch called Goetz and was told there was just no way the boat could be built on time if further testing was necessary. Koch tightened the vice, telling Eric that he believed the designers were close to the breakthrough that would win the Cup and it was up to Eric to deliver that breakthrough. "The America's Cup is in your hands, you're the only man standing between an American victory or a win by a foreign country." Goetz was used to just about every type of owners' pressure tactics, but no one had ever said that to him before. The next morning he called Koch and said he'd build *America³* on time.

The extra days of testing confirmed Koch's suspicion. What was thought to be the optimum speed point was proven to be bogus. The actual speed point was discovered and the final design was completed.

"Experimenting and testing found the optimums," said Koch. "Doing it again and again until you eliminate all uncertainty. That's the scientific way."

Goetz ran around-the-clock shifts and finished the yacht as the last grains of sand ran through the hourglass. Now the challenge was to get it to San Diego in time to be assembled, rigged, launched, and tested. To truck it to California would take valuable time away from preparing the boat and getting the crew on board and on the water. Flying it there would solve the problem. No American airplane had a cargo door large enough to accommodate the yacht, so the syndicate chartered a Russian Antonov 124 cargo plane that flew what they hoped would be America's best hope to San Diego. It arrived on January 25, two weeks before the start of Round 2.

In the few hours of sailing *America³* had against her stablemate *Defiant*, she looked a measure faster. But as she towed out for her first race against *Stars & Stripes*, there hadn't been time for even one practice spinnaker set. No matter. In very light air (5 knots), *America³* won the start and stretched out on every leg, winning by a whopping 6:23.

The more than six-minute victory produced a reaction in the yachting world similar to the 19-minute devastation *Matador²* loosed upon *Boomerang* just 17 months before in the race that had propelled Koch into Cup competition.

Over on *S&S*, there were obvious problems. In pre-start maneuvering, the blue boat slowed visibly after tacking or jibing. Going upwind, *S&S* was lower, slower, and side-slipped badly. The problem seemed to be rooted in

S&S's radical underwater appendages: an upside-down balance beam arrangement with twin tabs for steering. A conventional rudder was missing. While turning left with one wheel, Conner was seen turning his inner wheel to the right.

This keel arrangement — articulating twin keels with a long lead bulb hung between them — was not a new idea. A similar configuration had been noted on one of New Zealand's boats, and on Iain Murray's *Spirit of Australia* — when the ocean surface was calm enough for underwater objects to be discerned. America³ had tested the twin keel the previous fall in the wind tunnel. "We rejected the idea," Jerry Milgram said. "We thought it had possibilities, but it's very difficult to engineer. The two fins together can't be any bigger than one normal fin if you're going to avoid extra wetted surface. And the fins must have a thin core. With 30,000 or more pounds of lead hanging from them, it's hard to prevent the smaller fins from bending sideways under load."

From watching Conner trying to control his boat, steering with such a rig could also be tricky. As Melges said, only half in jest, "We didn't dare get too close to him." The New Zealanders obviously had control of their version of the double keel, but *S&S* was horribly out of balance, and *Spirit* had taken a 12-minute drubbing against *New Zealand* in its first race of challenger Round Robin #2.

Race 2 was *Defiant*'s turn against *S&S*. In keeping with Bill Koch's intention to constantly change crew assignments, he and Buddy were sailing on both America³ boats as a team in February. Navigator By Baldridge and tactician Andreas Josenhans were on *America³*; Bill Campbell (navigator) and Dave Dellenbaugh (tactician) were assigned to *Defiant*. The rest of the crews stayed more or less in place for the series. Again it was no contest. *Defiant* stretched out on every leg, winning by 4:16.

Race 3 was the best of the series, as *America³* (with Melges skippering) took on *Defiant* (with Koch skippering) and handed the Round 1 speedster her first defeat (:49). Scuttlebutt had it that *America³* was dragging its feet toward the end to make the boats appear more closely matched.

Race 4 was the clincher. In 10 knots of steady breeze, *America³* won the start and rounded the first weather mark 2:38 ahead of *S&S*. Some suggested that was a weather-leg record for two equally-rated boats in a fair breeze. As Buddy Melges said of *America³*, "This boat goes to weather like a scalded dog."

S&S was struggling. Several times on the weather leg the yacht rounded up so extremely that her mains'l battens popped inside out. At the finish, Team Dennis Conner was behind by 6:00.

While most of America³ rejoiced in their continuing success, Koch and Melges were concerned. They realized beating Dennis by such large margins was doing them no good. They needed closer competition, especially when the challengers' were winning and losing in the 5 to 30 seconds range. "They were getting battle-hardened," said Koch, "and we weren't. We were getting smug, overconfident, fat, and lazy."

Koch called Conner and made an offer: we'll let you modify your keel now if, at some time in the future, you let us modify ours. We'll get back to you was the response.

When Koch presented the offer to 14 of his own men, there was little enthusiasm to go along with it. As one participant observed, "A lot of these guys have run afoul of Conner in the past. They are enjoying having their foot on his neck."

TDC's response was to draw up a list of items they wanted modified, most of which had nothing to do with keel changes. Offered an inch, TDC negotiated hard for a mile, bringing in other issues. Koch was extremely upset, believing they were looking a gift horse in the mouth. "I finally told them to take it or leave it," says Koch, "and then I said look, here's what I'll do: I'll not only give you the mod, I'll donate $100,000 to your campaign. This will help you. It will improve your fundraising."

TDC accepted the deal, minus the financial donation.

It was both a sporting and pragmatic gesture on Koch's part, one with equal benefit to Conner, America³, and the defense. The most upsetting aspect of the situation for Koch was that the *San Diego Union-Tribune* printed news of the deal before Koch could inform the crew. It was a nervous president and skipper who faced his troops at the crew meeting the next morning, wondering if he'd be tarred and feathered or just received with stony silence.

"The decision has logic," Koch told them. "Maybe not the same as you're accustomed to in the sailing world, but what matters is winning the Cup. In these one-sided wins over Conner, our boats have not been sailed to their optimum. And focusing on killing Dennis Conner is dumb. He doesn't do us any good dead. One thing I've learned from a lot of nasty battles — forget about revenge. In Kansas we have a saying. When you go out for revenge, dig two graves — one for your enemy and one for yourself.

"We've got to focus on winning the Cup. DC is the tool that can help us. If the tool is sharp, it's useful. If it's dull, it's no good. We've got to improve our toughness, our ability to come from behind. If we can use DC to help us, then we will. We need him to push us, make us fight harder with fewer mistakes and bad tacks. That's the American way. When the sailing is close, every mistake matters.

"We're going to give DC a chance, but not much of one. I have ultimate faith in our design team. There's no way he'll catch us with what we have in house, unless we give up."

Koch's remarks were from the heart. At the end, as he apologized for the release to the press (which was not his doing), his face flushed with color and he paused, choking back emotion. He had worked long and hard to make this team believe in him. The moment's silence was shattered by spontaneous applause from the crew that lasted a full minute. Melges later said this was a key moment in the binding of America³ into a real team.

Koch's logic and forthrightness had won the team's support. But throughout the America³ organization, there were pockets of uncertainty. Too many veterans of past campaigns could recall watching in amazement as Conner had pulled an ace from an apparently empty sleeve. There were still a few who fully expected a second boat to arrive at Conner's compound, despite overwhelming evidence to the contrary; despite the fact that ESPN was already assembling footage for Conner's obituary.

"Wouldn't that be like him!" Jerry Milgram exclaimed, caught between the anxiety and the irony of a second boat appearing at TDC. "It's not something I would have done," Milgram said of Koch's decision. "Our stated aim has always been to beat TDC in the semis so we'd have our own two boats in the finals. Now that scenario is very unlikely."

Allowing the keel change was the first time anyone remembered in America's Cup history that one team helped a competitor it was racing to improve. Working all night in the driving rain, Team Dennis Conner amazed everyone by changing the *S&S* keel in less than 24 hours. The same exercise might have taken America³ as much as two weeks. The Cubens learned something from this.

TDC's new configuration, according to tactician Tom Whidden, was "similar" to the January configuration. The next day, with Conner out of town on business, Koch's wish to be pushed was fulfilled. John Bertrand drove *S&S* to a 55 second win over *Defiant* in a 14-16 knot southwest breeze and very sloppy seas left over from the previous day's storm. *Defiant*, which won the start and led for six legs, saw *S&S* close to within :19 at the end of leg 5. On leg 6 (the final weather leg), *S&S* showed good boat speed as the wind dropped to 9 knots. The blue boat slipped past *Defiant* to round the 7th mark 47 seconds ahead. *Defiant* fought back, regaining a slim lead on the last leeward leg before her spinnaker blew out.

"That was excellent," Melges said of the loss. "You learn nothing with 4-6 minute leads. Now we've got stuff to talk about. We don't have all the answers by any means. It's good we got pushed."

Over breakfast, Jerry Milgram and Harold Cudmore reviewed just what was learned. "We say we need two weeks to change our keel," Milgram said. "Conner did it in a day."

"When in doubt," Cudmore said, "fly a bigger sail on the reach. You can always change down."

Milgram: "Don't use the polyethylene spinnaker in a chop because it will break."

Cudmore: "Our program got out of whack when Conner fell over. They regrouped and beat us. Now we have to re-examine everything we do."

Melges said the boat had been noisy, unsettled during the loss to *S&S*, that a change of personnel on the bow and in the pit had caused some confusion. And there were numerous sail changes in this race. "There was a lot of yelling at the replacement guys from the back of the boat that was unnecessary. They know the jobs. They just do them a little differently." Melges said that was the price of constant crew fluctuation, which he nonetheless continued to support. "As the technology blossoms, keeping the whole crew up to speed is the way to go. In the end, we'll be able to pick a super, cohesive, 16-man crew. But right now we need lots of intelligent practice."

After a second day off while another in a series of storms pounded San Diego, *America³*, the "scalded dog," again showed her heels to TDC. It didn't matter to *America³* which keel *S&S* was using.

The following day in a breeze that freshened to 15 knots, *S&S* still had *Defiant*'s measure. Dave Dellenbaugh had been most impressive on the starting line. Jerry Milgram called him "one of the finds" of the program. Once again Dellenbaugh put *Defiant* out to the left ahead and to leeward of *S&S*. But after a dozen tacks, *S&S* crossed *Defiant*. By mark 5, *S&S*'s lead was 1:02. At the finish, *Defiant* had closed to :47.

Milgram thought *S&S*'s pass of *Defiant* in the lighter air toward the end of Race 5 was an anomaly, attributable in part to pre-race damage. Towing out, *Defiant* had smacked into a heavy sea so hard she lost the instrument package at the mast head, and her keel was shaken loose on its mounts. A postponement was granted, and hasty repairs were made on the water. The keel had wobbled most of the race.

But *S&S*'s speed in Race 7 was no surprise. "*S&S* is always fast in a breeze," Milgram said. "It's a wide boat with good stability, and it's longer as far as we can tell. *Defiant* is a great light air boat."

Because of two weather cancellations in the February series, it was arranged that the two races left between *America³* and *Defiant* would be sailed the same day on short courses. Koch steered America³, and Melges sailed *Defiant*. As expected, *America³* won the first race, windward/leeward twice around; eight miles total. But then *Defiant* took the second race — by 1:05. Wha...?

It turned out that everyone on *America^3*, from bowman to tactician, thought the boat had been over early. A red signal on the committee boat was misinterpreted as a recall. So *America^3* chose to restart. Perhaps her afterguard wanted to see just how fast she was. But USA- 23 never caught up over the 12-mile course.

At day's end, Bill Koch was ecstatic. With Josenhans in his ear, Koch had driven both starts and done well. But Dave Dellenbaugh had obviously used restraint on at least two potential contact situations. That was sound judgment. There's no gain in smacking your other boat around.

The *Union* dutifully used the word "UPSET" in the headline. A quote from TDC's operations manager, Bill Trenkle, generated a few chuckles around the America^3 breakfast table: "I'm not surprised (at the upset)," Trenkle said, "the boats are close enough."

And the *Defiant* win put another point in America^3's slot B coffer. Had *Defiant* lost, it would have had to sweep TDC in Round 3 to come out ahead. Now it must win two of three.

As for the *America^3* win, Koch loved to repeat Conner's quote about his grandmother being able to win if the boat was fast enough. Having a boat speed edge had been Koch's dream from the outset of the campaign. After taking USA-23 around the course from start to finish, Koch must have felt that his dream was coming true.

As a helmsman, Bill Koch improved daily. Josenhans said Koch constantly opened up more channels at the helm. "The experienced guy processes six or seven channels at a time," Andreas said: "speed, trim, tailer's comments, waves, tactician's and navigator's comments, wind shifts...and he can add up the scores as well. Bill added a channel or two this year, including a better sense of when to get off the helm."

Buddy said Koch's work in flat water was good, that he was getting his head off the boat, off the instruments. Who better to teach Koch those skills? Melges has honed his ability for 50 years at the highest levels of competition.

It's a measure of Koch's intelligence that he was arriving at decisions that a year ago seemed obvious to many Cup veterans. "Bill's insistence upon driving caused some problems early on," Louis Cabot said. "But Bill is clearly the boss. He knows the issues and he makes clear decisions, including when to sail and when not to. He's built a good, productive partnership between himself and Buddy."

The steering question probably wouldn't be resolved until an America^3 boat took to the water in actual Cup races beginning on May 9. In keeping with Koch's method of operation, the crew might not be announced until that morning. "Bill will make the right decision," Harold Cudmore said,

"I'm sure of it."

As the February trials ended, America^3 seemed to be in an enviable position. *America*^{3} was undefeated, *S&S* was offering *Defiant* good competition, and the syndicate's fourth boat being built — USA-28 — was slated for April launching.

When asked to define the biggest syndicate problem at this juncture, Louis Cabot said he worried what the alternative would be if America^3 didn't have a tough battle with Team Dennis Conner. "Figuring out how to drive ourselves to become faster and faster would be a big challenge," Cabot said.

To understand Louis Cabot's concern, all one had to do was cast an eye toward the Louis Vuitton challenger series. Round 1 hadn't proved much. But Round 2 was heating up. Four of the eight boats were competitive. New Zealand, Italy, Japan, and France were handling the two Australian teams, Spain, and Sweden, without a problem. New Zealand seemed fastest of the four. In one of the last races in February, she had beaten the formidable Italian team with apparent ease, seeming to find speed whenever she wanted. Before it was over, there would be some serious competition on the Louis Vuitton course. Whichever boat survived the trials would be well-tuned and thoroughly primed.

Fortune Amid Disaster

11

With only two victories in Round 2, and neither of them against America³'s new boat, Team Dennis Conner entered the third round clearly on the ropes. *Stars & Stripes*, even with the keel change, was beginning to demonstrate that she had been designed for a very specific range of conditions — winds of five to seven knots and smooth seas. The boat was wide of beam, in total contrast to *America³*, which was the narrowest boat in San Diego. *Stars & Stripes* caught the usual westerly sea swell with her girth when on starboard tack, while the slim *America³* knifed through the waves with better finesse.

Although the "scalded dog" had only six official races to her credit, the *America³* camp already believed she was the super boat the designers had promised. What's more, she performed exactly as they had said she would, further building confidence in the design team by the sailing team. What did come as some surprise was that the narrow boat performed exceptionally well when the wind speed increased, making her a boat for all seasons (spring, and the America's Cup finals, were still three months away). The A³ team entered Round 3, where each victory was now worth four points, with a certain sense of invincibility.

If America³ believed in their boat, that sentiment didn't extend to the media. Even after the first race of the new round held on March 3, when *America³* beat *Stars & Stripes* by 1:11 and produced the fastest time to date of any challenger or defender around the 20-mile course (2:16:16), a media poll was released in which Koch's speedster was said to be the fourth fastest boat in the Southern California city. *New Zealand*, *Il Moro di Venezia*, and *Nippon* were ranked ahead.

But what concerned the America³ camp more than the media's misguided mumblings was the performance of *Stars & Stripes*. Just a few weeks previous, *America³* had taken out *S&S* by times of 6:23, 6:00, and 4:33.

The concern heightened when in Race 2, TDC beat *Defiant* by 2:15 after *Defiant* suffered a broken spinnaker pole. Conner's time around the course, in 14 knots of wind, was almost a minute faster than the day before. Was this new display of speed a result of *S&S* adding wings to her keel and new sails, or was it Dennis beginning to remove his infamous sandbags and show his true colors?

A^3's worries were temporarily abated when the white wonder notched a 5:33 defeat of *S&S* in race four. Race 5 saw Dennis, who loves to take his opponent into the spectator fleet during pre-race maneuvers, hit a 70-foot luxury cruiser and cross the starting line well behind *Defiant.* Twenty miles later, TDC suffered their second loss in a row.

If Conner and company thought things could only get better, Race 7 quickly dispelled that notion. On one of the windiest days of the trials, *S&S* lost her mast at the first mark. In the water was $500,000 worth of carbon-fiber mast and a new $50,000 Kevlar mainsail.

After the dismasting in Race 7, Team Dennis Conner was forced to go back to its old mast and mainsail, a stiffer, fuller configuration. Conner lost to *Defiant* the following day. That was no surprise given there had been little time to tune *Stars & Stripes*' new rig. But observers noted that *S&S* was looking better upwind on port tack. There was a suspicion that the race committee biased the course 48 percent to starboard and 52 percent to port to benefit the hometown skipper.

"The course was balanced from a wind standpoint," said Koch, "but when the current was factored in, there was a definite bias. It was true Dennis was faster on the port tack, but that was because the waves were less on that tack." Added to this was the fact that the race committee started the races in light, fluky air which favored *S&S* and caused concern in the A^3 camp that there was a hometown bias among the starting officials.

After its dismasting, *S&S* had been towed in stern-first to prevent damage to the rigging. With no spares on the shelves, the rigging had to be salvaged for the other mast.

The mast had gone over the bow, good fortune amid disaster. Had the spar gone over to leeward, the rigging would also have been ruined, and *Stars & Stripes* might have been out for the series; maybe the duration. Word later circulated that during the stern-first tow, *Stars & Stripes*' trim tab had been bent. Could that have accounted for their port tack improvement? Had the Conner team stumbled onto something? Speculation ran rampant in the face of TDC's sudden improvement.

Races 10 and 11 offered perfect conditions for TDC. The hefty chop of the past two weeks, in which *Stars & Stripes* had been pitching noticeably upwind ("chopping wood"), had flattened out. The wind averaged 8-12 knots. The conditions were most favorable for the stiffer, fuller sail plan Conner was now using.

Starts on both *America^3* and *Defiant* were less than brilliant. And in both races, America^3 boats ended up on the least favored side of the course. Both times *Stars & Stripes* went left, got ahead quickly and seemed to sail its own race. Several times in each race, TDC left the rival America^3 boat uncovered, picking shifts in the erratic breeze with what tactician Andreas Josenhans called "uncanny accuracy." Some went so far as to wonder if Conner might have a helicopter at 10,000 feet calling the shifts.

The back-to-back wins got TDC the bonus point (slot C) it wanted for Round 4. America^3's slot A would have two bonus points; their slot B would have none.

TDC's surge was a reminder that the process of discovery in an America's Cup campaign is all-important. A brand new class of thoroughbreds like the IACC boats is a veil of mysteries shrouded in fog. The design and technical teams make the basic choices. If they are on the mark, the fine-tuning begins. The smallest adjustment or alteration to just one of the infinite number of go-fast possibilities can make a significant difference. He who discovers the most goes the fastest.

If further proof was needed, over on the challenger course the favorites were taking their lumps. France and Japan took turns beating New Zealand; Japan and New Zealand each handed Italy a defeat; and Japan beat France. The top four were the same, but the order was reshuffled. Japan — aided by four New Zealanders among the regular crew of 16 — had swept Round 3 and was leading the challengers as of March 15. Was a United States/Japan America's Cup match in the offing? If so, it would also be covered on the financial pages.

In the America^3 camp, TDC's surge was again viewed as a positive development. The peril of being front-runner is one of the oldest stories in sports. Getting nipped on the heels periodically is essential to maintaining top performance.

Nonetheless, Conner's two bullets ricocheted around the America^3 compound. *Defiant*'s loss could be explained by a perplexing move after the start. Crossing the line a full minute ahead of *Stars & Stripes* in the light air, *Defiant* tacked away to the right — the side favored pre-race by the *Firewater* brain trust. TDC got going, stretched to the left into the building sea breeze, and was ahead at the first crossing. "Yesterday, on the boat, I got bad information — go right," said *America^3*'s tactician Andreas

Josenhans. "Today I gave it. It wasn't quite as bad as hitting a spectator boat," Josenhans said of *Defiant*'s tack to the right, "but it was right up there."

America^3's loss was more perplexing. The "scalded dog" had seemed untouchable. That, it turned out, was the problem. Bill Koch, who with Buddy Melges had skippered and steered both boats during Round 3, had seen it coming. "Walking on the two boats I could feel the difference," Koch said. "The crew on *America*^{3} was cocky. Before the start there was lots of chatter and joking. On *Defiant* the mood was quiet, serious. Those guys knew they had to work harder to win. On *America*^{3} they had lost their fighting edge. They weren't trying as hard, and that doesn't make for a fast boat."

Koch also noted how much Conner had improved. "He learns every day he's out there. With one boat that's a necessity."

Josenhans mentioned Conner's improved sail trim in particular. "I've been saying since January that the reason Conner had no speed was that his sail trim was out of whack. Then he puts up that old mast with the old sail that's too round forward and he goes like hell in the flat water. Dumb luck? Maybe. We all profit from dumb luck. I also noticed that his jumpers were tipped forward at an angle identical to ours. We are providing Conner's data base, no question about that. And John Marshall [former president of North Sails and a Conner mainstay through three Cup campaigns] has been all over Conner in the press about his mains'l shape."

Team Dennis Conner had improved considerably. Even in defeat *Stars & Stripes* was being well-sailed. TDC's 100-degree reaching sails looked impressive, and the blue boat's crew work could not be faulted. At America^3, discussion about crew selection had been heating up throughout Round 3. The polished look America^3 had presented on the race course in Rounds 1 and 2 became slightly tarnished in Round 3.

Defiant's broken pole in Race 3 was the result of a timing problem, and there were a host of other, smaller things that compromised performance. Perhaps overconfidence was a factor, but from the crews' point of view, the constant shuffling of personnel was disruptive. Koch was under increasing pressure to keep successful crew combinations intact, or even to pick a #1 crew. He remained intent upon keeping his red/blue system. With the competition from Conner improving, crew selection became a more discussed issue.

And it was good that it did. One of the several positive surprises the IACC boats provided is the increased importance of crew work. The boats are so light for their sail area that they change speeds with amazing quickness. If the timing on a sail change was off by a few seconds on a 12-Meter, the momentum of those heavy displacement vessels wasn't critically affected. But a late set on an IACC boat will cost several boat lengths. And a perfect set is rewarded by a substantial gain.

Many thought the worth of Koch's crew shuffling system had run its course. Changes within the front five presented the most difficulty. The bow, mast, sewer man, and the two pit people are cogs in the same intricate machine. All have to know the others' instincts, strengths, habits, and preferences. Tailer changes were also causing problems. "All our guys are good," bowman Jerry Kirby said. "It doesn't make much difference who's doing the job when everything is routine. But it makes a huge difference in a crisis. Then you have to know exactly how the other guys will react. In the end, although frustrating at the time, all the crew changes were good. If we could survive that, we could handle anything the competition threw at us."

The crew decision was complicated by an embarrassment of equipment. Two days before Round 3 concluded, *Kanza* (USA-28) — America^3's fourth boat — was flown in from Goetz. The newest boat, named after the *Kanza* Indian tribe of Kansas/Oklahoma — "The Wind People" — was christened by the head of the tribal council, Wanda Stone. *Kanza* had been designed and built as a specialist boat for slightly heavier weather conditions — winds above 11 knots. She had been the recipient of hundreds of hours of tank and wind tunnel testing. Despite several long-range forecasts that called for lighter winds than usual, Koch reasoned he couldn't manage an America's Cup syndicate based on forecasts. If the winds did blow, he did not have a boat to handle them. He preferred to be prepared for all contingencies, so *Kanza* was built and she was now in San Diego.

Defiant Retired from Duty

Defiant was thus formally retired from serious racing after eight months of non-stop duty. *America^3* and *Kanza* would fight Round Robin #4 without her.

Having *America^3* and *Kanza* going head to head would be the culmination of all the design and technical work done over the last 17 months. *Defiant* was an increment faster than *Jayhawk*. *America^3* was an increment faster than *Defiant*. Hence, the fast boat in those pairings was never pushed to full potential. But *America^3* and *Kanza* were similar. Not identical, but close enough to push one another to the edge. And they were fast boats. As Buddy Melges said, "The design team has kept their word. Their claims are right. It's a marvelous situation."

If, as cautiously predicted, both *America^3* and *Kanza* beat TDC in the semifinals and set up an all-America^3 defense finals, it would be very important to discover which of the two boats was faster. If a first-string crew was named, could an afterguard be assembled on the other boat good enough to provide tough competition?

The additional pitfall of naming a first-string crew was to chance reducing the intensity of those not selected. But not picking a first-string at this juncture could jeopardize the Cup match itself. Buddy Melges found himself on the fence. "With red/blue, we've got two good crews, but not one great crew," Buddy said. "And there isn't enough time between the finals in April and the Cup in May [eight days] to make a team sharp enough to tangle with the challenger. I don't know the psychology involved here, but I know that we'll need 30 days to achieve the perfection of boat handling that we need.

"Picking an 'A' team could cause an in-house problem on the one hand. But if we don't have time to train a #1 crew we'll be in a compromising position. To get both boats up to speed we need a red/blue situation. It's a tough one. All I know is that if we don't have perfect crew work, we'll shoot ourselves in the foot and the system will have failed."

The day after the back-to-back defeats by TDC, *America³* and *Defiant* squared off in the last race of Round 3. [With the permission of the race committee, they again sailed two races on short courses that would count as two full races]. Koch, Melges, and Dave Dellenbaugh sailed *Defiant.* They lost twice to *America³,* with Bill Campbell steering and Kimo Worthington calling tactics.

That evening, at a full crew meeting, Koch addressed the problems. He said it was obvious that *America³* had not been up to speed in Round 3, and he put Melges in charge of finding out why. He told Buddy to order whatever he wanted for the boat, but he had only one day to figure it out. "Vincent said I was going to blow the budget to hell," Koch said. "I told him the budget was already blown to hell."

Tactics, which had become one of Koch's pet peeves, were next. He put Harold Cudmore officially in charge of tactical coaching and he told him to set up practice sessions over the next two weeks, "No holds barred — just get it done." Cudmore had to be pleased by that assignment. His big concern about the program had always been the lack of match-racing skills. The opposition had Cayard, Dickson, Davis, Eddie Warden Owen (coaching the Kiwis), Gilmour, Pajot, Bouet, and Conner. Most of them had been finishing in the money on the match race circuit. At America³, Dellenbaugh was closest to a match racer, and he is more practiced in fleet situations.

"Dellenbaugh is good," Cudmore said. "He just hasn't preprogrammed enough match racing moves into his memory. Match racing is a specific game like any other. That last race between *Defiant* and *America³*, *Defiant* had *America³* put away close to the finish. On the last downwind leg *America³*, on the right side, jibed onto port. *Defiant* was on starboard, coming across from the left slightly ahead. *America³* couldn't cross *Defiant*, so they jibed to starboard. At that point, *Defiant* jibed back to port. Wrong. *America³* is a faster boat! All *Defiant* had to do was sail deep during *America³*'s jibe, putting a bit more leeward gauge between them and *America³*, then come up and parallel *America³*'s course. *Defiant* could have pinned *America³* to the layline, jibed first, and led them across the line. It sounds easy, and it is. You just have to know the moves. Sometimes when you are behind, you must plan four legs ahead, then sail accordingly, limit damage so you'll be ready for the moment when it arrives.

"Our strength is our technology. Our weakness is match racing. We have to address the latter. This syndicate is so big it moves with glacial progress. But we're just in time, we hope...."

As for the crew, Koch stuck with red/blue. "I believe in hard work, faith in the ability to win, and the right attitude," Koch reiterated to the assembled sailors. "People have been talking to me about a #1 team, a dream team. I don't believe in a dream team anymore than I believe in a dream girl. If your dream girl ever materialized, she'd be a nightmare."

Koch said the crews on *Defiant* and *America³* had gotten to know each other, so he named them as teams that would stick together from now on. *Defiant*'s crew would transfer to *Kanza*. *America³*'s crew would remain on that boat. No more shuffling of players — with the exception of the afterguard. Koch and Melges (alternate drivers), Dave Dellenbaugh (starting helmsman and tactician), and Andreas Josenhans (main trimmer), would go from *America³* to *Kanza* when racing TDC.

A few days later, Koch announced that when the two boats raced each other, the alternate afterguard would be Bill Campbell, who had volunteered for the assignment and would drive, with Kimo Worthington as tactician and Michel Maeder navigating. Bill Rogers and Per Andersson would do the main. It was the first time anyone heard Koch use the expression, "trial horse." He thanked Bill Campbell for agreeing to take on the job and Campbell received a standing ovation from his teammates.

Here is how the two teams lined up for Round 4:

Kanza		***America³***	
Jerry Kirby	bow	Rick Burnham	bow
John Spence	sewer	Keith Renke	sewer
Mike Hein	mast	Peter Craig	mast
Beau LeBlanc	pit	Josh Belsky	pit
Dawn Riley	pit	Wally Henry	pit

Kanza		***America³***	
Rick Brent	grinder	Marty Steph	grinder
John Huffnagel	grinder	Larry Mialik	grinder
Rock Ferrigno	grinder	Peter Fennelly	grinder
T.A. McCann	grinder	Chad Van de Zande	grinder
Stu Argo	trimmer	John MacGowan	trimmer
Mike Toppa	trimmer	Bill Ruh	trimmer

Afterguard A	**Afterguard B**
Koch, skipper	Campbell, helm
Melges, helm	Worthington, tactician
Dellenbaugh, start and tactician	Maeder, navigator
Baldridge, navigator	Rogers and Andersson, main
Josenhans, main	

Bill Campbell said the crew welcomed Koch's decision. "They were upbeat, ready to go for the next set of trials." One could sense that it wasn't quite a final decision, but it was a way to proceed. A lot would depend on the outcome of Round 4. Koch was confident that if both boats made the finals, that series would afford plenty of practice time. He went so far as to tell Bill Campbell that whichever team won the finals would sail in the Cup — "with a few minor changes."

The defender semifinals were two weeks away. The new boat was a big plus going in, and there was another arrow in the quiver: America³ had caused a ripple even before Round 3 began by announcing the development of a revolutionary sail material that combined carbon-fiber and liquid crystals. The new sails appeared ten days after the Italians had announced their own new material.

The sail material project had begun 10 months previously when Bill Koch clipped an item about liquid crystal research from *Science News* and sent it to Heiner Meldner. Meldner asked scientists at Stanford University to get involved. "We checked out several dozen fibers," Meldner says. "The three we decided on were carbon-fiber; an extended-chain polyethylene along the line of the Spectra material made by Allied Signal; and the liquid crystals. The trick was combining them. We considered more than 200 combinations."

The previous November, Meldner had patches of the material sewn into a genoa that was tested frequently. "Word never got out," Meldner says with some amazement. "These were big patches — eight pieces 15 feet long and 3 feet wide. I knew the stuff would hold loads. We tested it. Its strength is phenomenal. I had fun handing a flimsy piece of the stuff to strong guys and asking them to tear it in half. It can't be done. What we had to find out was how it would react to sunlight, being creased, and chafed against the rigging."

Once the new material was perfected, it was up to Bill Shore, Director of Sail Development, and Win Fowler, the America[3] loft manager, to put it to use. As they know the sails as well as anyone, let them tell the story of how they were developed. The following was written by Shore and Fowler for publication in the English magazine *Seahorse:*

The America³ Sail Program

When Vincent Moeyersoms, America³ Foundation's executive vice-president, offered us the job of directing their sail development program in December of 1990, the International America's Cup Class was largely terra incognito. Not only was this an entirely new class of boat designed to an entirely new rule, but these boats were going to race on a new type of race course and do so with asymmetrical spinnakers — virtually a new order of off-wind sails. We knew that we faced a huge task, but we knew we would have the resources we would need to see the job through. Even so, the task proved more demanding (and more expensive) than we had ever imagined.

The early months of the campaign were spent playing catch-up. We were way behind, particularly relative to the Italians and Kiwis, in all aspects of the campaign, but especially in time on the water. We had acquired rights to IACC #2, known affectionately as "the French boat" or just "2," with other assets of the defunct Beach Boys group and used her hard as a training platform.

Her sail inventory, apart from the half dozen sails the French had built for her, and the early inventories for our own design team's first creation, Jayhawk, *were developed using the best guesses of our team of sailmakers. The process consisted of intense brainstorming sessions of sailmakers and sail-trimmers, during which time we would hammer out consensus target areas, profiles, and flying shapes for each sail in the inventory. The sails would be built to these specs at various lofts and then measured, flown, photographed, recut (if necessary) to achieve the targets, and finally assessed for effectiveness in their wind range.*

Feels Right / Looks Right Evaluations

This method of specifying sails was to continue throughout our campaign, but our tools, especially for assessing the effectiveness of different sails, got a lot better as time went on. The early evaluations were of the "feels right"/"feels wrong" "looks right"/"looks wrong" variety. Still, we had such a talented and experienced group that their best guesses proved quite accurate in a number of areas.

One subject we knew we had a great deal to learn about was the full-length mainsail battens. Together with Fiberspar, at the time primarily a builder of composite sailboard spars, we developed a system of interlocking carbon/s-glass tubular sections of varying flexibility that we could plug together like Tinker

Toys to build a huge array of batten tapers. While extremely versatile, this system suffered from some early teething problems. We suffered several joint failures early in the program that interrupted practice sessions, to the discouragement of the sailors and sailmakers alike.

We persevered with the system, however, and eventually were able to build full-length tapered mandrels for constructing our battens, and ended up with what we believe were battens of about half the weight of the solid rod or flat battens used by our competition. And although we feared broken battens, we never experienced the heart-rending failure the television cameras showed so vividly of the crewman aloft on Il Moro di Venezia *during the last race of the America's Cup finals, swinging from a harness 90 feet above the deck and trying to contain broken shards of carbon fiber batten.*

The 1992 IACC World Championships were a large milestone on the road to the America's Cup. Before that series we were struggling to get our act together just to field our two boats, get our base of operations built and staffed, and afterward we settled down to a long program of crew training and boat and sail testing.

Although Jayhawk *managed to win a race, our showing was not good. In the sail program we knew that our downwind inventory was grossly inadequate. At the post mortem sail meetings we hammered out specifications for an entirely different set of reaching and running asymmetricals. The Worlds had been a great opportunity to study the effectiveness of our competition's arsenal, and pointed out the importance of proper twist in these sails to accommodate the wind gradient over the 115-foot-tall rigs on these boats.*

At the same time we were rethinking our off wind inventory, we were enumerating the problems that we hoped to solve or eliminate in our sail testing program. The list grew quite long: There were questions of rig geometry. What was the right ratio of genoa to mainsail area? This was varied by changing the J dimension from headstay to mast. Bigger jibs and narrower jib sheeting angles of the long J arrangement meant a more efficient upwind sail plan. Short J and big mainsail mean more sail area off the wind. At an international gathering of the sailmaking crew late in the campaign, the Swedes arrived with T-shirts listing the seven or eight permutations of J length their boat had undergone, each of which implied many all-night sessions of sail recutting.

Next there was the question of the best mainsail profile. For the same sail area mainsail it was possible to build a sail with a huge roach and a short foot, or a long foot and a more conventional leech profile. The advantage of the former was area up high where the wind was. There seemed to be no doubt that this should be better, but could we build a sail with enough depth and twist up high?

To test these and many other more subtle questions we developed tools for extremely accurate real time sail shape measurement and for extremely accurate boat performance measurement. Differential GPS allowed placing two yachts within a few feet of their real position over the course of a 10 minute test run. As we homed in on fine details of the test to which we sought answers, such as the wind speed cross-over point between symmetrical and asymmetrical running spinnakers, the "scatter" in our data became more and more frustrating, especially to the sailors who had to endure what seemed interminable hours of straight line sailing.

Along with full-size testing, we had other tools to help us test sailmaking ideas, both mundane and very far out. We had a full-time programmer working on "flow code" for IACC sail plans. As our experience grew, his answers grew increasingly close to our on board experience and he could tweak shapes and suggest directions for full-size testing. Unfortunately, in the end the shapes he wanted were beyond our ability to build, but we were working on ways to achieve them down to the last days of the America's Cup finals.

We also had use of Amphitrete, MIT's Sailing Dynamometer. Known as "Bruce's summer camp," this craft had a 41% scale IACC rig attached to an internal frame that translated all sail forces to the hull through six load cells. When her computers were all tuned in she gave a very accurate reading of sail effectiveness: lift/drag ratios, and total force. We used her initially to tackle rig profile and sail shape issues. Near the end of the campaign she concentrated on off wind sails.

The final area of investigation, the most secret part of the sail program, was the development of improved sail fabric. This effort was undertaken by a team of Stanford researchers, headed by R.J. Downs, under the overall direction of Heiner Meldner. The early phases of development were confined to laboratories far from San Diego, but occasionally we would receive a swatch of material to run through the Instron tester and to sew into the leech of a genoa to see how it responded to the abuse of a 50-tack day.

When what came to be called "Cuben Fiber" emerged as the final material, we established a small and very secret manufacturing facility in an anonymous industrial complex in Rancho Bernardo, about 30 miles outside San Diego. There, an eclectic group of engineers and California surfers assembled 30-foot panels of the carbon fiber liquid crystal composite.

Paranoia surrounded this operation from the word go, with frequent reports of mysterious cars and even helicopters following personnel from the San Diego compound to this site. Next, when the material went to sail lofts to be turned into sails, it was never out of the sight of an America³ operative, whose job was to see that no scrap stayed behind to fall into the wrong hands.

The sails built from this material were truly remarkable. Although they weighed in at up to 40% less than high modulus aramid sails, we had to adjust the early sails because they did not stretch as aramid.

The problems presented were all new to us. The first genoas were flaked and rolled for shipment like conventional genoas. After tacking them a few dozen times we would often find a six or eight inch strip along one of the folding creases where the carbon fiber was all abraded through. We quickly changed the way the sails were prepared for shipping.

The biggest problem the Cuben Fiber sails faced were psychological ones. When we set the first Cuben Fiber mainsail early in 1992, the sailing crew's reaction was "well, it looks hot, and it sure is light, but we could never actually race with it because it is so untested we could never have confidence in it." As time went by and our experience with the material increased the attitude began to change. By the time the finals arrived we had reached the point when the sailors demanded we build one final Cuben Fiber code 2 genoa, with the argument that "we would be at a huge psychological disadvantage now if we had to use a Kevlar sail!"

Bill Koch had more confidence in his technical people than other syndicate heads seemed to. For this reason, technical decisions were made by technicians and sailing decisions by sailors. The Italians, for instance, never seemed to overcome their distrust of their carbon fiber sail material, and never used it in the finals until the last race. By then, the outcome was pretty much a foregone conclusion.

Sometimes a great result comes from a breakthrough boat or from brilliant sailing or sometimes even from magnificent sails. Of course we'd like to claim the last was responsible for America³ team's success, but we have to admit that Bill Koch's campaign had all the bases covered. Under Vincent Moeyersoms' direction, Jerry Milgram and his design team produced an extremely quick boat in America³. *Bill Koch, Buddy Melges, and the rest of the sailors performed close to flawlessly. But the sail program also contributed to the victory.*

Occasionally, we hear sailors complain of the colossal waste of an America's Cup Campaign. We believe that these campaigns make contributions that eventually benefit every sailor that appreciates advances in sailing performance. Already, A³ Technologies, Inc., an America³ Foundation spin-off, is bringing Cuben Fiber fabric to the marketplace. Fiberspar is building battens for many large offshore yachts, including most of the Whitbread fleet. Finally, the America's Cup asymmetrical designs are a huge leap forward for cruising sailors as well as racers.

Bay of Pigs Yacht Club

Early in the last America's Cup campaign, the America³ Foundation team came to be known around the San Diego waterfront as "Cubens." We were not then taken very seriously as Cup contenders, with the experts usually rating us as extreme long shots to defend, let alone defend successfully, and it was appar-

ent to us that this "Cuben" cognomen implied a certain disdain for our syndicate. However, we quickly adopted the name among ourselves and extended the concept. Our little corner of San Diego Harbor became known as the Bay of Pigs, our compound became the Bay of Pigs Yacht Club, and the BPYC burgee, depicting a serene pig in sunglasses, became our battle flag.

So it was that when we unveiled the first sails constructed from our own carbon fiber composite, the press immediately dubbed that material "Cuben Fiber." In a previous article we discussed many aspects of the America³ sail development program. Here we'd like to focus on the development and characteristics of the sail materials that program spawned.

There were several reasons for pursuing improved sail fabric. Lighter weight aloft would translate into improved righting moment and reduced pitching. Moreover, the IACC rule limited the total weight of crew and sails, so reducing sail weights, if we could reduce them enough, might allow us to carry an extra sail or two during a race.

Lower stretch was another very desirable goal. Sails that don't stretch translate more force from wind to yacht. Sails that don't stretch needed fewer, smaller sail control adjustments to achieve their designed shape while flying. Sails that don't stretch are more likely to finish a race with the same shape they had at the start. Sails that don't stretch wouldn't need recutting as early or as often. Recutting, no matter how carefully done, always includes the possibility that the recut sail will be neither as strong nor as smooth as it was before the recut.

Finally, no really satisfactory material existed at all for the IACC boat's 5,000-square-foot asymmetrical spinnakers and reachers. All existing laminates, nylons, and polyesters were too stretchy, too weak, too heavy, too unmanageable, or all of the above.

We decided early in the campaign that lighter, stronger sails were a worthy goal. Not all the competitors in San Diego agreed. For instance, we understood that the Kiwis apparently felt that experimenting with sailcloth would prove a counter-productive distraction and stuck with very conservative, proven cloth technology. But early on it became obvious that at least the French and the Italians shared our belief in the need to tackle the sail material problem.

We settled on a three-pronged approach— working to improve the strength-to-weight ratio of conventional sail fabric, working to develop sail construction techniques that used fiber more efficiently, and finally, searching for an entirely new and radically improved material. It was this search — striking out into unexplored territory — that led to success and far greater success than we had dared hope.

The America³ Foundation had as its motto "talent, teamwork, and technology." Therefore, we were not averse to spending money on technology, especially technology that promised competitive advantage. But a technology that our competitors shared was no advantage. Therefore, our research was carried out with circumspection. The effort to develop superior materials for sails was no exception. It was known only by its code name — the "B Project."

Dr. Heiner Meldner, who headed development of A³'s keels and rudders as well as other special projects, was given overall direction of the "B Project". Heiner was a strong subscriber to the philosophy of "need to know" access. People high up in the A³ technical team would often ask him, "how is the 'B Project' coming?" in the hope of finding out what the "B Project" actually was all about, but Heiner knew very well how to keep his secrets and never succumbed to such pumping.

Heiner recruited a young composites engineer named R.J. Downs to handle the day-to-day research. R.J., with help from Allied Signal and Hercules Aerospace, went to work. Very early the decision was made to try to take advantage of the exceptional strengths of carbon fiber.

Incorporating this material into a flexible membrane was like the struggle of giving birth — a little too much so on one occasion, when R.J. found himself in an intense conference call on the progress of the "B Project" while in the waiting room of the hospital in which his wife was doing the real thing.

Heiner, R.J., and their team started producing sample materials toward the end of the summer of 1991. These were tested on the same equipment using the same protocols we used to test conventional sail fabrics. These tests were encouraging. By October we were testing large panels in the leech area of full-sized genoas off San Diego. These were the first sails ever to use carbon as the primary load-carrying fiber. Some of these panels failed, but some showed remarkable promise, and each new batch proved a step better than the last.

By January it was apparent that we were onto something. Our samples had reached the point where they were approximately twice as strong for the weight as the most advanced of our commercial sail fabrics. Bill Koch and A³ Executive Vice-President Vincent Moeyersoms gave the approval to begin production of "Cuben Fiber" in sufficient quantities to build some real sails. Bill Shore, Heiner, and R.J. worked out the specs for the first production styles of materials. The communication between sailmakers and engineers was made easier because the material's modulus, a property familiar to the engineers, almost exactly matched its Kevlar equivalent in deniers per inch, a concept that sailmakers could grasp.

Kevin Ryan and some volunteers from the sail loft set up shop in an anonymous warehouse unit of a huge industrial park in Rancho Bernardo, about 30 miles northeast of San Diego. There, the material was laboriously hand-assembled in a process much more like boatbuilding than weaving cloth. As the production demands increased, this team was augmented by an eclectic mix of unemployed surfers and materials scientists

The first sail constructed totally of Cuben Fiber was a mainsail. Our very first Kevlar mainsail, built more than a year earlier, had weighed in at over 250 pounds. The first Cuben Fiber sail was less than half that weight. When the sailors arrived at the loft that morning in late March of 1992 and hefted the Cuben Fiber mainsail onto their shoulders to carry it down to America³*, they refused to believe that what they were carrying was a mainsail.*

After the sail was bent on and proved to look and act like a mainsail, they refused to believe such a sail could last for any length of time. A few days later however, the sail survived several hours of thrashing around San Diego harbor in what passes for storm conditions in that part of the world — sustained winds of 25 knots with gusts over 35.

Gradually, other Cuben Fiber sails began to arrive — and to prove their mettle. One particular Cuben Fiber Code 1 genoa experienced the most abuse of any sail in our experience when Stars & Stripes *and* America³ *each executed 80 tacks in one race. The crew was convinced that the sail had no future but the trash pile, yet our sail video cameras could detect no change in the sail's flying shape. When we cut some samples from the leech for testing, the Instron showed them to be no different than when they were new.*

The Cuben sailors, like sailors everywhere, were a conservative lot. After all, the sea, as we have had drummed into us over a lifetime, is a stern taskmaster and will ferret out any weakness in boat, sails, or hardware. We were all too aware that the surest way to lose a race is not to finish. So they were slow to accept Cuben Fiber. But as sail after sail proved its merit the attitude changed first to grudging acceptance and eventually to something akin to addiction. By the Cup finals, America³ *was carrying about 50 percent Cuben Fiber sails, including virtually all her upwind sails, and probably would have been completely outfitted if there had been time to build enough fabric, and sails from it.*

In the end we had settled on seven different styles of Cuben Fiber. These varied in weight from about .75 oz. per sailmaker's yard (36" x 28.5") up to about 4.5 ounces. They ranged in strength from the equivalent of 6,000 deniers per inch of Kevlar up to almost 50,000 deniers per inch. We built mainsails, genoas, and reach asymmetricals for almost all conditions from these materials.

We did experiment with a true 1/2-ounce material and built a very light running asymmetrical from it. However, to achieve this weight we eliminated the film layer from one side of the laminate. As a result, some of the tiny, yet extremely strong polymer filaments tended to come loose when the sail was handled. Sewer man John Spence at one point became so entangled in these he claimed to be in fear for his life. We never built another of these sails.

A complete discussion of the mechanical properties of Cuben Fiber is beyond the scope of this article, to say nothing of the scope of the authors. The properties of carbon fiber don't need repetition here, but as we understand it, their full utilization in a flexible membrane was a real breakthrough.

The Italian Il Moro di Venezia *team, together with Montedison and North Cloth, succeeded in putting some carbon fiber together with Kevlar in a woven material that was then laminated to film in a very conventional sail fabric construction. But they never seemed to embrace this technology in the way that we embraced ours, perhaps because it did not leapfrog existing materials in the way ours did. In fact, while* America³ *used Cuben Fiber sails in every leg of every race of the America's Cup,* Il Moro *sported hers only in the last race.*

In this material, carbon and extended chain polymer monofilaments are imbedded in a polymer matrix film. The appearance from a few feet away is a lustrous silver-gray. The lightest styles were similar, but lacked the carbon. These were a pale milky white.

Conventional woven fabric stretches at least partially because of "crimp," the bending of the yarns inherent in the over and under weaving process. Even in conventional unwoven "scrim" laminates, the individual filaments are not perfectly aligned due to the twist used to keep the yarns together for handling prior to lamination. The filaments in Cuben Fiber have neither twist or crimp, so that they do not need to straighten out before taking their full load. Cuben Fiber of 3 oz. per sailmakers yard requires the same load to reach 1 percent elongation as a 6 oz. aramid (Kevlar) laminate.

Another important aspect of Cuben Fiber is its thickness, or, we should say, its thinness. Because it has no twisted yarns, the material is dramatically thinner than other laminates. This contributes greatly to its ability to flex without loss of strength. After being folded 250 times, a typical aramid laminate will lose more than 80 percent of its yield strength, while an equivalent-strength Cuben Fiber under the same loading conditions exhibits virtually no degradation after repeated folding.

After more than a year of ironing out patent details and adapting the production process to achieve useful quantities, America³ Technologies, Inc., a spin-off of the America³ Foundation, has announced the first commercial availability of Cuben Fiber, now officially christened F³ — for Filament Fortified Film — for January of 1994. While still a young and relatively dear material, F³ should be immediately attractive to a variety of sailors, most notably the captains of megayachts. For these giants, F³ promises extremely fast, durable, and UV-resistant sails at incredible weight savings.

As the 1992 America's Cup Campaign fades into history, at least one important legacy remains for sailors of today and tomorrow — the stuff they called Cuben Fiber.

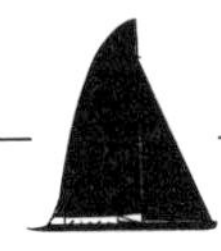

Pressure

12

Winning is easy. Losing is what tests the mettle of a sports team. After a fast start, *America³* lost two straight at the end of Round 3. As Round 4, the defenders' semifinals, began, Team Dennis Conner registered two more back-to-back wins — the first was against *Kanza,* America³'s brand new boat. *Kanza* took Race 4 from *Stars & Stripes.* But in Race 5, TDC again prevailed over *America³*, the white hope of February and early March.

When a team begins losing, fans and the press second-guess everything from management technique and overall game plan to specific tactical calls. On the inside, self-doubt can slip in on cat feet as all aspects of the team's program are re-examined.

With its exhausting schedules and diverse list of inner battles that must be engaged and won (yacht design/technology; sail development; crew training; maintenance; logistics; fundraising; press relations), the long Cup campaign is particularly susceptible to slumps. Turning them around is critical in playing this complex game. That job went to Bill Koch. Koch alone had his hands on every aspect of America³'s campaign.

"As in other sports," says Koch, "mental toughness is critical. We had to remain emotionally balanced, not get too high or too low as a result of winning or losing races. That may have been the most difficult aspect of personnel management. We're all people. We're happy when we win, sad when we lose. But we have to continually be aware, as Yogi Berra loves to say, it ain't over 'til its over, and it's essential for us to keep even."

Peaking at the right time is always the way to win. And as Dennis Conner proved in Fremantle, 1986/87, he knows all about peaking at the right time. Taken lightly for most of that campaign, he made significant changes to his boat in the last round, won the challenger finals, and brought home the America's Cup. So Conner's sudden surge in March struck an ominous chord.

Cup observers began to equate the Conner strategy of 1992 to his of 1986/87. While the America[3] strategy was to perfect boat speed by using science and to train hard for no crew mistakes, Dennis saw the early rounds of the defender trials, where the points counted the least, as training races. He reasoned this is where we can learn as much as possible about our opponent and use that knowledge to our best advantage in the later rounds, where the points count the most. It was a strategy that suited his limited budget, and one that came very close to being successful.

Yet even after the keel change Bill Koch allowed TDC in Round 2, *Stars & Stripes* remained in trouble. But now it became obvious that TDC had subsequently made significant improvements to *Stars & Stripes.* "Conner did the only thing he could do," Andreas Josenhans said. "He picked a corner and shot for it."

The niche Conner selected was light air — under 7.5 knots, and flat seas. And sure enough, the weather cooperated in the first four races he won. (*Kanza*'s win was in 10-13 knots, more to her liking.) As Bill Koch said after Round 4, "I'd like to have Conner's luck with my money."

Conner looked like Dennis the Menace of old, tacking smoothly, covering with a vengeance, taking large bites to weather with apparent ease, and picking shifts with confounding success. Conner's damage control — staying close when behind — was masterful. Winning or losing, *Stars & Stripes* seemed to be in charge of the race course, and that was disquieting.

It was predictable that the local newspapers would warm to another Conner comeback story. The same writers who had brutally castigated Conner in the past were suddenly embracing him as America's last hope. He had been reclaimed by his home town. Perhaps the local editors saw a Conner comeback as an antidote to San Diego's shaky America's Cup stewardship, which was foundering in a sea of financial mismanagement. Given its huge allocations for fireworks displays and six-figure salaries, the ACOC was on the brink of bankruptcy. The San Diego Yacht Club was embarrassed, and local merchants were bitterly vocal about overblown projections of Cup-generated business that had not materialized.

To Conner the sailor, Bill Koch was the enemy on the race course. But to Conner the businessman, Koch remained a potential client. Why alienate him with heavy flak ashore? From January on, Conner had been eyeing and praising Koch's fast white boats. There were several fantasies being entertained that could put Conner on board one of those fliers. At least that was a notion cherished by movers and shakers at the ACOC and the San Diego Yacht Club.

Conner and Koch wined and dined together more than once during the trials. For Koch, the dinners were opportunities to measure an adversary whom he considers best in the world and to form a friendship with him. For Conner, they were selling opportunities. He presented Koch with several suggestions for doing business together.

Koch said he may have leaned a bit too hard on Conner at one dinner. He told Conner, "We're better than you are. We're going to kick your ass." Koch admitted the remark got Conner angry, gave him new resolve.

With lots of shrugs, praise for the opposition, and sad smiles, the Big Bad Dennis that San Diego loved to hate had turned into a sympathetic character. He had a big assist from ESPN. "I would say we played up the underdog idea, helped make him into a hero," said Jed Drake, producer of the ESPN shows. "It was good for us. Heroes are easy for viewers to understand."

Newcomer Bill Koch, a rich guy with a four-boat program and the audacity to sail on his own team, made an easy target. Unpracticed before the media, Koch's initial effort to put up a strong front had been viewed as arrogance. Later, his sustained aggressiveness with the press was ill-advised. As design team member Jim Pugh observed, "America³ has done for Conner what he's tried to do for himself for 20 years."

Poor Dennis versus the rich bully, or as one newspaper writer alliterated, versus "the chemist from Kansas." It had a nice ring to it. The media strung its bow and let fly.

ESPN's producers were just trying to mold a potentially boring event into a salable television show. And some of it was flotsam from an America³/ESPN deal that went on the rocks. It began when ESPN wanted to shorten the race course to comply with its three-hour time slot. Too many light-air races were running long. America³ balked at this suggestion, pointing out that the course length (especially the three weather legs) had been a primary consideration for the design of the boats.

ACOC entreated America³ to agree. Koch responded with an emphatic no. "We don't dance to ESPN's tune," he said.

As a way to cut its losses, ACOC finally turned over its television rights to the Challenger of Record Committee (CORC), but ESPN was still pressing for shortening the course. Koch finally agreed, if America³ got something in return (free airing of spots for the Foundation was under discussion). ACOC told America³ a deal had been negotiated, but it turned out ESPN had not agreed to it. Koch then refused to give ESPN access to his syndicate and the all-sports network took a few shots at the sailor. For two months America³ and ESPN conducted a cold war until Gary Jobson was able to get Koch and ESPN president Steve Bornstein to sit down and hash out their differences.

Front-Runner Blues

As Conner surged at the end of March, there was a lot for the press to shoot at. America^3 was scratching its collective head. *The San Diego Union-Tribune*'s Don Norcross wrote, "The America^3 camp looks as fragile as a dime-store model airplane." Had the many options (boats, sails, rigs, and crews in all the possible combinations) of America^3's vast program become a liability? Suffering from a chronic case of front-runner blues, some Cubens were giving solemn credence to the notion that TDC's one-boat program was advantageous for the focus it demanded. The Cubens' mental stigmatism was understandable. At moments, the variables open to the America^3 brain trust appeared as so many twisted pathways in a killer maze.

The first surprise in Round 4 for America^3 was the initial performance of *Kanza*. This fourth-generation product of America^3's design team was aimed at a heavier wind range than America^3. While that was general knowledge around the compound, the fact was still perplexing. After the first day of sailing the new boat, the sailors were seen shaking their heads. Perhaps they had been spoiled by how fast *America^3* had come out of the box.

It was also known that there had been serious disagreement within the design team about the lines of *Kanza*. Bill Koch, who made the final decision about the yacht, made the decision based on the performance curves of the different boats in different conditions. Koch said his choice was based on being able to match whatever boat America^3 had to face in the finals, and in the Cup. "We had to cover ourselves. If we face a light-air boat in the finals, then we'll use *America^3*. If a heavy-air boat, we'll use *Kanza*. Who knows what the wind will do? If we have both boats, we'll race them enough to find out which one wins the most."

Vincent Moeyersoms would also defend the logic of *Kanza*. "It was an insurance policy," Vincent said later. "It turned out we didn't need it because of the conditions. But there was uncertainty about the weather. We thought *Kanza* would be useful in April, usually the windiest month of the spring. But El Nino came in, stuck around, and April turned out to be a dud. Yet if we had spent time on *Kanza*, changed it the way we changed *America^3*, *Kanza* could have won the Cup." In retrospect, the fact is that the weather during the Cup match was most conducive to *Kanza*!

Moeyersoms' reference to El Nino was to the warm-water current which flows in from the Pacific. America^3 meteorologist Chris Crabtree explained that El Nino is a warm cycle of sea surface temperature occurring in the Eastern Pacific on a regular basis. It moves westward along the equator. When the current reverses, it can send water toward the Western

Hemisphere. If it is strong enough, it deflects off South America into the northeast Pacific. That's what happened in 1992.

A study of the history of El Nino conducted by A³ showed that the phenomenon caused higher and lesser winds almost on an equal basis. Weather experts visited the compound with computer models and gave predictions. The team prepared for whatever conditions they might find.

In addition, big high-pressure areas stuck over San Diego during April, blocking storms which stir up cold water from below the surface. The result: a water temperature of 72 degrees — 10 degrees above normal.

The effect was to significantly reduce the strength of the sea breeze. On light-air days, the high bluff of Point Loma causes the breeze to separate well offshore. What's left is a potpourri of erratic, oscillating shifts and unpredictable, strong ocean currents. With his 40-odd years of experience sailing in San Diego, perhaps no one is better at negotiating what sailors called "The Coma Off Point Loma" than Conner.

At the time, TDC had a 2-1 lead in Round 4, but Koch had seen *Kanza* beat *Stars & Stripes* by :42 in 10 knots of breeze. In that race, Koch's boat looked higher and faster, and was never threatened over the 20-mile course. A good sign. But in the compound, how to improve both boats continued to be the number one topic of discussion among armchair designers. The major conundrum was this: if it is (in fact) easier to modify a light air boat upwards in wind range, why go with a heavier air boat that might have to be modified down? "Because," Harold Cudmore offered, "the program is driven by scientists, not yachtsmen."

The sailors were also struggling with the options for improving performance. "Now we have a new rig on *America³*," Jerry Kirby said. "I think we're changing too many things at once. We've got so many good sailors being swayed by so much input, so many opinions, that their basic instincts have become dulled. There are so many committees, so much talent...this thing has developed its own life. We have to consolidate.

"Vincent is getting out on the water, stepping in, and that's good," Kirby continued. "He's a sailor. He has a good feel. And he's cool. Everyone else is selling. Vince just absorbs information, makes decisions. He's the hope."

As the action on the water heated up, so, too, did the media's constant quest for controversy. At one press conference, Koch was asked yet again about his steering. "Gary Jobson has suggested that it would be best," said the reporter, "if you got off the boat and let Buddy steer all the time. What is your reaction to that?"

As Koch digested the question and fumbled for a public response, Melges leaned over the microphone and said "I'd like to answer that with one word, Bulllllsssshiiit!" The rest of the media in the room, in a rare show of unanimity, applauded.

Another subject for media scrutiny was crew selection. The lineup Koch had announced on March 20 lasted only three days into Round 4. The press jumped on this inconsistency with both feet. They also suggested that Koch was juggling crew to orchestrate the points accumulation of *Kanza* and *America^3*.

The media noise about America^3 orchestrating points was deafening at times. Never mind that America^3's two slots in the defense trials — and the possibility of an all-America^3 final — had been formally agreed upon by America^3, Team Dennis Conner, and the ACOC. Suddenly, outrage over the specter of foul play was the theme of the month. Hadn't Peter Gilmour admitted that the Kookaburras rigged their races in Australia? Wasn't Dennis Conner arguably the biggest sandbagger in the sport's history? Now here came Koch and what the *Union-Tribune*'s Bill Center was calling his "Evil Empire." The erratic Center, dubbed "Off Center" by the A^3 camp, provided the Wagnerian crash of cymbals: "It's just that the process — and the way Koch has used it — stinks so much that if Conner is eliminated by *Kanza*, Koch's effort will be tarnished and the bottom will fall out of what interest there is in the event's defense finals."

On the last day of March, amid the clatter from the press and the uncertainty in his own camp, Bill Koch stepped to the wheel of *America^3* after Dellenbaugh had won the start over *Stars & Stripes* and established a 10-second lead. Once again, the boss was making a statement and once again his team wasn't sure what it was. The usual routine was for Dellenbaugh to hand off to Melges for the first weather leg, especially in light air. Koch usually drove on the reaching legs.

"It wasn't a big deal," Koch later explained. "*America^3* hadn't beat *Stars & Stripes* since the 7th race of Round 3, and Dennis had reeled off three straight wins against *America^3*, *Defiant*, and *Kanza*. He had some momentum going and we were in a bit of a slump. I just wanted to shake things up a bit, see what happened."

What happened almost destroyed everything America^3 had accomplished to that point and once again held the Koch philosophy on management, crew selection, leadership, and teamwork in question. But in the end, it may have been the most significant race of the entire defender trials.

Although this was the time of year San Diego was supposed to begin experiencing its windiest conditions, El Nino was still in town and the day offered a maddening combination of light, fluky air with swells rolling in from astern. When Koch took the wheel, he was on the favored right side of the course. Conner went left to avoid the dirty air from his opponent and to search for more wind. He made some gains there, tacked, and headed for the right side. Koch asked the afterguard if he should tack. There was a brief discussion. Dellenbaugh said yes. Someone else said no. A third voice said wait to see what Dennis does.

Dennis crossed astern of *America³* and kept heading for the right side. Again, Koch asked what he should do. Again, no decision was forthcoming. Koch kept on the same course, Dennis continued to the right, caught a windshift *America³* missed and passed the white boat. Race over, *Stars & Stripes* by 45 seconds.

Here was the perfect example of why Koch wanted to be on the boat. Ashore, he wouldn't have known exactly what happened. Aboard, he was able to determine that the decision-making process in the afterguard had to be streamlined.

Hurricane Melges

Post race, the mood in the compound was grim. People gathered in small groups for guarded conversations. Melges stormed out of the afterguard meeting and cruised around the compound like a shark considering the dinner menu. Koch appeared a few moments later. "Cool off and come on back in," he said to Melges.

"I'm sick of this crap," Melges said as he followed Bill inside. "The team is so uptight they're shitting square bricks."

A few days later Buddy discoursed on a number of issues. "We're suffering from too many opinions," he said. "We're overcoached. I'm sick of having the afterguard ridiculed. If the coaches are so smart, let them sail the boat. And I don't mind crew changes, but sooner or later we've got to get everything set so we can get used to our jobs. I blew up because I wanted to shake the limbs. Bill's diplomatic. Every once in a while you need a little of the old Vince Lombardi."

Race 3 was intramural. Koch (with *America³*) and Melges (on *Kanza*), squared off on the water. *Kanza* was over early, but Melges had fire in his eye and veins in his teeth. The crew felt it. It was showtime on *Kanza*. Crossing the line a minute late, Melges and his dog pack ground down *America³* and came hunting them on starboard half way up the leg. Koch tacked too close. On ESPN, Jim Kelly suggested that if Melges protested his boss, Melges' next assignment would be on the television boat. Melges pulled the trigger, up went the flag. Koch was assessed a penalty turn, and that race was history.

Inside the compound, the atmosphere was frosty at best. Tension was thick, words were either whispered or shouted. To most of the crew, it seemed a power struggle was at hand and no one was sure who to follow: Koch or Melges.

"Buddy was pissed at the coaches and at me," Bill said. "I was pissed because it seemed everyone was blaming me for the last four losses to *Stars & Stripes*. Morale was down. Indecision was killing us. I saw the situation as a significant leadership and management problem. We had to get this straightened out immediately or chances of winning again weren't good."

Still stinging from the lack of direction from his afterguard in Race 2, Koch sought out Dellenbaugh for a heart-to-heart. The quiet tactician is tough to the core, and a smart sailor, but the least personally aggressive fellow around. One afternoon during a practice session, Dave spun around and shouted a curse at Harold Cudmore who had been nagging him to work on certain maneuvers. Cudmore was both amazed and delighted by Dellenbaugh's outburst. It was such a departure from the norm that the crew teased Dellenbaugh for days afterwards.

"I wasn't being strong enough about tactical decisions," Dellenbaugh says about his role on the boat. "I was getting one to four opinions about possible choices. I was in the middle, and being too influenced. What I needed were observations and information, not opinions. One person needs to decide tactics. You can't be sailing two or three different races.

"I saw this problem, and to his credit, so did Bill. Bill said to me, take charge, you make the decisions. I needed that. Buddy was willing to focus on steering and let me make the calls. We worked that out in the semifinals. And the others switched to providing information. I made stronger and quicker decisions after that."

Next, Bill attacked the subject that just wouldn't go away: his presence on the boat. "The afterguard meetings were getting ugly. Everyone on the afterguard had a dream team. In their hearts, none of them would put me on it. But I was going to be on the team. That's the price they pay. If not for me, they wouldn't be here."

In the past, Koch had told his team they were lucky to have him "because who else would be stupid enough to put up $50 million for a silly sailboat race." Now he walked into a crew meeting and told his team they were lucky to have him there because they had someone else to take all the heat. With that, he turn around and displayed a bull's eye target on the back of his shirt. The tension broke and the crew rolled with laughter.

"In our last three races," said Koch, "Buddy drove the first weather leg. In two of the races he drove the whole time. So in the second race I steered the first weather leg, and took the rap for four losses. There was bad chemistry somewhere," said the man with a Ph.D. in the subject.

Next, Koch announced he had undertaken an informal study of his effect on the boat's performance. He said that there was no correlation to winning or losing when he steered, when he was on board, or when he was ashore. Thus, from now on he would be on the boat when he chose to and there was to be no further discussion about that issue. He said he intended to take himself off the boat in light air. It was a promise he kept several times.

"One thing I know is how to make decisions," Koch told the crew. "And I will make them in the best interest of the team."

Afterwards, Carl Lessard gave Koch a nod. "I've been working for him for seven years," Lessard said, "and he always makes good decisions. And in that time, I've never seen him renege on a promise." Vincent Moeyersoms, eight years with Koch, was equally confident that Bill would do the right thing. So was Brad Robinson, America^3 vice-president and chief financial officer. "Wait and see," Robinson said. "When everyone stops pushing him, Bill will make the right decision."

Koch next addressed the problem of sail trim. The trimmers were getting mixed signals from a variety of sources about how to do their job. "Trim the way you see it," Koch told them. "If the boat is slow, it's your fault. If it's fast, it's to your credit. It's as simple as that."

Then there was the matter of the helm. "Buddy wouldn't give it up," Koch said. "I'd have to push for it. So we had a problem. We had to solve it or we couldn't be on the same boat. I was pissed to the point of considering two options: a radical restructuring of the afterguard, or total withdrawal from the Cup.

"I had told Buddy that if I wasn't on the team I would walk. He's seen my tough side. He knew I'd do it. On the boat I'm a mild-mannered guy who defers to all the talent and experience we've got.

"I needed to know Buddy would share the helm; and that if I screwed up, he would tap me on the shoulder. And he needed to know that if he did tap me, I wouldn't fire him. I told him he needed to stop yelling at people and threatening them, and compliment them once in a while, me included. He had to listen to me about management and motivation, and I'd listen to him about sailing.

"We got it worked out. We arrived at an excellent partnership."

Koch told the crew he and Melges had worked out the steering question. That was good news for the crew. As grinder T.A. McCann said, "I don't think there's a guy on this crew who doesn't think Bill should be on the boat. But he should rely on the helmsman to tell him when to drive."

Koch modified the teams he had announced the previous week. Kimo Worthington (helm), By Baldridge (navigator), and Per Andersson (main trimmer), would be permanently on *America^3*. Melges, Bill Campbell (navigator), and Andreas Josenhans (main trimmer), would be assigned to *Kanza*. Koch and David Dellenbaugh would shuttle back and forth between the boats.

Race 5 — *America^3* vs. *Stars & Stripes* — was a pivotal point in Round 4. Once again Conner got the wind he wanted: 8 knots, shifting radically and dying. As planned, Koch and Worthington shared the helm. Melges was on the bench. "We were just trying to sort things out," Worthington said. "We should have done it earlier. A four-man afterguard had been rotating from boat to boat. There was no leader on either boat, no camaraderie. So we had a meeting. Buddy would stay on *Kanza*, I'd stay on *America^3*. Bill and Dave would rotate. Great idea, but it only lasted one race."

Dellenbaugh's start was excellent. *America^3* lifted off as the two boats went up the left side. She stretched a couple times instead of covering, which made the coaches nervous, and led by only :09 at the mark. Downwind, *America^3* pulled away to lead by :41 at mark 2. Then disaster: on the second weather leg, the wind dropped to a whisper. While *America^3* went left, *Stars & Stripes* picked up a 50-degree shift on the right that brought them from :41 behind to :24 ahead. After that, the lead never changed.

TDC made the most of the win. At the press conference, tactician Tom Whidden crowed a little: "This kind of day is why Dennis makes the big bucks. He revels in the shifty, up-and-down stuff." Conner was quietly deferential: "In tank test conditions, we don't like what we see. In straight-line sailing, we still have a ways to go to catch up."

The press went on a second-guessing binge about why Melges was on the bench, why Koch steered upwind in light air, and why Kimo Worthington ("Kimo who?" one newspaper asked) was steering his first race at such a critical juncture.

Fifty-degree shift, wind conditions, media noise, and crew selection aside, *Stars & Stripes* was now 5-1 over the two newest America^3 boats since the blue boat's dismasting in Round 3. While America^3's afterguard was struggling to assess its options, TDC was jamming the airwaves with propaganda: Dennis will get tough...he hasn't been using his best moves up to now...Bill steers better than Buddy, or Bill Campbell, or Dave Dellenbaugh...*America^3* is fast. Dennis would like to defend the Cup with this boat.

Once again Buddy Melges went off like a hand grenade. "Our people were actually upset over this stuff. I blew up. I told them what the hell, you're all grown men and you can't understand what those guys are doing?"

"Blame No One, Do Something"

Bill Koch admitted his program wobbled for a moment under the pressure. The afternoon before a lay-day after an intramural race between *Kanza* and *America³* (*Kanza* broke a spinnaker pole, *America³* passed and won), Koch addressed his weary team. "We have two excellent boats and two excellent crews. If we are going to win, we must act as one team. Blame no one, do something...."

Koch again said the team was lucky to have him to take the blame. He said he understood where the buck stopped. Then he turned to display a large, red and white bulls-eye on the back of his T-shirt. The crew cracked up. The boss still had some humor.

Koch took action on two fronts. He sent *America³* into the shed for a mid-round modification that would improve light air performance. The right to change the keel was the result of the earlier agreement between the two camps when TDC was losing by such large margins. It was one of the smartest deals America³ negotiated throughout the entire competition.

And he addressed the team selection question. He said that in the *Matador²* program he had five years to get the crew fully evolved. Dennis Conner has had 25 years to make his team work. "Here we've only had 17 months. So we've mixed it up. I refused to go for a 'first team' early because some of our best guys who developed slowly would have been cut.

"It's time to fish or cut bait," Koch said at the morning meeting. The crew was collectively sprawled in its chairs. Faces were sour. They already knew who the first team was. Many had seen the list on the ESPN show the previous evening. Someone had leaked it. Parents and friends had already called long distance expressing delight or offering sympathy, catching sailors who hadn't seen the show totally off-guard.

Koch named a "central" team that he would build around. He said there would be lots of substitutions depending on race conditions and how people felt. The grinders would be rotated each race to prevent burn-out. "Some of these decisions were very tough," Koch said. "It came down to attitude, teamwork, and loyalty. I truly believe that both teams were good enough to win the Cup."

While *America³* was in surgery, *Kanza* met *Stars & Stripes* in Race 7, one of the most exciting and controversial races in the defender series. The breeze freshened just enough on the last weather leg for *Kanza* to shift into passing gear after trailing *Stars & Stripes* throughout the race. As *Kanza* approached the mark, *S&S* tacked to port, to the stern of her opponent. Following traditional match-race strategy, *Kanza* tacked immediately to keep herself between the mark and *S&S*. With approximately two boatlengths to the mark, *Kanza* had "buoy room" and should have been given room to round the mark. But Conner saw a small opening and, believing he had a right to maneuver under a technical amendment to the buoy room rule, tacked to starboard, forcing the issue. When *Kanza* tacked to round the mark, a slight collision ensued and *S&S* bounced off the A3 yacht into the mark.

Both boats immediately flew protest flags and the on-the-water umpires went into a huddle. They green flagged (gave no penalty) the incident, but they did penalize Conner for hitting the mark. *Stars & Stripes* was now required to perform a 270-degree penalty turn at any time before the finish. Running downwind, Conner retained the lead, but as he turned to resolve his penalty, *Kanza* passed and took the gun.

Conner and crew were irate over the penalty call. Their view was that hitting the mark was obviously the result of the collision, so if that incident was green-flagged, so should hitting the mark. The umpire's call was reminiscent of a collision between *Stars & Stripes* and *America*^{3} in the second round. That situation occurred during pre-start maneuvering as Conner's bow bit into the port rail of the white boat. Damage was sustained to both yachts, but surprisingly, the incident was also green flagged.

With seven races in the books, *Stars & Stripes* and *Kanza* each had three victories and *America*^{3} had one.

Peter Grubb's pit crew completed a five-day job on *America*^{3} in 48 hours. Grubb was used to doing things others said couldn't be done. After one transatlantic crossing aboard *Matador*, he had six days to haul the boat, pull the mast, change keels, and prepare the boat for a regatta.

"The keel change involved filling 22 two-inch holes and drilling new ones," says Carl Lessard. "Guys from *Kialoa* told Peter it was impossible. But Peter had the boat on the starting line."

As a boy in Cornwall, England, Grubb and his mates built Mirror dinghies in wood shop and then raced them on the weekends. In the early 1980s he began sailing maxis and in 1985, when Matador skipper Vincent Moeyersoms left to run Bill Koch's overall racing program, Grubb took over the boat.

He's known for his ability to trouble-shoot problems and fix them. His fast reactions on board are also an asset in any race, as well as being potentially life saving. In one race Lessard was at the end of *Matador*'s spinnaker pole during a sail change in heavy air. In the confusion of the sail change and the rocking of the boat, someone kicked the topping lift out of the winch. Lessard ended up underwater, pinned to the submerged pole as the boat sped along at 13 knots. Grubb reacted first, finding the loose topping lift, quickly jamming it back on the winch, and cranking Lessard free.

During the Cup campaign, Grubb served as America^3's maintenance manager and coordinated the efforts of fifteen people in the compound to keep the temperamental yachts race-ready.

The modifications looked encouraging. In 10-12 knots, *America^3* won the start, covered well, and led *Stars & Stripes* around the course. The next day, in very light air, *America^3* put *Kanza* away by nearly two minutes. The score: *Kanza* 5; *Stars & Stripes* 4; *America^3* 3.

Again the air was light for Race 10. Daylight saving time, which arrived on April 4, had created a problem. San Diego's typical summer sea-breeze thermal doesn't fill in (when it does at all) until early afternoon. With the advent of daylight time, the 12 o'clock warning gun was sounding at 11 am, sea-breeze time. The race committee was in a daily quandary about setting a course in unsettled conditions. ESPN was forced to fill time while waiting for races to start (as viewers changed channels). It was strange that this annual advancement of the clocks hadn't been considered when schedules were being written.

For all its technological emphasis, the inevitable daylight saving time adjustment had slipped past America^3's braintrust unnoticed. "For some reason we thought the time change came at the end of April," Moeyersoms said. "We made a mistake." But evidently it was something Team Dennis Conner considered when modifying its boat for the lowest wind range. Pre-race, under full sail, *Stars & Stripes* would begin buzzing the race committee at 11:30 am, making "let's get started" signals in the patchy, mid-morning zephyrs. TDC's race committee representative was applying pressure on board, while America^3's delegate would be urging a delay until the breeze came in. Then here would come the ESPN boat, circling the race committee, asking when the start would be.

The general impression around America^3 was that the race committee all too often started races in light air conditions that favored Conner, rather than waiting until the sea breeze settled in. In Race 10 (4-5 knots after a postponement), Conner once again got the air he wanted. He also got a gift from *Kanza* at the start. Dave Dellenbaugh, who was batting well over .800 on the starting line, swung at a bad pitch. Dellenbaugh jibed onto port just as Conner jibed onto starboard in front of him. With little steerageway, *Kanza* was a sitting duck. After a red flag and a 270-degree turn, it was all over.

Race 11 also started light. *America^3* won the start, but dropped behind, playing the oscillating breeze up the first weather leg. Several times, *America^3* chose to let her opponent wander free. Covering too loosely, or sometimes not at all, had been a continuing weakness in America^3's afterguard. While not good match racing, stretching out in hopes of finding advantageous shifts or wind velocity was also part of the game in San

Diego's fluky conditions and it could also lead to disaster. On the race course the wind puffs could be as much as one to two knots stronger in velocity and the current could be as much as one to two knots different. That meant that if the leading boat went looking for wind shifts instead of covering the opponent, it might end up in an area where the wind and current affected it adversely, giving the opponent the opportunity to pass.

But *America³* was still struggling with that aspect of the tactics. Stretching at the wrong time had been costing them. Part of the difficulty was that so many of the sailors in *America³* were used to fleet racing, not match racing. Koch spent many a night trying to get the point across that a one second win counted just as much as a 10-minute victory. If we are ahead, he would repeat often, we will stay in the same water and the same air as the other guy.

In Race 11, *Stars & Stripes* led by :21 at mark 1. In the freshening breeze (13-16) and three-foot wind-generated chop, *America³* came alive on the second beat, passing *Stars & Stripes* and winning by :44.

At 5:45 a.m. the next morning Bill Koch was awake, struggling to get out of his bed. He heard voices he recognized from the walk in front of his house. "Nice race, Bill." "Yeah, nice race." It was Dennis Conner and Tom Whidden, out for their morning constitutional.

"Thanks, Tom. Thanks, Dennis," Bill said toward the open window, still prone, but now smiling. Whidden and Conner broke out laughing and then joined Koch for coffee.

Thus began a week-long series of private conversations which ultimately led to a suggestion by Dennis that some type of merger between the two teams might be in the best interests of the American effort. In fact, these conversations began to circulate among the two camps until finally, it seemed, half of Bill's crew believed that many of them might be expendable with replacements coming over from Conner's all-star crew. The newspapers began to fan the controversy. The morale at North Harbor Drive began to suffer.

Conner had opened one conversation by saying: "There is nothing worse than losing the America's Cup." This nefarious little injection of paranoia was followed by a series of conflicting suggestions. Conner said America³ had tactical problems. He said that Koch should loan him a boat for the finals. If he beat Koch, he would invite Koch to sail with him in the Cup. If he lost, he and Whidden would do whatever they could for America³.

At other times, Conner praised Koch's team, saying he wished he could be a part of it. Once when Koch began to discuss how Conner could join America³, Conner quickly backed down. As one insider saw it, Conner was trying to destabilize Koch's program, or get himself one of the white boats, or both. Given that Paul Cayard acknowledged, at the final press conference, that he had received help from Conner, that analysis has merit. When winning is at stake, there is no card Conner won't play.

After listening to Conner's ploys for several days, Koch cut off contact with his rival, against the advice of Harold Cudmore, who had urged Bill to continue attempting to acquire as much information from Dennis as he could and keep his options open. But Koch believed it was time to close ranks and demonstrate that he backed his own team.

"Whatever you have heard about some deal between me and Dennis," the skipper told his team, "you can forget. There is no deal and there won't be one. When we win the America's Cup, it will be with the people in this room right now. You have stood behind me. I'll stand behind you!"

With the score *America*³ 4, *Stars & Stripes* 5, *Kanza* 5, no sailoff would have been necessary if *Kanza* had beaten *America*³ in Race 12. But that didn't happen. *America*³ led up the first weather leg, and was increasing the time difference at every mark when *Kanza* suffered a near disastrous breakdown approaching mark 4. The aluminum weldment anchoring the aft end of the hydraulic mast ram broke, creating a one-foot crack in the deck. A reaching sail was up, and the pole was forward, fully-loaded aft at deck level. The compensating back pressure on the mast was gone. If *Kanza* had rounded and had done a jibe set, when the new sail filled it could have buckled the rig. The score was tied at 5-5-5.

Luckily, the repair wasn't complicated. *Kanza* was at full strength for the sailoff the next day. (It was *Kanza* in the sailoff because this boat was sailing in Slot A, where it enjoyed a two-win bonus going in). Once again, the 6 knots of wind was perfect for TDC's light air boat. Seas were flat.

Stars & Stripes was moving faster at the start. "We misread the current," Melges said later. *Kanza* was forced to tack at the gun in the light air, and floundered. *Stars & Stripes* went right, into fresher breeze, and all but disappeared. The delta at mark 1 was 4:09, a record for the defender trials. *Kanza* managed to cut *Stars & Stripes*'s lead to 2:12 at the finish. But Bill Koch's dream of an all-America³ final drifted away on a San Diego zephyr.

Also critical to TDC making the trials' final was the fact that the America³ camp never threw any of the races between *America*³ and *Kanza*, despite all the speculation and accusations that dogged the syndicate throughout the semi-finals. As these races came to a close, *Kanza* needed only one victory over *America*³ to knock Dennis out. It never happened.

ESPN just about collapsed with relief over Conner making the cut. Without the media's newly fashioned hero, reruns of famous croquet matches would have pulled better than ten days of America³ scrimmages. The ACOC dodged a bullet as well. Tom Ehman's guitar medleys never would have soothed San Diego's savage partisan breasts, not to mention the merchants. And the local newspapers went so far out on a limb in their praise of Conner that alien visitors might have thought the Lord had returned for a visit.

A *San Diego Union-Tribune* writer named Nick Canepa won the "Praise Him" contest hands down. "Conner embodies what we, as a nation, are supposed to be about in the eyes of the world," the starry-eyed Mr. Canepa wrote. *The Los Angeles Times*'s Dave Distel alone countered: "The monster is alive. This underdog stuff isn't going to stick. Dennis Conner fits in that role about as well as Anjelica Huston playing Mother Theresa. Big Bad Dennis has survived to become his usual ominous presence in America's Cup racing."

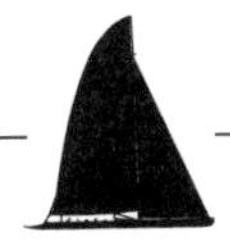

Showdown

13

It was a very subdued Bill Koch who faced his team after *Stars & Stripes* had clobbered *Kanza* in the sail-off of the semi-finals. Subdued, but hanging in there. "First Bill was in shock," Harold Cudmore said. "Then he came out fighting. He had a clear, realistic view. He knew what was wrong, and he knew how to turn it around."

"That was a tough day," Koch told the team. "Right after the race the wind came up. Now it's blowing 14. I'm disappointed, but I'm not unhappy. I started this syndicate 17 months ago as a first-timer. Now we're in the finals. We're in good shape technically. We have the equipment. We have to apply ourselves to it.

"We ate some humble pie today. Now the coaches are going to analyze tactical and crew mistakes, factually and objectively. No ego will be spared." Koch put Cudmore in charge of that touchy area because he had the respect of the crew and he had no ax to grind.

While Koch and the design team were sad to see their plan for an all-America³ final founder, everyone appreciated the competition Conner would offer. An all-America³ final might have produced good racing, but it would have been too incestuous. The killer instinct would have lost its edge. Whichever crew won the tough challenger final coming up between Italy and New Zealand would have its blood up. And Jerry Kirby probably spoke for the whole crew when he said, "It's nice we're down to one boat. We switched around so much we'd often forget which boat we were sailing."

The designers had long been caucusing about the details of the next modification to *America³*. The maintenance crew had four days to alter the boat for optimum performance against *Stars & Stripes*. That had to include the re-measurement process, and at least a day of sailing. It was a poker game. Conner was modifying his boat as well.

Koch said both the sailors and design team had to distinguish between perception and reality. "The perception is that the keel is too small and the boat is slipping sideways. The reality is that we have to learn to tack better."

Moeyersoms refused to go into detail about the modification. But he said it was aimed at overall improvement instead of a niche. And he was feeling confident about the results. "It took a while to make the sailors understand it wasn't up to them to suggest solutions. The boat is too technological for that approach. What we wanted from them was clear identification of the problems. Our technical guys could come up with the solution. Not, 'We need a new keel,' but, 'The boat is slipping sideways.'"

While *America³* was in the shed, coaches Cudmore, Spanhake, Campbell, and Hall had the team out drilling with *Defiant* and *Kanza*. Some thought a day off might be more productive, but not the sailors. "These boats are so tricky," Andreas Josenhans said, "that it takes 40 minutes of full concentration every day to get the boat in the groove. After a day off, it takes us two full days to get up to speed."

The "B" team, led by Bill Campbell and Kimo Worthington, was on the job every day to make sure the A boat was in tune. These were not happy campers on the B team. Their sustenance was humor black as pitch and caustic as battery acid. With the steady, reliable Campbell steering, and the glib Worthington running the program with non-stop patter that was as funny as it was effective, the B team did its job well.

"From the day I arrived I figured I'd be on the B team," Worthington said. "I told Koch he'd get 120 percent no matter where he put me. My attitude after the cut was, hey, we're still sailing. This was my third Cup. I've gone home early before. This was a much better deal. I told the guys, 'You're young, you're on a winning team, shut up.' Then I tried to keep 'em laughing, havin' some fun. But it wasn't easy."

Cudmore liked the boat modification. "The playing field will be level in the low ranges. We'll be better in 10 knots, and okay in 12." As for tactics: "We have to develop greater clarity on what we can and can't do out there. First we have to stabilize our act, and be efficient. If we see an area that needs improving, we have to fix it in a day. And we have to remember that Conner is fighting for his life. His options are narrow."

The possibility of 13 races loomed ahead for both America³ and Team Dennis Conner. Whoever was the first to win seven would take their boat into the America's Cup. That was what Bill Koch had planned for 17 months. It was what Dennis Conner had prepared for all his life.

At the beginning of the trials, no one gave Koch a chance. Midway through the races, Conner's obituary was filed in a thousand newsrooms. To date, a total of 54 races had been sailed. In head to head competition, A³ had 18 victories against TDC, while *Stars & Stripes* had won 13 times against his opponent's four boats. Now the two would face each other again with the whole shooting match on the line. Who had the faster boat? Who was the better sailor? Which team could handle the tactics and crewwork best? All answers lay ahead.

In sailing, the best laid plans depend on the weather, and perhaps never more so than in San Diego in the spring of 1992. The Saturday of Race 1, with a large spectator fleet on hand, was dead calm and flat. The race committee waited two hours, started the race but the boats never made it to the first mark so the committee sent everyone home. Overnight the breeze and "the lump," as the chop is called, returned. But on board *America³*, things were still a little ragged.

As Race 2 began, Melges took the helm from Dellenbaugh 20 seconds before the start and drove the boat over early. On the bow, Kirby was signaling like a man possessed, but Buddy wasn't seeing. *America³* was over by a full boatlength. Boatspeed and good tactical calls by Dellenbaugh brought *America³* within :15 at the first mark. *America³* passed *Stars & Stripes* downwind. On the second weather leg, Conner successfully fake-tacked *America³*, but he wasn't close enough to cash in on the move. *America³* won going away.

The modification to *America³* was applauded after the race. The new version was certainly fast in the 7-10 knots on the course. But the afterguard was still looking shaky. The helm transition between Dellenbaugh and Melges was addressed so that "startus interruptus" wouldn't be repeated. Everyone except Buddy seemed to know the boat was over early. As Kirby said, "Maybe I have too much respect for Buddy. Anybody else I would have gone ballistic, screaming at them to come down. He just didn't see my signal." Melges wasn't talking.

Race 3 was a great one. After an even start, the tactics up leg 1 were something to watch. *Stars & Stripes* looked good in downspeed tacking duels (a series of tacks made in quick succession before boatspeed builds), and seemed to spin and accelerate faster in all tacks. After some very close crosses, *America³* took a :09 lead at mark 1. On leg 3, the afterguard played it gutsy, barely crossing *Stars & Stripes* on port. Conner pinched up, took a big bite to weather and went hunting *America³* as it squeaked by, a technique Conner had perfected in these boats. This time he bit off too much and ran out of steam before he could nail *America³*.

The rest of the race, *America³* covered *Stars & Stripes*, which was reassuring. Although over on ESPN, anchor man Jim Kelly had this to say: "The bad news is that DC is falling further behind." Bad news? It made observers on *Firewater* wonder if Kelly thought *America³* was representing Mars.

Confidence continued to build on *America³* as the yacht took Race 4 by 4:20. With the score 3-0 against him, Conner finally notched a victory. El Nino was still influencing the conditions, conditions that had been paying off for him — 6 knots and flat water.

Two disquieting situations for *America³* arose from the race. First, Dellenbaugh had passed up an opportunity to take *Stars & Stripes* across the line early. *America³* lost the tactical game to Conner up the first weather leg, opting not to cover at one critical juncture. Covering in light air is difficult. It takes the boats a full minute to build speed after a tack, and by then the other guy is gone. And in San Diego, two boats crossing on opposite tacks can both be lifted. It's a maddening game.

Second, as the breeze built to 9-10 knots on the second weather leg, *Stars & Stripes* gained almost 20 seconds, confirming suspicions that Conner had raised his boat's optimum performance range.

Post-race Koch admitted to the press there had been some communications problems in the afterguard that were delaying decisions as much as 30 seconds. When asked for his version, Melges quipped, "Sometimes yes, and sometimes no." In-house, there was a discussion about Conner tacking onto starboard around mark 6 to cause the trailing *America³* to alter course.

Jim Pugh: "Did he make your life miserable?"

Bill Campbell: "Every time he could."

Pugh: "That's what we don't do."

Then *America³* won Race 6, and it was 4-1, and confidence blossomed. *America³* needed three wins to advance to the Cup match. Team Dennis Conner needed to double that.

On April 25, *Stars & Stripes* won the first of three straight races that would tie the series with *America³* at 4-4. It was the start of the most painful four-day period in the A³ syndicate's brief history.

Unprecedented Close Racing

Excitement was building. Never had America's Cup racing been so close. Never had tactical errors and crew mistakes been so visibly costly. On both the challenger and defender courses the tension was mounting. It was a field day for the press as the stories got juicier. The Italians were hammering the Kiwis with accusations of bad sportsmanship and cheating over the use of their bowsprit. The Kiwis fired back, outraged. Conner's comeback was being praised to the skies, while America³'s previous successes were being written off. In the America³ compound, long faces were seen from the docks to the retail store as Conner continued to roll.

In Race 7 (the sixth actual race; Race 1 had been canceled due to lack of wind), *America³*, which had been doing well on the left, unsuccessfully tried to burn through a Conner slam-dunk to get right. A puzzling move. Lead to Conner. Later in the leg, *America³* had gained considerably. She tacked on *Stars & Stripes*' hip and began to catch them. *America³* was moving faster, but Conner was taking bites all the time. *America³* got too close. Conner suddenly luffed hard, then again, and a third time, leaving *America³* to leeward and astern. End of race.

That night, Koch brought the afterguard to his house. "I've been studying these races on tape at night. I've got news for you. *America³* is fast in light air. The boat can point. We have good downwind sails. There are no excuses. It's up to us to make this boat come alive. We've been handing races to Conner. We've got the boat and crew to carry us the whole way. We just have to believe we can go out there and beat those guys."

In Race 8, *America³* fouled Conner at the start and had to do a 270-degree penalty turn after the gun. She never caught up. Score, 4-3.

With the turn of fortune, Koch began searching for answers. He had already given up reading newspapers and watching television because he believed they distracted his focus. "I needed to concentrate on the task at hand," he said. "I realized early that press reports affected me emotionally; if they were good I believed them, and if they were bad I'd get mad." So he returned to his house this night with a stack of tapes from the ESPN coverage under his arm, prepared to study them and note every mistake made aboard *America³*. This was to be his own observation, unclouded by the opinions of the commentators. So the skipper placed the tapes in the VCR, turned the volume off, and critiqued every tack and jibe, every mark rounding, every spinnaker set and douse that showed up in front of him. By the time he was finished, long into the night, he believed he had discovered a major flaw in how *America³* was going to battle. He began to formulate a plan on how to make his crew aware of the problem.

As the first signs of a Dennis comeback became apparent, some members of the San Diego Yacht Club chose to make their growing excitement public. A small group held a Team Dennis Conner rally at 5:30 am on Bill Koch's front lawn, right under his bedroom window. The partisan crowd hung a bra on one of Koch's bronze statues with a sign that said "We love Dennis Conner."

By the time Koch reached the America³ compound later that morning, he was not in the best of moods. He rounded up the afterguard for what he later termed a "come-to-Jesus" session. What he talked about was basketball.

"Red Auerbach, the great coach of the Boston Celtics, who won 11 NBA championships," Koch began, "would say to his team 'any one of you guys is good enough to score 35 points in any game, any night. But if you try to do that, we're going to lose every game because no one is going to be setting up plays, no one's going to be blocking shots, because you'll just be fighting for the damned ball.

"'So, Russell, you're going to block shots and get rebounds; Cousy, you're going to set up plays; Havlicek, you're going to score points.' To each of them he said that he knew damned well they could do all these things, that they were all multi-talented. 'But I want you to specialize and I will reward you for it,' Auerbach told his team and he made it work."

Bill stood up, walked around the room, and told his afterguard: "Now we are going to specialize even though you are multi-talented."

He went around the room, pointing at everybody, telling them what their job was and what their job wasn't. "By, your job is to tell us where we are on the race course, not to tell the trimmers how to do their job. David, you are to call the tactics and no one is to override you, except the skipper, and there is only one of them, me. Buddy, your job is to drive the boat as fast as possible, not to call tactics or tell the mastman or the bowman what to do. If any of you don't like this, I have five people waiting to get on the boat who will be happy to do your job, including me!

"Now let's go out there and do our jobs and win," said Koch. Then they went out on the boat but the tension was so thick you could cut it.

Recognizing their team needed something to ease the pressure, Vincent Moeyersoms and David Rosow jumped from *Firewater* into the harbor as *America³* passed by. The gesture was understood aboard the racing yacht, and while a momentary cessation of hostilities was achieved, the next few hours were as difficult as they had ever been during a race.

Buddy took Bill's words personally and believed they were directed at him. Despite several attempts by Koch to bury the hatchet, Melges sailed a good part of the race in silence. Others aboard were subdued, if not outright surly. Koch wondered if he'd pushed too hard.

After an even start in Race 9 and a slim lead through several crossings, *America³* found herself once again on *Stars & Stripes*' hip as the boats went on a long port hitch. In the light air, the blue boat was sailing higher, and after several minutes, *America³* had to tack away. Conner led by 1:16 at the first mark, and at the end by 1:47. Incredibly, after nine races (Race 1 didn't count) the series was tied at 4-4.

On the way in, with the team growing depressed, Bill Koch said to himself: "It's clear that the 'come-to-Jesus' speech and the pep talk did not work. I'll have to try something different to make the afterguard more a part of the team."

Bill decided to invite them over to his house for a bottle of "cheap" wine.

He would serve his favorite Burgundy, La Montrachet, at $120 a bottle, hoping it might break down some of their preconceived notions and promote the idea that the team came first.

When the sailors in the afterguard arrived, they sat on Bill's porch and watched the beautiful sunset over Point Loma. Not much was said, as none of the individuals felt they knew what was going wrong and none of them wanted to venture an immediate opinion. They sat there gloomily looking at one another. Although *Stars & Stripes* was getting some of the benefit from the extreme light winds, the men from *America³* knew they were not sailing as well as they had been, and they were not sailing as a team. They also knew that because they had the faster boat and better crew work, there was, in Dennis's famous words, "no excuse to lose."

David Dellenbaugh talked briefly about the wind shifts that had occurred that afternoon and how the afterguard and the crew had reacted to them. Then there was a long silence. Finally Bill said, "Guys, we have come all this way, sailed together for so long and now we face a crisis. I'm asking you, now what are we going to do?"

By Baldridge answered, "Bill, it would be nice after this is over if we could all be friends."

Bill nodded and said, "Yes, that was one of my original goals when I decided to enter the America's Cup. But now I'm asking what can we do about winning?"

There was another long silence. Buddy Melges finally broke it. He had been sitting alone, staring at the floor, not saying anything. Finishing his wine, he focused on the group and said: "I guess...I guess the reason we are all here is that I somehow got a cob jammed up my rear end.

"I misunderstood what Bill was saying this morning. I thought he was telling me not to speak on the boat, that he did not want my input. But I cannot sail without talking. I even yell, but I don't mean anything by it. What Bill was actually saying is that each of us needs to do his job and rely on our teammates to do theirs.

"Bill has told me he wants my opinion and I'll give it, but I think we need to support each other, to support David, and to get behind the tactical decisions he makes."

The Wizard of Zenda had clearly moved everyone in the room. He called for team solidarity and he asked each man in the afterguard to stand and join hands with him. He told them that communication among each other was critical. And he gave one last plea for teamwork.

By Baldridge, David Dellenbaugh, Andreas Josenhans, Bill and Buddy stood in a circle, joined hands and looked into each other's eyes. A silent promise, a deep commitment to each other and to their task passed between them. Then Buddy spoke again: "Now let's get out there and beat the hell out of Dennis Conner."

The speech was over, Buddy's words flowing like so many glasses of the fine wine. Both the words and the wine had their desired effect. *America³* would not lose to *Stars & Stripes* again.

"I'll never forget that moment," says Koch. "Buddy put his ego below the ego of the team, and in doing so he brought us all together. After that, there was no doubt in my mind that we would go all the way. Nothing could stop us."

While many members of the public and press saw the specter of a Conner comeback rising out of the flat blue, windless Pacific, if the same vision haunted Koch, he never let on.

Teamwork, Technology, Magic

Instead, Koch resorted to a bit of Indian folk magic. A medicine man from the Kanza tribe had traveled to San Diego on his own accord and at his own expense with a crow feather that signified communication with the Great Spirit (Kanza medicine men don't communicate directly with the Great Spirit — they send the crow). Koch brandished the feather with pride, and brought it on the boat every day with reverence. And before Race 10, the race that may have been the most curcuial of the entire series as it would have a great effect on momentum, he had been seen alone on the bow sprinkling something over the side from a small packet. It was an offering of tobacco to the four wind gods. Koch said later that before he was being too skimpy for the gods. When he increased the amount of tobacco, *America³* began to win. "Teamwork, technology, and magic?" one sailor wondered.

Koch wasn't the only one with rituals. Most of the sailors had something going, from lucky shirts and pocket pieces, to pre-race love-making. Buddy carried lucky corn and coins. Jerry Kirby's son Rome provided a small yellow airplane that was taped each day to the boom vang in front of ESPN's mast camera. Several guys used the same shower every morning in the gym. And several of the sailors and shore crew made it a point to baptize the keel on race days before the boat was launched. Sailors have always been superstitious.

During Conner's revival, Vincent Moeyersoms had been coordinating efforts to reverse the tide. "We worked on sail shapes and tuning the boat with a light-air setup," Vincent said. "We worked on how to shift gears when the wind dropped. And we leaned hard on the afterguard to accept coaching and suggestions for making our tactics and positioning better. By addressing the realities, we kept the myth of Conner's invincibility from sneaking in.

"When Conner tied the score, that was the turning point. We had to make everyone accountable: designers, sailmakers, the crew, and the afterguard. The afterguard were not only missing beats, they were missing the same beat repeatedly. They were taking too many fliers; trying things that weren't possible with these boats, like living on the other guy's hip; tacking or jibing with too little time left before the start; trying to break through slam dunks.

"Until that moment, the afterguard hadn't been willing to accept enough criticism to make it work. We kept putting ourselves in the same position on the course. We weren't reacting correctly and adjusting our game plan. When the rest of the crew saw that the afterguard was also held accountable, they performed better."

At the morning crew meeting of April 29, weatherman Chris Crabtree spoke prophetic words: "There's a change coming." It wasn't much — 6 to 10 knots instead of 5 to 7 — but it was the final item that put *America^3* back in the game.

Even so, Race 10 was a nail-biter, with the lead changing hands seven times. *America^3* went right after the start and looked buried. But one of the 20-degree oscillations that prevailed all day went in their favor, putting them only two to three boatlengths back of *Stars & Stripes* on the first cross. With *America^3* on Conner's hip (once again!), both boats went off on a long starboard tack. Then the breeze built to the promised 10 knots, and the white boat began to roll.

America^3 led at mark 1. *Stars & Stripes* led at mark 2. Going up leg 3, *America^3* handed Conner some of his own medicine. The white boat parked under him and drove him off its hip. If Conner's tack looked a bit sloppy, it was because he was distracted. ESPN's on-board camera caught Dennis staring at *America^3*. "That's really a rocketship," he was saying wistfully, to no one in particular. "That boat is so fast, there is nothing I can do."

America^3 held the lead through the Z-legs. (In all the trial races, there was only one pass on a reaching leg.) But trailing around mark 6 by only :09, Conner pulled off one of the prettier moves in sailing, a double (fake) tack that bought him the left side of the course. For a few minutes, Conner was looking good. *America^3* covered briefly to consolidate, but Dellenbaugh and Company liked what they saw on the right.

Splitting tacks was a gamble for Conner, one he lost. On the right, *America^3* once again picked up a favorable shift, and took the lead for good. Tacking behind the white boat, *Stars & Stripes*' jib sheet flew off the clew, costing them another couple boatlengths. *America^3* won by 1:08.

The momentum was back with the Koch syndicate, and it would stay there. The next day the seabreeze filled in early. *America³* led all the way for win #6 by 1:43. The sleek white yacht now needed only one more victory to win the defender finals and enter the best-of-seven series for the 1992 America's Cup.

America³ had won three straight races to start the series and they believed there was no reason why they couldn't close out the series by repeating the same feat. By now almost everyone within the compound on North Harbor Drive knew that the forces of nature would be the determining factor in the potential final race. To a person they believed they had the faster boat in almost any conditions other than 6 knots of wind or less and flat seas. They also believed that by now their crew had been tested by fire, both at sea and on land, and that it had proven itself at least equal, if not superior, to the veterans aboard *S & S*.

As the sixteen men who would sail *America³* this day made their way through the compound and the cheering throngs, the determination on their faces was more noticeable than usual. There was a sense that this series had already gone on too long, that despite Conner and company's great skill, they just weren't a match for the proud Cubens and their "scalded dog" of a yacht. As a line was thrown from *Firewater* to the racing yacht and cleated on its bow for the tow to the course, some ashore spoke of a palpable feeling that today, May 1, would be something special.

Even before *America³* reached the ocean off Point Loma, it was apparent nature favored the white yacht. The breeze freshened by the moment and the lump had returned. During the pre-race maneuvering, Koch thought he noticed expressions of concern on some aboard *Stars & Stripes*. Dennis, Mr. America's Cup, the "greatest sailor in the world," ever the competitor, wore his game-day face as he sailed on the edge of elimination. Koch admired the fight in his competitor, but as he searched the faces of each man on his own team, he knew they were ready to deliver the death blow.

And what a blow it was. The "scalded dog" howled from start to finish, reveling in the building wind. Dellenbaugh, relaxed and with total concentration, called an almost-perfect race. Buddy and Bill steered flawlessly. The crewwork never missed a beat. Tacks and jibes were executed with no mistakes.

As each mark was rounded, *America³* added to her lead. Soon the race became, in the term often used in sports to describe a blow out, "a laugher." *America³* was simply too quick, too fast, too perfect, for *Stars & Stripes*. The final delta was 5:08, the largest margin of the defender finals. "We were so far ahead I couldn't see the advertisements on Dennis's sails," said the Corinthian Bill Koch. His team had clearly saved the best for last.

When the white sloop returned to the compound, a great celebration ensued. The team Las Vegas labeled as 100-1 underdogs was going into the America's Cup match. The computer nerds, the techies, the no-way, José sailors had beat the world's greatest helmsman and his team of Cup veterans. Champagne bottles were uncorked, heart-stopping music blared at full blast, the compound gates were thrown open to allow entrance to anyone with congratulations on their lips. Among the visitors were Malin Burnham and Tom Ehman, the two ACOC principals who, in their heart of hearts, never believed this day would come. Conner supporters to the end, this was the end and in a gesture of sportsmanship they came to shake the hand of Bill Koch. Forgotten for the moment was their slight when Koch had offered to build a 120-foot yacht to battle the Kiwis in 1988. Put aside for now was the campaign to pressure Bill into a merger with Dennis. Now there were smiles and hugs and pats on the back. And there was the great tradition of the dunk to fulfill. So as the former M.I.T. basketball player spoke to the president of ACOC, he smiled and said, "You know, Malin, there is something I've always wanted to do...." With that he grabbed the San Diegan and the two flew into the water. Moments later the newly crowned victor had Ehman by the waist and the two were launched into the Pacific among hails of laughter.

Finally, Dennis Conner had been vanquished.

On the challenger course, Italy was sailing well after dropping the first race to New Zealand on April 21. The crew aboard *Il Moro di Venezia* was out of sync throughout the day, crossing the starting line 18 seconds after the gun and later discovering their on board sail inventory didn't fit the conditions.

Italy's Race 2 was sufficient to silence for all time the analogy that watching boats race is like watching grass grow. This was heart-pounding stuff. The two boats were never more than two or three boatlengths apart over the 20-mile course. Cayard took the start by one second and sailed the right side of the course towards the first mark. Rod Davis, at the helm aboard *New Zealand* found a little more breeze on the left and rounded the mark 13 seconds in the lead.

Then *Il Moro* began to catch up, showing her superior downwind speed. By the second mark the Kiwis' lead was just five seconds, and they picked up another three seconds on the second weather leg. Davis continued in the lead through the Z-legs continually feeling the presence of Italy's bow whipping across his stern like a killer scimitar that was coming ever closer.

On leg 7, Davis slam-dunked his rival Cayard. Too late. Cayard steered perfectly, putting the bow down a little for speed, then coming up and burning Davis off. It was great sailing. Cayard buried Davis the last five minutes on the wind, leaving *New Zealand* two boatlengths behind as he turned for the finish.

The light *New Zealand* sled got rolling off the wind as usual, and closed at the finish line in a replay of their semi-final photo-finish. This time, *New Zealand* was not eliminated for hitting the mark. But she lost anyway. Italy, to weather, snuck her bow across first and won by just one second. Not lost in the excitement was an ominous note: whichever of these teams survived would be superbly tuned for the Cup match.

By the afternoon of April 25 it looked like the Italians would soon be making reservations for an early return to Europe. Races three, four, and five had gone to the Kiwis, who profited from their own superb sailing and from a number of blunders by Italy. *Il Moro* let a 33 second lead in Race 3 evaporate by refusing to cover Davis as he went right. Soon, the wind followed the Kiwi boat and *Il Moro* fell behind, eventually losing by 34 seconds.

New Zealand won the fourth race by a whooping 2:26 and then, on the 25th, the men from down under surged to a 4-1 advantage with a 2:38 victory. The race was remarkable for two incidents. One, the Italians held a 4:20 lead going into the last leg. As the breeze died and the current increased, Davis and crew set up their yacht perfectly and placed her exactly where they wanted to be. On that one leg *New Zealand* gained an incredible six minutes and 58 seconds on her opponent to win the race.

The Great Bowsprit Debate

The other remarkable thing that happened is that Paul Cayard, realizing the Kiwis needed only one more win to advance to the Cup match, chose this afternoon to raise the protest flag; claiming an infringement of Rule 64.4. Thus began the great bowsprit debate.

The small white spar appeared on Bruce Farr's fourth design for *New Zealand*, and was a controversial item from the outset. Beginning in January, 1992, the Louis Vuitton jury, the International jury, the ACOC, the CORC, and the *New Zealand* and Italian syndicates exchanged enough paper on the subject to fill a set of encyclopedias. There were numerous hearings from which rule clarifications, decisions, amended decisions, and revised definitions were issued. Even the most knowledgeable sailors found themselves pondering a sea of technicalities.

On March 5, between Rounds 2 and 3 of the challenger trials, the America's Cup International jury made a ruling that served as the basis for the Cayard protest of almost seven weeks later. Requested by the Challenger of Record Committee and the America's Cup Organizing Committee to review the issue, the America's Cup jury knew their opinion was non-binding on the Louis Vuitton Cup jury. This in itself was controversial. In essence, the L.V.C. jury was saying "think anything you want, you'll get your turn soon enough, but right now, we're in control."

Regardless of who had the power at the moment, the America's Cup jury, led by Goran Petersson, opined that to attach the gennaker sheet to the bowsprit was a violation of Rule 64, which reads, in part, "...No sail shall be sheeted over or through an outrigger..." At the time the ruling had no impact because the L.V.C. jury refused to be bound by their counterpart's decision. "Here we are contesting the most prestigious sailing regatta in the world," said an angry Peter Blake, head of the *New Zealand* syndicate, "but the referees can't agree on the rules. Where does that leave the competitors?"

Where it left them was in the jury room on the evening of April 25. Cayard, armed with video tapes, diagrams, and a rule book, spoke long into the night. Davis, weary from a day of racing, protested the protest. In the end, the L.V.C. jury, citing several technicalities, ruled "...For approximately eight seconds, the tack of the gennaker was being controlled by a line from the tack of the gennaker through a block near the end of a bowsprit." While they affirmed Cayard's protest, they did not give him the race. Instead, *New Zealand*'s win that day was "annulled" — the first annulment of a yacht race in anyone's memory. The Kiwi lead was cut from 4-1 to 3-1 in what would mark the beginning of the end for Sir Michael Fay's third challenge.

Analysis of the bowsprit issue in the America³ camp tended more towards the psychological than the technical. The Americans believed Cayard had the faster boat, but the Kiwis sailed theirs better. Cayard's bowsprit gambit, so the thinking went, was a ploy more to upset the Kiwi crew than to have the use of the bowsprit outlawed. In the end, he did both. America³ saw the maneuver as a clever head game which resulted in the Kiwis losing confidence in their sailing technique. The small, light-displacement flier that Bruce Farr designed as New Zealand's fourth generation boat had looked like a winner from the moment it was launched. With its plumb bow, bowsprit, open transom, and double keel/double steering-fin arrangement, it was unique on the race course. And it won more races than any other challenger. Given its success, it was difficult to criticize *New Zealand*.

Yet America³'s design team, using the same words Paul Cayard had used to describe his impression of the America³ design, said if the Farr boat was right, they (and the French, Japanese, and Italians) were wrong. "It was a slow boat," said Peter Wilson, who had worked with former *New Zealand* teams. "I give tremendous credit to Rod Davis and his crew for getting as much out of it as they did."

Koch agreed. "The Kiwis had the best sailors out there. They got the most out of an average good boat. That's why the racing was so close."

The boat was admittedly a handful to steer, but skipper Davis seemed to have mastered that art. With tactician David Barnes making good calls; the highly-reputed, poker-faced Kiwi crew looking fierce in black; and Michael Fay's low-profile, darkly militaristic system in place in Coronado (no wives in the compound, among other rules), *New Zealand* was an early popular favorite.

What happened? A replay of 1987, for one thing. That year, after compiling a formidable 37-1 record, *New Zealand* lost to the USA in the challenger finals, 4-1.

This year it was a combination of things. One was the bowsprit, the most contested item in America's Cup XXVIII. The way the Kiwis were using the bowsprit to trim and jibe reaching sails was unique. "We had to practice a whole new technique in the middle of the finals," Rod Davis said after Cayard's protest was upheld.

As Jim Pugh pointed out, the rest of the boats were loading their poles with 8,000 pounds aft pressure when reaching with an asymmetrical sail in medium breeze. With the bowsprit, the Kiwis were down to around 800 pounds. Cutting out the bowsprit could have an enormous effect on rig and gear.

In hindsight, the bowsprit was a good idea. The next time perhaps everyone should have one. It facilitates sail handling, and it's probably safer. But why did *New Zealand* persist in using something that offered such obvious grist for the protest mill in the world's most litigious regatta? Because, as one *New Zealand* partisan says, it had been approved. And like other departures before it (the winged keel, for instance), the Kiwis considered it a progressive, worthwhile innovation. It was still risky business. Aside from last-minute boat-handling changes, the psychological effect perpetrated by Cayard was, as Rod Davis said, "Intimidating. Having the win taken away ticked everybody off. It was a harsh penalty...."

Another factor was the role of Peter Blake, the well-known Whitbread skipper, who was brought in as *New Zealand*'s sailing coach. Blake shattered Fay's understated media image by losing his cool more then once at press conferences. Ashen-faced and nearly trembling with rage, Blake once said *New Zealand* felt "shafted" by the reaction to its bowsprit, and suggested an American-based conspiracy was at work. Blake didn't appear at press conferences after that, but the damage was done.

Perhaps boosted by their protest coup, the Italians began sailing inspired races. And the loss of the bowsprit issue definitely took the Kiwi's minds off their sailing. After *Il Moro* tied the score at three-all, Blake replaced Davis and Barnes with helmsman Russell Coutts and tactician Brad Butterworth. It was a move that betrayed *New Zealand*'s desperation, and the shattered psyche of their compound. Rod Davis' deft public response to a situation that must have shaken him to the quick was admirable. He was the total sportsman and a gentleman to the end as he faced the camera with a clear eye.

True, Davis had lost two straight. New blood might make a difference. But Coutts had obvious problems handling *New Zealand*'s tricky steering. Meanwhile, Cayard and his crew continued to improve, winning starts and sailing smart, mistake-free races. Down 3-1, they won four straight, took the Louis Vuitton trophy and the right to challenge for the America's Cup.

One *New Zealand* insider says it was lack of leadership that really cost his syndicate. He points out that Blake was behind a desk; Fay could run the business but he isn't a sailor; and Davis, while a super sailor, isn't a strong leader. On the other side, Cayard was running the show and the boat, and that made the difference.

As the *New Zealand* effort unraveled, Cup observers compared the management styles of Sir Michael Fay and Bill Koch. Fay chose to run things from shore, practicing the hands-off approach. Koch insisted from day one he would be aboard, involved in every aspect of the campaign. The observation was made that if Fay was closer to the racing situation he may have made different decisions. One wonders if Koch had stayed on land would he have had the same information needed to make the critical decisions he made. The difference in management techniques may have been the difference in winning and losing.

In the days leading to the America's Cup match, Cayard tried to play his psych-out card again, this time against America^3. At a meeting of the judges, called to iron out minor discrepancies in the interpretations of the rules, the Americans came in with one page of queries. The Italians arrived with about 50 pages, 80 per cent of them complaining about the A^3 method of jibing, and the way in which they changed the position of their pole.

Harold Cudmore immediately recognized the tactic as similar to Cayard's using the bowsprit issue to shake up the Kiwi camp. He told Bill and the crew not to worry about it; the coaches will handle it. They collected film of Cayard's jibing tactics and took the crew out on the water, spending two hours with the crew, perfecting the technique. At the next meeting of the judges, Cudmore said simply: "There is no problem here. We will jibe exactly the same way they do." The strategy completely defused the Italian tactic. The issue was never raised again. "Harold handled the whole thing perfectly," says Bill. "None of us got upset, in fact, we didn't even think about it because we knew Harold had it under control."

Koch also asked Cudmore to negotiate other protocol aspects with the Italians such as who would leave the dock first. There had been some talk that the bowsprit issue was just the first sign of the kind of acrimony which had so spoiled the 1988 mismatch between Dennis and the Kiwis. When the Italians turned up with their "booklet" of rule questions, Koch thought he might be in for a long siege and whatever prestige the event may have regained since 1988 could be in jeopardy of losing again. Koch admonished Cudmore to stand strong for America^3, but, in the end, to do what he felt was best for the Cup. The two men had had long discussions on this issue and Koch believed Cudmore wanted the event to be run with as much style and class as he did. Cudmore believed that it was in everyone's best interest, and certainly in the best interest of the Cup itself, that the event be conducted in a gentlemanly fashion and that any disputes be worked out privately. He worked out a protocol without an angry word said or even a mention in the press. The only battle anyone outside the inner circles of the two syndicates knew about was the one about to occur on the water.

So it was to be *America^3* vs. *Il Moro di Venezia* in the Cup match, the preferred rival for the Americans. "I think our boat compares favorably to *Il Moro*," Melges said. "Probably better than she would have against the Kiwis." And yet even though the Kiwi boat was more radical than the yacht the Italians would sail, the hull of *Il Moro* was different enough from that of *America^3* to raise the question of which concept best fit the San Diego conditions. In the simplest terms, *America^3* was deep and narrow and *Il Moro* was shallow and wide. In fact, when Italian skipper Cayard saw *America^3* for the first time, he wondered aloud: "If she is right, than all of us are wrong." His statement, while repeating the words of the Marquis of Anglesey upon seeing the schooner-yacht *America,* make one wonder if Cayard knew the famous quote of philosopher George Santana: "Those who cannot remember the past are condemned to repeat it."

By the end of the defender finals, the "scalded dog" — the *America^3* of Round 2 and 3 — was back, sniffing victory. The howling had to be heard in the *Il Moro* camp just a stone's throw across Fisherman's Harbor from the America^3 compound.

Even as the defense victory celebration went on into the night at the America^3 compound, *America^3* was quickly hauled by the shore crew, unrigged and rolled into the shed for final modifications.

Goodbye blue boat; hello red boat.

It was the red boat that captured the media's imagination. On May 8, the day before the first Cup race, the *Los Angeles Times* polled 29 members of the yachting press. Twenty-two picked *Il Moro* to win by as much as 4-0.

Only seven picked *America³*, and only one — Australian Robert Keeley — correctly predicted the score. The poll gave Koch, the manager, one more opportunity to drive home a favorite theme of his.

"There is a great difference between perception and reality," he liked to tell his team. "Here are twenty-two so-called experts who are convinced we're not going to win. Seventeen say we have the better boat and fifteen say we have the better crew, but twenty-six say *Il Moro* has the better helmsman. This is the perfect example of the myth that one crew member, one star will win a race and that he is more important than the crew or the boat. That's perception, folks. The reality is that the better boat and the better crew wins! Now let's go out and prove it!"

For Bill Koch, the victory over Dennis was perhaps more a relief than an affirmation of his team's achievement. When asked by ESPN's Jim Kelly what advice he'd give future defenders or challengers, Koch smiled and said "Don't do it." Why, asked Kelly. "Too much money," said Koch. Kelly persisted, asking now what it felt like to have won the defender trials. "I'm reminded of one of the guys who climbed Mt. Everest," said the sailor. "He was asked what he felt when he reached the peak, what was the first thing that crossed his mind. 'How to get down, was his response,'" said the ever-pragmatic Koch.

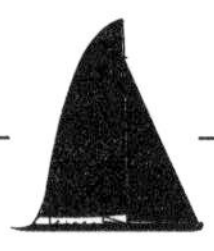

Defending

14

Thirty-two men met the dawn of May 9, 1992 with blood-pounding anxiety and knotted stomachs. In just a few hours they would be the focus of the sporting world. Their actions, and the responses of their boats, would determine who would win the 28th sailing of the America's Cup.

As hints of light began to break the early morning darkness, things began to stir in the compounds of America³ and *Il Moro di Venezia.* Maintenance crews and security guards shared the first cups of coffee as responsibilities for the boats changed hands. Given the time, to say nothing of the importance, of the day, conversation was muted. What talk there was was mostly of the weather, which forecasters predicted would be partly sunny, mid-60s, winds out of the southwest at 8-14 knots. Almost perfect conditions in which to begin the first race.

To sail in the America's Cup is perhaps every serious sailor's dream and there was no mistaking an electric excitement inside both camps. While supremely confident in the face of their challenge, the sailors' optimism was somewhat blunted by moments of doubt and question. Am I as prepared as I need to be? Can I deliver my best? Will our team work to its fullest potential? Is their boat faster?

It was that question, the question of boat speed, that most concerned both the Americans and the Italians. It was the question the sailing world had waited five months to have answered. Out of the 28 boats from 8 nations that came to San Diego seeking sailing's greatest prize, which was the fastest? Today, after so many hours sailed and dollars spent, two boats, two teams, would make their way to the starting line to begin to answer the question.

The defenders of the Cup had reason to believe *America³* was the fastest boat in the world. The result of the enormously successful five-year

Matador Program, she was formed from a mountain of data collected in laboratories, wind tunnels, water tanks, computers, and at sea. She had clocked the second fastest time around the course (*Il Moro* had the record, but it was set on the breeziest day of the entire competition), she had beat the defending champion and probably the world's most experienced America's Cup team, and she entered the final match with a record of 24-9. By contrast, *Il Moro* went to the finals starting line with a record of 26-13.

There was another reason the Americans believed their boat would prevail. It had to do with the set up of each yacht. Eyewitness information revealed the Italians would go into battle with a carbon-fiber keel and rudder, both of which were larger than those *America^3* had fixed to her hull. In fact, the size, weight, and composition of these appendages had been subject number one for Vincent Moeyersoms and his design team for some time now.

A theory had been forwarded by Peterson and Milgram, suggesting changing the keel from carbon-fiber to a smaller steel one. As the scientists and designers considered this and the forthcoming races, they decided to make the change. It was a bold risk, that when added to a new mast, new sails, new hull wings, and new partial rigging, reconfigured the boat considerably. While the move has been viewed by many as audacious, it should have come as no surprise from a syndicate so deeply rooted in the practice of science.

The new keel bulb was smaller, slimmer, more streamlined. While it would mean sacrificing stiffness and perhaps some stability, it offered less wetted surface and thus, less resistance, particularly in light air. Computer modeling proved the validity of the theory and Koch, whose belief in testing had long ago been confirmed, gave the go-ahead. Moeyersoms called the foundry and ordered an overnight casting. He was told there wasn't enough time to let it cool. "Ship it hot," was Moeyersoms' response.

The changes sent many of the San Diego Yacht Club members into apoplexy. Their view was "if it ain't broke, don't fix it." This was the boat that beat Dennis. What greater confirmation of its speed does anyone need? But Koch pointed out that the defender finals showed a weakness in *America^3*'s light air performance. Their computers showed them how to correct the weakness, but the syndicate had never tested the configurations the computer was spitting out. For a team that had put such a precedent on testing, in fact had built their entire design and sailing teams around testing, this was risky stuff. But Koch said simply, "We have confidence in our science and we want to win, so we'll make the changes."

In actuality, the change was probably not as big a gamble as it may have appeared. America^3 had collected so much data, had conducted so many tests, had relied so heavily on science, that they could design an optimum boat for any set of conditions the winds and waves off San Diego brought them. The only problem was that each set of conditions required a different boat. The scientists then collected 40 years of wind and wave history at the approximate location of the race course, and put it into a probability model, called the Monte Carlo model, which they then used to determine which design and configuration had the greatest chance of winning four out of seven races. They believed they had that design and it would soon be on the water.

If *America³* believed they had the fastest boat, *Il Moro* believed they had the best skipper. Paul Cayard is one of the bright, talented young helmsmen who has built a reputation as one of the world's best during the past decade. One of the first Americans to leave his country for the big dollars offered by a foreign syndicate, it appeared he fit seamlessly into the Italian program. During his more than two years in Italy, he had developed the trust of his mentor Raul Gardini and the loyalty of his crew. Far more than just a skilled driver, his imprint was on every phase of the Italian effort.

Cayard, like the vast majority of sailors in the 1992 America's Cup, had been sailing since he was a boy. His disdain for Koch, in his eyes a newcomer to the sport, was voiced on more than one occasion. The gulf between the two men was further enhanced by the rivalry between Gardini and Koch, which had grown during their years on the maxi circuit. It reached a boiling point during the controversy over *Guzzini* and the many accusations of spying. Cayard was outraged by what he believed to be a clear violation of sportsmanship, to say nothing of breaking the rules. Koch, who was receiving great pleasure from the entire *Guzzini* charade and the success of the psychological ploy, was nonetheless angered by the recriminations hurled at him by Cayard and seconded by Chris Dickson. As the charges began to fly, Koch shot back: "Cayard and Dickson are hired guns.... They're the ones who've given up their nationalities and their national pride to sail for foreign countries for dollars. They don't like what they think we're doing because it could harm their business careers."

The Golden Wizard of Zenda

Lost in the furor was the importance of Buddy Melges. While press and partisans keyed in on the developing Cayard/Koch dispute, the skills and natural abilities of the most experienced sailor on either team seemed overlooked. Of the 32 sailors who made their way to the starting line that spring day, no one had been in more races or won more races than Melges. And he was the only man aboard either boat who could display an Olympic Gold Medal as testament to his competence.

But Cayard had caught the imagination of the public and press (26 of the 29 journalists responding to the *L.A. Times* poll listed him as the better helmsman over Melges). Hollywood handsome, articulate, and confident, if not a touch arrogant, he symbolized the new America's Cup. His syndicate had built five boats and spent more than an estimated $200 million. The efforts and money had paid off. This was the first time in Cup history Italy had competed in the final match.

And now as the full rays of the sun began to heat the California city, traffic towards the waterfront built to a standstill. Over the past several weeks San Diego had filled to near capacity as the Cup attracted its fans. Thousands boarded some 800 spectator craft of all kinds, rowboat to luxury liner, as millions more prepared to view the world-wide television broadcast.

As the fleet maneuvered from dock to viewing area, all eyes followed *America³* and *Il Moro* as they were towed into open water. Speculation among the viewers was rife. Wasn't the red boat lower in the water? Didn't the white boat look much narrower? Overhead, a dozen helicopters jockeying for position over the starting line made a racket like as many carpenters hammering. There was a festive atmosphere to this small patch of ocean off Point Loma, a combination of excitement and curiosity. The America's Cup was about to begin. As Bill Koch said at that morning's meeting, "This is what we came for. We'll succeed if each of us does his own job and relies on the others to do their jobs."

The first few minutes of the first race in the America's Cup match always have yachtsmen on the edges of their seats. Until the two competitors enter the starting area at the ten-minute gun, no matter how much the other side thinks it knows about the other boat, challenger and defender are meeting for the first time. No one really knows which one will have the edge. But on May 9, 1992, the two hardly got acquainted.

Dellenbaugh did his job, handling the more aggressive Cayard well in the pre-start. With one minute to go, both boats were at the committee boat end. Dellenbaugh came up under Cayard on port and took him over the line. Cayard tacked and reached off for the pin end. Dellenbaugh did a circle and hardened up on port at the boat end, hitting the line at the gun at full speed. At the pin, Cayard came up two seconds too soon. Over early. After the race he blamed the false start on his misjudging the current as only half a knot when it was a full knot.

By the time *Il Moro di Venezia* restarted, *America³* had sailed without interference to the favored side of the course and was :30 ahead. The finish delta was also :30, and that had tongues wagging. Were these boats dead even? Cayard naturally implied as much at the press conference. Koch and company thought otherwise.

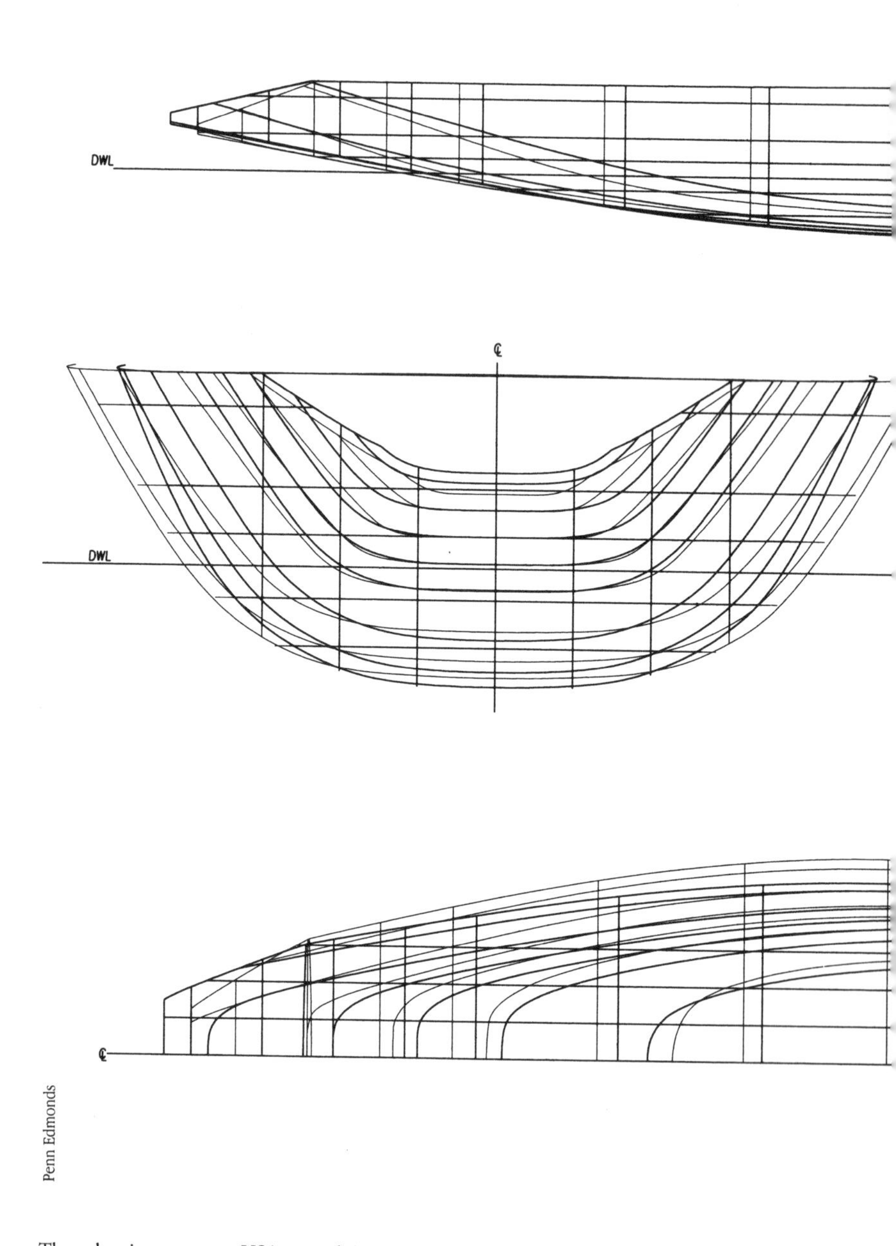

These drawings compare USA-12 and ITA-15, showing section, elevation, and plan views. USA-23 is longer overall but has a shorter waterline length. The plan and section views show that USA-23

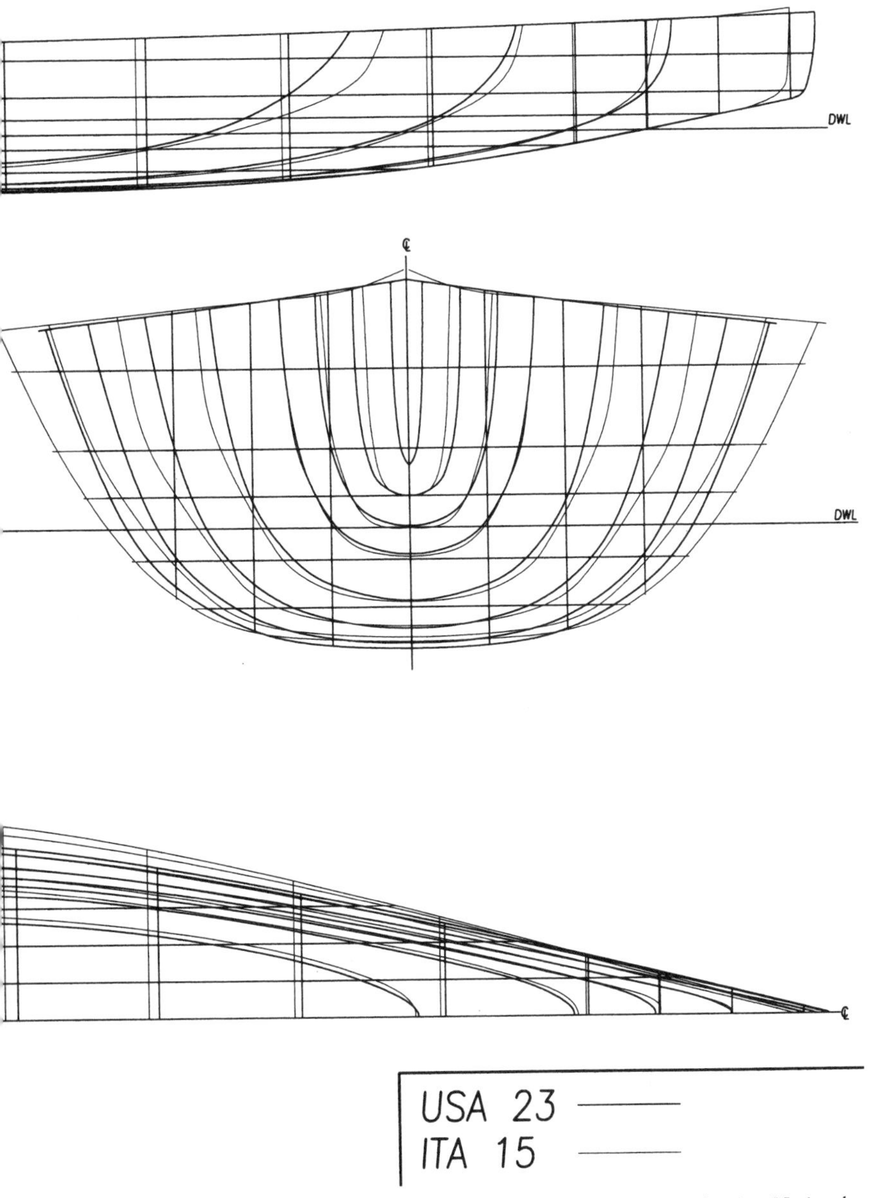

is significantly narrower at both the sheer and waterline, yet deeper in the midsection. Notice also the angle of the topsides.

Koch missed the press conference because during the race he had taken a blow to the head that briefly put him on the deck. In the past months, the 6-foot 4-inch Koch had been hit several times by the boom, especially after the boom had been lowered by increased mast rake for better light air performance. A month ago the crew had glued a foam rubber patch on the boom that bore an uncanny resemblance to their skipper's profile, and a local disk jockey had presented Koch with a San Diego Chargers football helmet. Koch had taken the ribbing in good spirits.

But in this case it was the runner block that got him. He ducked to avoid the boom, which had been flung in by a wave. As he came up, the swinging lazy runner block nailed him. He had a headache that lasted 36 hours, but no concussion.

Melges had the press in stitches describing the incident. "It sounded like...BONK!," Buddy said. "It was a different sound than the runner hitting the hollow boom...."

The next morning, a healthy Koch appeared at the crew meeting wearing a metal, winged helmet and smiling broadly.

Race 2 would become an historic event. In a light to moderate breeze of 8 to 10 knots, the start was virtually even, with *Il Moro* several boatlengths to weather. But if Race 1 was *Il Moro*'s folly, Race 2 would see the Cubens discovering their lack of jibing expertise. At the start, Cayard came out aggressive again, going at *America³* whenever he had a chance. Dellenbaugh, who held the wheel for each start in the finals, continued to steer defensively, playing for position and looking to avoid confrontations with the red boat. Today's start was virtually even, although Cayard took the committee boat end and may have had a slight advantage.

Neither boat had an advantage until the third encounter, when *America³* could not clear *Il Moro* as the Americans tried to clear to the favored right side. Cayard crossed on starboard, blocking *America³* as Melges, now at the helm, tried to burn through. Moments like these test the mettle of helmsmen and tacticians alike. If *America³* could clear *Il Moro's* bow and gain the favored side, she would gain a huge tactical advantage. If she didn't make the pass, she would foul out of the race before the boats even reached the first mark. At the last possible second, Melges opted for the safer course and ducked below his opponent's stern. Cayard threw the wheel of *Il Moro* to the left and completed a text book slam-dunk. *America³* was virtually trapped and was forced to follow *Il Moro* up the rest of the leg. The Italians had lifted off nicely and led by :33 at mark 1.

Downwind, *America³* showed stunning speed with the larger spinnaker, closing the gap before the leg was half over. But when Melges began a series of jibes to put him in position to round the second mark, the tactic backfired on him. Moving a huge, oversized spinnaker from one side of the boat to the other is a delicate maneuver practiced thousands of times. But this wasn't practice and Cayard and crew were unforgiving. On each jibe, *America³*'s spinnaker collapsed, losing the boat valuable headway. Then, trying to jibe on *Il Moro*'s air, *America³* got too close and Cayard pounced on the opportunity. *Il Moro* spun to her right, luffing the white boat into a head to wind jibe. The American's spinnaker collapsed once again. It was a perfect move by Cayard, stopping *America³* in her tracks. At the same time, the Italians hoisted a protest flag, claiming the Cubens had touched their boat. The umpires disagreed and signaled them to fight on. Now in total control, *Il Moro* sailed away and led by :32 at mark 2.

The second weather leg was a dogfight. *Il Moro* defended her lead tenaciously, covering and stretching. But *America³*, bouncing back from the stall, fought back, gaining confidence and position. At mark 3, Cayard's lead was cut to :20. By now the pundits were nodding their heads in unison: *America³* was faster upwind, considerably faster downwind. Reaching, the boats were close.

Going upwind the last time, *America³* threw 32 tacks at *Il Moro*, including a downspeed series that slowed the boats to less than 5 knots. *America³* fought all the way back until only one boatlength separated the two teams. Finally, Cayard let *America³* go left. *Il Moro* got a lift. When *America³* tacked back, she was on *Il Moro*'s weather hip, and once again she could not hold that position. The resulting two extra tacks *America³* needed to fetch the mark, plus some good velocity for *Il Moro* gave Cayard a :31 advantage going into the last leg. Would it be enough?

Not if *America³* had completed its last jibe smoothly. But jibing had been a problem all day for the white boat, and the final maneuver was not one of the better ones. *Il Moro,* on the favored side, eased spinnaker sheets and beat *America³* across by :03, the closest finish in Cup history. (Previous record: *Gretel* def. *Weatherly* — :26, 1962.)

Immediately after reaching the dock, the *America³* crew gathered in the meeting room. Soon it became a full house. Discussion about lodging a protest against *Il Moro* for purposely releasing the spinnaker to break the plane of the finish line was in full, emotional swing. Photographer Phil Uhl's video tape of the finish was being played repeatedly. David Rosow was struggling to hold a string against the screen to show the line. Necks craned and eyes strained to capture the instant. It was inconclusive.

Debate raged. Bill Koch arrived. So did Tom Ehman and Gene Trepte of the ACOC, and umpire Cy Gillette, who had joined *America³* as an advisor after his official duties during the trials were finished. A messenger arrived from downtown with the ESPN video of the finish. Now the room was jammed. The adrenaline was pumping. Dellenbaugh was quietly studying the rule that covered finishing. Voices were raised. Time, someone suggested, was the issue: get the protest written and lodged before time ran out. It could always be retracted.

Rosow ran the new tape half a dozen times, advancing it frame by frame as the boats hit the line. It clearly showed *Il Moro* finishing ahead. Harold Cudmore shrugged. There was no issue. *Il Moro* may have broken the rules by easing her sheets to fly the chute across the line. Even so, *Il Moro* bow obviously crossed before *America³*'s. After a frantic half hour, the meeting was over.

The score was tied at one-all.

The World's Second Best Sailor

At the press conference, Koch acknowledged his team's bad jibe at the finish, and complimented Cayard's brilliance. "He's the second best sailor in the world," Koch said of Cayard, purposely inflating his adversary's ego. Who was best? "I've always thought Conner was the best," Koch said. One journalist wondered where that left Melges, whose face remained impassive under the bright lights.

"He's good enough to be in the America's Cup," Koch said. "And he's a wonderful human being." No one asked where that left Cayard.

While the media focused on Koch's remarks, no one seemed to realize Buddy was going through a slow burn. Not because of what Koch had said, but because of Cayard's attitude and words as the press conference continued. The *Il Moro* skipper had reason to feel elated. After his re-start in the first race, he'd lost no time and now he'd won the second race.

Cayard's comments about the victory tended to be direct criticisms of Melges' helmsmanship. "Buddy gave us a Christmas present…Buddy made a mistake here…Buddy should have done this…." While Melges kept his cool on stage, Koch later described him as furious. The "Wizard of Zenda" knew well his performance was below par, and Cayard's words were salt in the wound.

If Cayard's press conference discharge was another attempt at a psyche-out, it backfired. Once he cooled off, Melges regrouped and rethought his actions.

The next morning, a lay day, America³ held an afterguard meeting. Koch had the film ready to roll and had prepared another "come-to-Jesus" session during which he was ready to spare no words or anyone's feelings. But then Buddy came in and announced he'd been up all night and he'd made a list of everything that went wrong the day before. He wanted the floor, but Koch said he had some things to discuss first. The two butted heads for awhile and then Bill asked Buddy what was on his list. Buddy read it and Bill, with a grin, said "it's your meeting."

Buddy stood before the afterguard and reeled off his list of 28 mistakes that he felt occurred during Race 2. "And out of these 28 mistakes," said Melges, "I'm responsible for at least 80 percent of them."

"He did the best thing anyone in an organization can do," Koch says. "He admitted his mistakes and got on with it. After that we were rolling. At the end, when Buddy was clicking as a team player, doing his job, he was wonderful."

The mistakes were boiled down to three or four major problems and practice on that lay day centered around those mistakes, with most of them devoted to jibing.

For Koch it was a long, but satisfying day which he felt was a major turning point for the entire sixteen men on board coming together as a team. As he returned home late, he was reminded of the 5:30 a.m. rally some members of the San Diego Yacht Club threw for him that morning. Koch, one of the world's more prolific art collectors, had had several of his multi-ton bronze sculptures from the hands of the Colombian Fernando Botero shipped from Florida and placed on his back lawn in San Diego when he first came to California. One statue in particular, an over-sized likeness of a full-figured woman, attracted the majority of public attention and was quickly dubbed "Roseanne" by the locals. It often served as a type of new age mannequin/billboard on which was fitted certain articles of women's clothing and messages to the Kansas skipper from Conner partisans, written in graphic language. Koch largely ignored the defacings, but on one occasion, when he felt the locals had gone too far, he threatened to turn "Roseanne" around so her backside would face the yacht club.

But on this day, all past actions were forgotten. Koch had been touched by the early morning pep rally. His young son Wyatt, remembering the previous rally for Dennis Conner, once again draped "Roseanne" with a bra. This time it read "We love Bill Koch."

Cautious optimism was the mood in camp as the day of Race 3 dawned. "When we're both going slower, *America³* is faster," Doug Peterson said. "We're faster in all conditions." Koch's long-term confidence in his equipment was well-founded. The sailors felt it. The media were the only ones still picking Cayard and *Il Moro*. No doubt they were wishing a trip to Venice for themselves.

"We've overcome some difficult obstacles," Koch told his team at the morning meeting: "The Race Committee, the media, the ACOC, ESPN, the San Diego Yacht Club. They were all biased toward Conner. And we beat him. I'm glad we made our mistakes early so we could correct them. It's in our hands now, and I'm optimistic."

Once again, Dellenbaugh controlled the start. With two minutes left, both boats on starboard tack, he stuck *America³*'s bow under *Il Moro*'s stern and kept it there, securing the left side of the course. At one minute, Cayard tacked away and started at the boat end. *America³*, five seconds late, tacked at the pin end and both boats went off on a long and puzzling port tack. Puzzling because drag racing *America³* was not in Cayard's best interest. Someone suggested Cayard wanted to make sure everyone knew he was up against a faster boat. Twelve minutes into the leg, *Il Moro* tacked. They weren't even close. The "scalded dog" was back and in full form.

"Great race," Jerry Kirby said. "The afterguard was perfect. They picked the left, held on until we sailed into a wall of wind, then steamed away. They played the shifts right all day, and the crew work was right on."

"Maybe Cayard's mistake was to agree to a 'nice' Cup match," Harold Cudmore said with one of his fiendish chuckles. "When the tension builds, he has nowhere to release it except internally."

Cayard would say after losing Race 4 that repeated selection of the wrong mainsail had been costing him. Mainsail selection is a critical pre-race decision. For *America³* it began every race day at 5 a.m. when meteorologist Chris Crabtree arrived at his office and began a routine he had been practicing for 17 months. A San Diegan, Crabtree is familiar with local conditions. "But for the hour-by-hour demands these guys made, I had to watch and refine and learn every day," Chris said.

By 9:30 a.m., when the boats left the dock, Crabtree was on board with forecast in hand. For the next two hours he watched and analyzed what he saw against the indicators, daily records, and models he constantly studied. At 11:30 a.m., it was showtime. The weather information was in from the tenders and the helicopter. The current buoys had been set and recovered. The *Firewater* brain trust had been talking all morning with navigator By Baldridge on the race boat. Now everyone turned to Chris Crabtree for the word.

"The first day we held tough with a lighter main. The Italians changed. If they had gone lighter, it would have been a factor. For Race 3, both boats selected heavy mains. It was the wrong call. If we'd used a lighter main, we might have won by 5 minutes. But it was blowing 9-13 in the morning. I saw a cirrus streak that puzzled me, and I lost a little nerve. I thought if it was blowing this hard now, what happens if that weak trough I had been watching came through. So I bumped the forecast to 11-14, and the afterguard went heavy. It was the first time we used the wrong main in 4 months. But it's best to err on the high side so people and equipment don't get hurt.

"Light air always makes me nervous because it can only build. I'm always nervous, like an expectant father."

The diligent Crabtree was taking modest satisfaction winning the meteorology war. *Il Moro*'s Australian weather man was said to rank himself first in his field.

After the first three races, it began to appear Cayard's only chance of beating the white boat was to take her decisively at the start. But in Race 4, Dellenbaugh once again sailed a great start. Cayard had him pinned near the Committee boat on starboard at 2:00. Dellenbaugh did a crisp tack-circle. Cayard followed, but came out to windward of *America*^{3} on starboard. Cayard dipped. Dellenbaugh dipped deeper. When they hardened up at the pin end, *America*^{3} was ahead and to leeward, right where she wanted to be.

America^3 carried a 30-second lead through most of the race, and that was lucky, because if it had been much less they would have lost it around mark 6. While removing the reaching strut, grinder Peter Fennelly stepped in a jib sheet loop. The spinnaker was being doused, blocking the developing crisis from most of the crew's view. In the flurry of activity that accompanies a sail change, Fennelly's foot was being ground into one of the winches.

A Crewman Saved

As the line pulled his foot, the grinder lost his balance and began to fall overboard, facing the possibility of losing his foot or being dragged upside down in the ocean and drowning. Suddenly, pitman Wally Henry grabbed Fennelly in a headlock and yelled for help. Bowman Jerry Kirby raced to his aid, knife in hand. Now both Fennelly and Kirby were over the side, Kirby hanging onto the rail and Henry holding onto Fennelly.

If Kirby cut the line, the sail would have blown and *America*^{3} probably would have lost the race. If Fennelly fell overboard, by the time the yacht had turned around to retrieve him, the regatta would undoubtedly be tied at 2-2. Kirby told him he'd cut the line if the pain was too much to bear. Fennelly later said that two thoughts were running through his mind. One was that if Kirby cut the line, his life would be saved, but the race would be lost and he'd wish he had died. If he didn't say anything, they'd win the race but he'd lose his foot.

At that point, trimmer Mike Toppa noticed what was happening and he eased the sheet enough for Kirby to pull it off Fennelly's foot. Teamwork had averted disaster and *America*^{3} won by 64 seconds.

The three sailors had the media howling when they restaged the event at the press conference, complete with head lock, knife-brandishing, and Fennelly's pithy narrative: "I was bummed out."

Score: 3-1.

It's always a bit scary to ice the champagne before the fat lady sings, but the mood the morning of Race 5 was definitely on the confident side. Koch repeated the litany — everyone do his own job, rely on the other guy, we've got a great team. "Let's smoke 'em today, have some fun tonight," Melges said. And there was a thick contingency plan (in case of a win) that included everything from handling the media to instructing the caterers. Lucky thing.

But there was still some excitement to be had. Throughout the campaign, *America³* had never done it the easy way. Why change at the last minute? With 13 minutes to the start, *America³* reported a broken mast ram. The hydraulic cylinder anchored in the deck that moves the mast forward and aft had torn off the back of the mast. Peter Grubb and the maintenance crew members assigned to *Firewater* to handle emergency breakdowns rushed below for parts and tools, and were waiting on the stern when the tender raced up. Meanwhile, a request for postponement was radioed to the race committee.

Two minutes had passed as the tender raced toward *America³*. They wouldn't make it. All shore personnel and radios had to be off the race boat by the ten-minute gun. Without a postponement, a repair would not be possible.

The request for postponement was denied by the race committee. All the maintenance crew had time to do was heave a coil of line onto the race boat. The mast would have to be lashed in place. Meanwhile the start was underway.

More trouble. With 5:45 left, Jerry Kirby was hauled aloft to do a tape repair on a torn mainsail seam. Dellenbaugh managed to stay away from *Il Moro*, yet position himself well in the starting area.

Riding in the cat bird seat as 17th man was Vincent Moeyersoms. Even though he couldn't participate, it was better for him to be on board witnessing the problems first hand than biting his nails on *Firewater*. The previous day, Koch had turned down a donation of $125,000 for the 17th man seat for Race 5. He didn't want to take a stranger on board, he said. Mainly, he had reserved the seat for Vincent.

After an even start, with *America³* on the left side, the two boats sailed the best weather leg of the series. After 20 tacks each, and a disallowed protest (tacking too close) by Italy close to the mark, *America³* led by :18. That was as close as *Il Moro* would get. Downwind it was *Il Moro* 's bowman aloft, applying tape to prevent several broken battens from tearing through the sail. Breaking battens were a constant problem for *Il Moro* .

As the wind freshened to 14 knots, *America³* kept gaining. A blown chute for *Il Moro* on leg 4 dropped the red boat further behind. Late in the race, ESPN microphones picked up a perturbed Paul Cayard. "We're losing our ass here," Cayard said, and indeed, that was the case. Approaching the finish line, Bill Koch and Buddy Melges looked at each other and in a simultaneous action that was both a celebration of victory and a statement of the growth of their personal relationship, both grabbed the steering wheel while yelling "give it to me, let me steer." The gun ended America's Cup XXVIII as *America³* crossed 44 seconds ahead of *Il Moro* . What followed were several hours of pandemonium.

America³ rubber chase boats descended upon *America³* from all directions, bearing wives, children, girlfriends, and syndicate members. Soon there were several score of people crammed onto the race boat, whooping and shrieking, embracing, and spraying each other with champagne. The night before, Vincent Moeyersoms had said no one would be allowed on the boat after the finish. Crew only. He was concerned about damage. Now Moeyersoms could be seen in the thick of it, hoisting a huge bottle of champagne, his unshakable composure happily shattered by the impossible dream come true.

The victory parade into the harbor was a breathtaking sight, as more than 400 spectator boats churned the wide, deep channel into white froth, and created a cross-chop fierce enough to broach the unwary. *Firewater* and the chase boats had their hands full keeping the area around the race boat clear. Everyone wanted a close look at the winners and the mad victory scene on board. There were some near misses.

One chase boat delivered a large blue bag to *America³*, and soon a new spinnaker was broken out. Emblazoned on the all-white chute was a huge yellow sunflower, the official flower of the state of Kansas. Koch obviously enjoyed this homage to his boyhood home.

After the wake-strewn victory ride past Point Loma, *America³* made a pass by the San Diego Yacht Club where the balconies were crammed with well-wishers. Bill Koch spied the America's Cup displayed on the dock. It was time. He turned to his son who stood by his side, caught up in the joyous calamity. "Watch this, Wyatt. No one has ever done this before." He leapt into the water and swam to the dock to claim the prize. Koch hoisted the gleaming old trophy over his head and let loose a Kansas whoop that echoed across the crowded anchorage. The whole crew followed their leader into the water and onto the dock.

On *Firewater*, after the initial celebration, there was a moment of calm as the realization sank in. "To tell the truth, I had trouble getting psyched this past week," Peter Wilson said. "I wondered how I would feel if we won. But after the gun went off, I was all choked up. Dirk Kramers came up to me and just stood there with a big grin and tears in his eyes. All those hours, all that table-pounding...." Wilson shook his head.

America³ had successfully defended the America's Cup. Moreover, Bill Koch had done it his way, and that would take a while to sink in. Not only had Koch come late as a new player into a complex game with a bunch of interesting notions, but in *America³*'s first public outing at the World Championships, his effort had looked bad enough to be permanently discounted in some people's minds. In some ways that was to his advantage. In terms of media ridicule, it became an obstacle, one he compounded with impulsive statements and terse rejoinders. In overcoming the obstacle, Koch proved just how tough he is.

There were two issues critics were certain would be Koch's undoing. One was his insistence upon steering. The other was his refusal to select a first team until the very end.

"Having the one team for so long was advantageous," Kimo Worthington says. "We kept racing each other and getting better and better. The A/B selection, when it came, was a tough hit. It was hard on the crew. And the politicking to get on the boat was ugly. But everybody came back up at the end.

"Lots of people thought Bill was our biggest hindrance. In reality, he was our biggest asset. He took all the pressure from the media and elsewhere. He had faith in the design team, and he kept modifying the boats all the way to the end. Italy didn't do that. For a time I thought there were too many changes going on. But in the end we really knew what we were doing. That last modification was finished only two days before the Cup. The bulb was still warm when it was delivered. We only had two days to sail the boat. But it was right. It was a step forward. *America³* was a rocket at the end."

The team selection scenario will long be debated. There are no easy solutions to this problem in a multi-boat campaign. And this was a personal matter with Koch. "If the boat had been fast enough, the team structure would have been different," Vincent Moeyersoms says. "Not only at the helm, but with the crew. Bill's ideal was to have a big crew rotation."

As for steering, having an inexperienced helmsman like Bill Koch driving a Cup yacht invited comparisons like renting Carnegie Hall for a concert after a couple years of violin lessons. Within the syndicate, the subject became on obsession. "There is nothing worse than people spending 80 percent of their time discussing other people's problems and not addressing what they have to do themselves to make the system better," Moeyersoms says.

Koch at the Wheel

As a helmsman, Koch progressed rapidly. He steered very well in certain conditions and situations. And critics underestimated his perception for knowing when not to steer. Buddy regularly drove the first two, often three legs of a race. Koch drove the reaches, and often legs six and seven as well. If the race was close, or if Koch felt he wasn't doing well, he would hand off to Melges. ESPN's on-board camera showed Koch asking Melges to step in for the tricky rounding of mark 5 in one race. And in the final Cup race, Koch willingly handed off to Melges for the last two legs.

Louis Cabot says that America³ backer and maxi racer George Coumantaros once told Koch he should steer as much as possible. "I was concerned that advice might feed the problem," Cabot says. "Then George added: by doing so, Bill would know how good everyone else was. It was a wise thought."

Involvement was at the heart of Koch's management method. "That's the difference between Koch and *Il Moro*'s Gardini," Cabot says. "Bill was involved in every aspect of the program. He understood the team, tactics, design, technology, and steering as much as anyone."

The press loved to hammer Koch's management system. Even from inside, America³ management looked helter-skelter on occasion, but perhaps that was because of the broad scope of the program. Since money was not a primary consideration, America³ expanded into a good-sized business, with 200 employees and contractors, hundreds of suppliers and manufacturers, and dozens of associated research projects going on. As David Lowry said, "Koch is the only one who knows everything. Some of the other guys think they do, but they have no idea."

Koch says he appoints managers and gives them both authority and parameters. "I stick my nose in whenever. If they go outside the boundaries, I jump on them. If not, I leave them alone. Vincent knows how I think. He understands the priorities. He brings bad news right away. It has to do with trust, confidence, and limits."

One problem with a team approach like America³ is the bureaucracy it generates. "It takes longer to get things done," Koch admits. "Dictatorship works best for start-ups and crises. Teamwork is better in the long run. My style is to dictate when appropriate, use teamwork the rest of the time. Maybe I don't dictate enough...."

Decisions often did seem to take a long time coming. In the nick of time is when most were made. But that's the American way, especially on the high end, when more with more is the prevailing policy. Crisis management is a bigger American national pastime than baseball. Moeyersoms takes mild umbrage at that implication. "We couldn't make good decisions until

Race Highlights

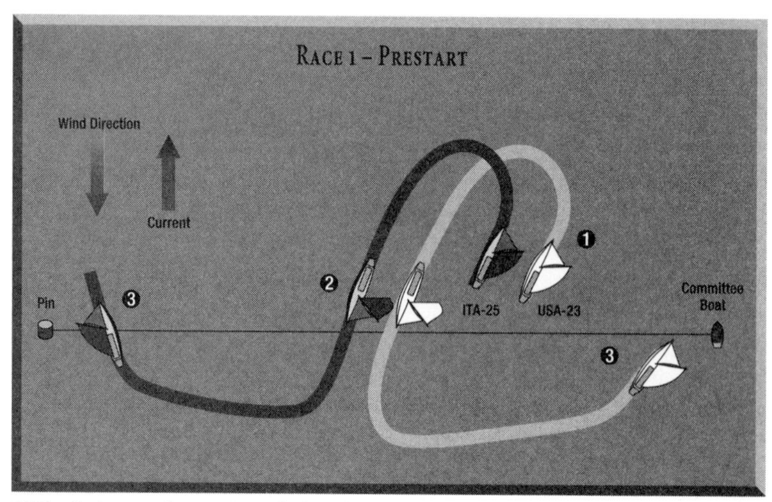

With a little more than a minute before the start of Race 1, both boats are above the line, luffing on port tack with A^3 on the right (shown in position 1). In position 2, *Il Moro* tacks and bears off on starboard to dip below the line as A^3 follows. After the two boats cross back under the line, they separate on opposite tacks, the Italians heading toward the pin end and the Americans favoring the committee boat end. Position 2 shows *Il Moro* over the line and A^3 getting a perfect start. Cayard later said he misjudged the current, costing his boat 30 seconds as he had to restart.

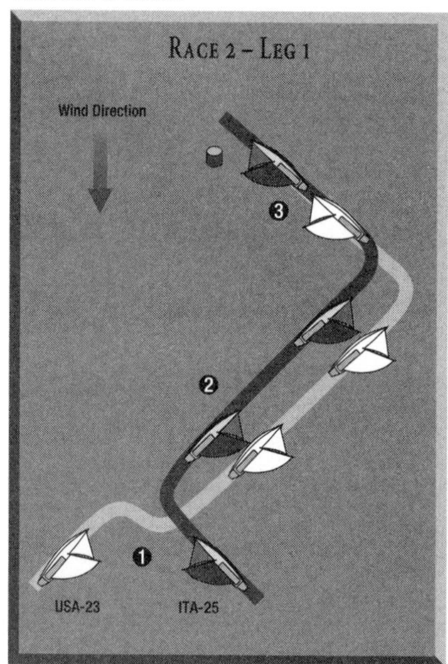

By sailing lower and faster, A^3 pulls even with *Il Moro* on the first run of Race 2. Position 1 shows A^3 attempting to jibe on *Il Moro's* air, but the boat comes out of the jibe too slowly. In position 2, *Il Moro*, with more speed sharply luffs A^3 with spinnaker collapsed. A^3 loses 30 seconds on her way to the leeward mark.

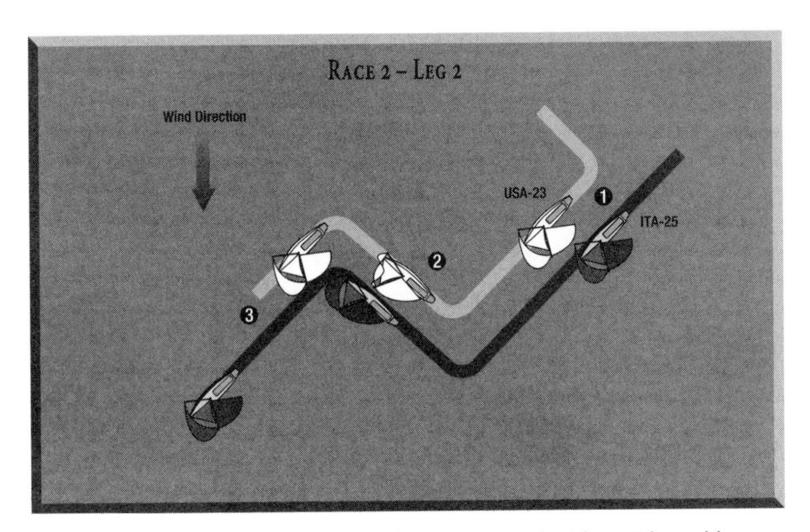

As the yachts sail upwind after the start, Melges is on port tack without rights and he must decide whether to sail on or attempt to cross *Il Moro* or bear off and take her transom. Position 2 shows Melges opts for the safer route under his opponent's stern. Cayard takes advantage of the opportunity and "slam dunks" Melges. In position 3, A^3 is unable to power through and is forced to follow *Il Moro* for the remainder of the leg. The difference at the mark is 33 seconds, *Il Moro* in front.

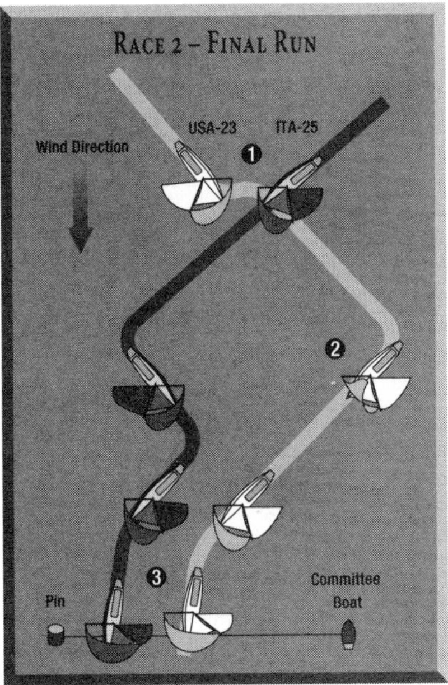

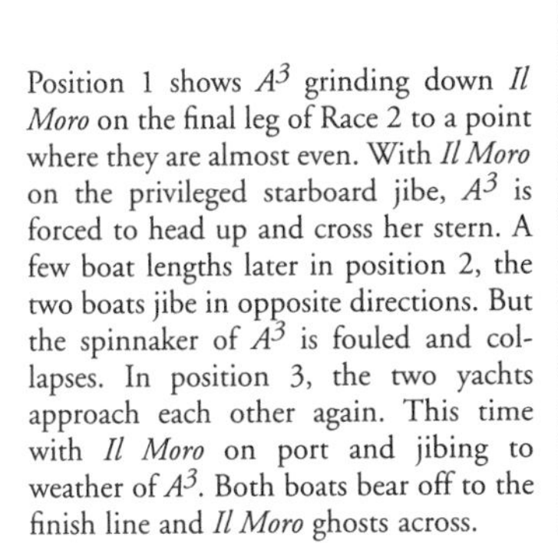
Position 1 shows A^3 grinding down *Il Moro* on the final leg of Race 2 to a point where they are almost even. With *Il Moro* on the privileged starboard jibe, A^3 is forced to head up and cross her stern. A few boat lengths later in position 2, the two boats jibe in opposite directions. But the spinnaker of A^3 is fouled and collapses. In position 3, the two yachts approach each other again. This time with *Il Moro* on port and jibing to weather of A^3. Both boats bear off to the finish line and *Il Moro* ghosts across.

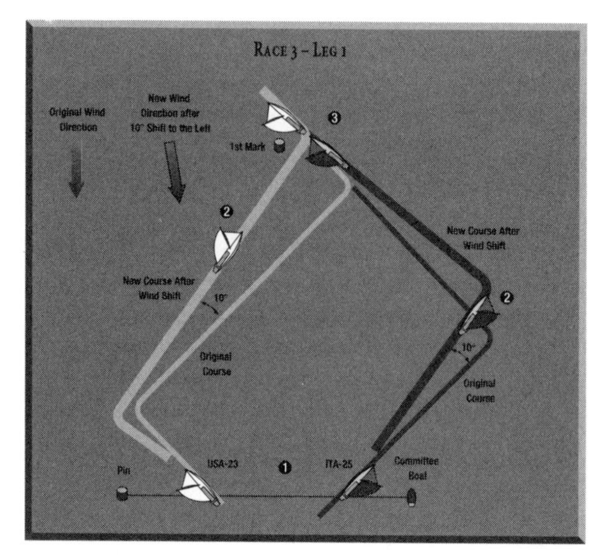

Position 1 shows the situation following *Il Moro's* winning the start by 2 seconds, but positioned at the unfavored committee boat end while A^3 starts at the pin end with solid pressure. A few minutes into the first beat, the wind shifts to the left 10 degrees. The windshift favors the boat on the left, allowing A^3 to sail a shorter distance to the mark (after tacking), which results in a 47-second lead when rounding the mark and heading downwind for the run.

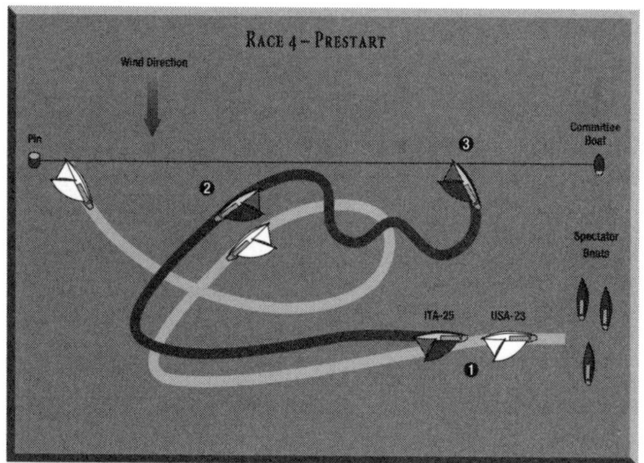

After maneuvering among the spectator boats outside the starboard end of the line, *Il Moro* leads A^3 back on starboard. Both boats favor the pin. In position 2, A^3 tacks with about a minute to go before starting. Both boats sail close-hauled with *Il Moro* to weather and slightly overlapped. A^3 bears off and rolls into a jibe, earning starboard tack rights. *Il Moro* tries to bear off and jibe inside A^3, but can't and is forced towards the unfavored end. In position 3, *Il Moro* tacks back to starboard before the start and both boats are even as the gun goes off. A^3 is on the favored left side and later catches a wind shift and leads at the mark.

TRUE WIND SPEED AND DIRECTION DURING RACE

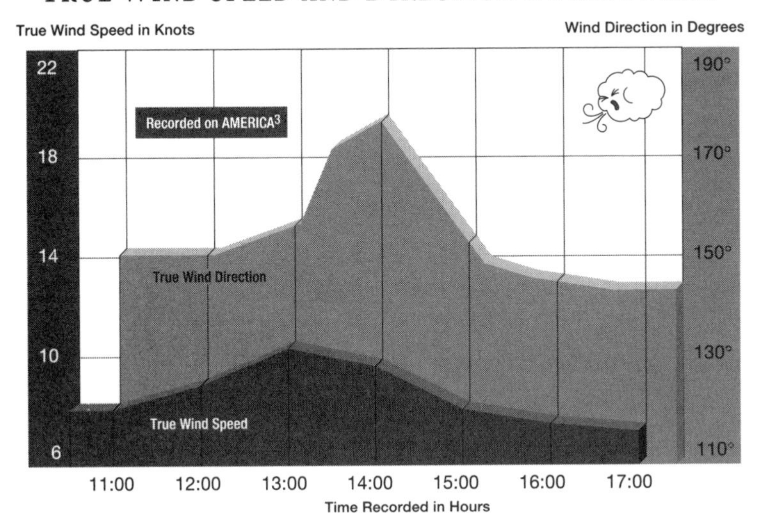

This chart represents the wind speeds and directions recorded on *America³* during a typical race day in San Diego. The wind speed averaged about 8 knots in the morning, increased to about 10 knots at about 1 p.m., and then decreased to about 7 knots in the late afternoon. Wind direction was fairly constant until the noon hour, then it began to shift as much as 40 degrees (from 180 to 140) in the afternoon.

TRUE WIND SPEED DISTRIBUTION

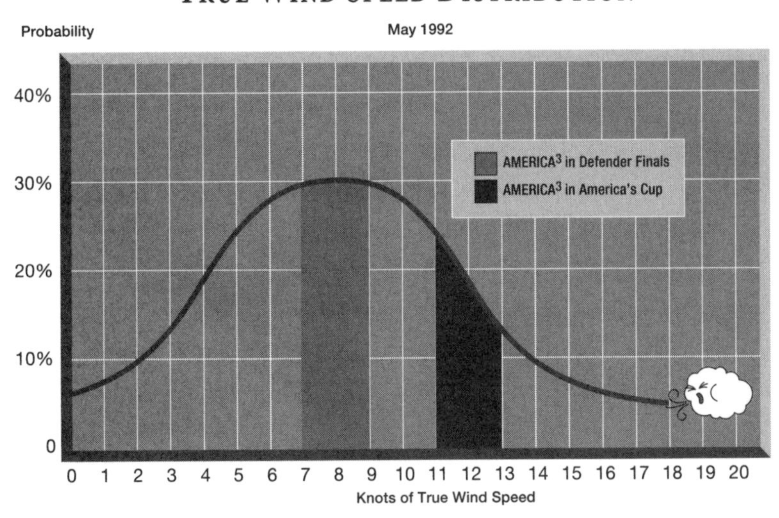

we had finished testing, had all the facts in, knew how things would evolve. You can't decide what's best until you try it." he says. But he agrees that the luxury of so many options delayed the game.

"We tried to do so many things that any question that could wait until tomorrow did. It's how the President runs the country. You can't decide everything today. Later in the program when we had a better handle on what the effect of our actions would be, things went quicker and smoother."

It was this learning-curve management approach that drove America³. "Italy was skipper-driven," Doug Peterson says. "That's why Cayard got the huge rudder he wanted. Mistake. So was Nippon. The sailors ruled the French. Another mistake. The designers ran the Kiwis. Bad news.

"*America³* looked owner-driven, but it was better than that. We had good management. Vincent is not a designer. He's an evaluator. That's a good thing. He kept egos under control. You need egos, but you need management above to make everyone keep working and producing. Vincent did this.

"Bill made the team the thing from the beginning. Credit always went to the team. This was consistent. That he wanted to steer was strange, but the rest was so positive, so correct, that it worked. He never wavered. He laid out a plan and stuck to it. Back a few months I agreed there was lack of leadership. I was wrong. It was there all the time.

"The amount of money spent made it look inefficient, and it was. But we were last in. We had to build four boats in a year. That we got it all done is a miracle."

Harold Cudmore agrees. "Bill changed Cup methodology. I'm a convert. He influenced me at the end. Dennis led people down the skipper-driven path, but then he's very good at that system. If good management had prevailed over Cayard, he might have won.

"A man in Bill's position is accustomed to advisors. But Bill's advisors have to support his philosophy. He has a broad strategy. And he kept to it. Amazing. He took a bunch of mostly average sailors, and some good guys who pretended to be team players, and a few good guys who were, and made them into a winning team. He evolved along with them. I think he undervalued relationships on the boat. People need time to learn about one another. But he made it work."

Koch often said that a program like his was designed to weed out all but the toughest players. One who survived from the outset was Dave Dellenbaugh. He never cracked. He delivered a steady product day after day. In an America's Cup scene of rampant egos, macho attitudes, sneaky politics, and bulging muscles, Dellenbaugh stood out.

"He's so calculating, such an artist," Buddy Melges says of him. "He always knew what the next three moves were. He had a great handle on the rules, and he always knew where he was on the course. When we let Dave be aggressive in his own inimitable fashion, he did great. He won three starts in a row against Dennis, and four in a row against Cayard."

Dellenbaugh bristles slightly when his starts are singled out. "Calling the races was a bigger deal than the starts," he says. "And I called every tack, every jibe. My training is classic match racing. But in San Diego a gain in the shifts outweighed everything else. You couldn't just tack on a guy. We did a good job in that area. Sailing against Dennis made us better at it."

Dellenbaugh echoes Josenhans about the nature of the tactician's job, especially in America³. "I saw it as a no-win situation for me," Dellenbaugh says. "Bill was counting on technology to win. There was always a stake in believing the boat would be faster. There was a strong designer lobby that belittled the sailors, saw them as robots. If we won, it would be boat speed. If we lost, my fault."

After it was over, Italy's tactician, Enrico Chieffi, was among the first to praise Dellenbaugh. "Speed makes life easier," Chieffi said, "but in my opinion Dave Dellenbaugh is the man who won the America's Cup."

Amid the victory celebration, *America³* design-team member Jim Taylor sought Dellenbaugh out. "Thanks," Taylor told the red head, "for making us look good." Dellenbaugh smiled and offered his hand. "No," he said. "Thanks to you. You designers made us sailors look good."

"When I first joined America³," Dellenbaugh said, "I decided to trust Bill Koch and the process. It's amazing how sensible that turned out to be."

Buddy Melges was another survivor. At the end, he was not all smiles, but then how could he be? A man who had ruled his own destiny all his life, Melges' conversion to cog in a team operation was often painful. Perhaps this was the first time in his adult life he had deferred to anyone on the water, or agreed to a partnership at the helm. His usual ride is a two- or three-man boat, often with his sons crewing. He's the boss, the Wizard of Zenda, the King of Zenda. Buddy has gotten used to being regarded as such.

"My stock was pretty low until the January trials when we compiled a 6-0 record in *Defiant,*" Melges says. "They thought I was full of crap until then. I took the bull by the horns in some cases, about sails, battens, crew work — especially when I knew I was right. I created my own niche."

Neither Koch nor Melges escaped their successful, odd-couple relationship without a few bruises. But that was to be expected. There were other pockets of unrest that not only stayed intact, but contributed to the winning effort. The Heiner Meldner/Jerry Milgram relationship was never smooth. And Peterson and Milgram frequently went at it.

"At the end, when the system began to click, everyone clicked with it," Moeyersoms says. "The nicest thing for me to see was Jerry and Doug falling into each other's arms after it was over. They had tough moments. But both brought their best to the effort."

The Meldner/Milgram Equation

Moeyersoms says there was an advantage to the Meldner/Milgram friction. "Both were on the theoretical end, but their approaches were totally different. Heiner flies into things. Jerry is methodical. If one of them suggested something, I knew the other was really going to check the numbers his own way on his own system. If they both agreed, I was happy. When Jerry, Doug, and Heiner all agreed, I knew it was okay."

Koch admits that one of his major personal disappointments is that he didn't have more time on the helm. But as a helmsman, he has only the skipper to blame. That's the trouble with wearing two hats. "Buddy gave me a great compliment," Koch says. "Above 12 knots of wind, he said he couldn't tell the difference when I was steering. If it had only blown a little harder," Koch says wistfully.

At the end, Koch's oft-repeated "Talent, Teamwork, and Technology" slogan had been expanded to include art; the art of sailing the boat. The blending of art and science. This tickled Doug Peterson.

"At one of the last design meetings Bill said it had to be a blend of art and science, but that science would win out. I said, 'I agree, but it hasn't yet.' Bill flung a plastic water bottle at me."

Looking back, Koch says the campaign was a much tougher endeavor than he could have imagined. "The time was staggering, the amount of money obscene, the effort immense," he says. "And the real skill needed wasn't sailing. It was leadership. Being able to recognize problems and go after them. Being able to pinpoint mistakes and correct them. Being able to stimulate people, encourage people to find better ways, find their own way. Being able to put aside secondary things.

"I regret some of the enemies I made. I regret the terrible amount of time I took away from my son, Wyatt. But it was fulfilling. It changed my life. People ask me for autographs, ask me to speak. I'm a mini celebrity. And winning — proving we were right — was gratifying.

"I learned a lot about myself. I learned I could do a lot more than I thought I could."

Aftermath

The final press conference of the 1992 America's Cup was held amid minor chaos as reporters and friends congratulated *America*³ team members and consoled *Il Moro* sailors and officials. Once the principals got settled on the stage, the questions began. Many were routine, but the one that drew the most interest and seems to have been best remembered was directed to Bill Koch, whose son Wyatt sat on his lap throughout the affair.

Would the skipper return for the next America's Cup in 1995, a reporter wanted to know.

Bill answered: "You'll have to ask my son Wyatt if he'll let me do the next one."

"Okay, Wyatt, how about it? Will you let him do the next America's Cup?"

"NO!"

"Why not, Wyatt?"

"Because it takes too long!"

There was perhaps no more significant statement made concerning the future America's Cup than those few words spoken by a six-year-old boy. Bill Koch, defending champion, owner of the just-proven fastest Cup boat in the world, custodian of enough scientific and technological data to float a fleet of speedsters, had been put on notice by his son that his father's involvement in another campaign would not be acceptable. Koch senior agreed; time away from his son was one of the things he hated most about the America's Cup. Before Wyatt went to bed that night, the man who had that day won the most prestigious prize in the sailing world, promised the young redhead he would never again be apart from him for that long.

The next day the entire *America³* crew, including Wyatt and Bill's wife Joan, dressed in blue blazers and white pants for the final sail of the campaign aboard the sleek white sloop that had just made history. Their destination was the San Diego Yacht Club where award ceremonies were to be held. It was a short, but very emotional sail.

At the yacht club, after some introductory remarks by club officials, Paul Cayard tearfully spoke about international relationships and his great respect for his mentor, Raul Gardini. Gardini spoke next and was gracious in defeat.

Then Bill Koch stood and addressed the crowd. During his talk, he said: "Throughout the entire campaign, I was asked why I insisted on being on the boat. I was told I was just an amateur sailor, not in the same league with Paul Cayard or Dennis Conner. I have three answers, one is real and two are facetious — you figure out which is which. First, I am a good sailor and I present my credentials as the winner of two maxi World Championships during which I drove 75 percent of the time. Second, if I'm providing the bulk of the financing, I'll do whatever I damn well please! And third, if I am on the boat, I can see for myself exactly what is going on and I don't have to rely on reports filtered through other people's agendas.

"When we first came to San Diego, things were very tough for us. We were considered a joke, my neighbors didn't appreciate my sense of art, the sailing establishment didn't appreciate our reliance on science, the community thought we were here to steal the Cup from San Diego, the media ate us for breakfast, and the America's Cup Organizing Committee urged us to merge with Dennis. All that made us stronger and allowed us to stand up to the toughest racing we've ever had, provided by Dennis and Paul. The Kanza Indians have a saying that the greatness of your tribe is determined by the greatness of your enemies. We have had some great enemies out here and that makes me feel very proud. I'd also like to say that holding a grudge only hurts the person who holds it."

With that said, Koch then announced he would like to honor a number of the men involved in the 1992 America's Cup by making them honorary members of America^3. He began by recognizing Gary Jobson and presenting him with the syndicate's official blazer patch. Another was given to Malin Burnham, who had pressured Bill in the beginning to merge with Dennis. A patch was presented to San Diego Mayor Maureen O'Connor, who had watched the races from Raul Gardini's yacht. Others were given to SDYC Commodore Fred Delaney and many members of the race committee, the same race committee which had been on watch during the mysterious and controversial mark moving incident which benefitted hometown hero Dennis Conner in one of the trial races. Paul Cayard was next, and then Koch took off his own patch and presented it to Raul Gardini, saying, "Raul has great spirit, élan, charm, and he is as fierce a competitor as there is.... It is an extreme honor for me to give this to my good friend."

At the Monday team meeting three days after the victory, Koch announced that the team was leaving for the Mauna Lani resort on the Hawaiian Island's Big Island (Hawaii) on Thursday, returning the following Monday.

At the appointed hour, 285 America^3 employees and their families embarked for Hawaii on a chartered L-1011. An hour into the flight a massive pillow fight started when six-year-old Wyatt Koch launched a feathery missile at his father. The fight lasted a full 30 minutes, with Wyatt in the middle of it all and as much laughter as pillows filling the plane's interior. Flight attendants said only one group they had encountered had been more rowdy: servicemen returning from Desert Storm.

"It was a primal scream of release, of victory at last," said Jim Draper, a scientist who had been working on a top secret project at the end of the campaign.

The three days in Hawaii were blissful. The championship golf course was almost as popular as fish-watching. Helicopter flights allowed one to peer into the mouth of an active volcano, and marvel at the changing topography of the amazing island. But perhaps the highlight of the trip was when Shannon (lead) and Kelli Crawford, Sarah Lessard, and Libby Toppa jumped onto the bandstand during the Mauna Lani's complimentary cocktail party, and belted out a sensational version of "Love Shack" as if they had been practicing with the band for a week.

Like so many things at America^3, it happened at the last minute, and it worked.

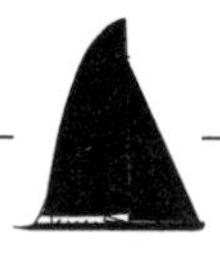

Managing to Win

15

In the months following the improbable victory, the physical presence of America[3] dissolved with much greater speed than it had evolved. The people that made up that team — sailors, designers, technicians, engineers, meteorologists, fund-raisers, administrators, directors, cooks, tender drivers, lawyers, maintenance and security men, coaches, physical trainers, retailers, and volunteers — scattered to the fifty states to resume their lives. Miles of line, tons of equipment, mountains of sails, were packed and warehoused. The compound on North Harbor Drive was swept clean one last time, the doors were locked, and the offices, sail loft, maintenance shed, and boat house left to an eerie silence. The syndicate's first IACC boat, "*F2*" bought from the French and dubbed "The Scud" had long been sold back to the French. *Jayhawk* was donated to the city of Wichita, Kansas, where Bill Koch was born and raised, and now is the principal exhibit at the city's new boathouse (a gift from Koch) on the Arkansas River. *Defiant* was donated to the America's Cup Hall of Fame at the Herreshoff Marine Museum in Bristol, Rhode Island. *Kanza*, the last of the Cup yachts built by the syndicate, joined the champion "fastest boat in the world" *America*[3] in storage in the Nevada desert.

Bill Koch returned to his world of science and business, adding to an already demanding schedule an appointment by the Governor of Kansas to form a commission to find innovative ways to reduce crime in his home state. Buddy Melges went duck hunting, then returned to Melges Boat Works where he oversaw the introduction of the Melges 24, perhaps the hottest racing boat in its class. Dave Dellenbaugh resumed his duties at North Sails, later to resign and begin his own successful publication on sail-boat racing. Vincent Moeyersoms, Rick Wrightson, and Ellen Bloom opened new America[3] Foundation offices in Newton Lower Falls, Massachusetts and continued the work of developing Cuben Fiber sails, contributing to sailing programs that benefited the physically disadvantaged, youth, and Olympic sailors. Jerry Milgram and Heiner Meldner resumed their academic careers at M.I.T. and Stanford, respectively. David Rosow went back to running a bank and building golf courses around the world, including Singapore and China. Bowman Jerry Kirby and sail trimmer Mike Toppa celebrated a 24-year-old pact they had made when sailing in junior programs in Newport, Rhode Island, where the two promised each other one day they would sail together to win the America's Cup.

Of the more than 400-person team, most of the individuals had come together as strangers and had forged friendships or at least working relationships. Many say they left with a feeling of family.

As time passed, the oft-asked question of what role, if any, America^3 would play in the 1995 America's Cup received ever-increasing attention in the media and among team members. Koch had already stated in an ESPN interview on the eve of his duel with Italy that knowing what he knew then, he wouldn't have sought the Cup in the first place. He felt the amount of money spent was obscene, the time away from family and business was too consuming, and the personal antagonisms between competitors and former friends that seem to occur during every Cup to be largely unnecessary. But now that he had won and had hoisted sport's most historic trophy, Koch was ready to wipe the slate clean and reflect on the accomplishment.

Considering the time limitations, the inexperience, the personnel problems that arose, and the strength of the competition, the range of accomplishments was truly outstanding. The syndicate was born two years after most of the challengers and it had had only 15 months to grow and mature before the first of the defender races began. In that short window of time, America^3 developed its own technology to use in the design and construction of four racing yachts in a class new to the America's Cup. It recruited and trained a group of Americans to sail the boats, a crew which underwent personnel changes throughout the campaign and one whose bodies and egos needed to be considered and dealt with continuously. The syndicate found, arranged permits for, and constructed and equipped a compound in San Diego Harbor. And it developed an organization that took care of the myriad activities off the water needed to support the racing: raising money, selling merchandise, repairing and maintaining the boats, entertaining donors, dealing with the press and public, managing the technological development, and providing security for the boats, crew and compound. It did all this in a hostile environment in which America^3 was viewed as the enemy to the city's favorite son. No wonder the Cubens lit up Las Vegas tote boards at 100-1!

And through it all, the team set a number of America's Cup records. It is the only team in modern history to win the Cup in its first attempt. It was the first team to include a woman who participated as an active crew member in the defender trials. It was the first team to have two African Americans on the crew. It was the first team to include two crew members who had never sailed before. And it was the first team to have as its organizational head and crew skipper someone who had started sailing only eight years before at the age of 44.

As Koch considered all this, he also reflected on what was wrong with the America's Cup. It seemed to him that public interest in the event had declined sharply since the Fremantle high-water mark in 1987. He considered a number of possible reasons for this and postulated that the ever-increasing costs, the apathy of Southern California residents to the event, the unexciting racing off San Diego, the dirty tricks and espionage all contributed to people looking elsewhere for entertainment.

In a position to attempt to improve the event, Koch suggested to the San Diego Yacht Club, still the holders of the Cup, that America^3 would form a committee to examine possible cost-cutting measures that might increase the number of teams participating in the 1995 competition. Vincent Moeyersoms was made chairman of the committee which was composed of potential defenders, challengers, and individuals with a keen sense of Cup history and concerns about its future. Koch also, on his own, commissioned a series of focus groups throughout the country made up of ordinary Americans which discussed how they perceived the event. Additionally, he hired a market research firm to survey potential donors and corporate sponsors to determine what would motivate them to invest in the 1995 races.

While this information gathering was proceeding, Koch began to receive a number of requests to speak about the 1992 victory, and what followed was a series of more than 150 motivational lectures given to overflowing audiences from Peoria to Paris. One of his first invitations came from the University of California. The speech was well accepted, if unpracticed and perhaps a bit raw. It was the skipper's immediate reaction to a series of events that seemed so improbable, so unbelievable, that he had yet to fully digest or comprehend them all. What followed were more requests to speak, appeals that prompted his analytical mind to action. "When people started asking me to speak," said Bill, "I thought I'd better really understand exactly what we did and why. First I did an economic analysis and then I combined that with a business analysis. What I discovered gave me a better understanding of exactly what it took to win the Cup, from both a monetary and a management perspective."

Analyzing the Costs

Koch had been stung by the initial utterances from some detractors that he had "bought the Cup." This notion has often been expressed in the past by critics of the amount of money spent on a sailboat race. The criticism is not unique to the America's Cup, especially during the last decade as players' salaries in baseball, football, basketball, and other major sports have escalated beyond imagination, leaving team owners subject to the same opprobrium after world championships are won. Unfair or not, the charge that he bought the Cup, not won it fairly and squarely, pushed Koch into an exhaustive analysis of 1992 America's Cup finances; both his and those of the other competitors.

Koch's analysis confirmed one of his early suppositions: the costs associated with the 1992 America's Cup far exceeded the initial projections of most of the organizations involved. Privately, he and many of the syndicate leaders had been shocked at the mountain of bills accumulated during the separate campaigns. America^3's original budget was $15 million, with a $5 million contingency fund. When the last dollar was spent, the total had ballooned to $68.5 million (see Chart A).

How could this happen? The syndicate had established strict budgets and controls in the very beginning and pledged to abide by the management credo that these would be adhered to come hell or high water. An independent finance department produced monthly statements comparing actual performance to each budget item. Koch saw early in the game where the money was going, but as he often said, "once you mount the tiger, how do you get off?" He realized that if he was to have a shot at winning, and that above all else was the goal of the syndicate, he would have to devote the necessary emotional and financial resources to the effort. There was no halfway, he had to commit himself entirely. If not, someone else would and he would win.

Because this was a new class that allowed exotic materials, the research and development costs were much higher than anyone expected. This was the largest portion of the America^3 expenses (see Chart A). Although America^3 had the extensive data from the *Matador* program, the syndicate's technicians and designers soon discovered that there were far more dissimilarities than similarities between maxi boats and IACC yachts, which meant that not much of the R & D information gained from *Matador*^{2} could be used in creating their America's Cup racers. Outside of the scientific tools already developed, it was pretty much back to the drawing boards.

Each boat that was built cost more, over $5 million, than originally estimated. Expenses attendant to the building and maintaining of these high tech racing machines were also escalated: the large size of the boats necessitated increased real estate for compounds, a large number of crew and support staff — everything was bigger. And because these large, fragile boats were constantly pushed to their limits, the costs for maintaining them, their sails, and their equipment were extraordinary.

"We made the conscious decision to go over budget," says Koch. "Once we had decided to make a run at the Cup, we built our entire organization around the principle that winning would take a total effort. That meant giving everything we had, both financial and personal. There is no such thing as being half pregnant. There is no such thing as winning the Cup with half an effort." But Koch was also aware, from lessons learned in his business career, that if too much money, too many resources, were thrown at a project, waste and gross inefficiencies resulted. Even more important, a soft attitude was created in which success or winning was not the primary objective.

Chart B lists all 1992 America's Cup syndicates ranked in order of their boat speed. Also included is the estimated amount of money each campaign spent. Approximately $498 million was spent by all competitors, not counting the $15 million consumed by ACOC in running the event. Koch believes this kind of financial commitment is indicative of most nations perceiving their America's Cup involvement as a symbol of their country's pride in its technology, management skills, and athletic prowess.

To Koch, what is fascinating about his analysis is that the Italians spent $238 million and came in second, the Japanese came in for $90 million and finished fourth, the New Zealanders anted up $50 million for their third spot, and America^3 won the entire affair at a cost of $68.5 million. To measure the efficiency of how each campaign used their resources, Koch divides the dollars spent by the boat speed each syndicate achieved, resulting in dollars spent per knot (see Charts B & C). Comparing each syndicate by this method, one sees that America^3 was more efficient than the Italians or Japanese, but not as efficient as the Kiwis. And for money spent versus how far each team went in the challenger and defender competition, Team Dennis Conner out-performed everyone by a huge margin.

By plotting each syndicate's money spent versus boat speed in this way, Chart D shows an interesting phenomenon commonly called the law of diminishing returns. To be competitive in the 1992 America's Cup, a boat had to achieve 9.235 knots of speed. This required an expenditure of approximately $35 million. To achieve the winning boat speed of 9.3 knots, just .065 of a knot more, required an additional expenditure of approximately $33.5 million. However, it isn't true that by simply investing that much, a syndicate would automatically achieve the necessary boat speed to

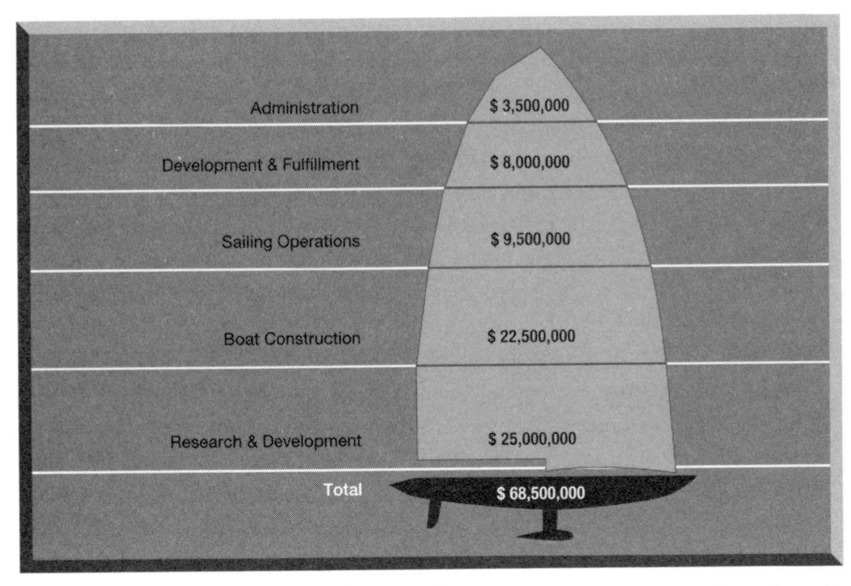

Chart A illustrates the amount of money America[3] spent on the Cup campaign and how the total was allocated.

1992 AMERICA'S CUP COMPETITOR'S EXPENDITURES AND RESULTING BOAT SPEED

TEAM	Boat Speed (in Knots)	Expenditures $'s (in Millions)	Millions of $'s (per Knot)
AMERICA[3]	9.300	$68	$7.31
ITALY	9.275	$238	$24.8
NEW ZEALAND	9.250	$50	$5.41
JAPAN	9.235	$85	$9.2
FRANCE	9.235	$35	$3.79
TEAM DENNIS CONNER	9.210	$12	$1.30
SPAIN	9.180	$12	$3.49
AUS. CHALLENGE	9.160	$32	$1.31
AUS. SPIRIT	9.150	$8	$.87
SWEDEN	9.100	$6	$.66
		Total $498	

Chart B lists each of the competitors in the 1992 America's Cup and how much each syndicate spent. The final figures on the right were derived from dividing the syndicate's expenditures by the boat speed of their yacht. The result is how much each knot cost.

win the Cup. The Italians and Japanese proved the point: you can't buy the Cup, you have to win it.

So if amount of money spent didn't automatically equate to victory, what did? With his economic and business analysis almost complete, Koch reflected on that question; the question that would be fundamental to any of the speeches he was being asked to give.

He returned to his premise that history proved Cup winners achieved their victories by producing a fast boat and fewest crew mistakes. His belief that boat speed is a science and sailing is an art led him to the two management principles that dominated the America^3 campaign: test for boat speed and practice to eliminate mistakes. The paragon of all testing was the concept of constantly improving boat speed. To do so, within a short time and with limited money, meant developing scientific tools which could analyze the myriad ideas generated by the A^3 designers and scientists and accurately predict the performance of certain designs under a variety of wind and sea conditions. The tools developed helped produce a progression of boats that were demonstrably faster around the race course (see Chart E). During the period of just one year, America^3 was able to improve the time around the course by an astounding 6.5 minutes, or 5%. As Chart F shows, *America^3* was by far the fastest boat in the 1992 America's Cup fleet.

Koch believes that one of the most important management decisions in the entire competition was when America^3 decided to play the final race between *America^3* and *Kanza* straight. Because of the way the defender trials had been structured, if America^3 threw the race, both of their boats would make it through to the defender finals. Instead, *Kanza* was beaten and *Stars & Stripes* met *America^3* at the starting line. The resulting competition revealed afterguard weaknesses in Koch's camp as well as boat speed problems. Chart G indicates that *Stars & Stripes* was faster than *America^3* in 7 knots of wind and flat seas. The America^3 team also realized that the races against Dennis were won and lost on the upwind legs.

And it was the competition, particularly against Dennis, that Koch feels was one of the most important ingredients in winning the America's Cup. He would tell the team that "competition makes you strong, do not be afraid of it. Listen to your competitors, try to understand what motivates them and then use what you learn to beat them."

While America^3 emerged from the defender finals to meet Italy in the Cup, the Americans knew their weakness in light air could be exploited. This led to a complete reconfiguration of the boat including a new keel, winglets, rudder, etc, all to the great befuddlement of the defense committee at the San Diego Yacht Club, which operated on the theory "if it ain't broke, don't fix it." The change was made without any tank testing or on-

Cost of Boat Speed
in Millions of Dollars per Knot

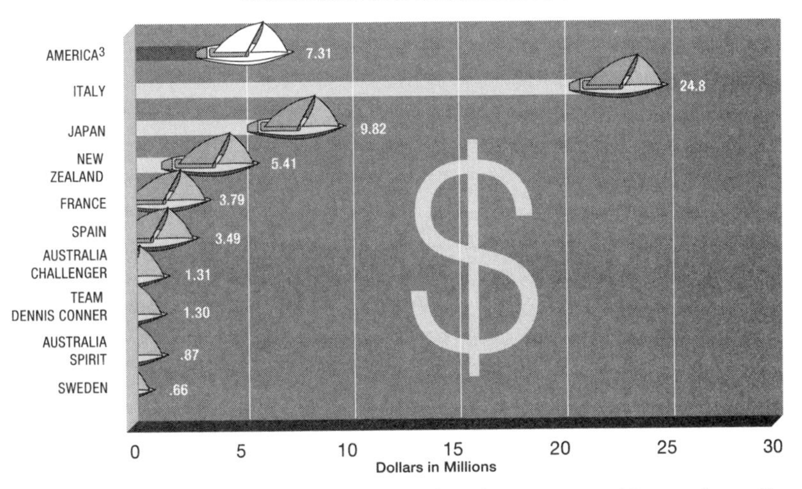

Chart C is another representation of how much each syndicate spent to achieve one knot of boat speed.

Law of Diminishing Returns
Investment vs. Boat Speed

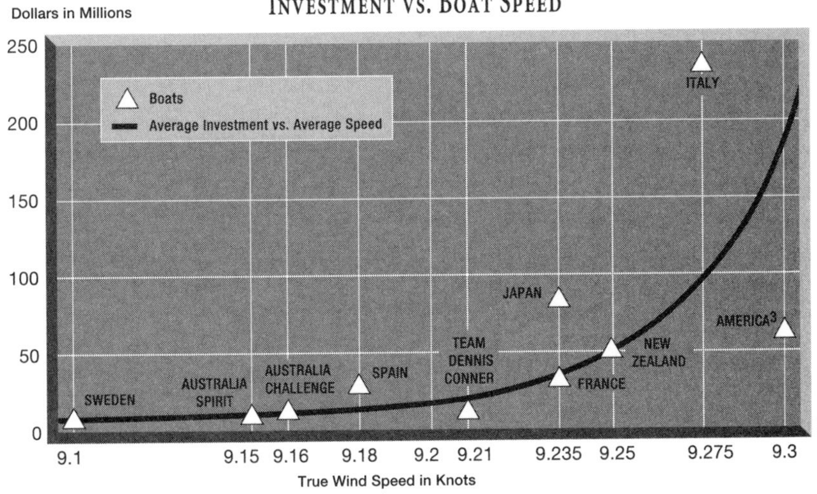

Chart D shows the phenomenon called the Law of Diminishing Returns. Based on plotting each syndicate's money spent versus boat speed, to be competitive in the 1992 America's Cup a boat had to achieve 9.235 knots of speed. This required spending approximately $35 million. To achieve the winning boat speed of 9.3 knots, an additional expenditure of $33.5 million was necessary.

the-water testing. It resulted from complete confidence in the tools that had been developed and which told the America[3] technicians that the new configuration would cure the light wind problem. Chart H shows that 30 seconds was taken off *America³*'s time in light air, at a cost of only 6 seconds in heavier winds.

With his studying and reflection now behind him, the skipper cum speaker was ready for the public. In an attempt to articulate just what winning the America's Cup meant to him, and what the lessons he learned might mean to others, Bill Koch hit the road carrying a video tape, a carousel filled with slides, and a briefcase bulging with notecards. As he criss-crossed the country, he delivered a message laced with humor and emotion, one with a common theme that seems to move audiences as varied as yacht club members, Rotarians, Air Force Academy students, and Bell South executives. Winning the America's Cup, finding triumph in an international sporting event, became for Koch a metaphor for successful management techniques. As he translated the 18-month whirlwind of business, scientific, and athletic activity he'd experienced to Kansas farmers, Texas ranchers, California surfers, Detroit auto workers, and Washington politicians, he told them the management approach he used to achieve victory in the Pacific Ocean was one they could apply to their lives and to their businesses.

"We came to understand that managing an America's Cup effort is like starting a high-tech company, running a political campaign, or conducting a war," he likes to say. "What these endeavors have in common is that they all require similar management techniques. To wage an effective battle a manager must identify the key success factors, assemble the necessary resources, and allocate them efficiently. He needs to establish simple goals everyone can understand and embrace, then focus on them, constantly reminding all individuals, and himself, of the ultimate importance of those goals. Finally he must make and implement decisions in a way that increases the chance of achieving the goals, and encourage innovation and constant improvement as a way to reach the goals."

Ordinary People Doing Extraordinary Things

Koch on the stump is part evangelist, part comedian, part professor, part patriot. He has a knack for making the complicated, technical aspects of science and sailing understandable. He wants you to believe in yourself, your country, your personal goals. At the heart of his message is his strong belief that ordinary people can do extraordinary things. There is a fervency in his midwestern directness as he appeals to what he believes is the winner within us all.

"We won the Cup because one of the most fundamental things we did differently from the competition was to take American management know-how from the land and apply it to the sea. We took management processes, some proven, many rising from our own philosophies, and we applied them to our team in San Diego."

Perhaps the one management philosophy that most flew in the face of proven processes was Koch's insistence on eliminating the hierarchical structure of the America^3 organization. Business-college deans and management specialists have told Bill they were particularly intrigued with his "we're a team and everyone from janitor to chairman is of equal value" philosophy. Successful organizations are built on hierarchies, the gurus say. Men are taught from childhood how to respond to the different layers of authority in group environments. Little League teams have captains, managers, and coaches. The Boy Scouts have progressive ranks. College fraternities have officers. U.S. military service is built on the hierarchical structure. American business has entry-level positions. There is a reason "the ladder of success" has become a cliché. But on Bill's team, at least theoretically, there was no ladder.

As on the *Matador* team, America^3 held frequent awards ceremonies during which individuals were recognized for their attitude and teamwork. Selections were made by previous award winners.

The thinking is simple. If there is one goal and everyone believes they can help achieve it, they will concentrate on that one goal. If three managers have three different goals, it is difficult for the employee/sailor to know to which one he should devote his energies. The trick is to align everyone's agenda with that of the single goal.

"Good American management style," Koch tells his audiences, "was entirely contrary to the sport of yachting and entirely contrary to what had happened in the past. For example, we had a single goal: Win the America's Cup. Do it fairly, do it right, do it the first time out. Winning the Cup was our focus, our concentration, our commitment.

"It started with me and extended to the entire team. I really believe that battles are won and lost in the minds of the commander. I was determined to win. That focus on winning was one of the things that set us apart."

The focusing technique actually began before Koch decided to enter the Cup. In deciding to do so, he himself focused on the question: Can we win? Once he became convinced they could, he never swayed from that conviction. He wrote about being focused in the manifesto and he reminded his managers and his team of the concept repeatedly. By constantly reinforcing that no other agenda mattered, not who drove the boat or which company made the sails, Koch attempted to keep his team focused on the goal. And

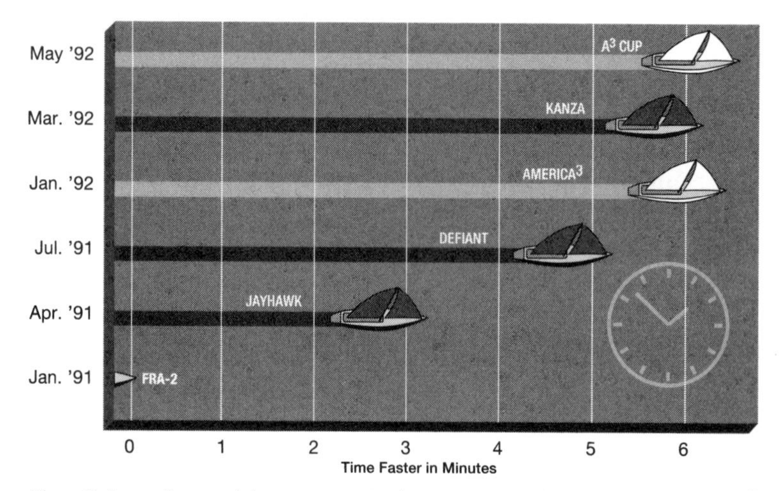

Chart E shows the speed improvement in the progression of boats built by America³ throughout the campaign after the syndicate purchased FRA-2. During the period of just one year, America³ improved the time around the course by an incredible 6.5 minutes, or 5 percent.

from that focus grew a clarity about making decisions. They were based on the answers to two questions: does it make the boat go faster and does it make the crew better? If the answer was no, the decision was no.

The dismissal of Gary Jobson is another example of focusing, or perhaps better said, of preventing the loss of focus. While Jobson ostensibly accepted Koch's determination to be on the boat and to steer during certain legs, he continuously campaigned with board members and team members to get the skipper off the boat. This not only undermined confidence in Koch, but also made a mockery of his management philosophies. The threat Jobson lodged, and the gamble Koch took, was that Jobson had a loyal following that would leave with him. The fact that no one did indicates just how much of an impression the boss's determination to win had made. The crew was more focused than even Koch had known; so much so they weren't about to let such a major disruption distract them.

In addition to being focused, one needs to be committed to be successful. The story Koch tells to illustrate the concept of commitment is about the America's Cup Ball, held two days before the first challenger race was to begin. The team had workouts every morning at 6:30. After the two hours of physical training they'd get on the boats and sail for 10 to 12 hours, with only 20 minutes off for lunch. After sailing, the boats were put

Times Faster Around Race Course of All Competitors versus Slowest Boat

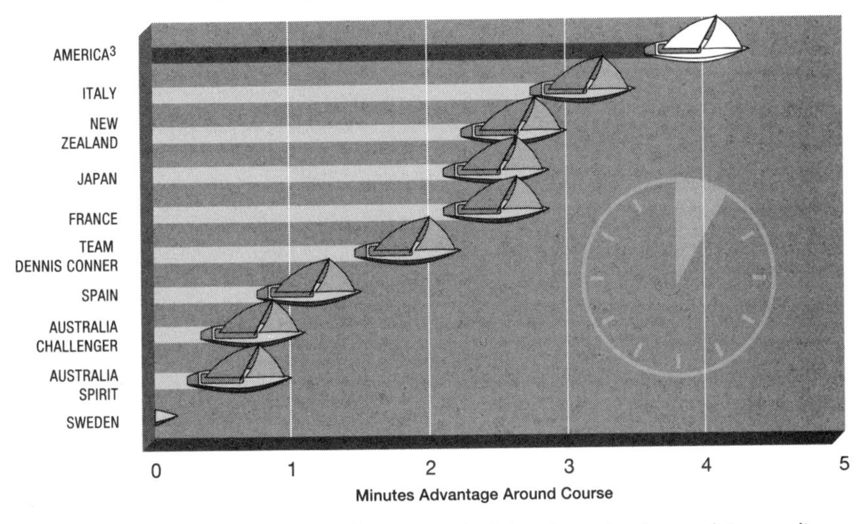

Chart F compares the slowest boat, *Sweden,* versus each of the other yachts that raced, in ascending order. The chart shows the number of minutes faster than *Sweden* around the course of each yacht.

Total Time Difference Around Race Course Between America³ and Stars&Stripes in Defender Finals

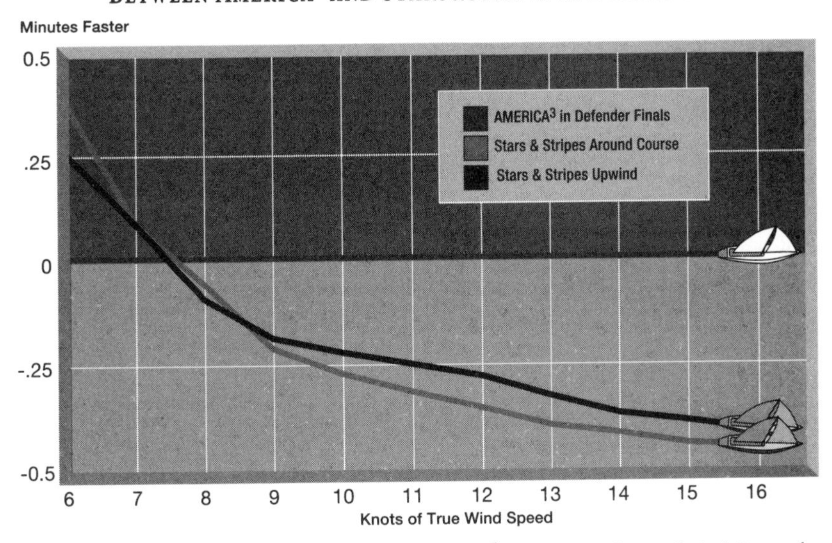

Chart G shows that *Stars & Stripes* was faster than *America*^{3} in less than 7 knots of wind. But as the wind increased, the *S & S* advantage decreased. The defender finals revealed other A^3 problems.

IMPROVEMENT IN A3 BETWEEN DEFENDER FINALS AND AMERICA'S CUP

TOTAL TIME DIFFERENCE AROUND RACE COURSE BETWEEN AMERICA3 AND IL MORO

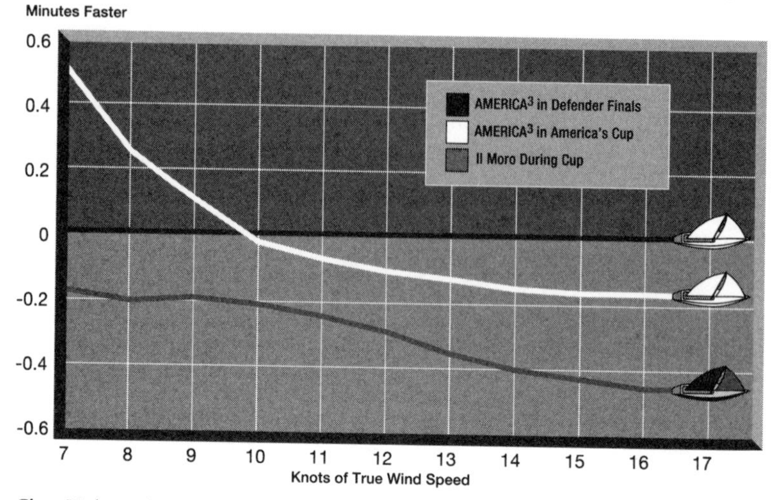

Chart H shows the results of the changes made to *America3* after the defender finals, done without any testing other than computer modeling, resulting in a new configuration to the yacht. The chart shows that the changes took 30 seconds off the yacht's time in light air, at a cost of only 6 seconds in heavier winds. Although *A3* prepared for lighter air, Cup winds were heavier than studies predicted.

away and usually the day ended around 8 p.m. with a crew meeting. That was the schedule, day in and day out, for 18 months, with a day off every ten days, two days off for Christmas and five days for Thanksgiving.

The morning of the Ball the skipper was informed there would be no workout the following morning because everyone was planning on going to the Ball and they anticipated they would be in no shape to make a 6:30 a.m. appointment.

Koch fumed. "We're here to win the Cup, not to go to a party. We did not spend $68 million to have fun. Dennis Conner says you have to be committed to the commitment to win the Cup. Those of you who feel you're committed and want to sail with me in the America's Cup on Saturday will be here at 6:30 a.m. I have to go to the bloody Ball, but I made a deal with the organizers that I can leave in time to be in bed by 10 o'clock. I want to work out tomorrow because I want to be in shape to race on Saturday. That's why we're here."

After Koch calmed down, he said if the team won the Cup, he would throw, at his expense, the best party anyone had ever been to, anywhere in the world. The Ball was held, the entire team worked out the next morning, the Cup was won, and Koch kept his promise by taking the entire team with spouses, children, and friends to Hawaii for three days of non-stop reveling.

Another element of the America^3 management philosophy was born from Koch's scientific background. His belief that boat speed is a science and sailing and designing are art forms drew him away from the prevailing wisdom that fast boats come from big name designers. In the mind of the man with three degrees from M.I.T., using science and developing technology were the keys to producing a fast boat. And the key to the scientific process was experimenting. Technology was the key to developing boat speed, and it was used to advance scientific tools and simulations. Everyone was encouraged to come up with new ideas. These were then objectively evaluated with the use of the tools, and, when tested, they established new boundaries and limits. The net result of America^3's technological approach was discovering new paradigms in considerably less time than other syndicates had done in the past.

Koch believed testing was the only method available to make up for the tremendous disparity in preparation time between the defenders and the challengers. Because of the legal wrangles arising from the previous Cup, challenging nations had a two-year jump on the U.S. defenders. America^3 had just 18 months to prepare their entire program while many of the challengers were afforded a 40-month window of opportunity.

Yet even in the intensity of testing so many different ideas as the clock continuously ticked, America^3, under the direction of Vincent Moeyersoms, checked and double-checked every calculation before anything was finalized. This procedure was indicative of one of the syndicate's greatest strengths — which was that although it had an overall strategy, it paid particular attention to the details. It realized from the beginning that it was one thing to have the big picture in mind, but it was necessary to compose that picture by concentrating on every brush stroke. As the architect Van de Roth once said: "God is in the details."

At podiums around the country, Koch becomes particularly animated when he discusses one of the subjects closest to his heart. "Our strategy was to get many scientists and designers together, have them come up with as many good ideas as possible, and then let the science and the logic pick which idea would produce the fastest boat. Generally, the fastest boat or the fastest car wins the race.

"We tested more than 120 different hull configurations and over 140 different keels. Thousands of hours were spent running boat models through wind tunnels and testing tanks. We tested every idea we thought had any validity. We tested new composite building materials, searching for the perfect balance between weight and strength, rigidity and flexibility. We developed in less than six months a revolutionary new sail cloth material called Cuben Fiber, made from carbon fiber, liquid crystals, and high density polymers."

Experimenting was also key to developing the sailing team. Koch refused to name an A and B team until the last possible moment, choosing instead to constantly rotate the crew into different positions, attempting to discover who worked best together. He would tell his team, "Dennis has had 20 years to find out who works best together; we have less than a year." Here, America³'s criteria for crew selection was attitude, teamwork, and talent.

No Individual Stars

"On *America³,* we had no individual stars. One person can't win an America's Cup race, but one person's mistake can cause a loss. The helmsman is a team member like everyone else. His job is to drive the boat fast. The tactician is the quarterback who calls the shots. The navigator tells us where to go. Each person must do his job the best he can and rely on his teammates to do their job the best they can. When the team wins, everyone is a star. On a team, if one person tries to be a star, he ends up with different goals than his teammates and ultimately his actions will hurt, not help, the team. That's why we de-emphasized the individual and talent. Instead, we concentrated on attitude and teamwork. A rating of ten in sailing ability could not counteract a two in teamwork. It is far easier to train a person with a great attitude to be a good sailor than it is to change the attitude, and make a team player, of someone who believes he's a star." The perfect example of this philosophy is the fact that Chad Vande Zande, who had never sailed before he tried out for the America³ team, not only made the team but sailed in the Cup match.

Koch believes that once an attitude, good or bad, takes hold in an organization, it perpetuates itself and soon becomes part of that organization's culture. Bad attitudes, such as blaming others for your mistakes or resentment growing from inter-organizational politics, can cripple the organization if allowed to spread. A good attitude, such as promoted on America³ by its managers and the grinders union, AKA "attitude police," is as effective a tactic at building teamwork as there is.

The testing process, whether it be at Hydronautics in Maryland or on a boat off San Diego, proved to be the system Koch the scientist best understood. It also proved to be unique to the America's Cup both in its approach and its results. No one had ever tested science and technology the way America³ did. No one had ever eschewed the star-sailor system the way America³ did. Testing produced the fastest boat and the most coordinated team. It worked.

While the victory is proof of teamwork, Koch likes to tell the story of how teamwork may have saved crew member Peter Fennelly's life, when his foot got caught in the jib sheet. Wally Henry's quick reaction was the result of his watching out for a teammate. Jerry Kirby hurtling to the rescue was the result of his being aware a teammate needed help. Mike Toppa's easing the sheet was the result of his immediate understanding of the situation. All of this was done without anyone uttering one word.

Koch believes that a person's attitude is the most important characteristic in building teamwork, and that teamwork is built over a period of time. Working together on a day to day basis helped each member realize the importance of the jobs all the other members were doing. Another technique Koch employed to instill the concept of teamwork was his insistence that everyone, from the security guard to the skipper, wear the same team clothing. The visual statement helped to reinforce the value of each person on the team, regardless of position. Everyone wins, or no one wins.

While Koch and his managers stressed teamwork, they also made an effort to encourage each individual to strive for continuous improvement. All team members — from scientists and engineers to fund raisers, maintenance managers, and retail sales people — were encouraged to do well and were given every opportunity to do so.

By concentrating on doing the job better each day, a creative environment was established in which innovation and improvement were by-products of the team's labors. Mistakes were expected and, in fact, encouraged. They are a by-product of innovation and they were accepted as a part of training. The saying was: "Any mistake is a good one, as long as you learn from it and don't sink the boat." In real races, mistakes were expected to be left on the dock. It was often said that the team which won was the team that made the least mistakes on the race course. The idea was that training and crewwork develop a team that makes no mistakes. To reinforce that point, Koch would quote the French Foreign Legion: "Train so hard that war is easy."

The managers defined each individual's authority and then each individual was asked to define his or her own job. Management's job was to acquire the resources necessary for the individual to perform his job. If the individual has to be told what his job is and how to do it, he is the wrong person for the job. In business, this is called giving an individual authority along with responsibility, and then holding him or her accountable for the results. To be held accountable, the individual's performance must be measured as objectively as possible and a meaningful reward granted if the established criteria for the performance is met or exceeded.

Another management principle Koch often refers to is the idea that, in many cases, the past should be ignored. Study it, learn from it, use what you can from that knowledge, but don't let it cloud your perception of what needs to be done in the present to prepare for the future. If Koch relied on the past, he would never have entered the Cup; no first-time effort, excepting *Magic* which won the first America's Cup in 1857, had been victorious in the event.

As a manager, both in business and sport, Koch urges his organizations to concentrate on the difference between perception and reality. The fact that he, his managers, and all of America³ did so many things differently than had been done in the past often caused the perception among the press and public that they didn't know what they were doing. No doubt the most often cited example of this was Koch's insistence that he should sail on the boat. Owners, organizers, money men, syndicate chiefs, just didn't do that. Koch didn't understand history, said the critics. He had no business on the boat. That was the perception.

The reality was that Koch believed part of his job was to be a leader, a hands-on manager. "Troops in battle fight harder when they see their commander on the point," he would say.

Several months after the Cup was over, an America³ study determined that more than 45,000 articles mentioning the syndicate had been written worldwide and that 40,000 of them had had something negative to say. Despite the continued bad press he received and the near crew mutiny his persistence caused, Koch remained determined to be on the boat. He said there were three reasons for this. "One is serious, the other two are facetious. You figure out which is which. First, I am good enough to be on the boat. I'm not the best, nor the worst, sailor in the world, but I've won two world championships and I know how to win. The second is if I'm financing the bulk of the effort, I'll do what I damn well please! And the third is if I'm on the boat I can see what is happening, I don't need an interpreter.

"That reminds me of a joke," the skipper says during his speeches as he warms to the story that regularly draws the greatest laughter. "Years ago a Mexican slipped across the Texas border and robbed a bank. The authorities sent their best Ranger after him. The Ranger eventually caught the bandit deep into Mexico and handcuffed him to a tree. He began to interrogate him, only to learn he didn't speak English. The Ranger went into town, found the most prominent, knowledgeable citizen who also spoke English and took him out to the bandit.

"Please ask him his name," said the Ranger.

The interpreter did so and then said "His name is José."

The Ranger said, "Ask José where he hid the money."

The interpreter came back and said, "José says he will never tell you."

The Ranger pulled out his pistol, put it to José's head, cocked it, and said "Ask him again."

José whispered in a very meek voice to the interpreter, "Okay, I hid it in the town well."

The interpreter turned to the Ranger with a very sad face and said, "José says he's not afraid to die."

Koch tells his audience that a good manager has to be part of the team and has to know for himself what goes on so he can make decisions on the basis of first-hand information. In Koch's view, effective managers shouldn't spend all their time behind their desks. They need to be on the assembly line, to work in the factory, to take sales trips.

A leader needs to be part of the daily process, do the same jobs everyone else is asked to do, be held to the same standard. In this, as well as in the emphasis on team and the de-emphasis on stars, the leader is helping to build an egalitarian organization. But as a leader, he must assume leadership responsibilities as well. He must have the capacity to rise above the group, not as a star but as a leader, and take on certain functions that will improve the team and move it forward. In America[3], theory became practice as Koch continuously strived to reinforce goals and values, to reinforce the importance of everyone and everyone as part of the team, to make sure the criteria developed for success was constantly applied and applied equally, to inspire confidence, to make sure everything was done well, and to make the tough decisions that no one else wanted to or could.

Never Give Up

The leader must always demonstrate his belief that the team will achieve success. He can never show signs of giving up, no matter how bad things may look. Mental toughness is an attribute a leader/manager must develop. A loss, whether in business or on the race course, has to be seen as only temporary. A true leader will inspire his team to come back the next day, the next month, the next year. When Dennis Conner was the first American to lose the America's Cup in 1983, many "experts" wrote him off as a has-been. He quietly went about his business, assembled his team, convinced himself and them they would win, and in 1987 in Fremantle, Australia, did just that.

Koch learned from Dennis, just as he did from his fellow Kansan, the great World War II general Dwight Eisenhower. When Ike, as commander of the European forces, witnessed the loss of one of the early battles of the war, he was depressed for several days. As he visited the troops over the next few days, he noticed his depression had spread to his men. The revelation shocked him and was the genesis of his developing the famous "Ike grin."

He worked on this technique to show the troops that nothing bothered him, that tomorrow was another day, that he had confidence his team would win. Koch experimented with similar methods throughout the campaign.

Managing individuals in a business enterprise, Koch tells his audience, is not very different from skippering an America's Cup boat with 16 crew. He often alludes to his experience at his own corporation, Oxbow. In the days when he was beginning to build the company, he fell victim to the "star system" he so emphatically castigates today. He hired three star executives whom he did not know especially well, except by reputation. He trusted their talent without paying attention to their personal agendas, which eventually came to encompass huge personal gain at the expense of the company's capital structure.

"It was a $35 million management error," he says, "but it taught me to never become overly dependent on talent alone."

Today, Oxbow's management is quite different in part because they place a great deal of emphasis on getting to know the individuals well in both business and social situations. They spend a good deal of time trying to understand individual goals and to align these with the goals of the corporation.

When Koch made the decision to take on the America's Cup challenge, he turned Oxbow over to three executives with instructions to improve the company's ongoing business operations, but not to leap into new territory. In 1991, when he was away from Oxbow for the full year, the company's profits doubled from 1990. He jokes that in 1992, when he was absent for only half the year, the companies profits rose by only 50 percent.

"This kind of performance could only have resulted from selecting the right people who could do the job better than I could," says Koch. "The selection process is exceedingly important in creating the right team, and that was especially true for America^3. More than 500 people applied for fewer than 40 places on the crew. We started with extensive interviewing, not only of the applicants but of others who sailed or worked with them. The process lasted two months, at the end of which we selected the 40 individuals, from which we selected a final crew of 16. As skipper, my job was to make sure the right people were in the right position."

Koch's task was made easier by the management lessons he had learned in building Oxbow. As in his company, he chose people from America^3 who could do the job better than he. While he insisted on being on the boat, he knew few helmsmen in the world are better than Buddy Melges, so he had Buddy steer most of the time. While he insisted on setting the racing strategies, he knew he needed an experienced tactician on the water so he recruited David Dellenbaugh and supported him throughout. While he insisted on a scientific approach to research and development, he knew Jerry Milgram and Heiner Meldner had had more experience in conducting technological programs affecting boat speed, so he put them in charge. While he insisted on a coordination of R & D, boat construction, sail development, and operations, he knew Vincent Moeyersoms had the right background and temperament to manage the program. While he insisted on a Corinthian approach to fund raising and making sure that the value of each sponsor's investment was more than the dollars contributed, he knew David Rosow was best qualified to head up that endeavor. While he insisted on a professional approach to media relations, he knew when a change of direction was needed and he brought in Will Robinson to direct it. And when he realized his sailors needed coaching on match race tactics, he brought in Harold Cudmore to give them just that. He also asked Cudmore to coach him as well, telling the Irishman that even the skipper needed an objective advisor.

Koch is often asked what mistakes he made during the campaign, to which is stock answer is "Too many to remember, but they were less than the competitors'!" But he'll add that perhaps his biggest mistake is that he didn't establish and make known an exact date on which he would select the crew to sail in the America's Cup. "Failing to do this, although it was a preconceived strategy, it caused some disappointments which I regret very much. I believe everyone on the sailing team was capable of being on the final boat. The strategy of not naming an A team worked to the point of everyone giving their best throughout the campaign and allowing us to see who worked best together. However, not announcing a clear selection date caused a distraction and some internal political and morale problems. The final decision broke some hearts and maybe I could have done it a better way. What I learned from this is the importance of communication. To be effective, you have to communicate constantly, openly, and honestly about exactly what your goals are, what your approach is, what your values are, what your criteria for judging people are, and how you see your strategy evolving into success."

Communication among and between everyone of the team was continuously promoted. The more ideas the better, believed the America^3 management. Different opinions, even controversy, would grow into solutions. "Out of the competition of ideas comes the very best in thinking," says Koch. Because so much was new — the boat, the crew, the course, the syndicate itself — no one was thought to have a monopoly on how things should be done. Everyone on the team was encouraged to have a say.

Koch is also often asked what his personal weaknesses are and how he deals with them. Like his mistakes, he answers, there are too many to recount, "but I try to recognize them realistically and deal with them. I believe my biggest weakness is that I tend to fall in love with my dreams. But that is also my biggest strength."

In the end, it is difficult to say what business management lessons were learned from leading America^3, and which sailing team lessons were learned from building Oxbow. And perhaps that is a question better left to historians or management gurus or efficiency experts. Perhaps it is enough said to realize that as far as the 1992 America's Cup was concerned, Bill Koch was the right man in the right place at the right time.

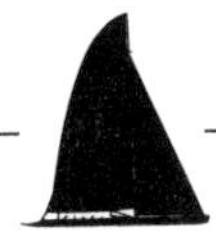

Epilogue

There is a belief among America's Cup participants and observers that once someone is bitten by the Cup bug, a mysterious malady known as "America's Cup fever" results, a fever for which there is no apparent remedy other than participation in each ensuing event. Although Bill Koch had stated publicly a number of times that he would not personally compete in the 1995 Cup, there was widespread speculation that as the event approached, he would be unable to resist. Despite his promise to his son, despite the fact that another entry would prove nothing, and despite his constant denials, numerous speculators had him mounting another campaign. Fuel was added to this fire when word got out that officers of the America³ Foundation were seen in discussions with San Diego Yacht Club officials responsible for organizing the defense of the '95 Cup.

What was really happening was Koch's effort to communicate the results of the studies America³ had independently underwritten to take the pulse of America on the subject of the America's Cup. This nationwide study on the Cup is believed to be the first of its kind conducted on so wide a scale. Koch and the Foundation managers believed that what the study discovered should have an impact on how the 1995 event was organized and run. And along with the results came a number of recommendations from America³, the reigning America's Cup champion.

The study showed that Americans by and large believed that the Cup was too expensive, took too long, was not exciting enough, had too few defenders, that the competitors were too spread out and inaccessible to the public, that there was a lack of impartiality and friendliness in San Diego, and that there was a visible lack of professionalism in managing a world class event. Some of these reactions could be attributed to the differences between the event held in Fremantle and the one in San Diego, as well as the dampening of interest resulting from the court cases of 1987-1989.

Historical America's Cup Participation and Spending

	ALL DEFENDERS		ALL CHALLENGERS	
Year	Syndicates	$ Amount Spent	Syndicates	$ Amount Spent
1958	4	$ 745,000	1	$ 225,000
1962	3	$ 850,000	1	$ 350,000
1964	2	$ 745,000	1	$ 450,000
1967	4	$ 1,500,000	1	$ 600,000
1970	4	$ 3,450,000	2	$ 2,000,000
1974	3	$ 4,500,000	2	$ 3,700,000
1977	3	$ 5,200,000	4	$ 7,100,000
1980	3	$ 5,600,000	4	$ 12,000,000
1983	2	$ 7,800,000	7	$ 25,500,000
1987	4	$ 36,000,000	12	$ 106,000,000
1988	1	$ 12,000,000	1	$ 17,000,000
1992	2	$ 80,000,000	8	$ 418,000,000

Chart I lists the number of all defender and challenger syndicates that competed in the 12 America's Cup events from 1958 to 1992, as well as their aggregate spending. Note that since 1977, the number of challengers has always been equal to, or greater than, the number of defenders. This fact is also represented by Chart J.

America's Cup Participation

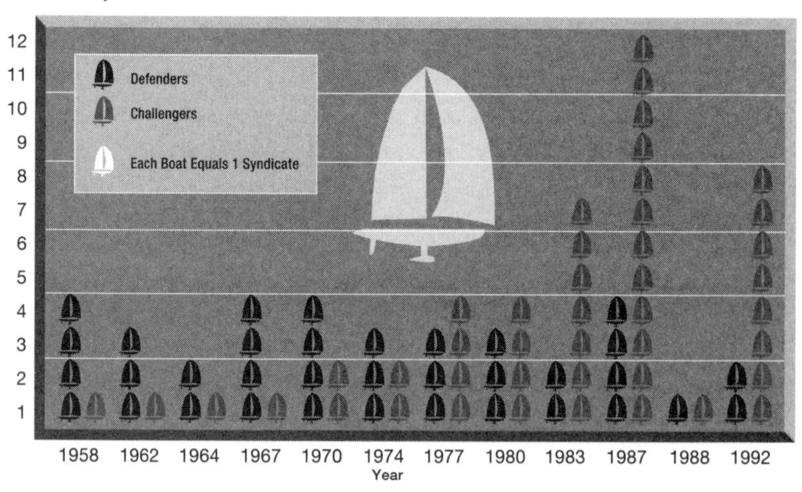

A study undertaken by the America[3] Foundation after the 1992 event found that the Cup is viewed by foreign countries as a symbol of a nation's pride and strength in management, technology, and athletics.

America's Cup Spending

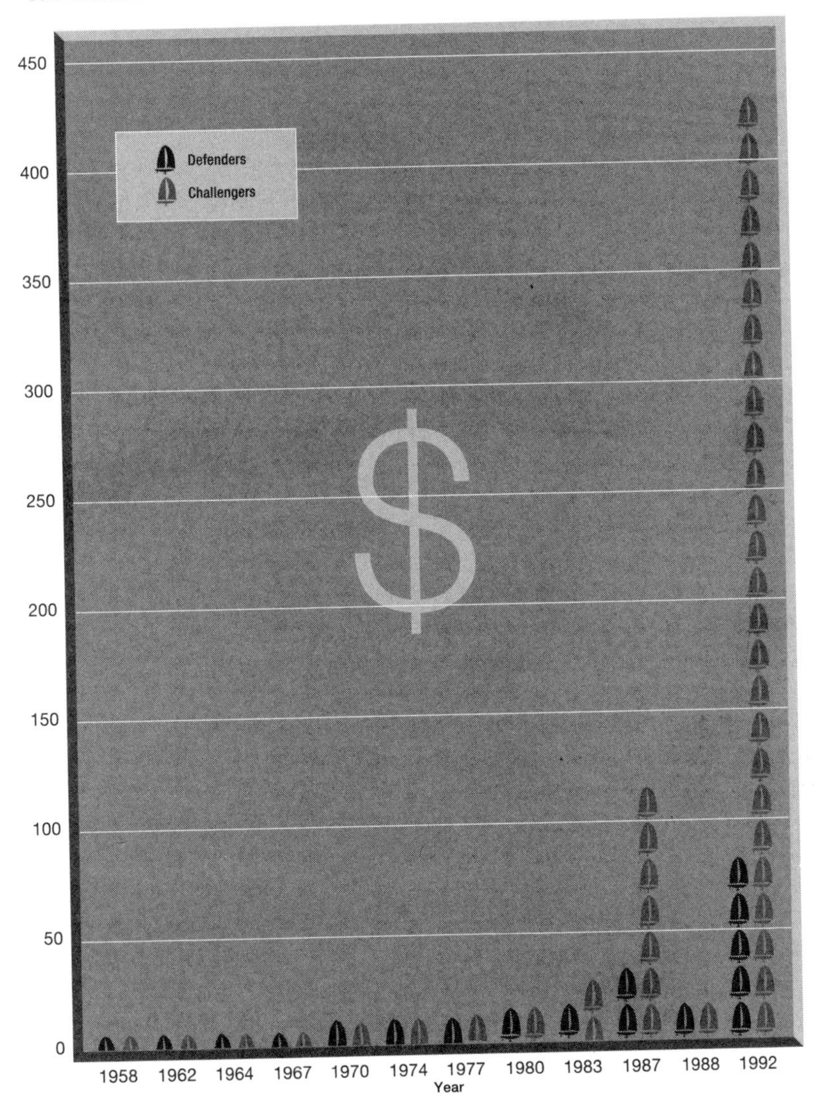

Chart K is the estimated expenditures of the Cup defenders and challengers. It shows that the challengers have greatly outspent the defenders and the combined costs have risen dramatically.

Americans in general view the America's Cup as a rich man's sport sailed in the backwaters of an exclusive yacht club. But internationally, other countries view the Cup as a symbol of a nation's pride and strength in management, technology, and athletics.

This may be one reason that in recent years the number of challengers has been increasing while the number of defenders has been decreasing (see Charts I & J). This fact also points to an interesting phenomenon about the America's Cup: the winning team doesn't make money from their victory, yet the host city often stands to rake in millions of tourist dollars. While this is not a hard and fast rule (San Diegans will tell you the Cup didn't fill their coffers in '87 or '92), challengers do believe they have something to gain by winning the Cup, and therefore usually outspend the defenders (see Charts I & K).

While the criticisms that arose from the focus groups tended to paint a not-so-rosy picture of the America's Cup, a great majority of those questioned responded that they believed the event had great potential to rise above its difficulties and resume its place as one of sport's premier spectacles. Whether this was a result of the event's unequaled tradition, the excitement it generated in Fremantle, or a variety of other positive factors was unclear, but what was evident was if handled correctly, the audience could grow significantly.

This potential was not lost on Koch or America^3. While his victory was sweet, Koch couldn't help but wonder if it had helped restore at least some luster to a Cup some felt was becoming increasingly tarnished. And if his maverick ways did have some impact on increasing interest, then might some of his ideas about improving the event be equally worthwhile? He believed so, but it wasn't so easy convincing the SDYC.

Growing out of the marketing study was a detailed, comprehensive plan to enhance the appeal of the America's Cup. In brief, the major points were to simplify the race course and improve spectating, enhance tourist appeal by centralizing docking facilities for all defenders and challengers, and locate the media, merchandising, sponsorship, and viewing areas immediately adjacent to the boats. In other words, make the event more "spectator friendly." Specifics on simplifying the race course included: drop the reaching legs on the course, shorten the course, use the same course for defenders and challengers, impanel a impartial jury made up of an umpire pool and international race committee, and penalize rule infringers with a headsail drop versus a 270-degree turn. The call to centralize docking facilities suggested March 19, 1995 as the date when all competitors would be located in one "America's Cup Village" type of area. Another recommendation was to assure that no spying would take place and that concealing boats and keels would be illegal after a specific date; again March 19 was suggested.

Also included in the plan were a number of recommendations for reducing costs. Shortening the length of the event headed the list, followed by allowing the building of only a predetermined number of new boats per syndicate, no change of boat after March 19, at which time all boats must be declared and open for public view, and predetermining the number of sails to be used.

The most controversial recommendation was that SDYC consider changing the venue for the 1998 Cup should a defender win in 1995. The idea was born from the growing discontent among competitors and spectators with San Diego. At sea, the conditions simply do not make for very exciting racing, especially when compared to a Fremantle, a Hawaii, or a Sardinia. On land, there are so many other enjoyable attractions in and around San Diego, the focus on the Cup was often obscured. Additionally, Americans tend to be regional fans. They are more prone to be avid followers of the Red Sox/Yankee rivalry than they are to get excited about international competitions, with the possible exception of the Olympics.

To earn the venue after 1995, it was suggested, a potential defender must win the trials and the Cup match, pay SDYC $2 million within 90 days, keep SDYC as trustee, and agree to return to San Diego for the next Cup should they successfully defend.

Already stung by the embarrassment of ACOC mismanagement and bankruptcy, as well as increasingly vocal criticism of their fair city, the SDYC was initially reluctant to even hear, much less discuss, any of the reigning champion's ideas. However, as time passed and it became increasingly apparent that the defense effort would be seriously diminished without America^3's involvement, members of the defense committee realized starting a dialogue would be in everyone's best interest.

In the meantime, history began to repeat itself. Just as Bill Koch was on every Cup hopeful's lips in the year or two leading up to 1992, so too was he the talk of the sailing world in late 1994 and early 1995. Here was the man with the fastest IACC boat in the world, a loft full of sails, tons of equipment, a well-trained team, and deep pockets (although Bill likes to say he may have deep pockets, but he has short arms!). Just as before, when Cuppers realized how easily the *Matador* program would translate into the America's Cup, Koch's phone and doorbell started ringing. There they were again, ready to deal, to beg, borrow, or steal all or any part of the recently proven program.

But Koch, although he himself would not compete, was considering making history yet again, not just repeating it. During the trials, Koch was approached by a woman from San Francisco who wanted to buy *Defiant.* She told him she dreamed of fielding an all-woman's team to compete in 1992, even if it was a token effort. This was not the first attempt at mounting such an effort. As far back as 1972 a Connecticut woman had actually formed a syndicate and began raising money for a team to be made up entirely of female sailors. Through the years other fledgling efforts began only to end as all had ended — unable to find the necessary resources.

But after the 1992 Cup, as information about public opinion was gathered, Koch began to seriously consider the idea of a women's team. He was intrigued with the notion. He had just finished a rugged campaign during which Dawn Riley had proved she could do her job as well as a man. Koch began to wonder why a boat full of Dawn Rileys couldn't do just as well as an all-men's team. He also saw this as a perfect way to illustrate his philosophy that attitude and teamwork, not individual stars, are the major components of winning. He also recognized that because of the cost reductions approved for the next Cup, and the fact that so much of the research and development costs of the new IACC boats had already been spent, the cost of a successful campaign would be closer to $20 million than $70 million. And from a personal perspective, he saw a women's team as a tribute to his mother who had been an outstanding sportswoman, excelling in golf, tennis, hunting, and fishing. It all seemed to fit.

Initial talks were held with potential managers and possible crewmembers. Announcement dates were set and then postponed for a variety of reasons. If this was going to happen, said Koch, it had to be set up just right from the very beginning. It had to be a serious, professional effort with a good chance of winning. An all-women's team was sure to shake up the sailing establishment even more than his "novice" team of 1992. One false step along the way could result in a major set-back.

As word of the all-women's team began to leak into the press, members of America^3 and the SDYC were in negotiations on many of the issues mentioned above. The club wanted Koch and his resources in, but they weren't too sanguine about this all-women plan. On the other hand, they knew enough about history to know that one of the reasons the New York Yacht Club had held the Cup for 136 years was because the defending boat or crew usually returned following their triumph. Experience had always been one of the defender's greatest strengths.

As these things happen, some of the rules and conditions of the 1995 America's Cup were changed in late 1993 and early 1994, but America^3 was never publicly acknowledged as being responsible for the alterations. In fairness it should be said that not all the recommendations made by America^3

were unique to them. Some of the issues had been discussed so many times by so many people that credit for origination would be dubious at best. However, it is interesting to compare the plan presented to the SDYC by America^3 to the changes made.

In 1995, the race course was to be windward/leeward only — no reaching legs, and measure 18.5 miles. Each syndicate might build only two new boats. Spying and secrecy were to be greatly limited to no aerial reconnaissance, and viewing on the water could take place no closer than 200 yards. A common declaration date for defender and challenger boats was established, keels were to be exhibited on that date, and the public will have greater access to crews and compounds. A limit on the number of sails to be used was established.

On March 9, 1994, Bill Koch and members of America^3 gathered at New York's Plaza Hotel for the announcement of the historical all-women's team which would compete in the 1995 America's Cup. The public and press reaction was nothing less than astounding. Interest in the Cup grew exponentially. Sources at ESPN reported that immediately after the announcement, an increase in advertising for their live Cup programming was realized.

The question of how well the women will do is left for time to answer. While there have been and certainly would continue to be detractors of the concept, Bill Koch stood steadfast behind the management principles used to bring victory to his 1992 team. "Our goal," he said, "is to empower women with this same formula for success. We believe that with the right focus, technology, teamwork, dedication, and desire, women can not only compete with the best men in the world, but they can also win."

A month after the 1992 America's Cup was over, Bill Koch made a startling discovery. A relative of his had been in the afterguard of *America* when she won the Cup in 1851. "I'm a direct descendent of Alexander Hamilton on my mother's side," Koch explained. Hamilton was secretary of the treasury in 1789 under President George Washington. He was killed in a duel by Aaron Burr (then Vice President) in 1804.

"Colonel James Alexander Hamilton, Alexander's son, was in *America's* afterguard," Koch says. Col. Hamilton was also father-in-law to George Schuyler, scholar, sailor, and member of the original *America* syndicate. It was he who wrote the original Deed of Gift and presented the Hundred Guineas Cup to the New York Yacht Club.

"I didn't even know this," Koch said, loving the coincidence, the prickly sensation of fulfilled destiny. "Heck," he said. "I was raised in Kansas!"

Bill Koch did, after all, have a reason to be in the America's Cup.

Appendix

Manifesto

Goal

To win the 1992 America's Cup.

Winning Philosophy

To win the Cup in good taste and without commercialism using high standards of sportsmanship, ethics, honesty, integrity, and by combining teamwork with advanced high technology with entrepreneurial management with superior talent. The effort will not be built around any one individual, but around the team as a whole.

General

To win the 1992 America's Cup is a large challenge. This is not just a sailboat race. It is a fundraising race, a race of technology, a race of managerial skills, a race of sailing ability, and sailing strategy. It is an intensive, full-time, 21-month campaign that will require a wide range of skills brought together and coordinated to produce the very best. It will require total teamwork with values and objectives that are shared and supported enthusiastically by all.

This is a contest that has captured many people's imaginations in many lands. National honors are at stake. We shall be very much in the public limelight. This can become a liability if we are careless about what we do, say, and how we appear. It can be an asset if we look good and handle ourselves honestly, fairly, thoughtfully, respectfully, and with a consistent voice. We must have a sportsman's understanding that we will never air our natural disagreements to the press or the public. We must all have the same party line. Because of the image we wish to project, we shall say nothing bad about any of our competitors to the press. I, personally, shall be our principle spokesman with the press and the public and shall only delegate that function to others in a careful, selective, and disciplined way.

Management

To accomplish our goals and objectives, we need to have a very simplified, clear management structure. The organization will consist of a president, who will be the chief executive officer; a vice-president in charge of technical operations; a vice-president in charge of sailing; a vice-president in charge of fundraising and public relations; and a chief financial officer. The president will report to the small board of directors consisting of three to seven people with appropriate experience. Each vice-president will be given authority limits necessary for his particular responsibilities. In addition, there will be a board of trustees composed of prominent individuals who will advise the board of directors.

Throughout the organization it must be emphasized and re-emphasized that the success of this effort will require teamwork, good attitude, and an absence of hidden agendas.

Since this is a not-for-profit venture and since our resources are limited, modest salaries will be paid. However, there will be a bonus pool set aside from the funds raised to reward those individuals who have given outstanding performance and contributed greatly to the teamwork and attitude of the effort.

We plan to have periodic meetings to review the various important aspects of the entire program. Also, to ensure the best input and maximum teamwork, we plan to have the vice-presidents periodically review and comment upon all of the major decisions that have to be made in the program.

It cannot be emphasized enough that, in order to be successful, we must do every job well. In that regard, every person in the organization is important to the overall effort. This must be constantly reinforced and pointed out.

Technology and Operations

It has been shown clearly that a high-tech approach to yacht design can, indeed, produce a very fast boat. If you have a very fast boat, then your chances of winning are greatly improved. In order to produce the best and the fastest boat, we believe that we can take the design approach that was used in *Matador*^{2}, rather than going to a standard yacht designer. We can break the yacht design down into the following general areas:

1. (a) Hull shape (b) hull structure
2. (a) Keel shape (b) keel structure
3. (a) Deck structure (b) deck layout
4. (a) Mast structure (b) mast rigging
5. (a) Sail shape (b) sail structure
6. (a) Boat construction
7. (a) Boat optimization

We plan to use all the tools we developed in the *Matador*^{2} program: tank testing, wind tunnel testing of keels, sail design and testing on the sail force boat, VPP formulation, computer simulation, etc. Since all of these things cover a multitude of different disciplines, what we would do is to assemble a group of highly qualified experts in each individual discipline, and get them to work together as a complete team.

We have enough individual data already to design what we believe to be a potentially very fast boat. Our plan would then be to build one boat using standard yacht construction techniques, and then another of the same design using high-tech, aerospace composite structure techniques. While this is going on, we would be doing sail force testing to come up with the optimum rig and sail shape. Simultaneously, we would tank test additional designs to come up with perhaps a third optimal design.

As soon as the two boats are built, we will put them in the water and test them against one another. We will design them in such a way that we could change keels and masts readily to get real life testing to confirm our wind tunnel testing or various keels and appendages and mast shapes. We will also have a concerted effort to optimize each of the boats. After we learn which construction technique is better, which keel is better and which mast is better and, from the tank test data learn which hull shape is better, we would then plan to build a third boat.

In order to speed up the experimentation design process, we would want to do as much computer simulation and flow code work as possible. To get a good measure of the performance of the boats, we would need to develop our computer information system on board as well as our electronic measurement system. We need to develop a good meteorological database to assist our design program. Finally, we want to develop the best sailing information package to enable America^3 to present information to the skipper and tactician in such a way as to be the most user-friendly and meaningful as possible.

The operations department would oversee the research and development effort, the design of the boats, the construction of the boats and, finally, the optimization and operations of the boats and the support facilities.

To protect our R & D results, we need to have tight and continuous security procedures. We will also have signed confidentiality agreements with those involved in the program.

In bringing all these various disciplines together, we would need again to concentrate on teamwork and shared sense of values and goals.

Sailing Programs

We plan to put together the best crews possible. This does not mean getting the best sailors. It does mean, however, getting the best people that rate the highest in attitude, teamwork, and sailing ability. Working together as a team is absolutely critical to sailing a boat of this size well. In order to ensure a good system of teamwork, we will have each of the major heads of the sailing teams rate each potential crew member on a scale from one to ten according to attitude, teamwork, and sailing ability. We will then select those that have the highest overall scores. As it is generally the case that the boat that wins is the one that makes the fewest mistakes, we will want to concentrate on making sure that each job on board the boat is done exceptionally well and that everyone appreciates that each crew member is equally important as any other. What this will entail is not only putting the right person in the right job spot on board the boat, but also practicing over and over and over again, so that each maneuver becomes second nature to each crew member. This will require an extensive amount of sailing on the water, practice, and a great deal of physical fitness for each crew member. In fact, we should have a physical fitness test for each person who is going to get on the boat.

To ensure that we have a good racing strategy and make few tactical mistakes, all of the crews will be trained in match racing tactics and strategy. Furthermore, each crew member will be instructed to look out, as much as possible, for each wind shift. And further, to develop a good sailing strategy, we will need to develop as good a meteorological and current database as we possibly can. In our practices we will need to review and practice as many tactical situations as we can expect to find on the race course. After each day of racing we should have a tactical and strategic review of what went on that day.

Furthermore, we need to develop a crew manual and to choreograph each crew member's movements during the various respective maneuvers. Before each race and practice we will have crew meetings and after each race and practice we will also have crew meetings to review what we are going to do and what we did do.

To instill the team concept in everyone, we will have a standard crew uniform and during the races will insist upon everyone wearing the same uniform; shirttail tucked in and starting the race with clean uniforms. We will also insist upon a clean, shipshape boat.

Because these boats have not been sailed before, we will not select a final crew until late in the program. We will try out a number of different people for each spot, and narrow it down to two and a half squads less than half way into the sailing program. The final helmsmen will not be selected until late in the program. Instead, we will have a squad of helmsmen and from them select the best ones who fit the overall program.

Additionally, to further emphasize the necessity of teamwork, we will give out the *Matador*-type of prize to the crew member who best exemplifies our spirit of attitude and teamwork after each major regatta. We will attempt to house all of the crew in a crew house as appropriate and plan to have regular crew dinners and meals.

Technology and Operations

We need to develop an overall marketing approach in order to raise $10 - $15 million. The market segments that we should initially go after would be (1) donations from individuals; (2) donations from corporations; and (3) gifts in kind from corporations. With our concept of a clean boat, we will not be able, for both strategic reasons and for IRS qualifications reasons, to sell advertising space on the boat or spinnakers during the races. However, preliminary indications are that we can lease the boat for advertising purposes during non-race and practice sessions. The strategic reason for having a clean boat and no advertising during the race is not only to show that we represent the traditional standard values of yachting, but also to distinguish ourselves from the other competitors who are having to produce boats that look like Indianapolis 500 cars.

We need to develop a fundraising and marketing program that distinguishes us from the other two syndicates; the Beach Boy' and Dennis Conners. To this end, I believe we should concentrate and emphasize our overall corinthian effort, our entrepreneurial management style, our teamwork, and our use of high technology for a good national purpose. We also need to do a great deal of market research to see what each one of our various market segments wants from such an America's Cup effort as ours. Then we can determine whether we can deliver that or not. In this regard, we need to be very careful that we follow religiously the guidelines that we have given the IRS as to our fundraising efforts.

As far as any marketing program, it is essential that we gear up to fulfill the promises that we have made to our client. This would require having a staff to look after it. We also need to have an organization headed by one person who can then supervise individual fundraising, corporate fundraising, and gifts in kind. That person would also have to coordinate with the other activities of our group in order to bring the right person in to make the right presentation at the right time.

As a supplement to our marketing program we probably need to develop some marketing aides; such as video and perhaps a newsletter. We would also want to follow up and entertain our largest donors.

I think it is going to be important that we decide what target donations we are going after. We do not want to waste time and money going after small donations, and yet we do not want to spend a lot of effort going after low probability, very large donations.

Again, throughout this activity we want to emphasize good attitude and teamwork. The teamwork is going to come from not only all of the individuals involved in the fundraising, but also from those involved in the sailing, technical, and operations divisions.

In summary, we need to do the following:

1. Define ourselves.
2. Identify and segment our potential customers and clients.
3. Develop an approach to the various different marketsegments.
4. Establish goals for each market segment.
5. Line up presentations to each market segment.
6. Get on the road make marketing calls.
7. Evaluate results for possible strategy changes.

I believe our approach should not be too slick, nor too amateurish. It should be exceptionally professional and show that we are a high quality, highly ethical organization that is emphasizing the right values.

Finance and Accounting

Our group will have a chief financial officer, whose responsibility it will be to prepare not only the monthly financial statements, but also to provide management information, as well as to do various economic analysis for us. As far as the accounting is concerned, we will insist on very strict operational accounting controls with the appropriate authority limits and check signing responsibilities. We will have monthly statements, which will be broken down by the various different cost centers so that we will know what each activity is costing us. This would include the breaking down into sub-activities of the development, operations, marketing, sailing, and technical groups. Each vice-president in charge of his various different groups will prepare a budget and each month he will be given a financial statement comparing the actual expenditures versus budget, revenue received versus budget, and the variances.

The chief financial officer will also be responsible for assisting the vice-presidents in making cost/benefit analysis and studies on critical decision items.

To make sure that expenditures do not get out of hand, we will need to have very tight controls over commitments to spend money. As such, we need to develop strict authority limits.

The 1992 America³ Team

Board of Directors

Louis W. Cabot, Chairman
William I. Koch
Richard P. Callahan
David A. Rosow
Robert G. Stone
Thor H. Ramsing

Officers

William I. Koch, President and Skipper
Vincent C. Moeyersoms, Chief Operating Officer and Executive Vice-President
David A. Rosow, Executive Vice-President
David Lowry, Senior Vice-President
Frederick W. Wrightson, III, Vice-President
M. Brad Robinson, Chief Financial Officer and Vice-President
William Campbell, Vice-President

Design Team

Director: Dr. Jerome Milgram
Deputy Director: Fernando Frimm
Appendages: Marvin (Buddy) Duncan
Lines: George (Penn) Edmonds
Keels and Spars: Phil Kaiko
Tank Testing: Daniel La Mere and John Mass
Review: Doug Peterson
Boat Setup: Jim Pugh
Rating: John Reichel
Performance Analysis: Jim Taylor
Software: Rob Scala
Software Programming: Noah Eckhouse and Don Peters
Sail CFD: Steve Eurle and Jack Kleene
Appendage CFD: Dave Greeley, Ching-Yeh Hsin, Justin Kerwin, and Alexis Mantzaris
Sailforce Boat: Erich Steadman and Bruce Sutphen
Consultants: Karl Kirkman, Paul Sclavounos, Howard Wilson, and Quilong Wong

Technical Team

Director: Dr. Heiner Meldner
Composite R & D: R.J. Downs, George Springer, and Steve Tsai
Software: Ron Cusson

Aerodynamics: Robert Liebeck
Quality Control: Bill Roeseler
Special Projects: Barnum Lambert
FEA Modeling: John Hamilton, S.K. Ha, K.S. Lui, James Peterson, Dr. Alan Puckett, Craig Riley, James Ross, Kevin Ryan, Kevin Scott, Walter Scott, Todd Scully, Ken Sherrod, and Alix Tilson

Technical Administration

Manager: Ellen H. Bloom
Fridolf Hanson and Nancy White

Instrumentation

Director: Dr. William Unkel
Electronics: Rodney Ernst, Dave Frank, and Paul Roell
Software: Andreas Klein, Kam Sing Leung, Mike Prichard, and Olga Pustylnikov
Analysis: Peter McCarthy and Betty Sherman
Meteorology: Chris Crabtree, Nicholas Graham, and Rea Strange
Special Projects: James Draper, Steve King, Harry Lee, Jim Nesbitt, Luis Quijano, and Mary Scott

Compound

Manager: Joel White
Team: Shannon Crawford, Bruce Durkee, Felix Gonzalez, Nick Kirby, Flynn McDonnell, Ron Wiswell, and Suzy Ziegler

Tenders

Manager: Tom McDonald
Team: Steve Connett, Mike Dailey, Todd Herrick, Rene Sagebien, Scott Sartrys, John Spengos, and Thomas McCarthy

Shore Crew

Manager: Peter Grubb
Foreman: Erik Soper
Team: Dave Bieling, Jay Christopher, Paul Cronin, Mike Eldred, Brent Foxall, Jack Guibilato, Steve Harrison, Gene Helsel, Brian Hutchinson, Toby Ingrey, Brad Johanson, Phil Keester, Jed Lowry, Bill Mattison, Jon Mulligan, Dale Schipporeit, J.T. Walsh, and Michael Walsh

Sail Program

Manager: Bill Shore
Loft Supervisor: John (Winn) Fowler
Loft Team: Marc Baxter, Marc Holzman, Marc Irwin, Virginia Leon de la Barra, Bridgite Lyle, Kenneth Peterson, Susan Peterson, and Bob Pettingill
Consultant: Paul Dimotakis
Design: Per Andersson, Andy Halsey, Dave Hirsch, Larry Leonard, Peter McCarthy, and Peter Wheeler

Construction

Manager: Peter Wilson
Assistant: Susan Gintling
Quality/ Weight Control: Sean Fawcett
Purchasing: Joe Milner

Chief Engineer: Dirk Kramers
Engineering: Jim Antrim, Steve Baker, Phil Craven, Ed Frank, Rodger Martin, and Carol Vernon
Spar Engineering: Ed Chase and Mike Feldman
Boatbuilders, *Eric Goetz:* Adam Aleicho, Dave Aleicho, Doren Almon, Randell Bagwell, Dennis Baxter, John Bradshaw, Fred Brodzinski, George Chase, Steve Coughran, Frank Eckhart, Carl Evans, Jim Foster, Bucky Frost, Jeff Green, John Hawkins, Rob Henry, David Hopton, Bill Koffler, Glen Longstreet, Kelly McMillan, Henry Mackaol, Carlos Medeiros, Vinny Medeiros, Dave Mellish, Kevin Monahan, Bucky Morgan, Vinnie Pard, Gary Patz, Robbie Pelletier, Joe Quaresma, Fred Richardson, Matt Sledge, John Telfyan, Will Vanderlande, Prentice Weathers, George Walker, Larry Tuttle, Don Watson, Dave Walworth, and Gary Wolfang
Model Construction: Walter Greene and Dave Hulse
Appendages: Henry Elliott, Mark Lindsay, and Dave Schwartz
Booms & Poles: Jeffrey Kent
Hercules: Joe Cuglietta, Paul Oppenheimer, Bob Randolph, and Steve Wilde
Transport: Joe Boccia

Sailing Team

Afterguard: Bill Koch, Buddy Melges, Dave Dellenbaugh, James (Kimo) Worthington, By Baldridge, Bill Campbell, and Harry Melges
Trimmers: Michel Maeder, Per Andersson, John MacGowan, Andreas Josenhans, Stu Argo, Mike Toppa, Bill Ruh, Bill Rogers, and Bob Billingham
Grinders: John Hufnagel, Rick Brent, T.A. McCann, Chad Vande Zande, Rock Ferigno, Peter Fenelly, Art Price, Marty Stephan, and Larry Miaik
Pit: Dawn Riley, Chip Parris, Fred Curran, Beau LeBlanc, Wally Henry, Josh Belsky, and Larry Turner
Mast: Peter Craig and Michael Hein
Sewer: John Spence and Keith Renke
Bow: Jerry Kirby, Rick Burnham, and Carl Lessard
Coordinator: Beke Lubeach

Coaching

Strategy: Harold Cudmore
Tactics: Graham Hall
Testing: Grant Spanhake
Intelligence: Bob Campbell and Eric Johnson
Tuning: Lou Varney

Physical Fitness

Head Trainer: Dick Dent
Staff: Dave Disney, Paul Gordon, Mark Herschberger, Libby Toppa, and Diane Wall
Physicians: Ned Chambers, M.D., and Robert Leach, M.D.

Legal

Roy Bell, Lyman Bullard, J. Michael Smith, Robert Brewer, David Dick, Ned Hines, and Marion Freemont-Smith

Finance

Manager: Mary Chaundy
Judy Arnheim, Kelle Courton-Wright, Georgia (Emma) Klein, and Sally Robinson

Office Staff

Manager: Lynn Rodrigues
Vivian Burrola, Jennifer Kloos, Tina Maddox, Margaret Mellin, and Elva Pearse

Security

Consultants: Arthur Bourgue and Marc Nezer
Noel Apostol, Eduardo Guillergan, Jeff Karpiak, Policarpo Navarro, Tony Ortiz, Tony Ramos, William Sullivan, Alvin Thomas, Leslie Thompson, Steve Troupe, Walter Vasquez, and Lisa Ware

Donor Acknowledgment

Manager: Sue Maffei-Plowden
Victoria Ricketts, Susan Sanders, and Jeanine Spence

Public Relations

Director: Will Robinson
Sue Maffei-Plowden and Robert Harmon

Fundraising

Director: Peter dePenaloza
Mary Jo Riley, Jeanne Rosow, and Ann Crosby
Volunteer Coordinator: Astrid Moeyersoms
Gifts in Kind: Kathy Farrell
Direct Mail: William Kardash and Kristen Kardash

Book, Video, Photography

Photographer: Daniel Forster
Videographer: Phil Uhl
Book: Paul Larsen
Writer: Roger Vaughan
Assistant: Kip Requart

Food Service

Chef: Sarah Lessard
Adrian Castellano, Kelly Crawford, John Dela Cruz, Lance Shelton, and John Tarantino

Retail

Manager: Sally Cusack
Brook Burnell, Michelle Dent, Kezia Disney, Gordon Durkee, Liz Flacke, Laurel Hanson, Lieve Johanson, Megan Karpiak, Kathy LeBlanc, Hilary Moore, Sheila Roell, Susan Tully, Richard Walwood, and James Williamson

Catalog

Victoria Ricketts

The Official Record

Challengers and Defenders

Challenger Round Robin 1

January 25 – February 3, 1992
Total number of races: 28 Points per win:1

Day 1	Race 1	*Il Moro* def *Spirit* by 02:23
	Race 2	*New Zealand* def *Ville de Paris* by 00:56
	Race 3	*Espana 92* def *Challenge* by 02:15
	Race 4	*Nippon* def *Tre Kronor* by 03:30
Day 2	Race 1	*Espana 92* def *Tre Kronor* by 04:22
	Race 2	*Nippon* def *Challenge* by 08:52
	Race 3	*Il Moro* def *New Zealand* by 02:14
	Race 4	*Ville de Paris* def *Spirit* by 11:00
Day 3	Race 1	*Ville de Paris* def *Espana 92* by 06:24
	Race 2	*Spirit* def *Tre Kronor* by 13:13
	Race 3	*Nippon* def *Il Moro* by 03:55
	Race 4	*New Zealand* def *Challenge* by 05:03
Day 4	Race 1	*New Zealand* def *Tre Kronor* by 09:38
	Race 2	*Nippon* def *Ville de Paris* by 00:29
	Race 3	*Spirit* def *Challenge* by 02:18
	Race 4	*Il Moro* def *Espana 92* by 09:46
Day 5	Race 1	*New Zealand* def *Nippon* (DNF)
	Race 2	*Spirit* def *Espana 92* by 01:50
	Race 3	*Ville de Paris* def *Tre Kronor* by 05:18
	Race 4	*Il Moro* def *Challenge* (DNS)
Day 6	Race 1	*Nippon* def *Spirit* (DNS)
	Race 2	*New Zealand* def *Espana 92* by 04:16
	Race 3	*Ville de Paris* def *Challenge* (DNS)
	Race 4	*Il Moro* def *Tre Kronor* (DSQ)
Day 7	Race 1	*Tre Kronor* def *Challenge* (DNS)
	Race 2	*Ville de Paris* def *Il Moro* by 00:25
	Race 3	*New Zealand* def *Spirit* (DNS)
	Race 4	*Nippon* def *Espana 92* by 04:34

Standings after Round Robin 1:
New Zealand 6 points; *Il Moro* 5 points;
Nippon 6 points; *Ville de Paris* 5 points;
Espana 92 2 points; *Spirit* 3 points;
Tre Kronor 1 point; *Challenge* 0 points

Abbreviations: DNS: Did not start; DSQ: Disqualified; DNF: Did not finish; *Spirit*: *Spirit of Australia*; *Challenge*: *Challenge Australia*; *Il Moro*: *Il Moro di Venezia*

Challenger Round Robin 2

February 15 – February 23, 1992
Total number of races: 28 Points per win: 4

Day 1	Race 1	*Nippon* def *Ville de Paris* by 01:42
	Race 2	*Il Moro* def *Tre Kronor* by 13:32
	Race 3	*Espana 92* def *Challenge* by 05:46
	Race 4	*New Zealand* def *Spirit* by 12:12
Day 2	Race 1	*New Zealand* def *Espana 92* by 04:55
	Race 2	*Spirit* def *Challenge* by 02:28
	Race 3	*Il Moro* def *Ville de Paris* by 00:11
	Race 4	*Nippon* def *Il Moro* by 02:21
Day 3	Race 1	*Espana 92* def *Il Moro* (DNF)
	Race 2	*New Zealand* def *Nippon* by 02:21
	Race 3	*Ville de Paris* def *Spirit* by 01:48
	Race 4	*Il Moro* def *Challenge* by 06:57
Day 4	Race 1	*New Zealand* def *Il Moro* by 01:16
	Race 2	*Spirit* def *Tre Kronor* by 02:52
	Race 3	*Nippon* def *Challenge* by 03:33
	Race 4	*Ville de Paris* def *Espana 92* by 03:07
Day 5	Race 1	*Il Moro* def *Spirit* by 07:58
	Race 2	*Nippon* def *Espana 92* by 04:12
	Race 3	*New Zealand* def *Tre Kronor* by 05:37
	Race 4	*Ville de Paris* def *Challenge* by 07:18
Day 6	Race 1	*Nippon* def *Spirit* by 12:21
	Race 2	*Il Moro* def *Espana 92* by 13:58
	Race 3	*Tre Kronor* def *Challenge* by 06:59
	Race 4	*New Zealand* def *Ville de Paris* by 00:08
Day 7	Race 1	*New Zealand* def *Challenge* by 06:46
	Race 2	*Ville de Paris* def *Tre Kronor* by 02:02
	Race 3	*Il Moro* def *Nippon* by 00:46
	Race 4	*Espana 92* def *Spirit* by 01:25

Standings after Round Robin 2:
New Zealand 34 points; *Il Moro* 29 points;
Nippon 26 points; *Ville de Paris* 21 points;
Espana 92 14 points; *Spirit* 11 points;
Tre Kronor 5 points; *Challenge* 0 points

Challenger Round Robin 3

March 8 – March 19, 1992
Total number of races: 28 Points per win: 8

Day 1 Race 1 *Espana 92* def *Tre Kronor* by 04:39
Race 2 *Ville de Paris* def *New Zealand* by 01:21
Race 3 *Nippon* def *Spirit* by 04:45
Race 4 *Il Moro* def *Challenge* by 08:03
Day 2 Race 1 *Challenge* def *Spirit* by 02:45
Race 2 *Nippon* def *Il Moro* by 00:05
Race 3 *Ville de Paris* def *Tre Kronor* by 22:32
Race 4 *New Zealand* def *Espana 92* by 17:46
Day 3 Race 1 *New Zealand* def *Spirit* by 08:10
Race 2 *Espana 92* def *Challenge* (DNF)
Race 3 *Il Moro* def *Tre Kronor* by 04:57
Race 4 *Nippon* def *Ville de Paris* by 00:46
Day 4 Race 1 *Ville de Paris* def *Challenge* by 12:44
Race 2 *New Zealand* def *Il Moro* by 05:01
Race 3 *Nippon* def *Espana 92* by 04:13
Race 4 *Spirit* def *Tre Kronor* by 06:42
Day 5 Race 1 *Il Moro* def *Ville de Paris* by 03:14
Race 2 *Spirit* def *Espana 92* by 11:11
Race 3 *New Zealand* def *Challenge* by 42:38
Race 4 *Nippon* def *Tre Kronor* by 05:00
Day 6 Race 1 *Il Moro* def *Espana 92* by 02:14
Race 2 *Ville de Paris* def *Spirit* by 03:13
Race 3 *Nippon* def *New Zealand* by 01:02
Race 4 *Tre Kronor* def *Challenge* by 01:13
Day 7 Race 1 *Nippon* def *Challenge* by 09:55
Race 2 *New Zealand* def *Tre Kronor* by 06:11
Race 3 *Ville de Paris* def *Espana 92* by 01:38
Race 4 *Il Moro* def *Spirit* by 01:15

Standings after Round Robin 3:
Nippon 82 points; *New Zealand* 74 points;
Il Moro 69 points; *Ville de Paris* 61 points;
Espana 92 30 points; *Spirit* 27 points;
Tre Kronor 13 points; *Challenge* 8 points

Challenger Semi-Finals

March 29 – April 9, 1992
Total number of races: 18 Points per win: 1

Day 1 Race 1 *New Zealand* def *Nippon* by 01:43
Race 2 *Il Moro* def *Ville de Paris* by 01:24
Day 2 Race 1 *Ville de Paris* def *New Zealand* by 01:46
Race 2 *Il Moro* def Nippon by 02:04
Day 3 Race 1 *New Zealand* def *Il Moro* by 00:18
Race 2 *Ville de Paris* def *Nippon* by 03:30
Day 4 Race 1 *Nippon* def *Ville de Paris* by 02:00
Race 2 *Il Moro* def *New Zealand* (DNF)
Day 5 Race 1 *Ville de Paris* def *Il Moro* by 01:56
Race 2 *New Zealand* def *Nippon* by 02:49
Day 6 Race 1 *New Zealand* def *Ville de Paris* by 03:11
Race 2 *Il Moro* def *Nippon* by 01:53
Day 7 Race 1 *Il Moro* def *Ville de Paris* by 01:28
Race 2 *New Zealand* def *Nippon* by 00:31
Day 8 Race 1 *Nippon* def *Il Moro* by 01:53
Race 2 *New Zealand* def *Ville de Paris* by 03:30
Day 9 Race 1 *New Zealand* def *Il Moro* by 02:20
Race 2 *Nippon* def *Ville de Paris* by 00:24

Standings after Challenger Semifinals:
New Zealand 7 points; *Il Moro* 5 points; *Nippon* 3 points; *Ville de Paris* 3 points

Challenger Finals

April 18 – April 30, 1992
Best of 9 races

Day 1 Race 1 *New Zealand* def *Il Moro* by 01:32
Day 2 Race 2 *Il Moro* def *New Zealand* by 00:01
Day 3 Race 3 *New Zealand* def *Il Moro* by 00:34
Day 4 Race 4 *New Zealand* def *Il Moro* by 02:26
Day 5 Race 5 *New Zealand* def *Il Moro* by 02:38
Day 6 Race 6 *Il Moro* def *New Zealand* by 00:43
Day 7 Race 7 *Il Moro* def *New Zealand* by 00:53
Day 8 Race 8 *Il Moro* def *New Zealand* by 00:20
Day 9 Race 9 *Il Moro* def *New Zealand* by 01:33

Il Moro di Venezia wins the Louis Vuitton Cup

Defender Round Robin 1

January 14 – January 25, 1992
Points per win: 1

Day 1 Race 1 *Defiant* def *Stars & Stripes* by 01:34
Day 2 Race 2 *Stars & Stripes* def *Jayhawk* by 04:10
Day 3 Race 3 *Defiant* def *Jayhawk* by 03:47
Day 4 Race 4 *Defiant* def *Stars & Stripes* by 02:36
Day 5 Race 5 *Stars & Stripes* def *Jayhawk* by 00:30
Day 6 Race 6 *Defiant* def *Jayhawk* by 00:20
Day 7 Race 7 *Defiant* def *Stars & Stripes* by 00:50
Day 8 Race 8 *Stars & Stripes* def *Jayhawk* by 06:08
Day 9 Race 9 *Defiant* def *Jayhawk* by 01:59

Standings after Defender Round Robin 1:
Defiant (America^3 slot A) 6 points;
Stars & Stripes 3 points;
Jayhawk (America^3 slot B) 0 points

Defender Round Robin 2

February 8 – February 18, 1992
Points per win: 2

Day 1 Race 1 *America^3* def *Stars & Stripes* by 06:23
Day 2 Race 2 *Defiant* def *Stars & Stripes* by 04:16
Day 3 Race 3 *America^3* def *Defiant* by 00:49
Day 4 Race 4 *America^3* def *Stars & Stripes* by 06:00
Day 5 Race 5 *Stars & Stripes* def *Defiant* by 00:55
Day 6 Race 6 *Defiant* def *America^3* by 01:05
Day 7 Race 7 *America^3* def *Stars & Stripes* by 04:33
Day 8 Race 8 *Stars & Stripes* def *Defiant* by 00:47
Day 9 Race 9 *America^3* def *Defiant* by 00:38

Standings after Defender Round Robin 2:
America^3 (America^3 slot A) 16 points;
Stars & Stripes 7 points;
Defiant (America^3 slot B) 4 points

Defender Round Robin 3

March 3 – March 15, 1992
Points per win: 4

Day 1 Race 1 *America³* def *Stars & Stripes* by 01:11
Day 2 Race 2 *Stars & Stripes* def *Defiant* by 02:15
Day 3 Race 3 *America³*def *Defiant* (DNF)
Day 4 Race 4 *America³* def *Stars & Stripes* by 05:33
Day 5 Race 5 *Defiant* def *Stars & Stripes* by 01:19
Day 6 Race 6 *America³* def *Defiant* by 00:31
Day 7 Race 7 *America³* def *Stars & Stripes* (DNF)
Day 8 Race 8 *Defiant* def *Stars & Stripes* by 00:23
Day 9 Race 9 *America³* def *Defiant* by 00:55
Day 10 Race 10 *Stars & Stripes* def *America³* by 01:05
Day 11 Race 11 *Stars & Stripes* def *Defiant* by 00:38
Day 12 Races 12/13 *America³* def *Defiant* by 00:34/00:23

Standings after Defender Round Robin 3:
America³ (America³ slot A) 48 points;
Stars & Stripes 19 points;
Defiant (America³ slot B) 12 points

Defender Round Robin 4

March 28 – April 12, 1992
Kanza starts round with 2 points;
Stars & Stripes with 1 point; *America³* with 0 points
Points per win:1

Day 1 Race 1 *Stars & Stripes* def *Kanza* by 02:27
Day 2 Race 2 *Stars & Stripes* def *America³* by 00:45
Day 3 Race 3 *Kanza* def *America³* by 01:13
Day 4 Race 4 *Kanza* def *Stars & Stripes* by 00:42
Day 5 Race 5 *Stars & Stripes* def *America³* by 01:56
Day 6 Race 6 *America³* def *Kanza* by 00:34
Day 7 Race 7 *Kanza* def *Stars & Stripes* by 00:57
Day 8 Race 8 *America³* def *Stars & Stripes* by 02:08
Day 9 Race 9 *America³* def *Stars & Stripes* by 00:44
Day 10 Race 10 *Stars & Stripes* def *Kanza* by 01:11
Day 11 Race 11 *America³* def *Stars & Stripes* by 00:44
Day 12 Race 12 *America³* def *Kanza* (DNF)
Day 13 Sailoff *Stars & Stripes* def *Kanza* by 02:12

America³ and *Stars & Stripes* advance to Defender Finals

Defender Finals

April 18 - April 30, 1992
Best of 13 races

Day 1 Race 1 *America*^{3} def *Stars & Stripes* by 02:09
Day 2 Race 2 *America*^{3} def *Stars & Stripes* by 01:47
Day 3 Race 3 *America*^{3} def *Stars & Stripes* by 04:20
Day 4 Race 4 *Stars & Stripes* def *America*^{3} by 00:39
Day 5 Race 5 *America*^{3} def *Stars & Stripes* by 03:31
Day 6 Race 6 *Stars & Stripes* def *America*^{3} by 02:18
Day 7 Race 7 *Stars & Stripes* def *America*^{3} by 01:28
Day 8 Race 8 *Stars & Stripes* def *America*^{3} by 01:47
Day 9 Race 9 *America*^{3} def *Stars & Stripes* by 01:08
Day 10 Race 10 *America*^{3} def *Stars & Stripes* by 01:43
Day 11 Race 11 *America*^{3} def *Stars & Stripes* by 05:08

Standings after Defender Finals:
America^3 7 points; *Stars & Stripes* 4 points
America^3 wins the Defender Finals

Race Course Times Rounding Each Mark

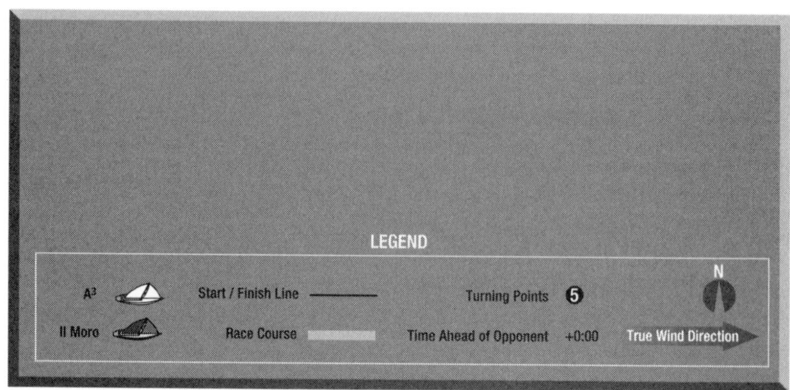

Day 1 Race 1 *America*³ def *Il Moro Di Venezia* by 00:30

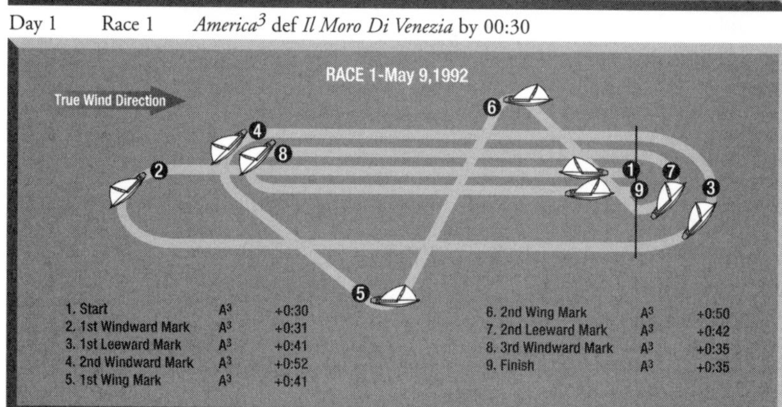

RACE 1-May 9,1992
True Wind Direction
1. Start A3 +0:30
2. 1st Windward Mark A3 +0:31
3. 1st Leeward Mark A3 +0:41
4. 2nd Windward Mark A3 +0:52
5. 1st Wing Mark A3 +0:41
6. 2nd Wing Mark A3 +0:50
7. 2nd Leeward Mark A3 +0:42
8. 3rd Windward Mark A3 +0:35
9. Finish A3 +0:35

Day 2 Race 2 *Il Moro Di Venezia* def *America*³ by 00:03

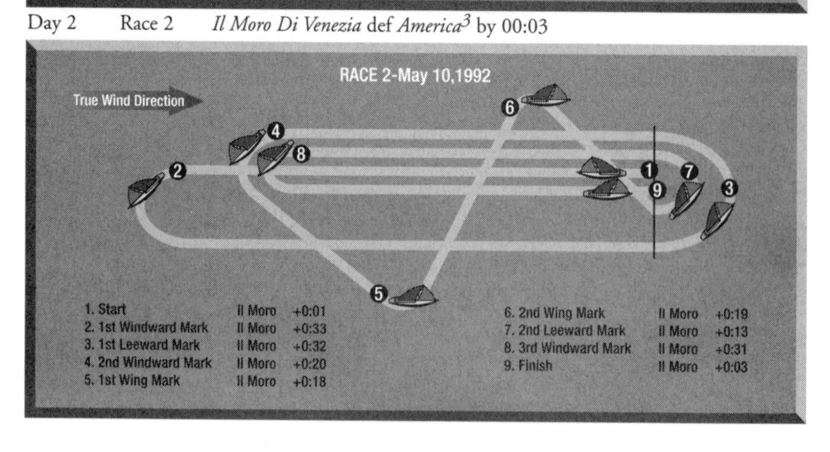

Race Course Times Rounding Each Mark

Day 3 Race 3 *America³* def *Il Moro De Venezia* by 01:58

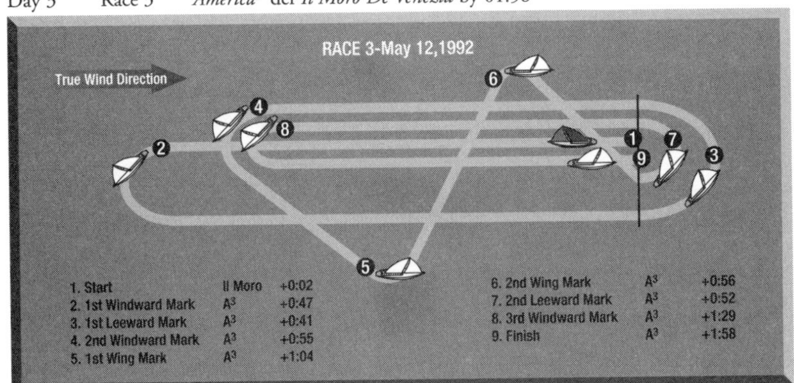

Day 4 Race 4 *America³* def *Il Moro De Venezia* by 01:04

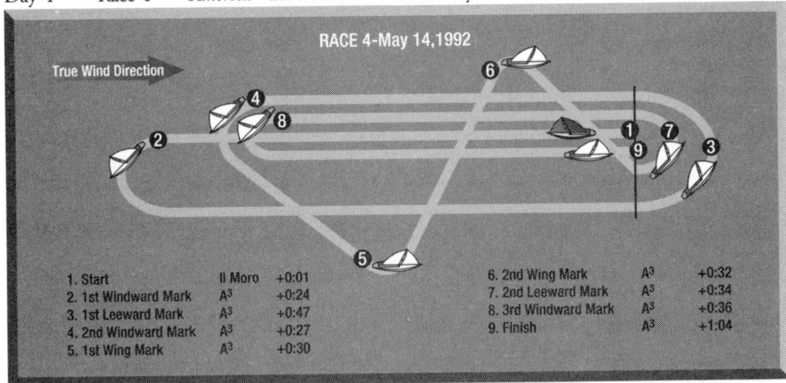

Day 5 Race 5 *America³* def *Il Moro De Venezia* by 00:44

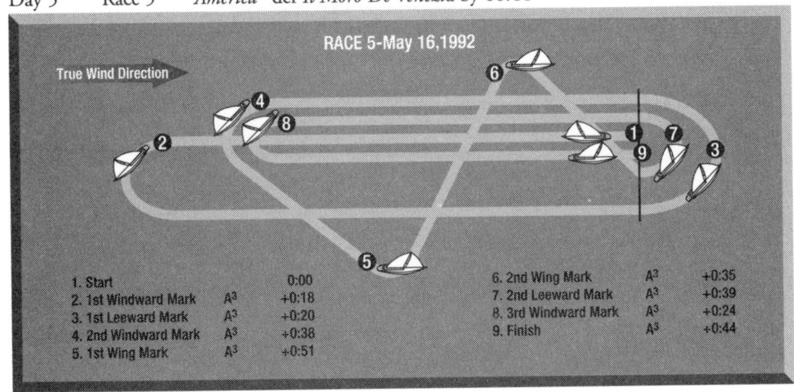

Defenders & Challengers 1851–1992

Year	Boat	Nation		Boat	Nation
1851	*America*	USA	def	*15 British yachts*	England
1870	*Magic*	USA	def	*Cambria*	England
1871	*Columbia/Sappho*	USA	def	*Livonia*	England
1876	*Madeleine*	USA	def	*Countess of Dufferin*	Canada
1881	*Mischief*	USA	def	*Atalanta*	Canada
1885	*Puritan*	USA	def	*Genesta*	England
1886	*Mayflower*	USA	def	*Galatea*	Scotland
1887	*Volunteer*	USA	def	*Thistle*	Scotland
1893	*Vigilant*	USA	def	*Valkyrie II*	England
1895	*Defender*	USA	def	*Valkyrie III*	England
1899	*Columbia*	USA	def	*Shamrock*	Ulster
1901	*Columbia*	USA	def	*Shamrock II*	Ulster
1903	*Reliance*	USA	def	*Shamrock III*	Ulster
1920	*Resolute*	USA	def	*Shamrock IV*	Ulster
1930	*Enterprise*	USA	def	*Shamrock V*	Ulster
1934	*Rainbow*	USA	def	*Endeavour*	England
1937	*Ranger*	USA	def	*Endeavour II*	England
1958	*Columbia*	USA	def	*Sceptre*	England
1962	*Weatherly*	USA	def	*Gretel*	Australia
1964	*Constellation*	USA	def	*Sovereign*	England
1967	*Intrepid*	USA	def	*Dame Pattie*	Australia
1970	*Intrepid*	USA	def	*Gretel II*	Australia
1974	*Courageous*	USA	def	*Southern Cross*	Australia
1977	*Courageous*	USA	def	*Australia*	Australia
1980	*Freedom*	USA	def	*Australia*	Australia
1983	*Australia II*	Australia	def	*Liberty*	USA
1987	*Stars & Stripes*	USA	def	*Kookabura III*	Australia
1988	*Stars & Stripes*	USA	def	*New Zealand*	New Zealand
1992	*America*^{3}	USA	def	*Il Moro di Venezia*	Italy

Teamwork, Technology, and Talent: The T^3 Approach[1]

William I. Koch

To compete successfully in an era of rapid change is a challenge that all American businesses face. The good news is that the playing field is expanding across the globe. The bad news is that the field is not level. In my experience as chief executive officer of an energy company[2] and chairman of a supercomputer manufacturer, I have found that competition is less a matter of superior resources than one of having the right management strategy. *The problem of competition is primarily a management problem.*

Nowhere was this fact more evident than in the 1992 race for the America's Cup, the oldest trophy in competitive sports. To even casual observers, there was no reason on earth that an amateur sailor who only started sailing eight years earlier, and a team with some members with no prior sailing experience, should have won the race. Las Vegas odds on our winning were a 100-to-1 longshot. Yet our America^3 team won the America's Cup because we approached the campaign as a management challenge. In fact, the name "America^3" represents the main elements of the management strategy I have used in my own businesses. To compete effectively, one must manage effectively using *teamwork, technology, and talent.*

For simplicity, I call this the "T^3" approach, and I have found T^3 to work consistently and successfully. Coming up with the right management approach required a great deal of study, hard work, and a lot of mistakes. Of the three, I have learned the most from making mistakes. Mistakes are necessary to the creative process. If you are not making mistakes, it means you are not trying new approaches. If you are not trying new approaches, you are not improving.

T^3 is a very straightforward approach to management. It strives to balance the best of human emotions, skill, and intelligence.

Teamwork

To accomplish almost anything in today's world requires the efforts of more than one person. It requires a team. The glue that holds a team together is a clear *focus.* In all of my business efforts, whether meeting annual financial objectives or increasing productivity in a pipe manufacturing plant, we set one or two simple goals each year that everyone can accept, and the achievement of which we can monitor. These goals are our constant focus — they are written down and reinforced constantly. We even post a simple chart that is visible to everyone in the company to show our performance. These are not the goals one usually finds in a mission statement, goals often forgotten in the rush of business. Instead, they become our final measures for decision-making.

1 This article first appeared in *The Corporate Board,* January/ February 1994.
2 Oxbow Corporation has become one of the 100 largest private corporations in the United States.

For example, in the America's Cup, our goal was simple: win the Cup. To do this, our analysis of previous races told us that we needed two things: a fast boat (since a slow one never won the race) and a crew that made few or no mistakes. Like most things in life, it is not the most brilliant who win, but the ones who are the most consistent and reliable. We ruthlessly judged every decision by two criteria: Does it make the boat faster, or make the crew better?

To achieve the established goals and create the reality of a team from the inside out, all members of the organization must be seen as equal in importance to all other members. Some executives will contest this statement on the grounds that companies are, by nature, vertical hierarchies with distinct pecking orders. While it takes more skill to be the chief financial officer than it does to be an accounting clerk, for an organization to succeed *every job must be done well and every job counts*. Because every job matters, every individual is equally responsible for the company's success, and those who contribute have the right to share in that success.

Team spirit and effectiveness can be reinforced by aligning the employee's financial gain with the corporate goals. At Oxbow in the mid-1980s, we instituted a financial bonus plan that resembles today's "gainsharing" plans. Everyone participates — from managers and engineers to the maintenance men and janitors. One result is that our geothermal plant in Nevada is one of the most productive energy plants in the country and regularly produces at 110 percent of capacity. The desire to perform well is promoted horizontally, not vertically, by employees working with each other. Either everyone wins, or no one wins.

Teamwork is also important in turning around a company. At a composite pipe plant in Oklahoma which we acquired, we were faced with a divisive, disgruntled workforce, low productivity, and catastrophic quality control. Our first priority was to build team spirit. Members of the R&D department, typically the "sacred cows" of an engineering company, were sent with salespeople on customer calls to understand the demands of the market. To build quality control and pride, every inspector was asked to sign his name to a completed length of pipe before it was shipped. As people began to work together and take pride in a shared accomplishment, new product development shrank from two years to six months, customer rejections declined by a factor of 10, sales tripled, and the annual red ink turned into monthly profits.

Teamwork in an organization requires constant reinforcement, and visual reminders can aid the process. During the America's Cup campaign, everyone on America^3 — from the security guard to the skipper — wore the same team clothing, whether or not their contribution was made on land or on sea. The visual statement helped to reinforce the value of each person on the team, regardless of position.

Technology

Despite the overwhelming importance of people, I am convinced that technology plays a huge role in competing effectively on a global scale. As a chemical engineer, I have seen repeated instances in which a technological edge has made the difference, not only in product development but in overall corporate management.

Technology has become increasingly important in formerly low- and non-technology sectors such as sailing. Until recently, sailing technology had been virtually unchanged for 100 years. Most people believed that yacht design is an art form, and it is true that yacht designers do create beautiful boats. However, boatspeed is a science governed by the principles of aero- and hydrodynamics. Since boatspeed is a science and sailing is an art, to win we needed to combine the art and the science. The trick was to know how.

In retrospect, our approach was simple. We applied highly developed technology from different disciplines to a business in which tradition said technology would not work. We ignored all the old rules of thumb and looked at what made our product better in relation to our goals.

We have taken a similar tack at Oxbow as well. For our large electrical generation plant in Nevada, we developed a highly sophisticated computer model of both the plant and the 12,000-foot-deep geothermal reservoirs. When we want to make improvements, anything from drilling a new well to changing a valve, we run the change through the model to determine how it will affect the bottom line of the entire operation. Technology enables us to continually improve our throughput without putting corporate resources at unnecessary risk. In so doing, we deliver the right product at the right price and maintain our competitive lead.

Talent

For many companies, talent is a first priority, but I view it as considerably less important than either teamwork or technology. Why? While skills can be taught to someone with the right attitude, a talented individual with a "me first/me only" attitude is a detriment to teamwork and ultimately prevents the organization from reaching its goals.

When it comes to talent, I follow two rules: Hire people who are better at their jobs than you are, and let them do the jobs for which they were hired. Hire talented people, but only if they have the right attitude.

Many managers put all their eggs in the talent basket and are willing to accept the demands of star players as a necessary consequence of getting some enormous load of talent. However, hiring stars can actually create problems, not solve them. In the early days at Oxbow in 1983, I hired three star executives whom I did not know especially well, except by reputation. I trusted their talent without paying attention to their personal agendas, which eventually came to encompass huge personal gain at the sake of the company's capital structure. It was a $35 million management error, but it taught me to never become overly dependent on talent alone.

The current Oxbow management team is quite different, in part because we now approach hiring differently. We get to know the individuals well in both business and social situations, and we usually hire for lower positions and give people a chance to prove their worth. Consequently, we promote heavily from within the corporation. We spend a great deal of time trying to understand individual goals and to align these with the goals of the corporation. By getting everyone to participate and buy into corporate goals, the two sets of goals — those of the individual and those of the corporation — merge into one.

With the current team, Oxbow has been able to grow at a fairly rapid rate. When I made the decision in 1990 to take on the America's Cup challenge, I turned the business over to three executives with instructions to improve our ongoing busines operations, but not to leap into new territory. When I returned a year and a half later, I found that 1991 profits (for the full year I was absent) had doubled from 1990. For 1992, when I was away for half the year, profits increased 50 percent from the prior year. When the press comments critically on this, I respond that I am quite proud of this feat. This kind of performance could only have resulted from selecting the right people who could do the job better than I could. Their performance allowed me, in turn, to pursue new areas which will ultimately benefit the company through increased scope and profits.

The selection or "hiring" process is exceedingly important in creating the right team, and that was especially true for America^3. More than 500 people applied for fewer than 40 places on the crew. We started with extensive interviewing, not only of the applicants but of others who had sailed or worked with them. From this group, we eliminated 340 on attitude alone, and then moved on to conduct tryouts with the remaining 160. A team of six people was chosen to rate each potential crew member on a 0 to 10 basis in categories we felt important: attitude, teamwork, and talent. To be considered, candidates had to achieve scores of 9 or 10 in each of the first two categories.

The process lasted two months, at the end of which we selected 40 individuals. For the America's Cup match, we selected a final crew of 16. Although they were virtually all amateurs, they proved to be the best team in the world.

One reason we competed successfully was a fundamental belief that there was no room for stars on the team. Each maneuver requires the coordination of 16 people working as one. The star sailor, on the other hand, tends to be intersted in one thing — his own glorification — and not how well the team works. If a mistake occurs, the star blames others, which in turn creates new problems.

As skipper, it was my job to make sure the right people were in the right positions, that they worked together well, and that they had the rsources to do their jobs to the greatest extent possible. Being a good leader also meant being part of the team and knowing the team's problems, just as in business it means knowing your customers' and suppliers' issues. It cannot be done from an office — being part of the team means being in the field and working with people. Effective leadership requires a delicate combination of hands-on and macro management.

In the America's Cup, I insisted on being physically on the boat, for which I received a tremendous amount of media criticism. However, by being on the boat I could see first-hand what mistakes were being made and by whom, and devise solutions to correct the problems. There was no need to filter information through someone else's agenda and risk receiving inaccurate information.

In contrast, the management cultures of our major competitors were quite different. Each chose a star who concentrated on his area of expertise. The Italians put a sailor in charge, and he concentrated on maneuvering and winning the starts. The New Zealand team chose a leader who was a yacht designer. He fell in love with his designs and would not accept improvements. Their personal biases and egos flawed their respective campaigns and contributed heavily, I believe, to their ultimate losses.

A successful campaigner from years past, General Eisenhower once commented that he spent 80 percent of his time dealing with his allies and only 20 percent fighting World War II. The same is unfortunately true for most of our large corporations, whose managers spend four days of the week concentrating on internal politics and one day on serving the customer and running the business. If we hope to win the global battle for business, we must change these priorities. If American businesses are going to compete effectively on a global scale, management must find new ways to use and strengthen the best of our human and technological resources.

T^3 is like a great partner — it helps bring greater success and prompts a constant review of the relationship between management style and performance. In the search for continual improvement, a few guidelines are steadfast reminders of the dynamic impact of the *teamwork-technology-talent relationship:*

- Develop team players according to the 80/20 rule: 80 percent attitude, 20 percent talent.
- Management's job is to keep the team focused, not perform subordinates' jobs.
- It is the team that wins. Management must be part of the team, along with customers and suppliers. Team members must have compatible goals and agendas.
- Everyone is equally important. The only ego that counts is the ego of the team.
- Along with teamwork, technology is the most effective tool to achieve your organization's goals. Technology can be especially effective when used in areas in which others are convinced it does not apply. This is how an organization can make tremendous gains over its competitors.
- Always improve. Mistakes are fine as long as you learn from them, and you "don't bet the farm."

Glossary

ABACK: Situation occurring when the wind is on the wrong side of the sail.
ABEAM: At a right angle to the hull's centerline.
AFT: Facing the rear or stern of the hull.
ALOFT: Overhead on the mast or in the rigging.
AMIDSHIP: The mid-section of the hull.
APPARENT WIND: The perceived direction and strength of the wind as judged from a moving boat. See also true wind.
ASTERN: In back of the boat.
BACKSTAY: A line, or wire, running from the top of the mast to the stern which secures the mast from moving forward. There are two types: permanent and running. The running backstay can be adjusted during a race to alter the shape of the mast, and therefore the shape or trim of the sails.
BALLAST: A weight placed in the bottom of the hull or keel for added stability.
BATTEN: A length of wood or plastic used to make the rear edge of the mainsail more rigid.
BEAM: A hull's breadth at its widest point. See also abeam.
BEAR AWAY: To change direction away from the wind.
BEARING: The angle between the centerline of the boat or a point on the compass and another object, such as a mark or an opponent. To gain bearing is to point closer and closer to an object. For example, in a race a windshift might allow you to sail more directly toward (gain bearing on) a mark.
BEAT: To sail to windward (also called "sailing close-hauled") as close to the wind as is efficiently possible. To reach an upwind mark in a race, a boat beats to windward by tacking back and forth. Before the wind: Sailing in the same direction that the wind is blowing. Also called sailing downwind or "on the run."
BENEATH: To sail beneath is to sail downwind, or to leeward, of another boat.
BILGE: The deepest, rounded part of a hull.
BLANKET: To take speed from another boat by coming between her and the wind. Your opponent's sails receive the weaker, turbulent air that spills downwind of your sails. Usually used to refer to trailing boat on a downwind leg when boat uses its spinnaker to blanket the boat in front. This strategy called "attacking."
BLOCK: Nautical word for pulley.
BOATSPEED: A hull's speed through the water. Compare Velocity Made Good.
BOOM: The horizontal pole that holds the foot of the mainsail.
BOOM VANG: A system which uses hydraulics or tackle to keep the boom from rising, which would cause the mainsail to point up, and slow the boat.
BOSUN'S CHAIR The canvas or wooden seat used to hoist a crewman aloft. Alternatively, a crew member can wear a web harness while racing that can be clipped to the line that will haul him aloft when needed.

BOWMAN: The crewman who works on the foredeck. His duties include attaching the jib to the forestay, bringing the jib onto the foredeck when it is lowered, managing the spinnaker pole, and calling distances to a mark or an opponent.
BROAD REACH: Sailing with the wind approaching from astern over one quarter or the other.
CENTERLINE: An imaginary line that runs from the tip of the bow to the center of the stern.
CHALLENGER OF THE RECORD: The Challenger for the America's Cup that takes responsibility for establishing the bona fides of all other challengers, scheduling of the races that will determine the best qualified boat, and establishing general procedures and rules that govern the Challenger series.
CHOP: Seas with small, angular waves.
CHUTE: Spinnaker.
CLEW: The rear corner of a sail, and the lowest corners of a spinnaker.
CLOSE-HAULED: Sailing as close to the wind as possible.
COCKPIT: The recessed aft deck area in which the helmsman, tactician, and navigator work during a race.
COFFEE GINDER: A large two-handled winch which trims sheets.
COME ABOUT: To change directions from one direction to another while sailing to windward. To tack is to come about. Compare jibe. See also port (tack) and starboard (tack).
COVER: To hold one's lead in a race by positioning one's boat between the opponent and the next mark, even if it requires one to sail a longer or slower course to do so.
DISPLACEMENT: The weight of water displaced by a floating boat.
DOWNWIND: To leeward, the direction that the wind is going.
DRAFT: The distance between the waterline and the deepest part of the keel. Also, a term used to describe the fullness of a sail.
DRAG: Resistance to boatspeed caused by the friction of water against the moving hull.
DUCK: To move behind the rear of a boat.
FEEDER: The groove in which the luff or forward edge of a sail passes as it is raised or lowered.
FETCH: The ability to reach a windward objective, such as a mark, without additional tacks. See also layline.
FLYING JIBE: See jibe.
FLUKY: Varying, weak wind.
FOOT: A sail's lower edge. To foot is to steer slightly off of a close-hauled course, which, since a reach is the fastest point of sail, allows you to increase boatspeed.
FOREDECK: The part of the deck between bow and mast.
FOREGUY: A line attached to the outer end of the spinnaker pole. It keeps the force of the wind on the spinnaker from raising the pole.
FORESTAY: The stay running from bow to mast on which the jib is set.
FOREWARD: Toward the bow.
FREEBOARD: The distance from the water to the deck.
GENNAKER: A large headsail that is a cross between a genoa and a spinnaker.
GENOA: A large jib whose clew (aft corner) extends aft of the mast. Larger genoas are designated by lower numbers.

GINDERS: Crewmen who operate the coffee grinder winches, which are used to trim the sails. A grinder must have great strength and endurance.

GUY: A line used to control a spinnaker pole. The after guy governs pole movement fore and aft, and the fore guy keeps the pole from rising upward.

HALYARD: A line used to hoist a sail.

HARDEN: To harden a sheet is to pull it in. To harden up means to point upwind.

HEADBOARD: A reinforced area at the top of a sail.

HEADER: A windshift whose direction moves further forward relative to the centerline of the boat. The usual response to a header is to tack or to bear off to leeward. The opposite of a lift.

HEADSAIL: A jib or genoa, which are sails set forward of the mast.

HEADSTAY: See forestay.

HEAD TO WIND: To point directly into the wind.

HEEL: A boat heels or tilts over on one side due to the force of the wind on the sails.

HELM: The boat's steering wheel.

IOR: International Offshore Rule. A series of specifications that govern the design of a certain class of racing yachts.

IYRU: International Yacht Racing Union.

JIB: Alternate term for headsail or genoa.

JIBE: To jibe is to change course while sailing downwind. Requires that one move the mainsail and spinnaker from one side of the boat to the other. When, for example, the sails are trimmed on the port side of the boat with the wing coming over the starboard side, the boat is said to be on starboard jibe. In a flying jibe, the boom swings quickly from one side to the other, placing great stress on equipment and sails.

JUMPER: A forward stay in the upper part of the mast.

KEEL: A protruding section under the boat that provides stability and prevents sideways drift.

KEVLAR: A material that ounce for ounce is stronger than steel. The gold-colored synthetic fiber is used in sailcloth, particularly in high-stress areas, and in ropes.

KNOCK: A header.

LATERAL RESISTANCE: Resistance to sideways drift. Is provided by the keel.

LAYLINE: An imaginary straight line tracing the course along which a boat can fetch a mark while sailing close-hauled. When racing to windward, competitors tack back and forth until they come to either the starboard or port laylines and then, unless the actions of the opponent dictate otherwise, each boat heads directly for the mark along the layline. If a boat sails upwind beyond the layline, it will have gone further than necessary (overstood) and, presumably, lost time. If a boat turns (i.e. tacks) toward the mark before reaching the layline, it will have to make a time-wasting tack again to round the mark. Starboard layline: the layline to the mark that is sailed on starboard tack. Port layline: layline to the mark along which one sails on port tack. The position of these imaginary lines is determined by wind direction.

LEEWARD: Downwind.

LEEWARD MARK: The downwind mark. Approached on a run.

LEG: The passage sailed between two buoys on a race course is known as a leg. An America's Cup course consists of windward legs (also known as weather legs or beats), leeward legs and reaching legs.

LEE BOW: To lee bow is to maneuver so as to direct the disturbed, weakened air spilling aft and to windward of one's sails toward the sails of one's opponent, thereby slowing him down. The correct position for using this tactic is just ahead and to leeward of one's rival.

LEE HELM: When a boat tends to head downwind unless steered up, it is said to have a lee helm.

LIFT: When a windshift moves aft or away from the bow, it is called a lift. When sailing to windward, it allows one to steer more directly toward the mark. The opposite of a header.

LUFF: A sail's leading edge. To luff is to point up into the wind so that the boat slows — sometimes a useful maneuver before the start of a race and in certain match racing situations.

LUFF ZIPPER: Main sails have a vertical zipper near the luff or leading edge, which, when opened, increases the area of the sail.

LOUIS VUITTON CUP: The trophy awarded the boat (*Il Moro Di Venezia*) that compiled the best record against all other Challengers during the 1992 America's Cup and so won the right to challenge the defender.

MAINSAIL: The sail hoisted aft of the mast. Its foot is attached to the boom.

MAINSHEET: The line used to trim the mainsail.

MARK: In a race, a buoy that one must sail around.

MAST: The vertical spar that holds up the sails and that is itself held up by stays.

MASTHEAD: The top of the mast.

MASTHEAD WAND: An antenna at the top of the mast.

MASTMAN: Crewman situated near the base of the mast whose responsibilities include control of the halyards.

MATCH RACING: Races involving two boats only as opposed to a fleet. Format used in the America's Cup.

MYLAR: A light, translucent material used in some sails and spinnakers.

NAVIGATOR: On a racing 12-Meter, the navigator assesses the boat's position, speed, and bearing with respect to the opponent and to the marks that must be rounded to complete the course.

OFFWIND: On a reach or a run you are sailing offwind.

ON THE WIND: Sailing as close to the direction the wind is coming from as you can. Close-hauled.

OUTHAUL: A line or tackle that pulls outward, e.g., the mainsail out haul pulls the mainsail toward the aft end of the boom.

OVERSTAND: To overstand a mark is to sail past the mark's port or starboard laylines, that is, to sail farther than necessary to round the mark. When the wind shifts, the laylines leading to the mark change too, and so a skipper may find that he now over stands the mark through no fault of his own.

PHASE: The match-racing textbook calls for the boat ahead to stay in phase with the boat astern, that is, to remain between her and the mark. If the boat astern is allowed to get out of phase, that is, go off on an opposite tack, then the boat ahead runs the risk of being of allowing the attacking boat to pick up a windshift, which could threaten his lead.

PIN: A buoy.

PINCH: To sail too close to the wind.
PITCH: Fore and aft rocking of a boat in heavy seas.
POINT: To sail close to the wind.The points of sail are the terms assigned to the directions you can sail with respect to the wind.
PORT: The left-hand side of the boat as you look forward.
PORT TACK: Sailing with the wind coming over the port side of the boat. The boom would, therefore, be the starboard side. Port tack does not mean tacking to the left.
PROPER COURSE: The course a boat would sail in the absence of other boats to finish a course as quickly as possible.
RAIL: The deck's outer edge.
RAKE: To bend the mask forward or aft by adjusting the rigging.
REACH: To sail with the wind abeam. On a close reach, the wind is somewhat foreword of abeam. On a beam reach, the wind is directly abeam. On a broad reach the wind is somewhat aft of abeam.
RHUMB LINE: A direct line between one mark and the next.
RIG: The way the spars, standing and running rigging, and sails are arranged. Spars and stays constitute standing rigging. Sheets and halyards are part of a boat's running rigging.
RUDDER: An underwater flap operated by the wheels in the cockpit that changes the boat's course.
RUN: To sail directly downwind, which occurs on the leeward leg.
RUNNER: Running backstay.
SDYC: San Diego Yacht Club.
SAIL PLAN: A boat's inventory of sails.
SEA BREEZE: Breeze blowing toward the shore as heated air over the sun-baked land rises and draws the cooler offshore air inland.
SET: To hoist and then trim a sail.
SEWER: The area under the foredeck where sails are stored. The sewerman organizes the sails down below and helps the bowman hoist and take them down.
SHACKLE: A fixture that fastens a line to a fitting, or one line to another.
SHEET: The line used for trimming sails.
SHIFT: See header and lift.
SHROUDS: Supporting wires on both sides of the mast. They give the mast lateral stability.
SLAM-DUNK: Maneuver used to deny a trailing opponent wind when maneuvering in close. Two boats approach each other on converging tacks. The leader (the boat that is likely to cross in front of the other) crosses in front of his opponent and then immediately tacks onto a course parallel to that of the trailing yacht. Downwind of the leader's sails the air is turbulent and weak; as the trailing yacht sails into this zone his boatspeed can be drastically reduced.
SPINNACKER: A light sail with three corners used when sailing to leeward. When set it has a balloon shape. It is flown with the aid of a spinnaker pole.
SPREADER: Struts on both sides of mast that spread the shrouds out from the mast as they travel down to where they're fastened to the edge of the deck amidships. Spreaders enhance the stabilizing effect of the shrouds.
STARBOARD: The right side of the boat as you face forward.

STARBOARD TACK: Sailing with the wind coming over the port side of the boat. When you're on starboard tack, the boom would therefore be trimmed to the portside. Starboard tack does not mean tacking to the right.

STARTING LINE: An imaginary line between the mast of the boat of the committee that supervises the race, and a buoy. In the America's Cup the buoy or pin end of the line is always on the left and each mark is kept on one's port side while sailing the course. The ideal starting line is set at a right angle to the wind direction and is directly downwind of the first windward mark. This is meant to ensure that both boats have an equal distance to sail to the first mark regardless of where they cross the line. But, for example, if the wind shifts to the right after the line has been established, a boat start ing on the right will have a shorter distance to sail on the beat to the first windward mark. In such a case the right side of the line is said to be favored. Until minutes before the starting gun sounds, the committee boat can adjust its position as the wind shifts to provide as fair a start as possible.

STAY: A wire that provides fore and aft support for the mast; part of the standing rigging.

STAYSAIL: Most often used during a run or a reach; it is a small jib flown between the spinnaker and the mainsail.

STERN: The part of the boat that is furthest aft.

SWELL: The long, heaving waves of the ocean, caused by a combination of currents and wind.

TACK: To tack is to change directions while sailing to windward by steering the bow of the boat through the wind from port tack (wind coming over the boat's port side) to starboard tack (wind coming over the starboard side) or vice-versa. Tack also denotes the foremost corner of the foot or bottom of a sail.

TACKING DUEL: In a close race, a tacking duel occurs when the boat that is ahead tries to maintain its lead by tacking whenever its opponent does in order to stay between the losing boat and the next mark that they both must round.

TACKLE: An arrangement of ropes and blocks (pulleys) that yields a mechanical advan tage and so makes it easier to pull or hoist.

TACTICIAN: The crewman who assesses actions of the opponent and offers tactical advice to the skipper, who concentrates on steering the boat.

TAILER: The port and starboard tailers are crewmen who trim the headsails. The port tailer, for example, is stationed on the port side of the boat and trims a jib or genoa when the boat is on starboard tack (in which case the wind blows over the starboard side and the sails are set on the port side of the boat).

TELEMETRY: Many of the vital moving parts and instruments of a modern IACC yacht are connected to sensors that detect movement or change and automatically send that information via telemetry, e.g., by radio to a computer on the tender or on land. An IACC yacht's own onboard computer can also digest such information and automatically display such key data as boatspeed and Velocity Made Good.

TENDER: A motorboat that holds spare equipment and sails for a yacht. America^3's tender was *Firewater.*

TIME-ON-DISTANCE: The act of precisely controlling one's boatspeed course, the distance to the mark, and the time remaining before the starting gun so as to cross the line with the greatest speed exactly when the gun sounds. When maneuvering against another boat, the fight for the controlling position tends to prevent one from attempting a perfect time-on-distance start.

TRANSOM: The back of the stern.

TRAVEL CAR: The mainsheet leads from the boom to the travel car, a device whose position along a track (the traveler) astern can be adjusted according to how one wishes to trim the mainsail. From the travel car the mainsheet passes eventually around a drum and into the hands of the mainsheet trimmer.

TRAVELER: A track perpendicular to the centerline along which the travel car can slide.

TRIM: One trims a sail by pulling in on a sheet.

TRIM TAB: At the aft end of the keel is a vertical, movable flap that acts as an additional rudder.

TRUE WIND: The actual velocity and direction of the wind. True wind combined with the wind one senses solely due to a boat's forward movement yields apparent wind.

TUNING: The act of adjusting a boat's sails, the shape of the hull and/or keel, and the rigging to optimize performance.

TURTLE: A bag that holds a folded spinnaker before that sail is set.

12-METER: A 12-Meter yacht is not 12 meters long, rather the term applies to a complex series of measurements and ratios having to do with various dimensions of the hull and mast, that when fed into a certain equation, must yield a sum of 12 meters. This class of boat used in America's Cup racing from 1958 to 1988.

UPWIND: Toward the direction from which the wind is blowing, to windward or to weather.

VANG: See boom vang.

VVP: Velocity Prediction (computer) Program.

VMG: Velocity Made Good. The actual speed one is making toward a mark as one tacks or jibes back and forth. VMG is affected by such factors as ocean current, leeway (side slippage), boatspeed, and course sailed.

WAKE: The turbulent waves a boat creates as it passes through the water.

WEATHER: In addition to the word's normal meaning, there is a nautical usage: to weather means to windward (upwind). The weather mark, therefore, is the windward mark.

WEATHER HELM: When a boat tends to head upwind unless steered away, it is said to have a weather helm.

WINCH: A drum around which one passes sheets or halyards; it enables one to trim or ease these lines even when they're under great strain from the pressure of the wind in the sails.

WIND SHADOW: The area of weakened, turbulent wind to leeward of a sail.

WINDWARD: Upwind, to weather, the direction from which the wind is blowing.

Index